Communications
in Computer and Information S

T0238514

Tianyuan Xiao   Lin Zhang   Shiwei Ma (Eds.)

System Simulation and Scientific Computing

International Conference, ICSC 2012
Shanghai, China, October 27-30, 2012
Proceedings, Part II

 Springer

Volume Editors

Tianyuan Xiao
Tsinghua University
Department of Automation
National CIMS Engineering Research Center
Beijing 100084, China
E-mail: xty-dau@tsinghua.edu.cn

Lin Zhang
Beihang University
School of Automation Science and Electrical Engineering
Beijing 100191, China
E-mail: johnlin9999@163.com

Shiwei Ma
Shanghai University
School of Mechatronics Engineering and Automation
Shanghai 200072, China,
E-mail: masw@shu.edu.cn

ISSN 1865-0929   e-ISSN 1865-0937
ISBN 978-3-642-34395-7   e-ISBN 978-3-642-34396-4
DOI 10.1007/978-3-642-34396-4
Springer Heidelberg Dordrecht London New York

Library of Congress Control Number: 2012949601

CR Subject Classification (1998): I.6, I.2, H.4, H.3, C.2, D.2, I.4

Typesetting: Camera-ready by author, data conversion by Scientific Publishing Services, Chennai, India

Printed on acid-free paper

Springer is part of Springer Science+Business Media (www.springer.com)

Preface

The Asia Simulation Conference and the International Conference on System Simulation and Scientific Computing 2012 (AsiaSim & ICSC 2012) was formed to bring together outstanding researchers and practitioners in the field of modeling and simulation and scientific computing areas from all over the world to share their expertise and experience.

AsiaSim & ICSC 2012 was held in Shanghai, China, during October 27–30, 2012. It was constituted by AsiaSim and ICSC. AsiaSim is an annual international conference organized by three Asia Simulation Societies: CASS, JSST, and KSS since 1999. It has now become a conference series of the Federation of Asia Simulation Societies (ASIASIM) that was established in 2011. ICSC is a prolongation of the Beijing International Conference on System Simulation and Scientific Computing (BICSC) sponsored by CASS since 1989. AsiaSim & ICSC 2012 was organized by the Chinese Association for System Simulation (CASS) and Shanghai University. In the AsiaSim & ICSC 2012 conference, technical exchanges between the research community were carried out in the forms of keynote speeches, panel discussions, as well as special sessions. In addition, participants were also treated to a series of social functions, receptions, and networking sessions, which served as a vital channel to establish new connections, foster everlasting friendships, and forge collaborations among fellow researchers.

AsiaSim & ICSC 2012 received 906 paper submissions from eight countries. All papers went through a rigorous peer-review procedure including pre-review and formal review. Based on the review reports, the Program Committee finally selected 298 good-quality papers for presentation at AsiaSim & ICSC 2012, from which 267 high-quality papers were then sub-selected for inclusion in five volumes published in the Springer *Communications in Computer and Information Science* (CIS) series.

This proceedings volume includes 63 papers covering five relevant topics including modeling theory and technology, M&S technology on synthesized environments and virtual reality environments, pervasive computing and simulation technology, embedded computing and simulation technology, and verification/validation/accreditation technology. All of these offer us plenty of valuable information and would be of great benefit to the technical exchange among scientists and engineers in modeling and simulation fields.

The organizers of AsiaSim & ICSC 2012, including the Chinese Association for System Simulation and Shanghai University, made enormous efforts to ensure the success of AsiaSim & ICSC 2012. We hereby would like to thank all the members of the AsiaSim & ICSC 2012 Advisory Committee for their guidance and advice, the members of the Program Committee and Technical Committee and the referees for their effort in reviewing and soliciting the papers, and the members of the Publication Committee for their significant editorial work. In particular, we would like to thank all the authors for preparing, contributing, and presenting their excellent research works. Without the high-quality submissions and presentations from the authors, the success of the conference would not have been possible.

Finally, we would like to express our gratitude to the National Natural Science Foundation of China, the Japanese Society for Simulation Technology, Korea Society for Simulation, the Society for Modeling and Simulation International, International Association for Mathematics and Computer in Simulation, Federation of European Simulation Societies, Science and Technology on Space System Simulation Laboratory, Beijing Electro-Mechanical Engineering Institute, Shanghai Electro-mechanical Engineering Institute, and Shanghai Dianji University for their support in making this conference a success.

July 2012   Bo Hu Li
                                                                Qinping Zhao

AisaSim & ICSC 2012 Organization

Honorary Chairs

Chuanyuan Wen, China
Sung-Joo Park, Korea

Robert M. Howe, USA
Myoung-Hee Kim, Korea

Osamu Ono, Japan
Mahammad Obaidat,
    USA

Sadao Takaba, Japan

Xingren Wang, China

Zongji Chen, China

General Chairs

Bo Hu Li, China
Qinping Zhao, China

General Co-chairs

Koyamada Koji, Japan
Qidi Wu, China
Xianxiang Huang, China

Jonghyun Kim, Korea
Song Wu, China
Khalid Al-Begain, UK

Axel Lehmann, Germany
Zicai Wang, China

International Program Committee

Chairs

Tianyuan Xiao, China
Lin Zhang, China

Co-chairs

Bernard Zeigler, USA

Tuncer Ören, Canada

Ralph C. Huntsinger,
    USA

Xiaofeng Hu, China
Satoshi Tanaka, Japan
Xudong Pan, China
Ming Yang, China
Jin Liu, China

Fengju Kang, China
Zaozhen Liu, China
Kaj Juslin, Finland
Xiaogang Qiu, China
Min Zhao, China

Soo-Hyun Park, Korea
H.J. Halin, Switzerland
Roy E. Crosbie, USA
Satoshi Tanaka, Japan
Shiwei Ma, China

Technical Committee

Agostino Bruzzone, Italy
Yu Yao, China

Anxiang Huang, China
Fei Xie, USA

Yoonbae Kim, Korea
Toshiharu Kagawa, Japan

Giuseppe Iazeolla, Italy   Mhamed Itmi, France   Haixiang Lin,
                                                    The Netherlands

Henri Pierreval, France   Hugh HT Liu, Canada   Shengen Zhou, China

Wolfgang Borutzky,   Jong Sik Lee,Korea   Xiaolin Hu, USA
  Germany

Yifa Tang, China   Wenhui Fan, China   Mingduan Tang, China

Long Wang, China   Doo-Kwon Baik, Korea   Shinsuke Tamura, Japan

Pierre Borne, France   Ratan Guha, USA   Reinhold Meisinger,
                                            Germany

Richard Fujimoto, USA   Ge Li, China   Jinhai Sun, China

Xinping Xiong, China   Gary S.H. Tan,   Francesco Longo, Italy
                          Singapore

Hong Zhou, China   Shin'ichi Oishi, Japan   Zhenhao Zhou, China

Beike Zhang, China   Alain Cardon, France   Xukun Shen, China

Yangsheng Wang, China   Marzuki Khalid,   Sergio Junco, Argentina
                          Malaysia

Tieqiao Wen, China   Xingsheng Gu, China   Zhijian Song, China

Yue Yang, China   Yongsheng Ding, China   Huimin Fan, China

Ming Chen, China

Secretaries

Ping Zhang, China
Li Jia, China

Publication Chairs

Huosheng Hu, UK
Fei Tao, China

Special Session Chair

Shiwei Ma, China

Organizing Committee

Chairs

Minrui Fei, China
Yunjie Wu, China

Co-chairs

Ping Zhang, China
Linxuan Zhang, China
Noriyuki Komine, Japan
Kang Sun Lee, Korea

Members

Shixuan Liu, China

Baiwei Guo, China

Yulin Xu, China

Xin Li, China

Qun Niu, China

Shouwei Gao, China

Xiao Song, China

Gang Zhao, China

Tingzhang Liu, China

Li Jia, China

Min Zheng, China

Ni Li, China

Yanxia Gao, China

Shaohua Zhang, China

Xin Sun, China

Ling Wang, China

Awards Committee

Chair

Zongji Chen (China)

Co-chairs

Axel Lehmann (Germany)

Soo-Hyun Park (Korea)

Wakae Kozukue (Japan)

Members

Satoshi Tanaka (Japan)

Sung-Yong Jang (Korea)

Wenhui Fan (China)

Yifa Yang (China)

Xiao Song (China)

Table of Contents – Part II

The Second Section: Computing and Simulation Applications in Education

The Third Section: Computing and Simulation Applications in Military Field

The Fourth Section: Computing and Simulation Applications in Medical Field

Table of Contents – Part I

The First Section: Computing and Simulation Applications in Science and Engineering

The Second Section: Computing and Simulation Applications in Management, Society and Economics

The Third Section: Computing and Simulation Applications in Life and Biomedical Engineering

Modeling the Power Generation Dispatching in Cyber-Physical Interdependent Perspective

Yi Xu and Guangya Si

National Defense University, No.3(A), Hongshankou, Haidian District, Beijing, China
{xuyi8899,sgy863}@163.com

Abstract. Modeling of the modern electric power infrastructure (EPI) which is a typical Cyber-Physical System has been an important method to analyzing the possible vulnerabilities in it and promoting its security. A modeling and simulation method based on Multi-Agent System (MAS) is proposed. And the modeling of generation dispatching in cyber-physical interdependent perspective has been completed first. The simulation experiment using the data coming from a real power grid system shows that our system could model the electrical characteristic of the real system and the generation dispatching according to the changing loads in reason.

Keywords: modeling, cyber-physical, economic dispatching control, automatic generation control.

1 Introduction

The modern EPI with pervasive embedded computation and communication devices and systems which serve as the control system is an extremely complex and geographically-dispersed system. It has now become a typical Cyber Physical System (CPS) [1], which has great benefits for improving the quality of electric power production and the efficiency of management. But the obscure cyber-physical interdependencies and the intrinsic vulnerabilities in information technologies also bring serious security threats to the EPI. The blackouts in North America and Italy in summer 2003, the one in West Europe in November 2006 and so on [2-4] are all examples which highlight the importance of analyzing the security condition of the modern EPI in the cyber-physical interdependent perspective.

Since the modern EPI is the most fundamental infrastructure, the correlative modeling and simulation works which are not only in the electric engineering but also in social simulation [5] have been the increasing interests in these years. The works in the electric engineering aim at promoting the security and reliability of the EPI. The U. S. government and the E. U. both attach great importance to the EPI protection due to the terrorism. The U.S. National Infrastructure Simulation and Analysis Center (NISAC) set up the National SCADA Test Bed (NSTB) project including many famous laboratories, which is in order to deeply recognize the vulnerabilities in the supervise control and data acquisition (SCADA) system which is widely used in the

T. Xiao, L. Zhang, and S. Ma (Eds.): ICSC 2012, Part II, CCIS 327, pp. 1–9, 2012.

EPI [6]. And the National Science Foundation project, Trustworthy Cyber Infrastructure for the Power grid (TCIP), is for the same purpose [7]. Beside this, the Electric Power Research Center of Iowa State University has been applying themselves to the assessment of the cybersecurity of the electric systems. And they have achieved good results in analyzing the cyber-physical interdependencies using the Petri net and the attack tree models [1, 8-10]. The E. U. supports the Critical Utility Infrastructural Resilience (CRUTIAL) project which focuses on proposing a resilient structure of the EPI control system [11, 12]. The French Grenoble Electrical Engineering Laboratory (G2ELab) in this project uses the Bayesian network evaluating the risk level of cyber attacks. And they combine the Power System Analysis Toolbox (PAST) which models the power flow, the SimPy which is object-oriented in Python to model the communication systems and the Matlab which modeled the control center to simulate the cyber-physical interaction in the EPI [13, 14]. References [15] and [16] which are also a part of the CRUTIAL project introduce the Stochastic Well-formed Nets (SWN) model and Stochastic Activity Network (SAN) model which are dedicated to analyze the cyber-physical interdependencies. The other relative works in the electric engineering are shown in References [17-20]. Unlike these works in the electric engineering, the social simulation always focuses on the reciprocal effects of the EPI and the social environment. It has been a powerful way of analyzing the complex evolvement of political, economic and social group behaviors due to the power blackouts in crisis. The Interdependent Energy Infrastructure Simulation System (IEISS) project sponsored by the U.S. Department of Energy is a famous one due to the needs. Its models are based on the Actors. The project has achieved the interactive simulations between the electric power models and the natural gas models. But it does not model their control systems [21]. However, the Sandia National Laboratory of the U.S. developed a simulation system based on the Virtual Control System Environment (VCSE), which is a part of the NSTB. They integrate the PowerWorld software to analyze the effect on the power grid which is caused by the cyber attacks. And they also integrated some software such as Regional Economic Account (REAcct) to analyze the impact of the power grid blackouts to the economics 0.

In order to understand the modern EPI deeply and insure our national security, we aim at modeling the EPI in a broad region and recognizing the reciprocal effects with the society. So we proposed a modeling and simulation method based on the multi-agent technologies with high level of abstraction. Beside the necessary agent models for the electrical resources, we developed some intelligent agent-models such as the control center agents which could model the behaviors of both the automation systems in it and the dispatchers. And we also modeled the control or automation systems in the power plant agents and substation agents. This paper focuses on the modeling and simulation of the generation dispatching we have achieved now. Unlike the References [15] and [22] in which the active power output of each plant is presumed, we successfully implement the Load Forecasting (LF), Economic Dispatching Control (EDC) and Automatic Generation Control (AGC) [23, 24] so that it is the optimal power flow in our simulation. It paves the way for the other simulations in the future.

The paper is organized as follows. Section 2 generally introduces our modeling and simulation method in cyber-physical interdependent perspective. Section 3 and 4 respectively introduce the modeling of the EDC and the AGC in detail. Section 5 gives a simulation experiment which analyzed a real power grid. The results showed that our simulation system could finely model the electrical characteristics of the real system. And it can smoothly perform the simulated function of generation dispatching.

2   Models and Simulation Mode

2.1   Modeling in Cyber-Physical Perspective

We model the EPI as two interacted layers. The cyber layer represents the control systems of the EPI, while the physical layer represents the power grid. We defined the interactions between them are **_information_** and **_control_** which are shown in Fig. 1.

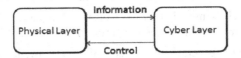

Fig. 1. The cyber and physical layers and their interdependences

The **_information_** coming from different models in the physical layer contain the status signals of breakers and the electric measurements. They are transmitted and processed in the cyber layer. The **_control_** is decided by all the information and some rules in the cyber layer. And the control signals are sent to the physical layer to modify the models' running states.

The information and control are both modeled by the messages among agents. The agents can read the messages and act accordingly.

2.2   Agent Models

The modeled objects in the simulation system are mainly the large power plants and the transmission systems with voltages in excess of 110KV. The other transmission and distribution systems with lower voltages are considered as consumer loads.

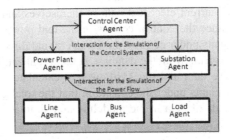

Fig. 2. The sketch map of the agents interactions

Fig. 2 shows the six classes of agents and their interactions in the simulation system. Beyond the dotted line, it is the cyber layer where the control center agents only interact with the power plant agents and the substation agents. They simulate the control systems. But under the dotted line, it is the physical layer where the five classes of agents which model the electrical resources and systems interact mutually according to the electrical connection in the real power grid. They simulate the power flow. And all the agents could also apperceive the environment to decide their running states.

2.3   Simulation Mode

The simulation is discrete. The changing load decided by all the load agents is the driven event at every simulation time. Then there is an EDC simulation at the beginning and every T_1 period, which decides the basic active power output of each power plant in the following T_1 period. This has the lowest costs of generation for the entire power system. And there is an AGC simulation at every T_2 period of the simulation time, which is modeled as the Constant Frequency Control (CFC). The period T_2 should be much shorter than the period T_1.

All the load agents generate the values of their current power consumption according to their attributes, the current time and the environment. The total load consumption of the entire system should be higher in the daytime, but lower at night. And it is also different because of the seasons. The consumption value of every load agent would multiply by a random number which obeys the law of the normal distribution with the average 1 for the simulation of the EDC. So this is the modeling of both the changing load and the LF. However, the key points of the generation dispatching simulation are the EDC and AGC, which are introduced below.

3   Modeling the EDC

The EDC is a main function of the Central Control Center Agent (CCCA for short) based on the Optimal Power Flow function in the MatPower. When it is the time to simulate the EDC, the load agents refresh their consumption values first. And then the other agents refresh their states by themselves' attributes and the interactions with the other agents. After that, the substation agents and the power plant agents would send the messages about the current electrical data of themselves and also the correlative agents to the CCCA. Since the control centers in the real power grid have the basic data of all the power plants under control, the CCCA would directly get the necessary data of the power plant agents from the database at the initialization stage. The CCCA then would use all these data and the MatPower to calculate the active generation power of all the power plants under the constraint that the total generation cost is the lowest. Two critical kinds of data in the modeling and simulation for the MatPower are introduced below.

The Maximum and Minimum Active Power of the Power Plant, P_{max} and P_{min}.
They are according to the principle of making generation scheduling in the real power grid. Table 1 shows the two values of different kinds of power plants. P_{ins} is the installed generation capacity of the power plant.

Table 1. P_{max} and P_{min} of each kind of power plants

Type of Power Plant	P_{min}	P_{max}
Nuclear	P_{ins}	P_{ins}
Hydro	Forced Power	P_{ins}
Thermal	Installed Power of the coal-fired units	P_{ins}
Pumped-Storage	0	P_{ins}
Wind	0	P_{ins}

Additionally, if the sum of all the power plants' P_{min} is much higher than the lowest total load, then P_{min} of the thermal power plants should be cut down.

Generation Cost Data. The generation cost data is important in the calculation. Here, only the generation costs of different thermal power plants are considered. The generation costs of the other power plants are ignored. The binomial model which is widely used is chosen in the simulation. And the three cost coefficients of different thermal power plants are according to the Reference [25].

The EDC simulation is not only at every T_1 period, but also when the AGC could not cope with the continuous change of the total load. And it always follows the AGC simulation to keep the optimal flow in the power system [24].

4   Modeling the AGC

The system frequency is considered to be normal after the EDC. Usually, the change of the total load is random in a period which is much shorter than T_1. But if there was a sharp change of the total load which causes a serious frequency deviation, it would be the duty of the AGC to keep the system frequency back to be normal.

We modeled the process according to the principle of the frequency control and the generation control. We ignore the processes of the primary control of the speed of generating sets in the simulation. But we estimate the frequency deviation after that as follow and consider it as the starting condition of the secondary control of the active power output.

$$\Delta f = -\frac{P_{L\_cur} - P_{L\_sta}}{\sum_n \dfrac{P_{Gn}}{f} \cdot K_{Gn*} + \dfrac{P_{L\_cur}}{f} \cdot K_{L*}} \tag{1}$$

In this expression, P_{L_cur} is the current total load, and P_{L_sta} is the total load at the last EDC or AGC simulation, which makes the frequency to be normal. P_{Gn} is the current active power output of each power plant. K_{Gn*} and K_{L*} are respectively the per-unit value of the unit power regulation of each power plant and the total load. Reference [24] gives their ranges. In the simulation, they are chosen by the average value of their own for simple because it is a calculation for sum. f is the frequency of the power system.

The frequency estimation is executed in some substation agents. And the values are included in the messages passing to the CCCA and other agents at every T_2 period. The agents would refresh their states according to the current Δf and the principle below:

- $|\Delta f| < |\Delta f_1|$. It is considered that the frequency offset after the primary control is small. It may be eliminated by the continuous random change of the total load. So, no agents would act.
- $|\Delta f_1| < |\Delta f| < |\Delta f_2|$. It is considered that the frequency offset after the primary control is very large so that there must be a secondary control.
- $|\Delta f| > |\Delta f_2|$. Start both the secondary control and the EDC.

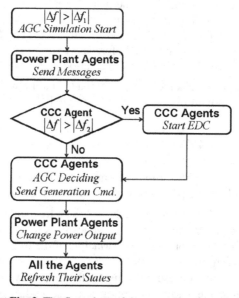

Fig. 3. The flow chart of the secondary control

Fig. 3 is the flow chart of the secondary control. The decision-making of the AGC is in the fourth step by the CCCA. It would command the primary Frequency Regulation Power Plants (FRPPs for short) to change their active power output immediately. If it could not remedy the load change, the CCCA would call the assistant FRPPs for help. The incremental power output of each FRPP is determined according to its adjustable capacity and property by the CCCA. The new active power output of each power plant would be used in the next simulation time. So T_2 should correspond to the response time of the secondary control in the real power grid. Furthermore, the FRPPs and their PRI are determined by the real power grid and recorded in the database.

5   Simulation Experiment

We built the database of a power grid system in China, which is a frequency regulation control region according to the principle of the hierarchical control. It contains the electrical data of all kinds of power plants and the transmission systems with 500kV, 220kV and 110kV voltage. The systems with the lower voltages are considered as all kinds of loads which are also in the database. The effects of the area tie-line are ignored. So the AGC is modeled as the CFC.

There are one central control center and one backup control center in the simulation which could go on working if the other is out of work. T_1 is one hour, and T_2 is one minute. $|\Delta f_1|$ is 0.05 Hz, and $|\Delta f_2|$ is 0.2 Hz. K_{Gn*} of the thermal power plants is 37.5 and the hydro power plants is 20.8. K_{Gn*} of the nuclear power plants and the thermal or hydro power plant which has no adjustable capacity is 0. And K_{L*} is 2. The primary FRPPs are two hydro power plants. And there are also some assistant FRPPs which include both the hydro and thermal power plants. In the simulation time of 25 minutes, the curve of the total active power output and the total load are showing in Figure 4. Because of the outage in the transmission system, the total generation is always higher than the total load. The outage in the simulation is about 4%~8%, which is much the same with the real system.

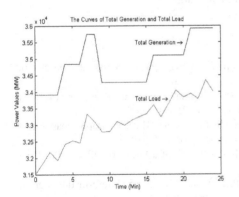

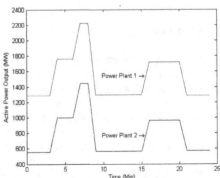

Fig. 4. The total generation and load

Fig. 5. The active power output of two primary FRPPs

Fig. 4 shows that the EDC and the AGC coordinately followed the continuous change of the total load. Since the total load is continuously rising, the AGC is executed at the 4th and 7th minute due to the sharp rising of the total load. Then, the CCCA executed the EDC automatically at the 9th minute. Fig. 5 is the curves of the active power output of the two primary FRPPs. The two figures show that although the total generation after the EDC at the 9th minute is higher than the beginning, the active power output of the two main FRPPs are just a little higher than the beginning. It means that the functions of the EDC are not only to keep the total generation cost as lower as possible, but also to keep the primary FRPPs having enough adjustable capacity. And the increment active power generation is assigned to the other power plants. At the 16th minute, there was an AGC simulation due to the continuous rising of the total load. And there is an EDC at the 21st minute automatically according to the current total load. Also, the active power output of the two main FRPPs are just a little higher than the beginning.

So the simulation experiments such as this one show that our simulation system can well modeled the generation dispatching which is executed by both the dispatchers and the control systems such as the Energy Management System (EMS).

6   Conclusion

The simulation system is suitable for analyzing the power grid operating and its impact on the society. Now, it can model the generation dispatching which is executed both by the automation system and the dispatchers in the real world. Although it is needed to be perfected, it has paved the way for the other simulations of the EPI. Next, the Automatic Frequency Control and some self-protecting functions of the generators would be modeled to perfect the generation dispatching. And more conditions will be considered in the EDC. The Substation Automation and the other functions of the control center, especially the Load Control & Management and the Security Analysis, would be the focus of our modeling work soon. After that, the communication processes in the control system would be a key point in our simulation works. Because analyzing the effect of the control system disabling is our ultimate target.

References

1. Siddharth, S., Adam, H., Manimaran, G.: Cyber-physical system security for the electric power grid. Proceedings of the IEEE 100(1), 210–224 (2012)
2. US-Canada, Power System Outage Task Force — Final Report on the August 14, 2003, Blackout in the United States and Canada: Causes and Recommendations (2004)
3. Sergey, V.B., Roni, P., Gerald, P., Eugene, S.H., Shlomo, H.: Catastrophic cascade of failures in interdependent networks. Nature 464, 1025–1028 (2010)
4. Pourbeik, P., Kundur, P.S., Taylor, C.W.: The Anatomy of a Power Grid Blackout. IEEE Power & Energy Magazineno, 22–29 (2006)
5. Xiao-Feng, H., Pi, L., Ming-Zhi, Z.: Social Simulation- New area of information warfare researches. Publishing House of Electronics Industry (2010)
6. May, R.P., Kenneth, R.: Cyber assessment methods for SCADA security. In: 15th Annual Joint ISA POWID/EPRI Control and Instrumentation Conference (2005)
7. Davis, C.M., Tate, J.E., Okhravi, H., Grier, C., Overbye, T.J., Nicol, D.: SCADA cyber security testbed development. In: 38th North American Power Symposium, pp. 483–488 (2006)
8. Chee-Wooi, T., Chen-Ching, L., Govindarasu, M.: Vulnerability Assessment of Cybersecurity for SCADA Systems. IEEE Transactions on Power Systems 23(4), 1836–1846 (2008)

9. Kevin, S., Chen-Ching, L., Jean-Philippe, P.: Assessment of Interactions between Power and Telecommunications Infrastructures. IEEE Transactions on Power Systems 21(3), 1123–1130 (2006)
10. Chee-Wooi, T., Govindarasu, M., Chen-Ching, L.: Cybersecurity for Critical Infrastructures: Attack and Defense Modeling. IEEE Transactions on Systems. Man. and Cybernetics- Part A: Systems and Humans 40(4), 853–865 (2010)
11. Laprie, J.-C., Kanoun, K., Kaâniche, M.: Modelling Interdependencies Between the Electricity and Information Infrastructures. In: Saglietti, F., Oster, N. (eds.) SAFECOMP 2007. LNCS, vol. 4680, pp. 54–67. Springer, Heidelberg (2007)
12. Dondossola, G., Garrone, F., Szanto, J.: Supporting cyber risk assessment of power control system with experimental data. In: 2009 IEEE/PES Power Systems Conference and Exposition (2009)
13. Tranchita, C., Hadjsaid, N., Torres, A.: Overview of the Power Systems Security with Regard to Cyberattacks. In: 2009 4th International Conference on Critical Infrastructures (2009)
14. Rozel, B., Viziteu, M., Caire, R., Hadjsaid, N., Rognon, J.P.: Towards a common model for studying critical infrastructure interdependencies. In: IEEE Power and Energy Society 2008 General Meeting: Conversion and Delivery of Electrical Energy in the 21st Century (2008)
15. Silvano, C., Felicita, D.G., Paolo, L.: Definition, implementation and application of a model-based framework for analyzing interdependencies in electric power systems. International Journal of Critical Infrastructure Protection 4, 24–40 (2011)
16. Marco, B., Silvano, C., Felicita, D.G., Susanna, D., Giovanna, D., Giuliana, F.: Quantification of dependencies between electrical and information infrastructure. International Journal of Critical Infrastructure Protection 5, 14–27 (2012)
17. Pederson, P., Dudenhoeffer, D., Hartley, S., Permann, M.: Critical infrastructure interdependency modeling: a survey of U.S. and international research. Technical Report INL/EXT-06-11464, Idaho National Laboratory (2006)
18. HadjSaid, N., Tranchita, C., Rozel, B., Viziteu, M., Caire, R.: Modeling Cyber and Physical Interdependencies Application in ICT and Power Grids. In: 2009 IEEE/PES Power Systems Conference and Exposition. IEEE Press (2009)
19. Deepa, K., Xianyong, F., Shan, L., Takis, Z., Karen, L.B.: Towards a Framework for Cyber Attack Impact Analysis of the Electric Smart Grid. In: 2010 First IEEE International Conference on Communications, pp. 244–249 (2010)
20. Igor, N.F., Andrea, C., Marcelo, M., Alberto, T.: An experimental investigation of malware attacks on SCADA systems. International Journal of Critical Infrastructure Protection 2, 139–145 (2009)
21. Bush, B., Giguere, P., et al.: NISAC ENERGY SECTOR: Interdependent Energy Infrastructure Simulation System. Technical report, Los Alamos National Laboratory (2003)
22. Andjelka, K., Drake, E.W., Laurence, R.P.: Cyber and Physical Infrastructure Interdependencies. Technical report, Sandia National Laboratories (2008)
23. Siddharth, S., Manimaran, G.: Data Integrity attacks and their impacts on SCADA control system. In: IEEE/PES General Meeting (2010)
24. Ming-Guang, Z., Yu-Wu, C., Qun-Feng, N.: Telecontrol and Dispatching Automation of the Electrical System. China Electric Power Press (2010)
25. Shi-Zheng, W.: Control and Dispatching Automation of the Electrical System. China Electric Power Press (2008)
26. Wen-Yuan, L.: Electric Power System functioning economically and in security: models and methods. Chongqing University Press (1989)

An Intelligent Method for Fault Diagnosis in Photovoltaic Array

Zhihua Li, Yuanzhang Wang, Diqing Zhou, and Chunhua Wu

Shanghai Key-Laboratory of Power Station Automation Technology,
Department of Automation, Shanghai University, Shanghai 200072, China
wangyuanzhangabc@126.com

Abstract. A new intelligent method is proposed to detect faults in the photovoltaic (PV) array. Usually, there is an obvious temperature difference between the fault PV module and the normal PV module. So, the temperature information of the PV modules is utilized to locate the fault in the PV array firstly. Then, the Artificial Neural Network (ANN) is applied to diagnosis the type of the fault. The current of maximum power point (I_{mpp}), the voltage of maximum power point (V_{mpp}) and the temperature of the PV modules are input parameters of the ANN. The output of the ANNunit is the result of the fault detection. Basic tests have been carried out in the simulated environment under both normal and fault conditions. The simulation results show that the outputs of the ANN are almost consistent with the expected value. It can be verified that the proposed method based on ANN can not only find the location of the fault but also determine the type of the fault.

Keywords: PV array, Fault diagnosis, ANN, Temperature.

1 Introduction

Solar energy recently has been attracted more and more people's attention as a kind of clean, inexhaustible energy. A photovoltaic (PV) system converts solar power into electrical energy directly. For PV systems are always installed in remote and poor environment. It is very important to improve the efficiency and reliability of PV system by detection and protection technology.

Fault diagnosis in PV system has been studied by many researchers. *Peizhen Wang et.al* proposed the diagnosis method based on the analysis of infrared image[1, 2]. In their method, the temperature difference between normal PV module and fault PV module is utilized. It had been showed that the technology of infrared image processing and data fusion is effective and feasible for fault diagnosis in PV array. But the proposed method needs the extra devices as the infrared camera and the cost is a little high.*Syafaruddin et.al* proposed an intelligent method for fault diagnosis in PV array using three layered feed forward neural network[3]. Several ANN models are developed as the diagnosis tool and the control rule is utilized to determine the fault location. The method only can find short-circuit location in one string. If faults occur in two or more different strings at the same time, the method is ineffective.

T. Xiao, L. Zhang, and S. Ma (Eds.): ICSC 2012, Part II, CCIS 327, pp. 10–16, 2012.

In this paper, temperature information of PV modules and ANN are combined to detect faults in PV array. The ANN here is the three-layered feed forward neural network. The proposed method can find more kinds of faults in PV array and no other extra devices are needed. The maximum power point voltage(V_{mpp}), the maximum power point current(I_{mpp}) and the module temperature(T) are used to analyze faults in PV array. Computer simulations have been carried out to verify the proposed method.

2   Configurationof the Proposed System

The basic framework of our method is shown in Fig.1. The configuration is composed of 3x2 PV array integrated with a boost circuit to trace the maximum power point using MPPT algorithm, DCload, ANN unit and output display.

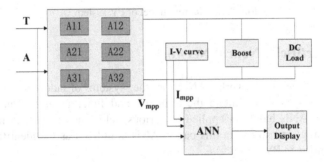

Fig. 1. Basic framework of the proposed method

Three kinds of fault shown in Table1can be detected by ANN unit in Fig.1. The serial number in Table 1 is supposed to be the expected output of the ANN.

Table 1. Types of fault

Serial number	Type of fault
0	Normal
1	Degradation
2	Short-circuit
3	Shading

In this paper, Matlab/Simulink is used to develop the simulation model of PV system shown in Fig.1. Simulink is one of the most important components in MATLAB. It provides an integration environment in which a dynamic environment can be modeled without some programs. Simulink has been widely applied to the complex simulation and design in control theory and digital signal processing. According to these reasons, simulation model of PV system is developedinMatlab/Simulink shown in Fig. 2.

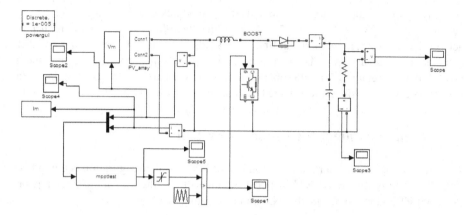

Fig. 2. Simulation model of PV system

3   The Artificial Neural Network

The Artificial Neural Network (ANN) is the system of adopting the physical implementation system to imitate the structure and function of human brain cell. Nowadays, the ANN has been applied to various fields such as pattern recognition, signal processing, and so on. In this paper, ANN is utilized as the identification tool for fault diagnosis in PV array.

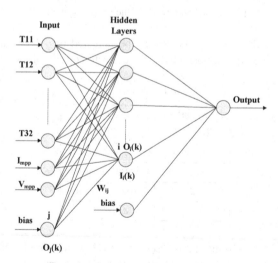

Fig. 3. Structure of ANN

ANN structure is shown in Fig.3. The type of the proposed ANN is a three-layered feed forward neural network. In order to reduce learning error, back propagation algorithm and descent gradient method for adjusting the weights are used. The advantage of ANN is its simple algorithm, fast computational speed and high accuracy of validation[3].

Generally, ANN method has three important stages. They are training data collection, data training process and validation of ANN respectly. The simulation model of PV system shown in Fig.2 is the source of training data acquasition.

To acquire the training data set, sampling points should be determined at first. The voltage and current data under the irradiance from $300W/m^2$ to 800 W/m^2 at an intervals of 50 W/m^2 and the cell temperature from $30°C$ to $40°C$ at an intervals of $2°C$ at maximum power point are recorded. As the result, about 264 instances data are recorded to train the neural network.

The activation function in the training process of ANN is the tangent sigmoid function which is demonstrated as the input-output characteristics of the nodes. For each node i in the hidden and output layers, the output $O_i(k)$ is showed in Equation (1)[3].

$$O_i(k) = \frac{e^{I_i(k)} - e^{-I_i(k)}}{e^{I_i(k)} + e^{-I_i(k)}} \tag{1}$$

Where: the term $I_i(k)$ is the input information to node i at the k-th sampling. The input $I_i(k)$ is given by the weighted sum of input nodes as following[3]:

$$I_i(k) = \sum_j w_{ij}(k)O_j(k) \tag{2}$$

Where: w_{ij} is the connection weight from node j to node i and $O_j(k)$ is the output from node j.

During the training process, based on the minimum value of the sum of the squared errors(SSE) described in Equation (3), the connection weights w_{ij} are tuned recursively until the best fit is achieved for the input-output patterns[3]:

$$SSE = \sum_{k=1}^{N} (t(k) - O(k))^2 \tag{3}$$

Where: N is the total number of training patterns, $t(k)$ is the k-th actual output and the $O(k)$ is the estimated number. In each training process of ANN, the error function is evaluated and the connecting weights w_{ij} are updated to minimize the error given in Equation (3). In this study, the simulation model of the ANN is developed in Matlab.

4   The Proposed Method

In a PV array, when a PV module is in an abnormal state like short-circuit, shading and etc., its temperature will be different from other PV modules in normal state. So the proposed method utilized the module temperature to determine the location of the fault at first. In an ideal condition, the PV module temperature can be expressed as Equation (4)[1,2] .

$$T = \left(\frac{\overline{\alpha}}{G + \overline{\overline{G}}} \cdot \frac{S \cos \Gamma}{\sigma} \right)^{1/4} \qquad (4)$$

Where: $\overline{\alpha}$ is the effective solar absorption rate for the PV module. S is the constant value for solar irradiance. Γ is the angle formed between the normal of the PV module and the line from the PV module to the sun. $\overline{G}$ is the effective outward radiance rate from the positive hemisphere, G is the effective outward radiance rate from the back hemisphere. σ is the Stefan-Boltzmann constant. T is the absolute temperature.

Generally, for a PV module, the effective solar absorption rate is 97% and the actual conversion efficiency is about from 8% to 13%. It is assumed that when the PV module is in normal state, the module temperature is $30\,°C$ and the conversion efficiency is from 8% to 13%. The temperature deference ΔT between the normal module and the fault module can be reached from $6.5\,°C$ to $11\,°C$. When the PV module is in abnormal state, the energy from the sun which originally converts to electrical energy through the PV module becomes the source to heat the PV module. Here, it is assumed that the temperature of the fault module always different from the temperature of the normal module. For thees above reasons, the proposed method utilizes the temperature information of PV modules to determine which PV module is abnormal. For simplicity of the input for ANN, the temperature of the fault PV module is labeled as number "1" and the temperature of the normal PV modules is labeled as number "0".

5   Simulation Results

The model of PV system in Fig.2 is established in the Matlab/Simulink as above. The program is also written in the Matlab to realize the proposed ANN. Eight kinds of information are utilized as the input of the ANN. They are the temperature of the six PV modules, the maximum power point voltage(V_{mpp}) and the maximum power point current(I_{mpp}).

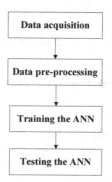

Fig. 4. The process to develop a ANN model

The data collected from the sampling points under various fault situations are utilized as the training data. And the data collected from other working points under various fault situations are utilized as the testing data. The proposed ANN model is developed according to the four steps shown in Fig 4.

The parameters of the neural network are shown in Table 2.

Table 2. Parameters of the neural network

Times of training	50000
Error of training	1e-5
Learning rate	0.01

The error curve is shown in Fig. 5. It can be found that the performance of the network meets the requirement after 687 times of training.

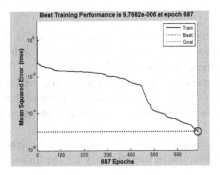

Fig. 5. The process of data training

To ensure that the proposed method is useful under physical environment conditions, different fault scenarios occurs in PV array are tested under different irradiance and cell temperature.

Table 3. Simulation Results of the proposed method

Environment Conditions			Simulation Results		
Type of faults	Temperature (^{o}C)	Irradiation (W/m^2)	Expected Value	Output of ANN	Approximate Value
Normal	33	400	0	-0.0019	0
	35	620	0	0.0002	0
Degradation	33	400	1	1.0108	1
	35	620	1	1.1324	1
Short-Circuit	33	400	2	2.0001	2
	35	620	2	2.2724	2
Shading	33	400	3	3.0033	3
	35	600	3	-1.8418	incorrect
	35	450	3	3.0124	3

The simulated results are given in Table3. The output of ANN represents the type of fault. The number "0" represents the PV module is normal, the number "1" represents the PV module is in degradation state, the number "2" represents the PV module is   in short-circuit state and the number "3" represents the PV module is in partial shading state. It can be found that majority outputs of ANN are consistent with the expected values.

However, the proposed method has some limitations. On one hand, at some special operation points or situations such as lower irradiation, the current and voltage at the maximum power point of the PV array with different kinds of faults are similar. This will lead to the result that ANN can not identify the fault exactly. To solve this question, more training data should be collected. On the other hand, when the structure of a PV array changes, ANN has to be retrained according to the new data generated from the changed PV array.

6   Conclusion

A new fault diagnosis method of a PV array is surveyed. First, the temperature information of the PV modules is utilized to determine the location of faults. Then, ANN is utilized to determine the type of faults.

The system has been tested in a simulated framework, where both normal and fault situations have been reproduced. Simulation results showed that the proposed method can recognize some kinds of fault situations such as short-circuit, degradation, and partial shading.

Although there are some shortcomings in the proposed method, it is still feasible to detect faults in PV array because of its simplicity for the training process of ANN.

Acknowledgments. This research is supported by the National Natural Science Foundation of China (Grant No. 51107079) and Shanghai Key Laboratory of Power Station Automation Technology, "11th Five-Year Plan" 211 Construction Project .

References

1. Wang, P., Wang, Q., Yang, W.: Research on infrared characteristic of the photovoltaic array. J. Hefei. Univer. Tech (Natural Science) 24, 769–773 (2004)
2. Yang, W., Wang, P., Zhou, L.: Study on fault diagnosis of the photovoltaic array. J. Anhui. Univer. Techn. 20, 345–348 (2003)
3. Syafaruddin, Karatepe, E., Hiyama, T.: Controlling of Artificial Neural Network for Fault Diagnosis of Photovoltaic Array. In: 16th International Conference on Intelligent System Application to Power System(ISAP), Hersonissos, pp. 1–6 (2011)
4. Zhao, Y., Yang, L., Lehman, B., et al.: Decision Tree-Based Fault Detection and Classification in Solar Photovoltaic Arrays. In: Applied Power Electronics Conference and Exposition(APEC), Twenty- Seventh Annual IEEE, Orlando, FL, pp. 93–99 (2012)
5. Ducange, P., Fazzolari, M., et al.: An Intelligent System for Detecting Faults in Photovoltaic Fields. In: 11th International Conference on Intelligent Systems Design and Application (ISDA), Cordoba, pp. 1341–1346 (2011)
6. Park, M., Yu, I.K.: A novel real-time simulation technique of photovoltaic generation system using RTDS. J. EC. IT. 1, 164–169 (2004)

Comparison of LOLE and EUE-Based Wind Power Capacity Credits by Probabilistic Production Simulation

Shaohua Zhang, Chen Zhao, and Xue Li

Key Laboratory of Power Station Automation Technology,
Department of Automation, Shanghai University, Shanghai 200072, China
eeshzhan@126.com

Abstract. To mitigate the global climate change and environmental issues, wind power generation is growing at a startling pace around the world. The wind power capacity credit can be used to measure the contribution of wind power resource to the capacity adequacy of a power system, thus plays an important role in development of wind power resources and expansion planning of power systems. Using the probabilistic production simulation technology, wind power capacity credits based on the capacity adequacy indexes LOLE and EUE are investigated and compared in this paper. The theoretical analysis and numerical simulation show that non-smoothness presents in variation of the LOLE index with load, while variation of the EUE index with load displays a good smoothness. This will lead to a difference in the EUE-based and the LOLE-based wind power capacity credits. In addition, the wind power capacity credits based on the LOLE index is non-monotonic for relatively small installed capacity of wind power.

Keywords: power system, capacity adequacy, wind power, capacity credit, probabilistic production simulation.

1 Introduction

In recent years, there is a strong growth in wind power generation capacity worldwide due to three main reasons [1,2]. The first one is the growing public awareness and concern about climate change and environmental issues related to other sources of energy such as fossil fuels. The second reason is awareness about oil and gas reserves depletion and the third one is the improvements in wind turbine technologies that have resulted in lower costs. China has become the nation with the largest installed and grid-integrated wind power capacity in the world since 2010. By the end of 2011, the total installed and grid-integrated capacity had reached 62.0GW and 45.05GW, respectively.

Generation system capacity adequacy refers to the issue of whether there is sufficient installed capacity to meet the electric load [3]. This adequacy is achieved with a combination of different power generation resources that may have significantly different characteristics. Capacity credit (or capacity value) can be defined as the amount of additional load that can be served due to the addition of a power generation resource, while maintaining the existing levels of capacity adequacy. It is central to determining a generation system's capacity adequacy. It is used by system engineers

T. Xiao, L. Zhang, and S. Ma (Eds.): ICSC 2012, Part II, CCIS 327, pp. 17–24, 2012.

for the assessment of a generation capacity deficit risk and the expansion planning of a power generation system.

Although wind power has features of strong randomness, volatility and intermittence, high wind power penetration still contributes a lot to capacity adequacy of power generation systems. Wind power capacity credit can be used to measure the contribution of wind power resources to the capacity adequacy of power systems. As such, it is very decisive to accurately estimate the wind power capacity credit when planning for high wind power penetration levels.

The capacity adequacy indexes of power generation systems mainly include the Loss of Load Probability (LOLP), the Loss of Load Expectation (LOLE), and the Expected Unserved Energy (EUE) [3]. LOLP is the probability that the load will exceed the available generation at a given time. LOLE is the expected number of hours or days, during which the load will not be met over a defined time period. The EUE weights the size of the outage with the probability of the outage. Simply put, the EUE is the average number of MWh of outage one could expect to incur. The LOLP (or LOLE) criterion only gives an indication of generation capacity shortfall and lacks information on the importance and duration of the outage. For a given generation system, an hour with 100MW of unmet load is logically worse than an hour with only 10MW of unmet load. The EUE index can not only reflect the possibility of power shortage, but also give the importance and duration of the outage, thus it is a more accurate capacity adequacy index than the LOLP or LOLE.

There is a large variety of definitions of the wind power capacity credit. For example, in [4], the capacity credit of wind power is defined as the amount of reduced capacity of conventional generators that can be saved due to the addition of wind power (or as the percentage of wind power installed capacity), while maintaining the existing levels of capacity adequacy. The effective load carrying capability (ELCC) is the metric used to denote the wind power capacity credit [5-10]. The ELCC is defined as the amount of additional load that can be served due to the addition of a new generator, while maintaining the existing levels of capacity adequacy. The ELCC is usually expressed in terms of the percentage of the installed capacity, and used in most of related references to denote the capacity credit of wind power. The comparison among several different definitions of wind power capacity credit was presented in [11]. It can be noted that up to now, the LOLE index is employed to estimate the wind power capacity credits in most of related references.

The objective of this paper is to compare the capacity credit of wind power based on different capacity adequacy indexes. Using the probabilistic production simulation technology, the differences of wind power capacity credits based on the LOLE and EUE indexes are investigated. Numerical simulations are presented to verify the validity of theoretical analysis.

2   Theoretical Analysis

2.1   Capacity Adequacy Indexes of Power Generation System

A power generation system, consisting of a certain number of conventional generating units, is considered as the existing generation system. Each conventional generating unit can be represented by a two-state available capacity model with a known forced outage rate (FOR). Using the probabilistic production simulation technology [12], the discrete probability distribution function of the system's available capacity after all the conventional generating units are loaded, $F(x)$, can be obtained as follows:

$$F(x) = \sum_{k=1}^{N} P(k)u(x - X(k)) \tag{1}$$

where, $X(k)$ and $P(k)$ represent the k-th available capacity state and the corresponding probability, respectively. N is the number of available capacity states. The available capacity states are arranged in strictly ascending order, i.e. $X(k) < X(k+1)$. $u(x)$ is the unit step function.

Assume that a time period of T hours is considered, $L(i), i = 1, 2, \cdots, T$ is the load demand in hour i. The LOLE and EUE during the time period T can be respectively given by:

$$LOLE_0 = \sum_{i=1}^{T} \sum_{k=1}^{K_i} P(k) \ . \tag{2}$$

$$EUE_0 = \sum_{i=1}^{T} \sum_{k=1}^{K_i} [L(i) - X(k)]P(k) \ . \tag{3}$$

where K_i is defined such that $X(K_i)$ is the largest available capacity state that would cause capacity deficiency for the given load $L(i)$, more precisely

$$X(K_i) < L(i) \le X(K_i + 1), \quad i = 1, 2, \cdots, T \ . \tag{4}$$

To illustrate the difference between the variations of the LOLE and the EUE with load demand, a generation system consisted of a 600MW generating unit with a FOR of 0.1 and two 300MW generating units with a FOR of 0.08 is considered. After all the generating units are loaded, the discrete probability distribution function of the system's available capacity can be expressed as follows:

$$F(x) = 0.00064u(x) + 0.01472u(x - 300) + 0.0904u(x - 600)$$
$$+ 0.13248u(x - 900) + 0.76176u(x - 1200) \tag{5}$$

Using (2) and (3), The LOLE and EUE in hour i can be respectively given by:

$$LOLE(i) = \begin{cases} 0.0 & \text{if } L(i) = 0 \\ 0.00064 & \text{if } 0 < L(i) \le 300 \\ 0.01536 & \text{if } 300 < L(i) \le 600 \\ 0.10576 & \text{if } 600 < L(i) \le 900 \\ 0.23824 & \text{if } 900 < L(i) \le 1200 \\ 1.0 & \text{if } L(i) > 1200 \end{cases} \tag{6}$$

$$EUE(i) = \begin{cases} 0.0 & \text{if } L(i) = 0 \\ 0.00064L(i) & \text{if } 0 < L(i) \leq 300 \\ 0.01536L(i) - 4.416 & \text{if } 300 < L(i) \leq 600 \\ 0.10576L(i) - 58.656 & \text{if } 600 < L(i) \leq 900 \\ 0.23824L(i) - 177.888 & \text{if } 900 < L(i) \leq 1200 \\ L(i) - 1092.000 & \text{if } L(i) > 1200 \end{cases}. \tag{7}$$

From (6) and (7), it can be noted that the variations of $LOLE(i)$ and $EUE(i)$ with the load $L(i)$ are different. The variation of $LOLE(i)$ with the load is stairwise, while the variation of $EUE(i)$ with the load is piecewise and presents a relatively good smoothness as compared to the variation of $LOLE(i)$ This will possibly lead to a distinction in wind power capacity credits based on the LOLE and EUE, as shown in the following simulation results.

2.2   Wind Power Capacity Credit Based on LOLE and EUE

Suppose that a wind power resource is added to the aforementioned existing generation system. To reflect the strong randomness in wind power output, the wind power resource is approximately represented as a generating unit by a multi-state available capacity model. After all the generating units including the wind power are loaded, the discrete probability distribution function of the system's available capacity can be expressed as:

$$F'(x) = \sum_{k=1}^{M} P'(k)u(x - X'(k)) \tag{8}$$

where, $X'(k)$ and $P'(k)$ represent the k-th available capacity state and the corresponding probability, respectively. M is the number of available capacity states. The available capacity states are arranged in strictly ascending order, i.e. $X'(k) < X'(k+1)$.

For the generation system with the wind power resource, the LOLE and EUE during the time period T can be respectively given by:

$$LOLE' = \sum_{i=1}^{T} \sum_{k=1}^{K_i'} P'(k) . \tag{9}$$

$$EUE' = \sum_{i=1}^{T} \sum_{k=1}^{K_i'} [L(i) - X'(k)]P'(k) \tag{10}$$

where K_i' satisfies:

$$X'(K_i') < L(i) \leq X'(K_i' + 1) , \quad i = 1, 2, \cdots, T . \tag{11}$$

Generally, addition of wind power resource to the existing system will enhance the capacity adequacy. Thus we have $LOLE' \leq LOLE_0$ and $EUE' \leq EUE_0$. Let ΔL denote the amount of additional load that can be served due to the addition of the wind power resource, while maintaining the original level of capacity adequacy ($LOLE_0$ or EUE_0 index). That is, ΔL satisfies the following condition (12) or (13).

$$\sum_{i=1}^{T}\sum_{k=1}^{K_i''} P'(k) = LOLE_0 \ . \tag{12}$$

$$\sum_{i=1}^{T}\sum_{k=1}^{K_i''}[L(i) + \Delta L - X'(k)]P'(k) = EUE_0 \ . \tag{13}$$

where K_i'' satisfies:

$$X'(K_i'') < L(i) + \Delta L \le X'(K_i''+1) , \quad i = 1, 2, \cdots, T \ . \tag{14}$$

In this paper, the one-dimensional search algorithm is employed to determine ΔL. For the LOLE-based capacity credit, the equations (2) and (12) are used. For the EUE-based capacity credit, we use the conditions (3) and (13).

Let C_w denote the installed capacity of the wind power resource. The capacity credit of the wind power resource based on the LOLE or EUE index is expressed as follows:

$$ELCC = \frac{\Delta L}{C_w} \ . \tag{15}$$

3   Numerical Simulations

In the following simulations, the power generation system in [13] that is patterned after the IEEE Reliability Test System [14], is employed as the existing generation system. The generating units' data are listed in Tab.1. A typical load curve consisting of hourly load data for a full year can be obtained by the week-day-hour load model in [14]. To achieve the standard LOLE index of 0.1 days per year for the existing generation system, the annual peak load takes a value of 7765MW, and the corresponding EUE index is 724.944 MWh.

Table 1. Data of the conventional generating units

Number of units	Unit size (MW)	Forced outage rate	Operating costs ($/MWh)
1	1000	0.1000	4.5
1	900	0.1034	5.0
1	700	0.0977	5.5
2	600	0.0909	5.75
3	500	0.0873	6.0
5	400	0.0756	8.5
1	300	0.0654	10.0
5	200	0.0535	14.5
7	100	0.0741	22.5
6	100	0.0331	44.0

3.1   Variations of LOLE and EUE Indexes with Load

Fig.1 shows the variations of the LOLE and EUE with annual peak load when a new 40MW conventional generating unit with a FOR of 0.1 is added to the existing generation system.

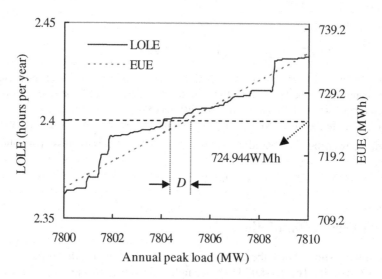

Fig. 1. Variations of LOLE and EUE with annual peak load

It can be observed from Fig.1 that the stairwise characteristics is presented in the variation of the LOLE index with annual peak load. The variation of the EUE index with annual peak load displays a good smoothness. This may lead to a difference in the capacity credits based on the LOLE and EUE. From Fig.1, it can be seen that using the LOLE index, the additional load (ΔL) that can be served due to the addition of the new generating unit while maintaining the original level of capacity adequacy, is different from the one that is based on the EUE index. The difference is denoted by D in Fig.1.

3.2   Wind Power Capacity Credit

A wind power resource which has an available capacity probability distribution listed in Tab. 2 is assumed to add to the existing generation system.

The LOLE-based and the EUE-based wind power capacity credits for different wind power installed capacity are given in Tab. 3 and Fig.2. It is obvious that there are difference between the EUE-based and the LOLE-based wind power capacity credits. In addition, it can be observed from Fig.2 that the LOLE-based wind power capacity credit is non-monotonic for relatively small installed capacity of wind power.

Table 2. Probability distribution of wind power's available capacity

Wind power's available capacity as the percentage of its installed capacity (%)	Probability
0	0.2971
12.5	0.1725
25.0	0.1273
37.5	0.1054
50.0	0.0829
62.5	0.0632
75.0	0.051
87.5	0.0443
100.0	0.0563

Table 3. Comparison of LOLE-based and EUE-based wind power capacity credits

Installed capacity of wind power(MW)		80	1200	2000
ELCC (%)	LOLE-based	32.248	21.266	16.325
	EUE-based	33.192	20.494	15.547

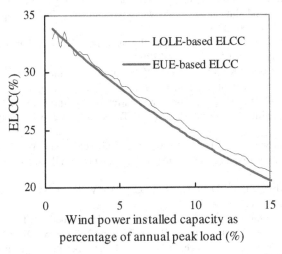

Fig. 2. Wind power capacity credits based on the LOLE and EUE

4   Conclusion

There is a need around the world to plan for high wind power penetration levels in power systems in order to mitigate the global climate change and environmental issues. In this regard, it is crucial to accurately estimate the wind power capacity credit. Using the probabilistic production simulation technology, wind power capacity credits based on the capacity adequacy indexes LOLE and EUE are examined and compared in this paper. The theoretical analysis and numerical simulations show that non-smoothness presents in variation of the LOLE index with load, while variation of the EUE index with load exhibits a good smoothness. This will lead to a difference in the EUE–based and the LOLE-based wind power capacity credits. In addition, the wind power capacity credit based on the LOLE index is non-monotonic for relatively small installed capacity of wind power.

Acknowledgments. Research grants from National Natural Science Foundation of China (No.51007052) and "11th Five-Year Plan" 211 Construction Project of Shanghai University are acknowledged.

References

1. Smith, J.: Wind power: present realities and future possibilities. Proceedings of the IEEE 97(24), 195–197 (2009)
2. Xu, J., He, D., Zhao, X.: Status and prospects of Chinese wind energy. Energy 35(11), 4439–4444 (2010)
3. Billinton, R., Allan, R.N.: Reliability Evaluation of Power Systems, 2nd edn. Plenum, New York (1996)
4. Castro, R., Ferreira, L.: A comparison between chronological and probabilistic methods to estimate wind power capacity credit. IEEE Trans. Power Systems 16(4), 904–909 (2001)
5. Milligan, M.: Modelling utility-scale wind power plants. Part 2: capacity credit. Wind Energy 3(4), 167–206 (2000)
6. Kahn, E.: Effective load carrying capability of wind generation: initial results with public data. Electricity Journal 17(10), 85–95 (2004)
7. Milligan, M., Porter, K.: The Capacity Value of Wind in the United States: Methods and Implementation. Electricity Journal 19(2), 91–99 (2006)
8. D'Annunzio, C., Santoso, S.: Noniterative Method to Approximate the Effective Load Carrying Capability of a Wind Plant. IEEE Trans. on Energy Conversion 23(2), 544–550 (2008)
9. Hasche, B., Keane, A., O'Malley, M.: Capacity Value of Wind Power, Calculation, and Data Requirements: the Irish Power System Case. IEEE Trans. on Power Systems 26(1), 420–430 (2011)
10. Keane, A., Milligan, M., Dent, C., et al.: Capacity Value of Wind Power. IEEE Trans. on Power Systems 26(2), 564–572 (2011)
11. Amelin, M.: Comparison of capacity credit calculation methods for conventional power plants and wind power. IEEE Trans. Power Systems 24(2), 685–691 (2009)
12. Sutanto, D., Outhred, H.R., Lee, Y.B.: Probabilistic power system production cost and reliability calculation by the Z-transform method. IEEE Trans. on Energy Conversion 4(4), 559–565 (1989)
13. Shih, F.R., Mazumdar, M.: An analytical formula for the mean and variance of marginal costs for a power generation system. IEEE Trans. on Power Systems 13(3), 731–737 (1998)
14. IEEE Committee Report, IEEE Reliability test system. IEEE Trans. on PAS 98(6), 2047—2054 (1979)

Modeling and High Performance Computing Analysis of Three-Dimensional Electromagnetic Environment

Yingnian Wu[1,2], Lin Zhang[1], Fei Tao[1], Yuewei Shen[1], Dengkun Liu[1], and Lan Mu[1]

[1] School of Automation Science and Electrical Engineering, Beihang University,
Beijing 100191, P.R. China
[2] School of Automation, Beijing Information Science & Technology University,
Beijing, 100192, P. R. China
wuyingnian@126.com

Abstract. Electromagnetic environment (EME) is important in both civil and military wireless communication systems design and radar testing. The key is on whether the EME model and algorithm is proper for the computer solution and how to make the algorithm actually work in computer or computer clusters. We have analyzed EME modeling by three-dimensional parabolic equation (3DPE) and discussed the finite difference method with it, then provide the idea of transforming the equation solving algorithms to parallel algorithms. The cloud computing simulation framework is given and discussed. The future work direction is shown in the conclusion.

Keywords: Electromagnetic environment simulation, High performance computing, Cloud computing.

1   Introduction

Electromagnetic environment (EME) is important in both civil and military wireless communication systems. It is realized that simulation of an electromagnetic environment is useful and can give much information in communication systems design and radar testing.

Some methods and models proposed for calculation of EME, such as ray tracing and the numerical solution of Maxwell's equations, require quite lots of computation time and huge capacity of memory.

The frequency domain Parabolic Equation (PE) method has been used widely for electromagnetic wave propagation predictions due to its computational efficiency. In most previous research of EME, two-dimensional (2D) parabolic equation (PE) simulation models have been used to represent three-dimensional (3D) EME simulation using an approximation to reducing the computation time. However, 3D effects should not necessarily be neglected and 3D models are required in many situations. [1] Thus, several 3D models have been constructed for electromagnetic wave propagation research. [6-7]

In order to simulate EME in computer, we must consider the computation time and capacity of the computer memory. These are the key issues in EME simulation. In this

T. Xiao, L. Zhang, and S. Ma (Eds.): ICSC 2012, Part II, CCIS 327, pp. 25–33, 2012.

paper, a 3D parabolic equation for wave propagation in Cartesian coordinates for three-dimensional EME simulation is derived. The resulting equation is then solved using the finite difference method. The parallel computing scheme is analyzed. Numerical simulations are conducted for three-dimensional wave propagation problems with different scale area. Examples of parallel computing are then included that demonstrate the effect of high performance computing. The cloud computing simulation framework is given and discussed.

2   Methods in EME Simulation with 3DPE

Numerical solutions of the 3DPE are primarily classified into two categories, the Fourier/split-step method (FSSM) and finite-difference method (FDM) approaches [1-4]. The FSSM allow for a relatively large range step. However, some complex boundary conditions for the terrain cannot be dealt with by FSSM. In the FDM, implementation of the appropriate boundary condition is usually straightforward. A disadvantage of FDM, however, is a requirement for fine sampling on the horizontal or range grid, which makes the calculations computationally intensive, especially for three-dimensional large-scale areas.

2.1   The 3-D Parabolic Equation Method

Based on the assumptions, in the following formulation, the atmosphere is assumed to vary in range and height only, which makes the field equations are independent of azimuth. At the same time, it is assumed that the time dependence of $e^{-i\omega t}$ in the field components. We begin with the parabolic wave equation for a flat earth [2-3].

Small angles three-dimensional parabolic equation (3DPE) can be obtained as follows:

$$\frac{\partial u(x,y,z)}{\partial z} = \frac{ik_0}{2}\left[\frac{1}{k_0^2}(\frac{\partial^2}{\partial y^2} + \frac{\partial^2}{\partial z^2}) + n^2 - 1\right]u(x,y,z) \qquad (1)$$

This SPE is suitable for large scale wave propagation problems. It has good computation precision for small angles, which is up to $15°$.

In vacuum, $n = 1$, a standard three-dimensional parabolic equation can be obtained as follows:

$$\frac{\partial u(x,y,z)}{\partial x} = \frac{i}{2k_0}\left(\frac{\partial^2}{\partial y^2} + \frac{\partial^2}{\partial z^2}\right)u(x,y,z) \qquad (2)$$

2.2   Five Points FDM in EME Simulation with PE

For the FD method [2-5], we start by defining the integration grid, which propagates in the x direction, the step is Δx. The square regular grid is adopted in the y - z plane, set step $\Delta y = \Delta z = h$. The grid scheme is showed in Fig. 1.

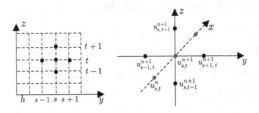

Fig. 1. Five Point Finite Difference Method Grid Scheme

Then we can get FD equation,

$$\frac{u_{s,t}^{n+1} - u_{s,t}^{n}}{\Delta x} = \frac{i}{2k_0}\left(\frac{u_{s+1,t}^{n+1} + u_{s-1,t}^{n+1} + u_{s,t+1}^{n+1} + u_{s,t-1}^{n+1} - 4u_{s,t}^{n+1}}{h^2}\right) \tag{3}$$

Let $\beta = i\Delta x \,/\, (2kh^2)$, we get

$$(1 + 4\beta)u_{s,t}^{n+1} - \beta(u_{s+1,t}^{n+1} + u_{s-1,t}^{n+1} + u_{s,t+1}^{n+1} + u_{s,t-1}^{n+1}) = u_{s,t}^{n} \tag{4}$$

The matrix equation can be expressed in the general form given by

$$Au^{n+1} = u^n \tag{5}$$

Matrix A has the form

$$A = \begin{bmatrix}
1+4\beta & -\beta \,\|\, 0 & 0 & 0 & \cdots & 0 & -\beta & 0 & \cdots & \cdots & 0 \\
-\beta \,\|\, 0 & 1+4\beta & -\beta \,\|\, 0 & 0 & 0 & \cdots & 0 & -\beta & 0 & \cdots & 0 \\
0 & -\beta \,\|\, 0 & 1+4\beta & -\beta \,\|\, 0 & 0 & & & & \ddots & & \vdots \\
\vdots & 0 & -\beta \,\|\, 0 & \ddots & \ddots & & & & 0 & -\beta & 0 \\
0 & \vdots & 0 & \ddots & \ddots & \ddots & & & & 0 & -\beta \\
-\beta & 0 & & & \ddots & \ddots & \ddots & & & & 0 \\
0 & -\beta & & & & \ddots & \ddots & \ddots & & & \vdots \\
\vdots & 0 & \ddots & 0 & & & & -\beta \,\|\, 0 & 1+4\beta & -\beta \,\|\, 0 & 0 \\
\vdots & & & -\beta & 0 & & & 0 & -\beta \,\|\, 0 & 1+4\beta & -\beta \,\|\, 0 \\
0 & \cdots & & 0 & -\beta & 0 & \cdots & & 0 & -\beta \,\|\, 0 & 1+4\beta
\end{bmatrix}$$

Where $-\beta \,\|\, 0$ means the element value of matrix A is $-\beta$ or 0, depending on if the corresponding grid point is boundary point or not.

The matrix A is five-diagonal symmetry matrix, as following

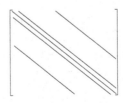

Fig. 2. Sparse Matrix Structure in the First Boundary Conditions

2.3   AGE FDM in EME Simulation with PE

For the AGE (Alternating Group Explicit) method, we start by defining the integration grid, which propagates in the x direction, the step is Δx. The square regular grid is adopted in the y - z plane, set step $\Delta y = \Delta z = h$, $r = \Delta x / h^2$. The grid scheme is showed in Fig. 3.

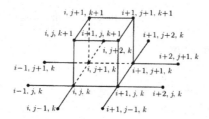

Fig. 3. AGE method scheme

Then we can get equation,

$$-ru_{i+1,j}^{k+1} + (1+2r)u_{i,j}^{k+1} - ru_{i,j+1}^{k+1} = ru_{i-1,j}^{k} + (1-2r)u_{i,j}^{k} + ru_{i,j-1}^{k} \qquad (6)$$

$$-ru_{i,j}^{k+1} + (1+2r)u_{i+1,j}^{k+1} - ru_{i+1,j+1}^{k+1} = ru_{i+2,j}^{k} + (1-2r)u_{i+1,j}^{k} + ru_{i+1,j-1}^{k} \qquad (7)$$

$$-ru_{i,j+1}^{k+1} + (1+2r)u_{i+1,j+1}^{k+1} - ru_{i+1,j}^{k+1} = ru_{i+2,j+1}^{k} + (1-2r)u_{i+1,j+1}^{k} + ru_{i+1,j+2}^{k} \qquad (8)$$

$$-ru_{i,j}^{k+1} + (1+2r)u_{i,j+1}^{k+1} - ru_{i+1,j+1}^{k+1} = ru_{i-1,j+1}^{k} + (1-2r)u_{i,j+1}^{k} + ru_{i,j+2}^{k} \qquad (9)$$

The equation can be expressed in the general form given by

$$\begin{bmatrix} 1+2r & -r & & -r \\ -r & 1+2r & -r & \\ & -r & 1+2r & -r \\ -r & & -r & 1+2r \end{bmatrix} \begin{bmatrix} u_{i,j}^{k+1} \\ u_{i+1,j}^{k+1} \\ u_{i+1,j+1}^{k+1} \\ u_{i,j+1}^{k+1} \end{bmatrix} = \begin{bmatrix} f_{i,j}^{k} \\ f_{i+1,j}^{k} \\ f_{i+1,j+1}^{k} \\ f_{i,j+1}^{k} \end{bmatrix} \qquad (10)$$

Then we can get

$$u_{k+1} = A^{-1} f_k \qquad (11)$$

Where

$$u_{k+1} = (u_{i,j}^{k+1}, u_{i+1,j}^{k+1}, u_{i+1,j+1}^{k+1}, u_{i,j+1}^{k+1})^T, \quad f_k = (f_{i,j}^{k}, f_{i+1,j}^{k}, f_{i+1,j+1}^{k}, f_{i,j+1}^{k})^T \qquad (12)$$

$$A^{-1} = \frac{1}{(1+2r)(1+4r)} \begin{bmatrix} 1+4r+2r^2 & r(1+2r) & 2r^2 & r(1+2r) \\ r(1+2r) & 1+4r+2r^2 & r(1+2r) & 2r^2 \\ 2r^2 & r(1+2r) & 1+4r+2r^2 & r(1+2r) \\ r(1+2r) & 2r^2 & r(1+2r) & 1+4r+2r^2 \end{bmatrix} \qquad (13)$$

2.4 The Boundary Conditions

In Y-Z plane, the irregular terrain is shown in Fig. 4.

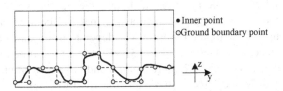

Fig. 4. The Grid Point Classification of Computational Field

If considering the ground boundary as the first boundary condition, and not considering the each direction component coupling, then structure of matrix A remains unchanging while the unknown grid points distribute on the irregular terrain.

If considering the ground boundary as the second boundary condition, then each direction component couple with each other, then structure of matrix A becomes irregular. [4]

Component in the form equation:

$$iku_x + \frac{i}{2k}\left(\frac{\partial^2 u_x}{\partial y^2} + \frac{\partial^2 u_x}{\partial z^2}\right) + \frac{\partial u_y}{\partial y} + \frac{\partial u_z}{\partial z} = 0 \tag{14}$$

Irregular boundary may result in some boundary not overlapping with the grid point, so the grid points are divided into inner points and boundary points. We adopt shift with the boundary value method and unilateral finite difference to deal with boundary condition difference discretization on the boundary points. Fig. 5 shows the boundary grid points unilateral finite difference, B_0 is the boundary point, the others are inner points.

Fig. 5. Boundary Grid Points Unilateral Finite Difference

The unilateral finite difference is as follows:

$$\left| \begin{array}{l} \dfrac{\partial u}{\partial z}(B_0) \sim \dfrac{u_{B_1} - u_{B_0}}{\Delta z} \\[3mm] \dfrac{\partial^2 u}{\partial z^2}(B_0) \sim \dfrac{u_{B_0} + u_{B2} - 2u_{B_1}}{\Delta z^2} \end{array} \right. \tag{15}$$

3 High Performance Computation Analysis

Computation time and capacity of the computer memory are the key problems in the simulation of EME by 3DPE FDM. The major limitation of the finite difference method is that it becomes computationally intensive in cases that require a very dense mesh.

The elements of the matrix A will not be in five-diagonal symmetry form for irregular terrain boundary. Furthermore, even though the matrix A will be sparse, the matrix elements cannot be arranged in such a way that will confine them to a narrow region [8]. Although the computation time will depend on the speed and memory of the computer, in general the solving of the 3DPE may be too time consuming when dealing with problems that require high resolution and large area simulation.

In order to calculate the huge matrix equation for EME simulation, we can use computer clusters, and solve the matrix equation which is the derivation using the FD method by parallel computing. A parallel cluster is built under the Linux environment, and MPI is combined base on the parallel cluster environment.

This method requires much higher arithmetic speed, timeliness handling accuracy, and fleetness of the computers. Therefore, a PC cluster system based on fleet technology and distributed store technology becomes an effective approach satisfying the high-performance data handling requirements.

3.1   The Parallel Computing Method

How to make better use of PC clusters, design high-effect and stable parallel algorithms for the EME simulation, is one of the hot spots in the computer simulation field at present, it also has a broad application background and practical value. The parallel scheme for the EME simulation: solving the 3DPE finite difference equation with GMRES iterative method and using computing cluster for parallel computing.

The Generalized Minimum RESidual (GMRES) method was proposed by Saad and Schultz in 1986 [9] in order to solve large, sparse and non Hermitian linear systems. GMRES belongs to the class of Krylov based iterative methods.

In order to expand the 3DPE simulation area, MPI parallel matrix computing is used to deal with the GMRES matrix computing.

3.2   The Computing Experiment Examples

In order to take advantage of FDM, computer clusters can be used to improve the computational level. Then we can both deal with complex boundary conditions and get high computation speed in EME simulation. We can compute the 3DPE using GMRES in computing cluster by MPI.

Software environment: Operation System: RedHatLinux5.4; MPI: MPICH2-1.2 Ver. Iterative Algorithm: GMRES
Hardware environment: Cluster: DAWNING TC4000L; Node: Dual CPU per Node, 54 Nodes; CPU: AMD Opteron™ Dual Core Processor 2.2GHz; Memory: 4GB
Parallel Computing Example 1:

Y-Z plane scale: $400\text{m} \times 400\text{m}$, grid size $\Delta y = \Delta z = 1\text{m}$.

Parallel Computing Example 2:

Y-Z plane scale: $1000m \times 1000m$, grid size $\Delta y = \Delta z = 1m$.

Based on the parallel computing example of one step simulation in x direction, we can estimate the whole simulation time in appointed area.

Y-Z plane scale: $1000m \times 1000m$, grid size $\Delta y = \Delta z = 1m$.

X direction scale: 1Km, 18Km, step size: 1m.

Parallel computing time is as follows:

Table 1. 3DPE Simulation Time Consuming Compare

Process Computing Time(Hour)	1	5	10	20	30	40	50
Per Step	1.017	0.309	0.205	0.091	0.075	0.062	0.087
1Km	1017	309	205	91	75	62	87
18Km	18310	5575	3686	1646	1358	1118	1580

From the Parallel Computing Example, we can see:

(1) The EME computing time related to simulation distance and height. Simulation of EME is a large-scale areas simulation, the larger distance and height is simulated, the longer computing time will be used. For one PC, because of the limit of memory and computing time, it is difficult to deal with large-scale areas and huge amount data. The computing time and memory consuming are decreased, which means we can simulate lager area by parallel computing.

(2) The parallel speed-up ratio is increased with more and more computing process number when the process number is from 1 to 40 (for the $1000m \times 1000m$ example). When the process number is bigger than 40, the parallel speed-up ratio is decreased and the computing time is increased. And the mass data need mass storage system to store. The main reason is that the communication time of the process is increased as the process number is increased. The more efficiency iterative algorithms and parallel computing methods should be adopted for the larger scale area.

3.3 The Cloud Computing for 3DPE Simulation

There is very little software designed for EME simulation, and they are not satisfactory to give a good EME simulation.

We give an EME cloud computing simulation framework here. The framework is shown in Fig. 6. There are three layers in the framework: Infrastructure-as-a-Service (IaaS), Platform-as-a-Service (PaaS), Software-as-a-Service (SaaS), and User Interface.

The IaaS is a base layer. The IaaS provider supplies the whole cloud infrastructure such as servers, clusters, routers, hardware based load-balancing, firewalls, storage and other network equipment. The customer can buy these resources as a service on an as needed basis.

The PaaS is core storage and computing platform layer. IaaS delivers computer and web infrastructure through virtualization. But the all infrastructure is of no use without a platform. This middle layer of cloud is consumed mainly by developers. The Data Analysis and Processing Platform is a core module, almost all computing tasks are in this platform. Here we can use the 3DPE model and FDM to simulation EME. To improve the speed, Parallel Computing Support is available here. It offers parallel programming and a computing environment such as MPI or PVM, etc.. Massive Distributed Database System can store and manage the data involving terrain data, atmosphere data, electromagnetic data, etc.. Data treatment can analyze the geography digital data and build the environment such as the terrain using these tools. Cloud Operating Systems such as Google App Engine and Windows Azure can provide operation environment for this layer.

SaaS is an application layer. EME Simulation Interface has the functions to implement all the module work patterns, simulation area setups, geography data setups and get data from the files. EME Visualization can give 2D and 3D displays application for the user. It can display the electromagnetic field strength with different colors and display the path from the transmitter to the receiver. It makes the invisible things visible.

The EME cloud computing framework gives general ideas to the EME simulation. It has a lot of modules in function, and some of them are independent in design, but must work together. So, we must consider the interface from one module to another.

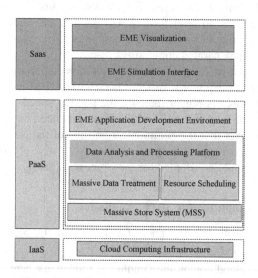

Fig. 6. Cloud Computing Framework for EME

4   Conclusion and Future Work

Three-dimension electromagnetic environment simulation has been mentioned in recent years. The key is on whether the EME model and algorithm is proper for the computer solution and how to make the algorithm actually work in computer clusters. The computer's speed and memory capacity is the bottleneck of the EME simulation.

We have analyzed EME modeling by 3DPE and discussed the parallel computing scheme with it, and provided the idea of transforming the equation solving algorithms to parallel algorithms. The cloud computing simulation framework is given and discussed.

It is a key issue on how to deal with massive data and parallel display them in 3D, using a high performance Graphics Process Unit (GPU) and developing new computer graphics rendering parallel methods. With more and more requirements for EME simulation; high performance computer, parallel modeling methods, cloud computing technology, parallel solving algorithms, feedback optimal computing scheme, energy saving methods, should all be considered together as one entity. The latest computing technology and optimal parallel computing algorithm should be used in EME.

Acknowledgement. Supported by PHR201108258 (IHLB); Pre-research Foundation; Beijing Education and Teaching - Personnel Training Model Innovation Experimental Zones Project - The Automation Application Personnel Training Mode Reform.

References

1. Zelley, C.A.: A three-dimensional parabolic equation applied to VHF/UHF propagation over irregular terrain. IEEE Transactions on Antennas and Propagation 47(10), 1586–1596 (1999)
2. Levy, M.: Parabolic equation methods for electromagnetic wave propagation. Institution of Electrical Engineers, London (2000)
3. Donohue, D.J., Kuttler, J.R.: Propagation modeling over terrain using the parabolic wave equation. IEEE Transactions on Antennas and Propagation 48, 260–277 (2000)
4. Apaydin, G., Sevgi, L.: Two-Way Propagation Modeling in Waveguides With Three-Dimensional Finite-Element and Split-Step Fourier-Based PE Approaches. IEEE Antennas and Wireless Propagation Letters 10, 975–978 (2011)
5. Wu, Y., Zhang, L., Tao, F.: Study on high effective simulation of complex electromagnetic environment. In: 7th EUROSIM Congress on Modeling and Simulation (2010)
6. Levy, M.F., Zaporozhets, A.A.: Target scattering calculations with the parabolic equation method. J. Acoust. Soc. Amer., 735–741 (1998)
7. Izquierdo, B., Alonso, J., Capdevila, S., Romeu, J.: A combined spectral-parabolic equation approach for propagation prediction in tunnels. In: 2010 IEEE Antennas and Propagation Society International Symposium (APSURSI), pp. 1-4, 11-17 (July 2010)
8. Strikwerda, J.C.: Finite Difference Schemes and Partial Differential Equations, 2nd edn. SIAM, Philadelphia (2004)
9. Saad, Y., Schultz, M.: GMRES: A generalized minimal residual algorithm for solving non-symmetric linear systems. SIAM J. Sci. Stat. Comput. (1986)

Modeling and Simulation of Electricity Markets under Different Environmental Policies

Xinhua Fu, Chen Zhao, Shaohua Zhang[*], and Xian Wang

Key Laboratory of Power Station Automation Technology,
Department of Automation, Shanghai University, Shanghai 200072, China
eeshzhan@126.com

Abstract. Renewable energy quota obligation has been enforced in many countries to mitigate greenhouse gas emissions and promote renewable energy. To fulfill the quota obligations, many countries have adopted environmental policies such as carbon tax (CT) and feed-in tariff (FIT) in their electricity sectors. This paper aims to examine the impacts of different environmental policies on the electricity market competition and the social welfare. For this purpose, Cournot equilibrium models for electricity wholesale market competition are developed taking into account the CT and the FIT policies. The nonlinear complementarity approach is employed to solve these equilibrium problems. In addition, an environmental policy that combines the carbon tax and the feed-in tariff (CT&FIT) is also proposed in this paper. Numerical simulations are presented to assess the performances of different environmental policies. Some practically meaningful conclusions are derived.

Keywords: Renewable energy, environmental policies, electricity markets, equilibrium model, simulation analysis.

1   Introduction

Increasing environmental regulation of the electricity sector has become a capital trend in all industrialized nations, and the rest of the world as well. As one of the important measures to curb global warming and encourage renewable resource development, the quota obligation has been enforced in many countries [1]. In the near future, this scheme will be applied in China. To meet the minimum targets set by the renewable energy quota obligation, environmental policies such as carbon tax (CT) [2] and feed-in tariff (FIT) [3] can be used. The CT scheme aims to impose carbon taxes on generation companies (Gencos) with CO_2 emissions. The FIT system deals with renewable Gencos such as wind power and solar power which need to be subsidized to compensate their relatively higher costs. These policies will inevitably impact the Gencos' strategic behaviors in electricity market. Equilibrium models have been widely used to analyze Gencos' strategic behaviors in oligopolistic electricity markets [4]. Therefore, equilibrium analysis of electricity markets under different environmental policies is of great

---

[*] Corresponding author.

T. Xiao, L. Zhang, and S. Ma (Eds.): ICSC 2012, Part II, CCIS 327, pp. 34–43, 2012.

significance to the environmental policy-making along with the design and operation of electricity markets.

A considerable amount of research has thus far been conducted on the impacts of environmental policies in power systems. The effects of CT on the generation mix and the risks of renewable resources are analyzed in [5] and [6] respectively. Downward [7] illustrates through a stylized tow-node system that overall CO_2 emission can increase after a CT is imposed. An overview of seven different ways to structure the remuneration of a FIT policy is presented in [8]. Moreover, the long-term effect of FIT and CT schemes on distributed generation is demonstrated in [9]. It can be noted that up to now, there is few research work to examine the impacts of different environmental policies on the electricity market competition and the social welfare.

Under the CT policy, the costs of fossil-fuel Gencos will increase, while in the FIT scheme the cost of renewable Gencos will be lowered. Thus the CT policy will reduce fossil-fuel Gencos' competitiveness and the FIT scheme will improve renewable Gencos' competitiveness in electricity markets. As a result, both of the two policies can mitigate the greenhouse gas emissions and promote renewable energy. From the standpoint of welfare economic [10], the fossil-fuel generation has negative externalities while the renewable generation has positive externalities, which can both affect the efficiency of resource allocation. The CT policy can be used to relieve the negative externalities caused by fossil-fuel generation. The FIT scheme can only mitigate the positive externalities of renewable energy. For this reason, a new scheme that combines the CT and the FIT (CT&FIT) is proposed in this paper to deal with both the positive and negative externalities.

This paper examines the impacts of different environmental policies on the electricity market competition and the social welfare. Cournot equilibrium models for electricity wholesale markets are developed taking into account the CT, FIT and CT&FIT policies. Then, the nonlinear complementarity approach is employed to solve these equilibrium problems. Finally, numerical simulations are presented to assess the performances of different environmental policies.

2   Theoretical Model

A pool-based electricity wholesale market with fossil-fuel Gencos and renewable Gencos is considered. Let B denote the set of the fossil-fuel Gencos, G the set of the renewable Gencos and N the set of all Gencos. The Cournot mode is assumed for the competition of these Gencos. This is, Gencos compete in the market by bidding their power outputs. The market demand is represented by a linear inverse demand function as follows:

$$P_e = A - \xi Q \tag{1}$$

where P_e is the market price, Q is the market demand, A and ξ are constants.

Assume that the cost of fossil-fuel Genco b is characterized by the following quadratic function:

$$C_b(q_b) = 0.5 u_b q_b^2 + v_b q_b + z_b, \quad \forall b \in B \tag{2}$$

where q_b is the output of Genco b, u_b and v_b are cost coefficients of Genco b, and z_b is the fixed cost of Genco b.

Suppose that the cost of renewable Genco g is characterized by the following linear function:

$$C_g(q_g) = v_g q_g + z_g, \quad \forall g \in G \tag{3}$$

where q_g is the output of Genco g, v_g is the constant marginal cost of Genco g, and z_g is the fixed cost of Genco g.

The CO_2 emission quantity of fossil-fuel Genco b is given by:

$$F_b(q_b) = e_b q_b, \quad \forall b \in B \tag{4}$$

where e_b is the emission rate of fossil-fuel Genco b.

2.1   Cournot Equilibrium Model for Electricity Market under CT Policy

The profit maximization problem for fossil-fuel Genco b ($\forall b \in B$) under the CT policy can be formulated as follows:

$$\max_{q_b} \left[A - \xi \left(\sum_{i \in N, i \neq b} q_i + q_b \right) \right] q_b - C_b(q_b) - P_t F_b(q_b) \tag{5}$$

s.t. $$q_b^{min} \leq q_b \leq q_b^{max} \tag{6}$$

The first order optimality conditions (KKT conditions) of the above optimization problem can be formulated as:

$$A - \xi \left(\sum_{i \in N, i \neq b} q_i + q_b \right) - \xi q_b - \frac{dC_b(q_b)}{dq_b} - P_t \frac{dF_b(q_b)}{dq_b} + \rho_b^- - \rho_b^+ = 0 \tag{7}$$

$$0 \leq \rho_b^- \perp q_b - q_b^{min} \geq 0 \tag{8}$$

$$0 \leq \rho_b^+ \perp q_b^{max} - q_b \geq 0 \tag{9}$$

where, P_t is the per unit tax price (hereinafter CT price) for CO_2 emitted by fossil-fuel Gencos, q_b^{max}, q_b^{min} are the maximum and minimum output limits of fossil-fuel Genco b, respectively. ρ_b^+, ρ_b^- are dual variables associated with the upper and lower bound of generation output, respectively. Complementarity conditions (8),(9) are presented in the form of $\alpha \perp \beta$, which means $\alpha \geq 0, \beta \geq 0, \alpha\beta = 0$.

The nonlinear complementarity method [11] is employed to deal with the complementarity conditions. A nonlinear complementarity function $\psi(\alpha, \beta)$ is introduced, which is defined as: $\psi(\alpha, \beta) = 0 \Leftrightarrow \alpha \geq 0, \beta \geq 0, \alpha\beta = 0$. This means if α, β satisfy the equation $\psi(\alpha, \beta) = 0$, then they are automatically satisfy the complementarity condition

$\alpha \geq 0, \beta \geq 0, \alpha\beta = 0$. In this paper, the nonlinear complementarity function $\psi(\alpha, \beta) = \alpha + \beta - \sqrt{\alpha^2 + \beta^2}$ is used, thus the complementarity conditions (8),(9) can be reformulated as the following set of nonlinear equations:

$$\psi(\rho_b^-, q_b - q_b^{min}) = 0 \tag{10}$$

$$\psi(\rho_b^+, q_b^{max} - q_b) = 0 \tag{11}$$

The profit maximization problem for renewable Genco g ($\forall g \in G$) can be formulated as follows:

$$\max_{q_g} \left[A - \xi(\sum_{i \in N, i \neq g} q_i + q_g) \right] q_g - C_g(q_g) \tag{12}$$

$$\text{s.t.} \quad q_g^{min} \leq q_g \leq q_g^{max} \tag{13}$$

Its KKT conditions are:

$$A - \xi(\sum_{i \in N, i \neq g} q_i + q_g) - \xi q_g - \frac{dC_g(q_g)}{dq_g} + \rho_g^- - \rho_g^+ = 0 \tag{14}$$

$$0 \leq \rho_g^- \perp q_g - q_g^{min} \geq 0 \tag{15}$$

$$0 \leq \rho_g^+ \perp q_g^{max} - q_g \geq 0 \tag{16}$$

where, q_g^{max}, q_g^{min} are the maximum and minimum output limits of renewable Genco g, respectively. ρ_g^+, ρ_g^- are dual variables associated with the upper and lower generation output constraints, respectively.

Using the nonlinear complementarity function, the complementarity conditions (15),(16) can be rewritten as:

$$\psi(\rho_g^-, q_g - q_g^{min}) = 0 \tag{17}$$

$$\psi(\rho_g^+, q_g^{max} - q_g) = 0 \tag{18}$$

The renewable energy quota obligation requires that the total renewable output must be no less than a designated proportion of the total generation output. Here the following quota obligation constraint is considered.

$$\sum_{g \in G} q_g \geq \alpha(\sum_{g \in G} q_g + \sum_{b \in B} q_b) \tag{19}$$

where α is the designated proportion for renewable output by quota obligation.

By gathering each Genco's first order optimality (KKT) conditions and the quota obligation constraint (19), a set of nonlinear equations can be obtained. Thus, the equilibrium results, such as each Genco's output, the market price and the CT price, could be derived by solving this set of nonlinear equations.

2.2   Cournot Equilibrium Model for Electricity Market under FIT Policy

The profit maximization problem for fossil-fuel Genco b ($\forall b \in B$) under the FIT policy can be formulated as follows:

$$\max_{q_b} \left[A - \xi(\sum_{i \in N, i \neq b} q_i + q_b) \right] q_b - C_b(q_b) \tag{20}$$

$$\text{s.t.} \quad q_b^{\min} \leq q_b \leq q_b^{\max} \tag{21}$$

Its KKT conditions are:

$$A - \xi(\sum_{i \in N, i \neq b} q_i + q_b) - \xi q_b - \frac{dC_b(q_b)}{dq_b} + \rho_b^- - \rho_b^+ = 0 \tag{22}$$

$$0 \leq \rho_b^- \perp q_b - q_b^{\min} \geq 0 \tag{23}$$

$$0 \leq \rho_b^+ \perp q_b^{\max} - q_b \geq 0 \tag{24}$$

The profit maximization problem for renewable Genco g ($\forall g \in G$) under the FIT policy can be formulated as follows:

$$\max_{q_g} \left[A - \xi(\sum_{i \in N, i \neq g} q_i + q_g) + P_f \right] q_g - C_g(q_g) \tag{25}$$

$$\text{s.t.} \quad q_g^{\min} \leq q_g \leq q_g^{\max} \tag{26}$$

Its KKT conditions are:

$$A - \xi(\sum_{i \in N, i \neq g} q_i + q_g) + P_f - \xi q_g - \frac{dC_g(q_g)}{dq_g} + \rho_g^- - \rho_g^+ = 0 \tag{27}$$

$$0 \leq \rho_g^- \perp q_g - q_g^{\min} \geq 0 \tag{28}$$

$$0 \leq \rho_g^+ \perp q_g^{\max} - q_g \geq 0 \tag{29}$$

where P_f is the per unit subsidy price (hereinafter FIT price) for renewable Gencos' output.

Using the nonlinear complementarity function,, the complementarity conditions, such as (23),(24),(28),(29), can be reformulated as a set of nonlinear equations. By gathering each Genco's first order optimality (KKT) conditions and the quota obligation constraint (19), the equilibrium results, such as each Genco's output, the market price and the FIT price, could be derived by solving a set of nonlinear equations.

2.3   Cournot Equilibrium Model for Electricity Market under CT&FIT Policy

The CT&FIT policy proposed in this paper requires that all the carbon taxes collected from the fossil-fuel Gencos are completely used to subsidize the renewable Gencos. Thus, the profit maximization problem for fossil-fuel Genco b ($\forall b \in B$) under the CT&FIT scheme can be formulated as follows:

$$\max_{q_b} \left[A - \xi(\sum_{i \in N, i \neq b} q_i + q_b) \right] q_b - C_b(q_b) - P_t F_b(q_b) \tag{30}$$

$$\text{s.t.} \qquad q_b^{\min} \leq q_b \leq q_b^{\max} \tag{31}$$

Its KKT conditions are:

$$A - \xi(\sum_{i \in N, i \neq b} q_i + q_b) - \xi q_b - \frac{dC_b(q_b)}{dq_b} - P_t \frac{dF_b(q_b)}{dq_b} + \rho_b^- - \rho_b^+ = 0 \tag{32}$$

$$0 \leq \rho_b^- \perp q_b - q_b^{\min} \geq 0 \tag{33}$$

$$0 \leq \rho_b^+ \perp q_b^{\max} - q_b \geq 0 \tag{34}$$

The profit maximization problem for renewable Genco g ($\forall g \in G$) under the CT&FIT scheme can be formulated as follows:

$$\max_{q_g} \left[A - \xi(\sum_{i \in N, i \neq g} q_i + q_g) + P_f \right] q_g - C_g(q_g) \tag{35}$$

$$\text{s.t.} \qquad q_g^{\min} \leq q_g \leq q_g^{\max} \tag{36}$$

Its KKT conditions are:

$$A - \xi(\sum_{i \in N, i \neq g} q_i + q_g) + P_f - \xi q_g - \frac{dC_g(q_g)}{dq_g} + \rho_g^- - \rho_g^+ = 0 \tag{37}$$

$$0 \leq \rho_g^- \perp q_g - q_g^{\min} \geq 0 \tag{38}$$

$$0 \leq \rho_g^+ \perp q_g^{\max} - q_g \geq 0 \tag{39}$$

Besides the quota obligation constraint (19), the following financial balance constraint (40) is also considered.

$$P_f \sum_{g \in G} q_g = P_t \sum_{b \in B} e_b q_b \qquad (40)$$

Using the nonlinear complementarity function, the complementarity conditions, such as (33),(34),(38),(39), can be reformulated as a set of nonlinear equations. By gathering each Genco's first order optimality (KKT) conditions, the quota obligation constraint (19) and financial balance constraint (40), the equilibrium results, such as each Genco's output, the market price, the CT price and the FIT price, could be derived by solving a set of nonlinear equations.

3   Numerical Simulations

Suppose that there are three fossil-fuel Gencos and one renewable Genco in a pool-based wholesale market. The parameters of each Genco are given in Table 1. In the market inverse demand function, the parameter A takes a value of $240.0/(MW \cdot h)$ and ξ is assumed to be $0.07/(MW)^2 \cdot h$.

Table 1. Parameters of Gencos

Genco	Type	Cost coefficients			Minimum output /MW	Maximum output /MW	CO_2 emission rate /t/(MW·h)
		u /$/(MW)^2h	v /$/(MW·h)	z /$			
1	coal	0.030	14.0	0	100	1000	1.20
2	coal	0.025	23.0	0	65	650	0.84
3	CCGT	0.020	50.0	0	60	600	0.45
4	wind	-----	90.0	0	0	600	0.0

3.1   CT Price and FIT Price under Different Environmental Policies

Fig.1 shows the CT prices under the CT and CT&FIT policies for varying renewable energy quotas. It can be observed that the CT price under the CT scheme is higher than

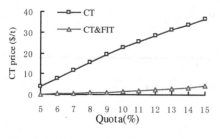

Fig. 1. CT Prices under CT and CT&FIT

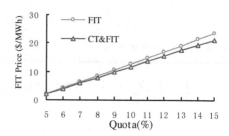

Fig. 2. FIT Prices under FIT and CT&FIT

that under the CT&FIT scheme, especially for high quotas. As the quota increases, the CT price under the CT policy rises quickly while the CT price under the CT&FIT scheme increases slowly. Fig.2 reveals that as the quota increases, the FIT price under FIT policy is increasingly higher than that under the CT&FIT scheme.

3.2   Gencos' Output and Market Price under Different Environmental Policies

The output of fossil-fuel Genco 1, the total emissions of CO_2, the output of renewable Genco 4, the total output and market price under different environmental policies are illustrated in Fig.3-Fig.7, respectively.

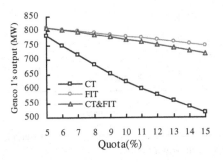
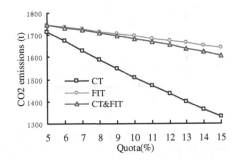

Fig. 3. Fossil-fuel Genco 1's output under different environmental policies

Fig. 4. Total CO_2 emissions under different environmental policies

From Fig.3, it can be seen that the fossil-fuel Genco 1's outputs under different environmental policies will reduce as the quota increases. Under the CT scheme, the reduction is most remarkable. This is because, under the CT policy, the higher CT price increases the costs of fossil-fuel Gencos which will lower these Gencos' competitiveness. Fig.4 reveals that the CT policy has the advantage of reducing emissions compared to the FIT and CT&FIT policy.

From Fig.5, it can be noted that the renewable Genco's output under different environmental policies will increase as the quota increases. The FIT and CT&FIT policies outperform the CT scheme in promoting renewable energy.

From Fig. 6 and Fig.7, it can be observed that under the CT policy, the total output decreases and the market price increases as the quota increases, while under the FIT and CT&FIT policies, the results are just the opposite. This is because under the CT scheme, the presence of carbon tax will equivalently increase the whole marginal generation cost, which will lead to a lower generation output. On the contrary, the subsidy in the FIT scheme will equivalently decrease the whole marginal generation cost, which will lead to a higher generation output. Although the CT&FIT policy has the characteristics of both the CT and FIT, it is more akin to the FIT scheme.

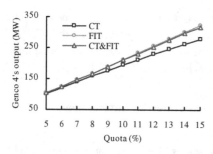

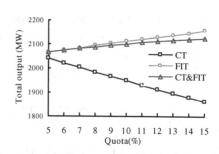

Fig. 5. Renewable Genco 4's output under different environmental policies

Fig. 6. The total output under different environmental policies

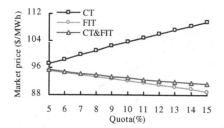

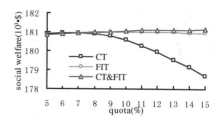

Fig. 7. Market price under different environmental policies

Fig. 8. Social welfare under different environmental policies

3.3   Social Welfare under Different Environmental Policies

In this paper, the social welfare is calculated as follows:

$$SW = R_0 - C_{gen} + R_{CT} - C_{FIT} - C_{carbon} \qquad (41)$$

where R_0 is the gross consumer surplus, C_{gen} is the total generation cost, R_{CT} is the carbon tax revenue, C_{FIT} is the subsidy for renewable energy, and C_{carbon} is social cost of CO_2. We assume the social cost of CO_2 is $50/t [12].

Fig.8 shows the social welfares under different environmental policies for varying quotas. It can be observed that for relatively lower renewable quotas, there is no obvious difference in the social welfares under the three policies. The social welfare under the CT&FIT policy will increase slightly with increasing the quota, while the social welfare under the CT scheme will decline dramatically after the renewable quota reaches a certain level.

4   Conclusions

This paper examines the impacts of different environmental policies on the electricity market competition and the social welfare. Cournot equilibrium models for electricity wholesale market competition are developed taking into account different environmental policies. The nonlinear complementarity approach is employed to solve these equilibrium problems. An environmental policy that combines the carbon tax and the feed-in tariff (CT&FIT) is also proposed in this paper. The performances of different environmental policies are compared in the numerical simulations. It can be shown that as compared to the FIT and CT&FIT policies, the CT scheme has the advantage of saving energy and reducing greenhouse emissions, while the FIT and CT&FIT policies outperform the CT scheme in promoting renewable energy. The total social welfare will increase under the CT&FIT policy when the renewable electricity quota increases, unlike the CT scheme where the total social welfare declines after the renewable quota reaches a certain level.

Acknowledgments. Research grants from National Natural Science Foundation of China (No.70871074, 51007052) and "11th Five-Year Plan" 211 Construction Project of Shanghai University are acknowledged.

References

1. Tsoutsos, T., Papadopoulou, E., Katsiri, A., et al.: Supporting schemes for renewable energy sources and their impact on reducing the emissions of greenhouse gases in Greece. Renewable and Sustainable Energy Reviews 12, 1767–1788 (2008)
2. Cansino, J.M., Pablo-Romero, M.d.P., Roman, R., et al.: Tax incentives to promote green electricity: An overview of EU-27 countries. Energy Policy 38, 6000–6008 (2010)
3. Mabee, W.E., Mannion, J., Carpenter, T.: Comparing the feed-in tariff incentives for renewable electricity in Ontario and Germany. Energy Policy 40, 480–489 (2012)
4. Ventosa, M., Bayllo, A., Ramos, A., et al.: Electricity market modeling trends. Energy Policy 33, 897–913 (2005)
5. Voorspools, K.R., Dhaeseleer, W.D.: Modelling of electricity generation of large interconnected power systems: How can a CO2 tax influence the European generation mix. Energy Conversion & Management 47, 1338–1358 (2006)
6. Green, R.: Carbon tax or carbon permits: the impact on generators' risks. The Energy Journal 29, 67–89 (2008)
7. Downward, A.: Carbon Charges in Electricity Markets with Strategic Behavior and Transmission. The Energy Journal 31, 159–166 (2010)
8. Couture, T., Gagnon, Y.: An analysis of feed-in tariff remuneration models: Implications for renewable energy investment. Energy Policy 38, 955–965 (2010)
9. Wong, S., Bhattacharya, K., Fuller, J.D.: Long-Term Effects of Feed-In Tariffs and Carbon Taxes on Distribution Systems. IEEE Trans. Power Systems 25, 1241–1253 (2010)
10. O'Connell, J.F.: Welfare Economic Theory. Auburn House Publishing, Boston (1982)
11. Wang, X., Li, Y.Z., Zhang, S.H.: Oligopolistic equilibrium analysis for electricity markets: a liner complementarity approach. IEEE Trans. Power Systems 19, 1348–1355 (2004)
12. Hammond, G.P., Ondo Akwe, S.S., Williams, S.: Techno-economic appraisal of fossil-fuelled power generation systems with carbon dioxide capture and storage. Energy 36, 975–984 (2011)

Overload Risk Assessment in Grid-Connected Induction Wind Power System

Xue Li, Xiong Zhang, Dajun Du, and Jia Cao

Department of Automation, Shanghai University, Shanghai, 200072, China
{lixue,zhangxiong,ddj,jiajia1222}@shu.edu.cn

Abstract. Aiming at the new uncertainties brought by wind farms connected directly into power grid, a novel approach to calculate overload risk in grid-connected induction wind power system is proposed. In this method, the probability and consequence of line flow fluctuations is fully considered, and a probabilistic wind farm model is firstly presented. The probabilistic load flow (PLF) calculation with correlated parameters is then used to analyze the randomness of system statuses. Furthermore, the severity function is applied to describe the impact of line flow fluctuations. Finally, the overload risk index is quantified and is treated as an indicator of power system security. Simulation results of the modified 5-bus system confirm the effectiveness of the proposed method.

Keywords: wind farm, overload risk, probabilistic load flow (PLF), correlate, risk assessment.

1   Introduction

To achieve fossil energy saving and emission reduction, more attention is focused on wind power that is playing an increasingly important role in power system. However, wind energy, with the characteristics of randomness, gap and fluctuation, is a kind of unstable energy. With the enlargement of wind farm and wind power unit capacity, it is urgent to study the security of power system connected with wind farms.

The conventional deterministic evaluation methods obtain the system security state in accordance with "the most serious accident decision criteria" in a particular state, which are commonly used in power system under the traditional regulated conditions [1]-[3]. However, the deterministic evaluation methods get usually much conservative results in overload analysis. Recently, risk theory is employed to power system, and the risk assessment method is gradually formed [4]-[7]. For example, a method to assess the cumulative risk associated with overload security has been proposed [7]. It quantifies the risk index reflecting the possibility and severity of risk occurrence. The safety status of the whole system can be reported.

There exist usually a large number of disturbances and uncertainties in the operation of power system. In a certain time, the state variables and control variables of system present the characteristic of stochastic variation. Specially, the bus

T. Xiao, L. Zhang, and S. Ma (Eds.): ICSC 2012, Part II, CCIS 327, pp. 44–51, 2012.

injections in grid-connected induction wind power system are fluctuated with the uncertainties of wind power and load. The line flows influenced by the bus injections are also uncertain [8], and overload often occurs. The probabilistic load flow (PLF) calculation [9] provides an effective tool to analyze the relationship between the bus injection fluctuation and overload and report the operation state of system. There exist some methods to solve the PLF calculation [10]-[12], and Monte Carlo simulation (MCS) [10] is the simplest method. Moreover, the correlation of load and wind power may bring the certain effect on the risk assessment results, so it is necessary to study the risk indices of the grid-connected induction wind power system considering the influence of correlated parameters [13][14]. Considering spatially correlated power sources and loads, a probabilistic power flow model has been proposed. The proposed model was solved using an extended point estimate method that accounts for dependencies among the input random variables.

The paper considers the uncertainty and correlation of load and wind power, and a PLF method based on MCS to solve overload is proposed. The paper is organized as follows. The probabilistic models in wind power generation system are presented in Section 2. Overload risk assessment is proposed in Section 3. The simulation results on the modified 5-bus system are analyzed in Section 4, followed by a conclusion Section 5.

2   Probabilistic Models in Wind Power Generation System

The wind turbine model is given by [15]

$$P_m = \frac{1}{2}\rho A v^3 C_p \tag{1}$$

where ρ is the density of air (kg/m^3), A is the area swept out by the turbine blades (m^2), v is the wind speed (m/s), and C_p is the dimensionless power coefficient. Here, C_p can be expressed as a function of the blade tip speed ratio and be obtained by interpolation method.

The wind speed are usually modeled as [15]

$$\varphi(v) = \frac{k}{c}(\frac{v}{c})^{k-1}\exp[-(\frac{v}{c})^k] \qquad (k > 0, v > 0, c > 1), \tag{2}$$

where v represents wind speed, and $\varphi(v)$ is the Weibull probability density function (PDF) with the shape parameter k and the scale parameter c. Weibull parameters can be obtained by the mean and standard deviation of wind speed. The induction generator is usually used in a wind farm, and its equivalent circuit can be simplified into equivalent circuit [15].

The real power and reactive power injected into grid generated by wind power generator can be expressed as

$$P_e = -\frac{U^2 r_2 / s}{(r_2 / s)^2 + x_k^2} \ , \tag{3}$$

$$Q_e = \frac{r_2^2 + x_k (x_k + x_m) s^2}{r_2 x_m s} P_e \ , \tag{4}$$

where $x_k = x_1 + x_2$, U is the generator voltage.

It can be seen from (3) and (4) that the reactive power absorbed by wind power generator has close relationship to the voltage U and the slip s when the real power P_e is certain. Moreover, note that the uncertainty of the mechanical power of the wind turbine induces uncertainty in the powers generated by the wind power generator.

3   Overload Risk Assessment in Grid-Connected Induction Wind Power System

3.1   Probabilistic Model of Overload

The overload possibility finds expression in random probability distribution. PLF calculation is a load flow analysis method that treats the known variables and unknown variables as random variables. It can be used for the analysis of probability distribution and various characters for power flow and node voltage. In this paper, PLF method is used to calculate the possibility of line flow fluctuations in grid-connected induction wind power system.

Let N_W denote the set of the buses connected with wind farm. Assuming that the wind farm is connected as bus i ($i \in N_W$), the corresponding PLF equations that are for grid –connected induction wind power system are given by

$$\begin{cases} P_{ei}(e_i, f_i, s_i) - P_{Li} - \sum_{j \in i}(e_i a_i + f_i b_i) = 0 \\ Q_{ei}(e_i, f_i, s_i) - Q_{Li} - \sum_{j \in i}(f_i a_i - e_i b_i) = 0 \ , \\ P_{mi} - P_{ei}(e_i, f_i, s_i) = 0 \end{cases} \tag{5}$$

where P_{Li} and Q_{Li} are the load real and reactive powers in ith bus, respectively, $a_i = G_{ij} e_j - B_{ij} f_j$ and $b_i = G_{ij} f_j + B_{ij} e_j$. P_{mi} and P_{ei} are the mechanical power of wind turbine and the electrical power of wind generator at the ith bus, respectively.

Load is described by the normal distribution. Note that when the uncertainties of wind speed and load are incorporated, the mechanical power, the real power and reactive power injected into grid generated by wind power generator are also described by the probabilistic equations. The mechanical power and electrical power in (5) can be calculated using (3) and (4), respectively. The Newton-Raphson algorithm is used to solve the unified iteration for the original state variables and the slip. In the correction equations of PLF, the corresponding elements of Jacobian matrix are modified [16], which retains the quadratic convergence characteristic of NR algorithm.

3.2   Severity Model of Overload

The severity for overload is related to line real power and defined specific to each line. The real power as percentage of rating (PR) power of each line determines the overload severity of that line [17]. As shown in Fig.1, for each line, when the real power at 90% of the rated value, the risk severity value is 0; when the real power at 100% of the rated value, the risk severity value is 1. The risk severity value of overload has linear relationship with the line real power. When the line real power is less than 90% of the rated value, the risk severity value is 0.

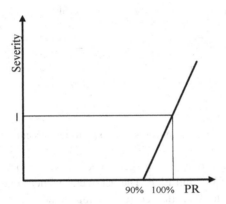

Fig. 1. Severity function of overload

3.3   Risk Index of Overload

Base on risk theory and overload definition, the overload risk r_{isk} of line i is the result of the probability p_r multiplying the severity of transmission line flow s_e :

$$r_{isk}\left(Z_i\right) = \int_{-\infty}^{+\infty} p_r\left(Z_i\right) s_e\left(Z_i\right) dZ_i \ , \tag{6}$$

where Z_i is the line flow, $p_r\left(Z_i\right)$, $s_e\left(Z_i\right)$, $r_{isk}\left(Z_i\right)$ are the probability, the severity and overload risk, respectively.

4   Numerical Example

The proposed method was applied to a modified 5-bus test system as shown in Fig.2. The equivalent wind farms were connected at the node 1 of 5-bus test system by the two step-up transformer and double circuit transmission line. The nodes 6 and 7 were added with the wind farms connected with the system. A computer program was carried out using MATLAB.

There are 20 identical wind turbines in the wind farm, each of which has the nominal capacities equal to 600KW. Its rated power factor is 0.89. All wind turbines are assumed equipped with induction generators compensated by a capacitor bank equal to 29.7% of their nominal capacity. The parameters of wind farm are given as follows. The density of air ρ is $1.2245kg / m^3$, the area swept out by the turbine blades A is $1840m^2$, the identical cut-in wind speeds, cut-out wind speeds and rated wind speeds of wind farm are given as $3m / s$, $20m / s$ and $14m / s$, respectively.

The parameters of a wind generator on the rated capacity base and the parameters of equivalent wind generator on a 100MVA base are shown in [15].

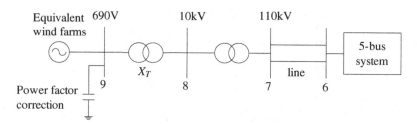

Fig. 2. Wind farm connected to 5-bus test system

The 10000 wind speed samples can be generated according to the shape parameter and the scale parameter of Weibull PDF. The parameter values are given as $k = 2$ and $c = 6.7703$. According to (2), the corresponding wind power outputs can be calculated. 10000 nodal powers random samples were generated according to the means and standard deviations of uncertain nodal powers. The means were taken as per-unit value and the standard deviations were taken as 5% of their means. Then, the wind power and nodal power samples were used to execute the MCS. The fiducial value was 100MVA and the upper and lower bounds of voltage were 1.1 and 0.9, respectively. Bound of line real power is listed in Table 1.

Table 1. Bound of line real power

line	Bound of real power/p.u.
1—2	1.7769
1—3	0.0721
1—7	0.0371
2—3	1.5266
2—4	5.5038
3—5	2.7625
7—6	0.0371

To analyze the influence of correlated parameters on risk indices, the MCS under different correlation were taken. The parameter p is correlation coefficient. Table 2 shows the mean and standard deviation results for a selected set of output random variables.

Table 2. Comparisons of power flow result of different correlation coefficient

Load flow results	$p = 0$		$p = 0.9$	
	μ	σ	μ	σ
P_{23}	1.3878	0.1854	1.3853	0.2649
P_{24}	-5.0034	0.2548	-5.0027	0.2553
P_{35}	-2.5114	0.2998	-2.5187	0.5347
P_{76}	-0.0337	0.0317	-0.0339	0.0317
P_{21}	1.6154	0.0899	1.6160	0.0802
P_{31}	0.0656	0.0918	0.0681	0.1452
P_{71}	0.0338	0.0317	0.0339	0.0317

From Table 2, it can be seen that the means and standard deviations of load flow solution are affected to a certain extent after considering the correlation. There are more effects on the standard deviation. For example, the means of P_{23} are 1.3878 and 1.3853 for different correlation coefficient, which are almost the same. However, the deviations are 0.1854 and 0.2649, respectively, which are completely different.

The PDFs of the real power of line 2-1 for different correlation coefficient are shown in Figs.3 and 4. This demonstrates the difference between the different correlation coefficient, i.e., the mean and standard deviation were 1.6154 and 0.0899 in Fig.3, while the mean and standard deviation were 1.6160 and 0.0802 respectively in Fig.4 when considering the correlation. Therefore, the probabilities were 0.0363 and 0.0219 when the real power just over the bound. This provides much effective information for security analysis in grid-connected induction wind power system.

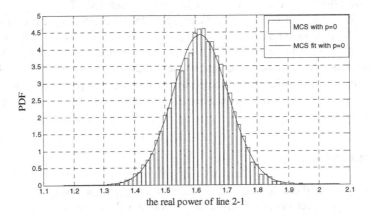

Fig. 3. PDFs of line 2-1 for $p=0$

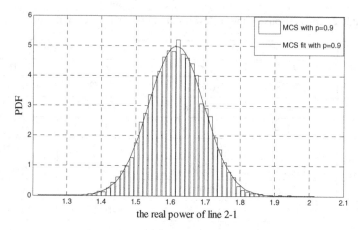

Fig. 4. PDFs of line 2-1 for p=0.9

Table 3. Comparisons of risk indices of different correlation coefficient

line	$p = 0$	$p = 0.9$
1-2	0.0150	0.0123
1-3	0.2952	0.7090
1-7	0.0687	0.0685
2-3	0.0633	0.1251
2-4	0.0399	0.0401
3-5	0.0928	0.2779
7-6	0.0690	0.0686

The possibilities of line overload can be got from Table 2 and the PDFs of Figs 3 and 4. The overload severity value can be also obtained from Fig.1. According to this known knowledge, the overload risk index was quantified. Table 3 shows the overload risk assessment results on different correlation coefficient. From Table 3, considering the correlation of load and wind power, the risk indices are different from that with the independent parameters. It can also be seen that the risk indices become bigger and the system risk becomes worse when considering the correlation. Consequently, the risk indices are affected by the parameter dependence. The results also indicate that the correlation between load and wind power has a major impact on the results of risk assessment.

5   Conclusions

Wind farms connected directly into the power grid have brought new challenges to the safe operation of power system. Considering overload and the correlation between bus injections problems, this paper presents a risk assessment method of overload in gird-connected induction wind power system. Using MCS for PLF to analyze the possibility and severity of overload, the proposed method can effectively overcome the disadvantages of the determined assessment method. The effectiveness of the proposed method is verified by the modified 5-bus system. Considering the correlation of load and wind power, The risk indices obtained can be a more accurate reflection of the system security, which can provide much effective information for the decision-maker.

Acknowledgment. This work was supported in part by the National Science Foundation of China under Grant No. 51007052 and 61104089, and Science and Technology Commission of Shanghai Municipality under Grant No. 11ZR1413100.

References

1. Duan, X., Yuan, J., He, Y., et al.: Sensitivity analysis method on voltage stability of power systems. Automation of Electric Power Systems 21(4), 9–12 (1997)
2. Dan, D.: A practical calculation method for power system voltage stability. Power System Technology 20(6), 61–63 (1996)
3. Zeng, Y., Yu, Y.: A practical direct method for determining dynamic security regions of electric power systems. Proceedings of the CSEE 23(5), 24–28 (2003)
4. Ming, N., McCalley, J.D., Vittal, V., et al.: Software implementation of online risk-based security assessment. IEEE Trans. on Power Systems 18(3), 1165–1172 (2003)
5. Hua, W., McCalley, J.D., Vittal, V., et al.: Risk based voltage security assessment. IEEE Trans. on Power Systems 15(4), 1247–1254 (2000)
6. Zhao, S., Zhang, D.: Risk assessment of smart grid. Power System Technology 33(19), 7–10 (2009)
7. Dai, Y., McCalley, J.D., Vittal, V.: Annual risk assessment for overload security. IEEE Trans. on Power Systems 16(4), 616–623 (2001)
8. Chen, W., Luo, L.: Risk assessment and preventive control for power system overload. East China Electric Power 36(7), 42–45 (2008)
9. Borkowska, B.: Probabilistic load flow. IEEE Trans. on Power Systems PAS (93), 752–759 (1974)
10. Rubinstein, R.Y.: Simulation and the Monte Carlo Method. Wiley, New York (1981)
11. Dopazo, J.F., Klitin, O.A., Sasson, A.M.: Stochastic load flows. IEEE Trans. on Power System 94(2), 299–309 (1975)
12. Allan, R.N., Al-Shakarchi, M.R.G.: Probabilistic techniques in AC load flow analysis. Proc. IEEE 124(2), 54–160 (1977)
13. Usaola, J.: Probabilistic load flow with correlated wind power injections. Electric Power System Research 80(5), 528–536 (2010)
14. Morales, J.M., Baringo, L., Conejo, A.J., Minguez, R.: Probabilistic power flow with correlated wind source. The Institution of Engineering and Technology 5(4), 641–651 (2010)
15. Li, X., Pei, J., Zhang, S.: A probabilistic wind farm model for probabilistic load flow calculation. In: Asia-Pacific Power and Energy Engineering Conference, APPEEC 2010, pp. 1–4 (2010)
16. Fuerte-Esquivel, C.R., Acha, E.: A Newton-type algorithm for the control of power flow in electrical power network. IEEE Trans. on Power Systems 12(4), 1474–1480 (1997)
17. Ming, N., McCalley, J.D., Vittal, V., et al.: Online risk-based security assessment. IEEE Trans. on Power Systems 18(1), 258–265 (2003)

Simulation Research on the Effect of Thermocline on Underwater Sound Propagation

Lin Zhang, Lianglong Da, and Guojun Xu

Navy Submarine Academy, 266071 Qingdao, China
zhanglinqtxy@sohu.com

Abstract. The thermocline has an important influence on sound propagation or underwater acoustic detection in shallow water. The beam-displacement ray-mode theory is used to analyze the effect of thermocline on underwater sound propagation. The peculiarity of this method is that the boundary effects on the sound field can be expressed by the equivalent boundary reflection coefficient. An improved new method for computing the upper boundary reflection coefficient in the theory is proposed based on the generalized phase integral eigen function and an univocal formulation of upper boundary reflection coefficient is deduced. An ocean environment model of thermocline is established. The effect of thermocline's depth, thickness and intensity on sound transmission loss is discussed. The research result shows that thermocline has an important effect on sound transmission loss. It is of practical guiding significance in sonar detection and underwater warfare.

Keywords: Sound propagation, thermocline, beam-displacement ray-mode theory, transmission loss.

1   Introduction

This paper discusses the influence of thermocline on underwater acoustic propagation in shallow water by the Beam-Displacement Ray-Mode (BDRM) theory. The propagation of acoustic waves is extremely complicated because of the multiplicity of spatial and temporal scales of variability in shallow water. In summer and fall, there often exists a strong seasonal thermocline in many shallow water areas. The seasonal thermocline has an important influence on sound propagation or underwater acoustic detection in shallow water.

In shallow water with a thermocline, the sea water can be divided into three layers. In the upper and lower layers the sound speed changes little as the depth increases, while it decreases sharply in the middle layer. In this kind of environment, the sound propagation characteristics will strongly depend on the thermocline's depth, thickness and intensity. Ref. [1] calculates the pulse waveforms by ray-mode theory with beam displacement for shallow water with an ideal thermocline. Using the concept of beam-displacement, the sound propagations in shallow water with a linear thermocline are discussed by Zhu and Zhang [2]. Ref. [3] introduces a normal mode method for propagation modeling in common horizontally stratified shallow water, which is called Beam-Displacement Ray-Mode (BDRM) theory. The peculiarity of this

T. Xiao, L. Zhang, and S. Ma (Eds.): ICSC 2012, Part II, CCIS 327, pp. 52–60, 2012.

method is that the boundary effects on the sound field can be expressed by the equivalent boundary reflection coefficient. For the calculations of shallow water sound field, the method has high accuracy and fast speed. An improved new method for computing the upper boundary reflection coefficient in the theory is proposed based on the generalized phase integral (WKBZ) eigenfunction and an univocal formulation of upper boundary reflection coefficient is deduced in this paper.

This paper is organized as follows. In section II, an ocean environment model of thermocline is established. Section III introduces the basic theory of the Beam-Displacement Ray-Mode (BDRM) theory and deduces the univocal formulation of the upper boundary reflection coefficient. In section IV, the influence of thermocline's depth, thickness and intensity on sound transmission loss is discussed, and simulations are made. Section V gives the conclusions.

2   Ocean Environment Model of Thermocline

In this section, an ocean environment model of thermocline is first established. We consider a realistic shallow water environment model of thermocline, that is, three water layers overlying a fluid bottom. The upper and the lower water layer are homogeneous, and in the middle water layer, the sound speed decreases linearly as the depth increases, as shown in Fig. 1.

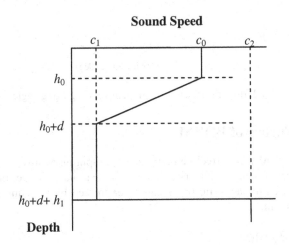

Fig. 1. Ocean environment model of thermocline

Above the thermocline is the surface homogeneous layer, whose thickness is h_0, and whose sound speed is c_0. The thickness of the middle layer, or the thermocline is d, whose sound speed decreases with depth. Below the thermocline is the lower isospeed layer, whose thickness is h_1, and whose sound speed is c_1. Assume that the water is the medium of constant density. The lower layer can be considered as the liquid waveguide and the other two layers as the outside of the waveguide. For this ocean model, the thermocline's depth is h_0 and thickness is d. We define $(c_0-c_1)/d$ as the thermocline's intensity I.

The bottom is the liquid half space, whose sound speed is c_2. The other parameters of the bottom is the dendity ρ and the absorption α. For this sea bottom, the reflection coefficient versus grazing angle is shown in Fig. 2. at different absorption α when $c_1=1480$ m/s, the density of water is 1.0 g/cm^3, $c_2=1680$ m/s, $\rho=1.95$ g/cm^3.

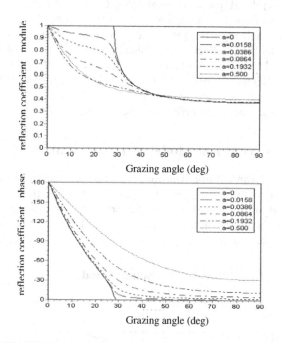

Fig. 2. Bottom reflection coefficient versus grazing angle

3   Basic Theory of BDRM

The theory of BDRM is an effective method for computing acoustic fields in shallow water. The advantages of this theory are not only fast and accurate, but also that the boundary effects on the acoustic fields can be expressed by the equivalent boundary reflection coefficient.

3.1   Theory of BDRM

In the common horizontally stratrified water, the sound field excited by a harmonic point source can be expressed as a sum of normal modes:

$$p(r, z_s, z; \omega) = \sqrt{\frac{8\pi}{r}} e^{i\pi/4} \sum_l \Phi(z_s, v_l) \Phi(z, v_l) \sqrt{v_l} e^{i\mu_l r - \beta_l r} \qquad (1)$$

where $v_l = \mu_l + i\beta_l$ is the complex eigenvalue, the real part μ_l is the horizontal wavenumber, and the image part β_l is the mode attenuation. The eigenfunction $\Phi(z, v_l)$ satisfies

$$\frac{d^2\Phi(z,v_l)}{dz^2} + (k^2(z) - v_l^2)\Phi(z,v_l) = 0 \tag{2}$$

and its boundary conditions.

The eigen-equation of the normal mode can be expressed as

$$2\int_{\zeta_{l1}}^{\zeta_{l2}} \sqrt{k^2(z) - \mu_l^2}\, dz + \varphi_1(\mu_l) + \varphi_2(\mu_l) = 2l\pi, l = 0,1,\cdots, \tag{3}$$

and

$$\beta_l = \frac{-\ln|V_1(\mu_l)V_2(\mu_l)|}{S(\mu_l) + \delta_1(\mu_l) + \delta_2(\mu_l)}, \tag{4}$$

where $\varphi_1(\mu_l)$ and $\varphi_2(\mu_l)$ are the phases of the reflection coefficients on the upper and lower boundaries. $S(\mu_l)$ is the cycle distance of eigen-ray, $\delta_1(\mu_l)$ and $\delta_2(\mu_l)$ are the beam displacements of the eigen-ray on the upper and lower boundaries.

By partial differential with respect to μ and ω on equation (3), the mode group velocity can be obtained as

$$v_l = \frac{\partial \mu_l}{\partial \omega} = \frac{S(\mu_l) + \delta_1(\mu_l) + \delta_2(\mu_l)}{T(\mu_l) + \tau_1(\mu_l) + \tau_2(\mu_l)}, \tag{5}$$

where $T(\mu_l)$ is the travel time along the eigen-ray, $\tau_1(\mu_l)$ and $\tau_2(\mu_l)$ are the time delays corresponding to the beam displacements $\delta_1(\mu_l)$ and $\delta_2(\mu_l)$ at the the upper and lower boundaries.The method using equations (3), (4) and (5) to calculate the sound field is called beam-displacement ray-mode theory.

The eigenfunction between the the upper and lower boundaries can be expressed by generalized phase integral (WKBZ) approximation [4].

$$\Phi(z,\mu_l) = \sqrt{\frac{2}{S(\mu_l) + \delta_1(\mu_l) + \delta_2(\mu_l)}} \times$$

$$\begin{cases}
\dfrac{\exp(-\int_z^{\zeta_{l1}} \sqrt{\mu_l^2 - k^2(z)}\, dz - \gamma)}{\left\{BE^{4/3} - DE^{2/3}\left[k^2(z) - \mu_l^2\right] + 16\left[k^2(z) - \mu_l^2\right]^2\right\}^{1/8}}, & z < \zeta_{l1} \\[4mm]
\dfrac{\sin(-\int_{\zeta_{l1}}^z \sqrt{k^2(z) - \mu_l^2}\, dz + \dfrac{\pi}{2} - \dfrac{\varphi_1}{2})}{\left\{BE^{4/3} - DE^{2/3}\left[k^2(z) - \mu_l^2\right] + \left[k^2(z) - \mu_l^2\right]^2\right\}^{1/8}}, & \zeta_{l1} < z < \zeta_{l2} \\[4mm]
\dfrac{(-1)^l \exp(-\int_{\zeta_{l2}}^z \sqrt{\mu_l^2 - k^2(z)}\, dz)}{\sqrt{2}\left\{BE^{4/3} - DE^{2/3}\left[k^2(z) - \mu_l^2\right] + 16\left[k^2(z) - \mu_l^2\right]^2\right\}^{1/8}}, & z > \zeta_{l2}
\end{cases} \tag{6}$$

where $B = 2.152, D = 1.619, E = \left| \dfrac{dk^2(z)}{dz} \right|, \gamma = -\ln\left[\cos(\dfrac{\varphi_1}{2}) \right].$

3.2   Method for Computing the Upper Boundary Reflection Coefficient

Computation of the upper boundary reflection coefficient is the core of BDRM theory. The computation accuracy of the boundary reflection coefficient can directly affect the eigenvalues precision, and further the accuracy of the acoustic fields.

The upper boundary reflection coefficient can be expressed as $V_1 = e^{i\varphi_1(\mu_l)}$. The upper boundary phase-shift $\varphi_1(\mu_l)$ can't be omitted easily or disposed approximately since the sound speed in the waters above the upper boundary changes rapidly. According to the distribution of horizontal wavenumber μ_l, the normal modes can be divided into 2 categories. One includes reversed normal modes, in which eigenrays are reversed below the upper boundary, that is $\mu_l \geq k_0$, where k_0 is the wavenumber at the upper boundary; the other is called reflected normal modes, in which eigenrays are reflected at the upper boundary, that is $\mu_l < k_0$.

For normal modes I, the phase-shift function $\varphi_1(\mu_l)$ of the upper boundary reflection coefficient can be expressed as [5]

$$\varphi_1 = \begin{cases} \dfrac{\pi}{2} + \arctan\left(\dfrac{Ai(t)}{Bi(t)} \right) + \arctan\left(\dfrac{Ai'(t)}{Bi'(t)} \right) & t \geq 0 \\[3mm] \dfrac{\pi}{2} + \arctan\left(\dfrac{Ai(t)}{Bi(t)} \right) + \arctan\left(\dfrac{Ai'(t)}{Bi'(t)} \right) - 2\omega_0 & t < 0 \end{cases} \tag{7}$$

where $t = \dfrac{\mu_l^2 - k_0^2}{b_0^{2/3}}$, $b_0 = \left| \dfrac{dk^2(z)}{dz} \right|_h$, $\omega_0 = \dfrac{2}{3}|t|^{3/2}$, $Ai(t)$ and $Bi(t)$ are Airy functions respectively.

For normal modes II, the phase-shift function $\varphi_1(\mu_l)$ can be obtained by means of the eigenfunction continuity at the upper boundary. The water for $0 \leq z \leq h+dh$ is vertically divided into $n+1$ equidistant grids, and the width of the grid is dh. And the differential form of the wave equation can be expressed as [6]

$$\left\{ 12 + dh^2\left[\dfrac{\omega^2}{c^2(z_j)} - \mu_l^2 \right] \right\}\Phi_j =$$

$$\left\{ 24 - 10dh^2\left[\dfrac{\omega^2}{c^2(z_{j-1})} - \mu_l^2 \right] \right\}\Phi_{j-1} - \left\{ 12 + dh^2\left[\dfrac{\omega^2}{c^2(z_{j-2})} - \mu_l^2 \right] \right\}\Phi_{j-2} \tag{8}$$

where $z_j = jdh$, Φ_j is the value of eigenfunction at grid j. It is assumed that the surface is a pressure release boundary and so $\Phi_0 = 0$, and Φ_1 is a random constant

ε'. Φ_n and Φ_{n+1} at grid n and grid $n+1$ are then computed from Eq.(8). The eigenfunction continuity at the upper boundary can be expressed as

$$\Phi_n = \varepsilon\Phi(h,\mu_l,\varphi_1) \tag{9}$$

$$\Phi_{n+1} = \varepsilon\Phi(h+dh,\mu_l,\varphi_1) \tag{10}$$

Where ε is a constant relative to ε', $\Phi(h,\mu_l,\varphi_1)$ and $\Phi(h+dh,\mu_l,\varphi_1)$ are eigenfunctions based on the WKBZ approximations. By defining

$$\Delta\alpha = -\int_h^{h+dh} \sqrt{k^2(z)-\mu_l^2}\,dz$$

$$\hbar = \frac{\Phi_{n+1}}{\Phi_n} \cdot \frac{\left\{Bb_{h+dh}^{4/3}-Db_{h+dh}^{2/3}\left[k^2(h+dh)-\mu_l^2\right]+\left[k^2(h+dh)-\mu_l^2\right]^2\right\}^{1/8}}{\left\{Bb_h^{4/3}-Db_h^{2/3}\left[k^2(h)-\mu_l^2\right]+\left[k^2(h)-\mu_l^2\right]^2\right\}^{1/8}}$$

where $B=2.152$, $D=1.619$, $b_h = \left|\frac{dk^2(z)}{dz}\right|_h$, $b_{h+dh} = \left|\frac{dk^2(z)}{dz}\right|_{h+dh}$

The phase-shift function for normal modes II is then expressed from Eqs (9) and (10) as,

$$\varphi_1(\mu_l) = 2\arctan\left(\hbar\csc(\Delta\alpha)-\cot(\Delta\alpha)\right) \tag{11}$$

In summary, the phase-shift function of the upper boundary reflection coefficient can be expressed as

$$\varphi_1 = \begin{cases} \dfrac{\pi}{2} + \arctan\left(\dfrac{Ai(t)}{Bi(t)}\right) + \arctan\left(\dfrac{Ai'(t)}{Bi'(t)}\right) & \mu_l > k_0 \\ 2\arctan\left(\hbar\csc(\Delta\alpha)-\cot(\Delta\alpha)\right) & \mu_l \le k_0 \end{cases} \tag{12}$$

4   Effect of Thermocline on Sound Propagation

In this part, using the ocean environment model of thermocline, we discuss the effect of thermocline's depth, thickness and intensity on sound transmission loss by the theory of BDRM.

Because the focus of our study is the influence of thermocline on sound transmission loss, the bottom parameters are fixed at $c_2=1680$ m/s, $\rho=1.8$ g/cm^3, $\alpha=0.6$ dB/λ. At first, we discuss the influence of thermocline's depth on sound transmission loss. The thermocline's thickness d is 15m, and the intensity I is 3.67/s. The thermocline's depth h_0 is from 15m to 40m at a space of 5m. The sound speed profiles are shown in Fig. 3. The source is taken to be at 10m depth, and two receivers are at

30km range, 10m and 80m depths respectively. In Fig. 4 are given the transmission loss curves versus source-receiver range at the frequency of 500Hz.

Secondly, we discuss the influence of thermocline's thickness on sound transmission loss. The thermocline's depth h_0 is 15m, and the intensity I is 3.67/s. The thermocline's thickness d is from 15m to 3m at a space of 3m. The sound speed profiles are shown in Fig. 5. The source is taken to be at 10m depth, and two receivers are at 30km range, 10m and 80m depths respectively. In Fig. 6 are given the transmission loss curves versus source-receiver range at the frequency of 500Hz.

At last, we discuss the influence of thermocline's intensity on sound transmission loss. The thermocline's depth h_0 is 15m, and the thickness d is 15m. The thermocline's intensity I is from 3.67/s to 0.3/s at a space of 0.67/s. The sound speed profiles are shown in Fig. 7. The source is taken to be at 10m depth, and two receivers are at 30km range, 10m and 80m depths respectively. In Fig. 8 are given the transmission loss curves versus source-receiver range at the frequency of 500Hz.

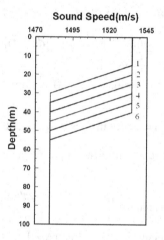

Fig. 3. Sound speed profiles with different thermocline's depths

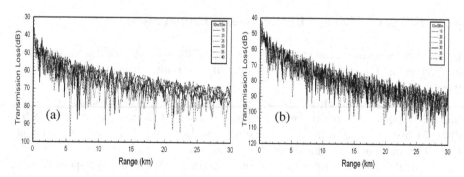

Fig. 4. Transmission loss versus range with different thermocline's depths. (a) source and receiver depths 10m/10m; (b) source and receiver depths 10m/80m.

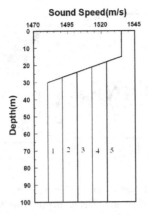

Fig. 5. Sound speed profiles with different thermocline's thickness

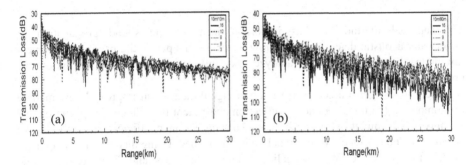

Fig. 6. Transmission loss versus range with different thermocline's thickness. (a) source and receiver depths 10m/10m; (b) source and receiver depths 10m/80m.

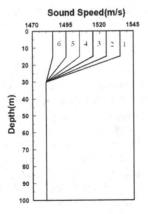

Fig. 7. Sound speed profiles with different thermocline's intensity

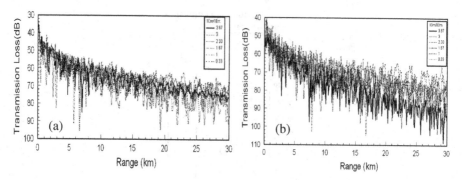

Fig. 8. Transmission loss versus range with different thermocline's intensity. (a) source and receiver depths 10m/10m; (b) source and receiver depths 10m/80m.

5   Conclusions

The seasonal thermocline has important influence on sound propagation or underwater acoustic detection in shallow water. In this paper, the beam-displacement ray-mode theory is used to analyze the influence of thermocline on sound propagation.

Based on the generalized phase integral eigenfunction, an improved new method for computing the upper boundary reflection coefficient in the theory is proposed and an univocal formulation of upper boundary reflection coefficient is deduced. An ocean environment model of thermocline is established. Using this ocean environment model, the influence of thermocline's depth, thickness and intensity on sound transmission loss is discussed.

From Fig.4, Fig.6 and Fig.8, the research results shows that thermocline has an important effect on sound transmission loss. This study is of practical guiding significance in sonar detection and underwater warfare.

References

1. Zhu, Y.: Theoretical analysis on waveform structures of pulse propagating in shallow water with an ideal thermocline. Acta Acustica 14(2), 133–140 (1995)
2. Zhu, Y., Zhang, R.: Pulse propagation in shallow water with thermocline. Science in China, Ser. A 26(3), 271–282 (1996)
3. Zhang, R., Li, F.: Beam-displacement ray-mode theory of sound propagation in shallow water. Science in China, Ser. A 42(7), 740–752 (1999)
4. Zhang, R., He, Y., Liu, H.: Applications of the WKBZ adiabatic mode approach to sound propagation in the Philippine Sea. J. Sound & Vib. 184(2), 439–452 (1995)
5. Murphy, E.L.: Modified ray theory for bounded media. The Journal of the Acoustical Society of America 56(6) (1974)
6. Li, F.: Beam-displacement ray-mode theory and its application in shallow water. National Laboratory of Acoustics (2000)

Study of Real-Time Wave Simulation in Virtual Battlefield Environment

Dinghua Wang[1,2], Fengju Kang[1,2], Huaxing Wu[1,3], and Wei Huang[3]

[1] School of Marine, Northwestern Polytechnical University, Xi'an 710072, China
[2] National Key Laboratory of Underwater Information Process and Control, Xi'an 710072, China
[3] Aeronautics & Astronautics Engineering College, Air Force Engineering University,
Xi'an 710038, China
wangdinghuad342@163.com

Abstract. Aiming at the requirements for virtual naval battle environmental simulation, we present an ocean wave simulation method. Firstly according to double superposition model based on the ocean wave spectrum and the linear ocean wave theory, using the acceleration algorithm for ocean wave numerical simulation, the method completes the three-dimensional shape of ocean wave, and then introduces vertex array graphics rendering into drawing ocean wave. Lastly, to improve the visual fidelity, with separate specular color and local viewpoint, we achieve ocean wave surface reflected light effects simulation. Through testing and validation, the method can quickly simulate ocean waves, and the simulation result is available.

Keywords: ocean wave simulation, vertex array, acceleration algorithm, visualization.

1   Introduction

With the naval battle increasingly prominent position in the future war, and naval weapons and equipment combat simulation technology research deepening, increasingly high requirements of marine battlefield environment modeling and simulation support technology get to a new level. Ocean wave modeling and rendering is one of the key technology and the difficulties in the virtual ocean battlefield environment simulation, because in the virtual naval warfare environment, the authenticity of the waves generated and real-time of ocean wave simulation have higher requirements.

To date, there are already many people to complete the simulation of waves. Early in foreign countries, Peachey [1] adopt a linear combination of sine function and quadratic function to simulate ocean wave frequency spectrum and directional spectrum formula, and implements an ocean wave shape based on wave spectral, Fournier [2] introduce parametric surfaces to simulate the crest curling waves, and achieves the analog ocean wave approximate shape. Such method is simple, intuitive and faster to compute, more obvious man-made traces, the narrow scope of application.

T. Xiao, L. Zhang, and S. Ma (Eds.): ICSC 2012, Part II, CCIS 327, pp. 61–69, 2012.

In the country, with wave spectral inversion linear superposition, HOU Xuelong and some other people[3-5] gets three-dimensional ocean wave field data, with calculation and display carried out separately, and large amounts of data read directly from memory, it greatly increased the consumption of storage space. Moreover, he realized three dimensional dynamic displays with about ten frames of image repeating play, and did not truly reflect the randomness of the ocean waves. Yang Huaiping[6] puts forward a wave real-time rendering method, whose ocean wave model is a small amplitude simplified model based on two-dimensional Stokes equations, he consider ocean waves as the result of a simple gravity waves superposition. But ocean waves usually refers to the storms and surges, they are generated by the wind, ocean waves reflected that the effect of the wind is more complex than the gravity, therefore, its simulation results can not reflect the real situation of the ocean wave fluctuations.

Aiming at the requirements of virtual ocean battlefield and a certain algorithm shortcomings, we bring forward a dynamic ocean wave generation method, and get a large number of high-precision ocean wave data which meet image fidelity and speed two key indicators.

2   Ocean Wave Numerical Simulation

2.1   Algorithm Principle

Based on ocean wave spectrum and linear wave theory, using linear double superposition method (different frequencies and different directions sine wave superposition), it inverse ocean wave data to achieve ocean wave numerical simulation. This method can be a true reflection ocean wave random nature, and its physical concept is clear.

2.2   Ocean Wave Frequency Spectrum and Direction Spectrum Selection

2.2.1   Frequency Spectrum Selection

Ocean wave spectrum is on behalf of the wave energy distribution relative to the composition wave frequency, and easily get through observation, so far it have been proposed a lot of frequency spectrum, the simulated ocean waves adopt JONSWAP spectrum based on 'Joint North Sea Wave Plan' system measurements carried out by Germany, Britain, the United States, Netherlands and other relevant organizations in 1968 - 1969. The following formula:

$$S(\omega) = \alpha \frac{g^2}{\omega^5} \exp\left\{-1.25(\frac{\omega_0}{\omega})^4\right\} \gamma^{\exp}\left\{-\frac{(\omega-\omega_0)^2}{2\sigma^2\omega_0^2}\right\} \tag{1}$$

Where, g is the gravity acceleration; ω_0 is the peak frequency; γ is the elevated factor, which is defined the ratio of spectral peak value E_{max} and P-M spectral peak value $E_{(PM)\max}$ for the same wind speed; σ is known as the peak shape parameters, α is dimensionless constant. The JONSWAP spectrum is limited by ocean wave spectrum of the wind zone state, the scale coefficient α the peak frequency ω_0 and peak elevated factor γ are related with wind speed and wind zone.

2.2.2   Directional Spectrum Selection

The directional spectrum used to represent energy distribution of different direction and frequency composition wave. Generally it can be written as the following forms:

$$S(\omega,\theta) = S(\omega)G(\omega,\theta) \tag{2}$$

Where $S(\omega)$ is frequency Spectrum, $G(\omega,\theta)$ is direction distribution function, referred to as the direction function. According to the three-dimensional ocean wave observational project, direction function used in this paper is the formula as follow:

$$G(\omega,\theta) = 1/\pi(1 + p\cos 2\theta + q\cos 4\theta) \tag{3}$$

2.3   Numerical Simulations Based on Superposition Method

We consider actual ocean waves as the superposition result of different frequencies, different spread direction, different wave height and different initial phase sine wave. Wave surface function $S(\omega,\theta)$ described by directional spectrum is as follows:

$$\eta(x,y,t) = \sum_{m=1}^{M}\sum_{n=1}^{N} a_{mn}\cos[\omega_{mn}t - k_{mn}(x\cos\theta_{mn} + y\sin\theta_{mn}) + \xi_{mn}] \tag{4}$$

Of which: a_{mn}, ω_{mn}, k_{mn}, θ_{mn}, ξ_{mn} are parting unit regular wave amplitude, angular frequency, wave number, spread direction and phase; M is frequency partition number and N is direction partition number.

2.3.1   Parameter Setting

(1) Wave amplitude is $a_{m,n}$, According to the formula (2)

$$a_{m,n} = \sqrt{2 * S_{m,n} * \Delta\omega_m * \Delta\theta} ;$$

(2) Angular frequency is ω_{mn}. As the wave energy is mainly distributed in a narrow band, we abnegate 3% of the total energy in the high-frequency side and low-frequency side, and get a frequency range, then in this range $M \times N$ different frequencies Value based on the energy part principle;

(3) Wave number is k_{mn}. According to the linear wave theory $k_{mn} = \omega_{mn}^2 / g$;

(4) The direction angle is θ_{mn}. Direction angle is an angle engendered by the unit wave propagation direction and x axis in the $[-\pi/2, \pi/2]$ uniform selection.

(5) The initial phase is ξ_{mn}, which randomly obtained by mixed congruent method in the $[0, 2\pi]$.

(6) frequency division number is M and direction partition number is N, In general, the larger M and N is, the more abundant the wave details is, the more smooth the wave surface is, but at the same time it increase the amount of calculation and impact wave real-time rendering were taken for 10 as a better fit point between the real-time and visual realism (with the PC configuration differ).

2.3.2   Acceleration Algorithm Design

Known by the formula (4), when M and N are taken for 10,we should calculate 10×10 cosine function to get height $\eta(x, y, t)$ at the point (x, y) on time t, with selecting 100×100 wave surface grid, computing a screen will be carried out one million times cosine calculation, such a large amount of computation will seriously affect the process efficiency and image quality.

Cosine sum formula can be a good solution to this problem. when the time changes, It's easy to find that in the wave surface point (x, y), a composition wave frequency ω_{mn} Cosine meet tolerances for Δt arithmetic sequence, according to the summation formula of the cosine function:

$$a_{m,n} \cos(\omega_m t_{i+1} + \zeta) + a_{m,n} \cos(\omega_m t_{i-1} + \zeta) = 2 \times a_{m,n} \cos(\omega_m t_i + \zeta) \times \cos(\omega_m \times \Delta t) \qquad (5)$$

Among $\zeta = k_m(x \cos\theta_n + y \sin\theta_n) + \xi_{m,n}$, as each component wave only need to calculate the first two moments function value of each point, the follow-up time function value can be obtained by subtraction and multiplication, without calculating the cosine, the acceleration algorithm can significantly improve program efficiency. But only for the purposes of a wave, waves of different frequencies and cosine without meeting the conditions of arithmetic sequences over time should give a separate calculation and wave superposition.

3 Waves Draw Method

All objects are described as an ordered collection of vertices in OpenGL, while rendering primitives, you need to call a lot of OpenGL functions, if you selected 10000 point to draw 100×100 wave surface mesh, and at least you need to call the 10002 function. At first you call glBegin () function, and then successive draw each vertex, and finally call a glEnd () function. In addition, the additional information (polygon boundary line flag, texture mapping and surface normal, etc.) makes an increase call some function for each vertex, such as glTexcoord 2f (), glNormal 3f (), which makes a function call the number an increase of three to five times, greatly increases the system overhead, and slow down the graphics rendering speed.

In addition, when continuous triangle approximation method implements irregular polygons, there is common vertices redundancy between the adjacent triangles.

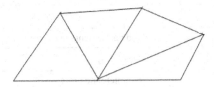

Fig. 1. Irregular polygons

Figure 1 show that the polygon has four faces and six vertices, unfortunately, the common vertex in the use of each triangle must assign once, we only need to deal with the six vertices, but we actually deal with 12 vertices.

Vertex arrays can solve the above problems, OpenGL provide vertex array functions to render graphics, you can only use a few array to designate a large number of vertex-related data, and then use the same amount several functions to access data. Vertices array can reduce the number of function calls, and improve the wave surface grid rendering speed and application performance.

Vertex array rendering ocean wave surface requires three steps, first we should use a list of parameters to activate the array, including the wave surface grid array, texture mapping coordinates array and surface normal array, then calculated data is loaded into the active array, the wave surface grid data obtain by using equation (4) and (5), texture mapping coordinates can get by using the texture perturbation method, vector dot metrix product surface normal array. the List of all data in this article are compose of the individual data elements, we does not introduce cross-array to avoid confusion, therefore the load function span parameters stride unified set to 0. Finally, we lift the pointer index of the data elements list to complete the wave surface.

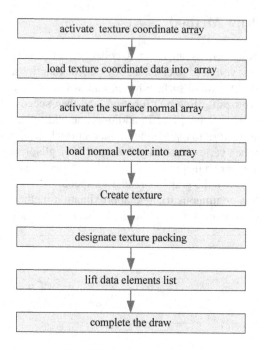

Fig. 2. Drawing flow chart

4   Wave Surface Illumination Effects Rendering

In order to improve the visual fidelity of three-dimensional ocean wave effects, lighting effects of the wave surface are simulated. Mapped lighting calculations consider the environment and scattered light, at the same time, and focuses on the effect of specular reflection simulation. Specular light reflection is different from the reflection of ambient light and scattered light, the reflection of ambient light and scattered light don't affect ocean wave surface color by the viewing position, while specular reflection produce a highlight area in the wave surface, and it's   related to surface material, light source and viewpoint.

Due to the ocean wave surface texture mapping is carried out after the light handling, specular light lose its effect and can not reflect the effect of ocean wave surface light specular reflection. Therefore, when the illumination model is specified, we should separate specular color, environment color and scattering color, for each vertex, the light produce two colors including main color by all non-specular light and subordinate color by the specular light. During texture mapping, we only combine main color with texture color, after texture operations we combine the results with subordinate colors, and then the wave surface will form a relatively significant specular light.

in addition to depending on the vertex normal and the direction of the vertex relative to light, A particular vertex specular reflection brightness relate to the direction of the vertex relative to view point, when view point is infinity, any direction of the vertex relative to view point in the scene are constants, although computation and rendering will be relatively quick and easy, a true reflection is not as good as the local viewpoint. The default location of the viewpoint is set at infinity, in OpenGL, calling glLightModelf (GL_LIGHT_MODEL_LOCAL_VIEWER, GL_TRUE) will be placed the view point on the human eye coordinate system (0, 0, 0) point.

Finally, the corresponding parameters set the mirror reflection highlighted area attribute including specular reflection exponent, light specular reflection color and material specular reflection attribute. A simulated wave surface reflection effect is shown in Figure 3:

Fig. 3. Wave surface and the specular reflection effect

5   Ocean Waves Procedure Performance Test

In order to verify the dynamic ocean waves proposed method validity and the ocean wave data authenticity, we test the program efficiency of accelerated algorithm to obtain the ocean wave data and vertex array rendering ocean waves.

5.1   Wave Data Validation

Test that stimulant ocean wave data statistical characteristics and actual observations information are consistent, we sample the wave surface height at equal intervals on a certain time, and then apply the fast Fourier transform algorithm (FFT) to made spectrum estimation, the results shown in Figure 4. The red line indicates the target spectrum; the blue line shows the estimated spectrum of the simulation results. Visible, simulation spectrum and target spectrum is very close, meaning that the results of ocean wave simulation and linear random ocean wave theory is consistent.

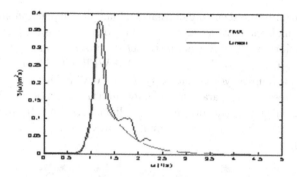

Fig. 4. Linear estimation spectrum and target spectral contrast

5.2   Procedure Performance Testing

A single animation frame time test outcome show in Table 1(in milliseconds).

Table 1. Procedure performance comparison

a single animation frame Computation time	wave surface height	wave surface rendering	umulative total
not using acceleration algorithm and vertex array	566	31	597
using acceleration algorithm and vertex arrays	41	15	56

Visible, acceleration algorithms and vertex array greatly reduce the computation time and rendering time, improve the efficiency of the program, and basically meet the requirements of real-time rendering.

6   Conclusions and Future Work

Aiming at building distributed virtual marine battlefield environment, through the research and experiment of the ocean wave spectrum inversion wave theory, we successful inverse ocean wave field data and complete the ocean wave field three-dimensional modeling. On this basis, with well-designed data solver, image rendering method and three-dimensional display continuing optimization, the ocean wave fluctuation effects simulation can get a successful realization.

Since the current simulation only apply to small-scale waves, it can not meet the requirements of large-scale wave real-time simulation, therefore the next step is to study the waves modeling and display method under the conditions of multi-resolution.

Acknowledgments. This work supported by the ship pre-research support technology foundation, China (11J4.1.1) and the basic research foundation of Northwestern Polytechnical University, China (NWPU2011JC0242).

References

1. Peachey, D.R.: Modeling waves and surf. Computer Graphics 20, 65–74 (1986)
2. Fournier, A., Reeves, W.T.: A simple model of ocean waves. Computer Graphics 20, 75–84 (1986)
3. Hou, X., Huang, Q., Shen, P.: Ocean Wave Real-time Simulation Method Based on FFT. Computer Engineering 35, 256–258 (2009)
4. Yao, H., Bao, J.-S., Jin, Y.: Study of Real-time Wave Simulation in Virtual Battlefield Environment. Acta Armamentari 29, 697–702 (2008)
5. Yin, Y., Jin, Y.: Realistic Rendering of Large-Scale Ocean Wave Scene. Journal Of Computer-Aided Design & Computer Graphics 20, 1617–1622 (2008)
6. Yang, H.-P., Sun, J.-G.: Wave simulation based on ocean wave spectrums. Journal of System Simulation 14, 1175–1178 (2002)

Numerical Modeling for Venus Atmosphere Based on AFES (Atmospheric GCM for the Earth Simulator)

Norihiko Sugimoto[1], Masahiro Takagi[2], Yoshihisa Matsuda[3],
Yoshiyuki O.Takahashi[4], Masaki Ishiwatari[5], and Yoshi-Yuki Hayashi[4]

[1] Research and Education Center for Natural Sciences, Keio University, Yokohama, Japan
[2] Faculty of Science, Kyoto Sangyo University, Kyoto, Japan
[3] Department of Astronomy and Earth Science, Tokyo Gakugei University, Koganei, Japan
[4] Department of Earth and Planetary Sciences, Kobe University, Kobe, Japan
[5] Department of Cosmosciences, Hokkaido University, Sapporo, Japan
nori@phys-h.keio.ac.jp, takagi.masahiro@cc.kyoto-su.ac.jp,
ymatsuda@u-gakugei.ac.jp, {yot,momoko,shosuke}@gfd-dennou.org

Abstract. In order to elucidate phenomena of Venus atmosphere, an atmospheric general circulation model (AGCM) for Venus is being developed on the basis of AFES (AGCM For the Earth Simulator). As a first step toward high resolution numerical simulation with realistic physical processes, we investigate unstable modes on the condition of super-rotation by nonlinear numerical simulation with simplified physical processes. At initial state zonal super-rotation is assumed to exist. We use the relaxation forcing of the meridional temperature gradient to maintain the zonal flow. In the time evolution of this experimental setting, baroclinic modes grow in the cloud layer with small static stability. The structures of unstable modes are similar to those obtained in the linear stability analysis. We discuss resolution dependency of the results.

Keywords: Venus atmosphere, baroclinic instability, Earth Simulator, numerical modeling, geophysical fluid dynamics, planetary sciences.

1   Introduction

The structure of the general circulation differs significantly with each planetary atmosphere. It is one of the most interesting and important open questions of the atmospheric science and fluid dynamics to understand the physical mechanisms causing structures of the general circulations of planetary atmospheres. The purpose of our research project is to elucidate the dynamical processes that characterize the structure of each planetary atmosphere by numerical simulation of general circulation model (GCM) with a common dynamical core of the AFES (Atmospheric general circulation model For the Earth Simulator) [1]. AFES is highly optimized for the Earth simulator which is one of the world's largest vector super-computers provided by Japan Agency for Marine-Earth Science and Technology (JAMSTEC). In the present study we focus on the phenomena on Venus atmosphere.

T. Xiao, L. Zhang, and S. Ma (Eds.): ICSC 2012, Part II, CCIS 327, pp. 70–78, 2012.
© Springer-Verlag Berlin Heidelberg 2012

Venus atmosphere is quite different from Earth one, while Venus is similar to Earth in its radius, mass, and gravity acceleration. Venus has a thick CO_2 atmosphere with surface pressure of 92 bar. Surface temperature is about 730 K due to the strong greenhouse effect of these massive CO_2. In addition, optically thick clouds of sulfuric acid droplets cover over the whole planet from 47 to 70 km. It is considered that solar heating at the cloud layer may be one of the energy sources driving circulation of Venus atmosphere. While the solid part of Venus rotates at extremely slow rate with the period of 243 Earth days, the atmosphere at cloud-top level (about 70 km) rotates about 60 times faster in the same direction. This fast zonal flow is called as "super-rotation" and one of the most interesting phenomena in the planetary science.

There are at least two mechanisms, the Gierasch mechanism [2] through meridional circulation and the thermal tides mechanism [3] through wave mean flow interaction, that can generate super-rotation in the numerical simulations using Venus-like atmospheric GCM [4,5]. However, these studies used only coarse resolutions and involve simple physical processes. It should be examined whether the previous results could hold in the case of realistic numerical simulation of AFES with high resolution. Although our final goal is to understand the fundamental mechanism of the super-rotation, we have to check developed numerical model before performing long time simulation. As a first step we investigated unstable modes by the nonlinear numerical simulation using idealized initial state of the super-rotation with realistic static stability. The results are compared with those obtained in the previous study of linear stability analysis [6].

2   Experimental Settings

We construct a full nonlinear dynamical model for Venus atmosphere on the basis of AFES. The primitive equations in sigma coordinates on the sphere are used for the basic equations. Values of physical parameters are set for Venus. We replace physical processes for Earth atmosphere by the simplified version for Venus atmosphere. Experimental settings are basically based on the previous linear stability analysis [6]. We use several horizontal resolutions, T10, T21, T42, and T63, while vertical resolution is fixed to L60 (60 grids). 32 times 16 (T10), 64 times 32 (T21), 128 times 64 (T42), and 192 times 96 (T63) grids are used in the longitudinal and meridional directions, respectively. Vertical domain extends from the ground to about 120 km with almost the constant grid spacing of 2 km. The model include vertical and horizontal diffusions. Horizontal eddy viscosity is represented by the second-order hyper viscosity. The e-folding time for the maximum wave number component is set to about 0.8 day in order to prevent numerical instability. Vertical eddy diffusion coefficient of 0.015 m^2 s^{-1} is set in the model. We do not use Rayleigh friction (or sponge layer) in the present model except at the lowest level, where the surface friction acts on horizontal winds. In addition, the dry convective adjustment scheme is used to restore the temperature lapse rate to the neutral one when an atmospheric layer becomes statically unstable. We fix the specific heat at constant pressure to the constant value of 1000 J kg^{-1} K^{-1}.

In the present study we exclude the solar heating for simplicity, but scheme of the solar heating based on the previous works [7] and [8] is also prepared for future realistic simulation. The Venus international reference atmosphere (VIRA) data [9] is also prepared for vertical distribution of the specific heat at constant pressure. The radiative forcing in the infrared region is simplified by Newtonian cooling. The relaxation coefficients are based on the previous study [8]. The temperature field is relaxed to the prescribed zonally uniform but meridionally gradient field. The thermal relaxation to a meridional gradient temperature field is considered as an alternative to the zonal component of the solar heating. It is also possible to take a realistic temperature profile from the VIRA data. We are also constructing the scheme of realistic radiative forcing for future investigation.

We set the realistic but idealized static stability based on the observations [10]. Figure 1 shows vertical profile of the static stability. The lower Venus atmosphere near the ground is weakly stable; 5.0×10^{-4} K m^{-1}. There is a layer (from 55 to 60 km) with almost neutral stability in the cloud layer where vertical convection takes place; 1.0×10^{-4} K m^{-1}. At the bottom of the cloud layer atmosphere is stable, and the stability has a maximum value at around 45 km; 4.0×10^{-3} K m^{-1}. Above the cloud layer (from 70 km) atmosphere is stratified strongly, as in the case of the stratosphere on Earth. It is expected that unstable baroclinic modes appear in the cloud layer, as the previous study [6] suggested.

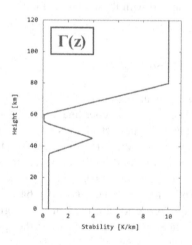

Fig. 1. Vertical profile of the static stability

We set an idealized super-rotating flow at the initial state. Figure 2 shows latitude - height cross section of zonally uniform zonal flow. The zonal velocity linearly increases with height from the ground to 70 km. Its maximum is 100 m s^{-1} at 70 km at the equator and above there it is constant. Meridional distribution is assumed to be solid body rotation. We set temperature to be in balance with the zonally uniform flow (Fig. 2), namely, gradient wind balance. Meridional temperature difference from equator to pole is about 5 K at the top of cloud layer. Figure 3 shows latitude – height cross section of zonally uniform temperature. Initiated from this idealized basic state of super-rotation, we perform nonlinear numerical simulation of AFES for a period of 5 Earth years. The leap frog method is used for the time integrations with an increment of 600 s. We exclude computational modes by the Asselin filter.

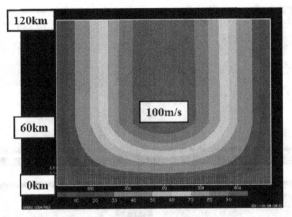

Fig. 2. Latitude - height cross section of zonally uniform zonal flow used for the initial basic state of idealized super-rotation

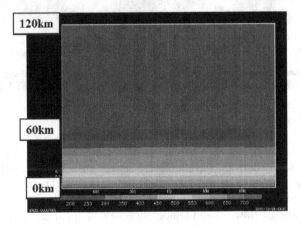

Fig. 3. Latitude - height cross section of zonally uniform temperature used for the initial basic state of idealized super-rotation

3   Results

We first show the results of T42L60. The results are typical and easy to understand. Figure 4 shows time evolution of the latitude - height cross sections of zonal-mean zonal velocity. While super-rotation in the upper layer quickly stops due to disturbances from the lower layer, super-rotation is gradually decreasing in the cloud layer (40 to 60 km) from mid-latitude to the pole. Initial strong deceleration at the upper layer (above 60 km) is mainly because of small density in this region. In contrast, small deceleration from mid-latitude to the pole in a height range of 40 to 60 km is due to another reason. Meridional distribution of super-rotation holds more than 4 years under the cloud layer (under 40 km).

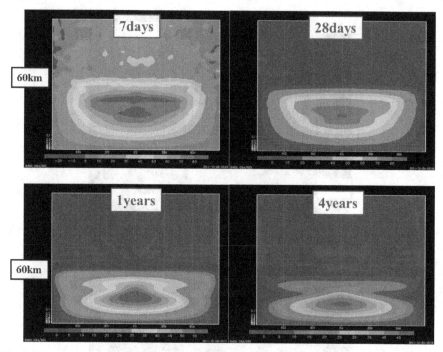

Fig. 4. Time evolution of zonal-mean zonal flow. Latitude - height cross sections are shown for 7 days, 28 days, 1 year, and 4 years.

Figure 5 shows snapshots of horizontal cross section of vorticity disturbance at 54 km for 300 days. Vortices of wavenumber 3 and 4 grow at the mid-latitude. They have significant amplitude at the later stage (not shown). These growing vortices decrease super-rotation where they evolve. Figure 6 shows longitude - height cross sections of meridional flow (a) and temperature deviation (b) at the section of 40 °N where unstable modes grow (dotted line in Fig. 5). The phases of these disturbances are tilted from down-east to up-west and out of phase. This implies that cold air flows down and southward, while warm air flows up and northward using available potential energy. This is the typical structure of baroclinic instability. The results are consistent with those of the previous linear stability analysis [6]. Thus we conclude that baroclinic modes decrease super-rotation in the cloud layer (40 - 60 km).

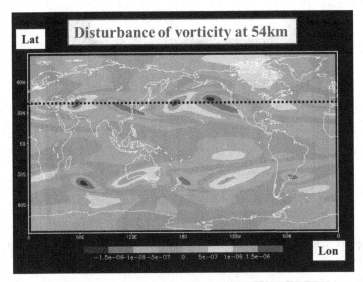

Fig. 5. Snapshots of horizontal cross section of vorticity disturbance at 54 km for 300 days

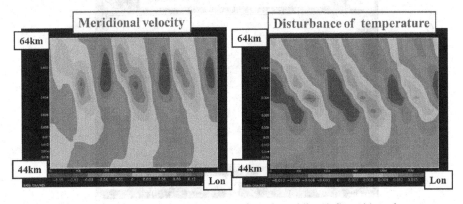

Fig. 6. Longitude - height cross sections at 40 °N of meridional flow (a) and temperature deviation (b) for 300 days

In order to check the resolution dependency of the results we show the results of T21L60 and T63L60 in Figures 7 and 8, respectively. Although we use the same condition except for the resolution (and therefore the horizontal diffusion), the flow field for T21L60 is quite different from that of T42L60. Only large scale vortices appear and there is no filament structure of vortices for the case of low resolution. It takes more time for unstable modes to grow in T21L60 simulation than in T42L60 one. The structure of vortices is different from typical baroclinic modes (not shown). On the other hand, the flow field and the structure of vortices for T63L60 are qualitatively similar to that of T42L60. The trains of baroclinic modes appear and evolve rapidly, while there are many small scale disturbances in T63L60 simulation. It is suggested that we have to use higher resolution than T21L60, as is done in the present study, in order to investigate the roles of baroclinic modes quantitatively.

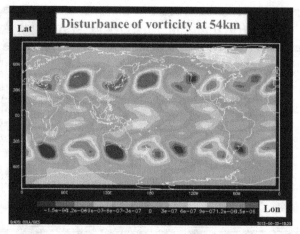

Fig. 7. Snapshot of horizontal cross section of vorticity disturbance at 54 km for 500 days using T21 resolution

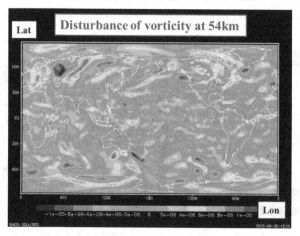

Fig. 8. Snapshot of horizontal cross section of vorticity disturbance at 54 km for 48 days using T63 resolution

4   Summary and Discussion

We developed an AGCM for Venus on the basis of AFES. As a first step, we investigated unstable modes in the idealized super-rotation by nonlinear numerical simulation of AFES with several resolutions. In the results of medium resolution of T42L60, vortices of baroclinic modes appeared at the mid-latitude in the cloud layer, where super-rotation is fast and meridional temperature gradient is large. The structure of unstable modes is similar to that of the previous linear stability analysis [6]. They develop using available potential energy. While the simulations with low resolution of T10L60 and T21L60 did not reproduce these phenomena appropriately,

T42L60 andT63L60 showed qualitatively similar results. Traditionally, numerical simulations performed by GCM for the Venus atmosphere used only T10 or T21 resolutions. However, as shown in Figure 7, the effects of baroclinic modes are not represented correctly in the results obtained by the coarse resolution simulations. T42 or higher resolutions of GCM would be necessary in order to investigate baroclinic instability on Venus atmosphere.

So far, there are no observational studies of baroclinic instability on Venus atmosphere, though this instability is considered to exist and have important roles. This study suggests that the baroclinic modes could exist in the cloud layer with small static stability. It is also expected that the baroclinic modes have a significant impact on the general circulation on Venus through momentum and heat transports in the meridional direction. Quantitative estimation of the roles of baroclinic modes by the numerical simulation with high resolution would be one of the promising ways.

For future work, we plan to improve the realistic radiative processes. The present study examined only an initial growth of baroclinic instability. But realistic solar heating will maintain meridional temperature gradient and super-rotation in the cloud layer. This enables us to examine the life cycle of baroclinic waves and interaction between the waves and the mean zonal flow. As is frequently discussed on Gierasch mechanism, several unstable modes are candidates to transport momentum from pole to equator [11]. Long time numerical simulation initiated from the super-rotation [12] would be valid to investigate roles of disturbances, including baroclinic modes, on the super-rotation.

Acknowledgements. This study was conducted under the joint research project of the Earth Simulator Center with title "Simulations of Atmospheric General Circulations of Earth-like Planets by AFES". The author acknowledge to the Earth Simulator Center for providing large computer resources. The GFD-DENNOU Library was used for drawing the figures.

References

1. Ohfuchi, W., Nakamura, H., Yoshioka, M.K., Enomoto, T., Takaya, K., Peng, X., Yamane, S., Nishimura, T., Kurihara, Y., Ninomiya, K.: 10-km Mesh Meso-scale Resolving Simulations of the Global Atmosphere on the Earth Simulator, -Preliminary Outcomes of AFES-. Journal of the Earth Simulator 1, 8–34 (2004)
2. Gierasch, P.J.: Meridional circulation and maintenance of the Venus atmospheric rotation. J. Atmos. Sci. 32, 1038–1044 (1975)
3. Fels, S.B., Lindzen, R.S.: The interaction of thermally excited gravity waves with mean flows. Geo. Fluid Dyn. 5, 149–191 (1974)
4. Yamamoto, M., Takahashi, M.: The fully developed superrotation simulated by a general circulation model of a Venus-like atmosphere. J. Atmos. Sci. 60, 561–574 (2003)
5. Takagi, M., Matsuda, Y.: Effects of thermal tides on the Venus atmospheric superrotation. J. Geophys. Res. 11, D09112 (2007), doi:10.1029/2006JD007901
6. Takagi, M., Matsuda, Y.: A study on the stability of a baroclinic flow in cyclostrophic balance on the sphere. Geophys. Res. Lett. 33, L14807 (2006), doi:10.1029/2006GL026200

7. Tomasko, M.G., Doose, L.R., Smith, P.H., Odell, A.P.: Measurements of the flux of sunlight in the atmosphere of Venus. J. Geophys. Res. 85, 8167–8186 (1980)

8. Crisp, D.: Radiative forcing of the Venus mesosphere: I. Icarus 67, 484–514 (1986)

9. Seiff, A., Schofield, J.T., Kliore, A.J., Taylor, F.W., Limaye, S.S., Revercomb, H.E., Sromovsky, L.A., Kerzhanovich, V.V., Moroz, V.I., Marov, M.Y.: Models of the structure of the atmosphere of Venus from the surface to 100 kilometers altitude. Advances in Space Research 5(11), 3–58 (1985)

10. Gierasch, P.J., Goody, R.M., Young, R.E., Crisp, D., Edwards, C., Kahn, R., Rider, D., del Genio, A., Greeley, R., Hou, A., Leovy, C.B., McCleese, D., Newman, M.: The General Circulation of the Venus Atmosphere: an Assessment. In: Venus II: Geology, Geophysics, Atmosphere, and Solar Wind Environment. University of Arizona Press (1997)

11. Iga, S., Matsuda, Y.: Shear instability in a shallow water model with implications for the Venus atmosphere. J. Atmos. Sci. 62, 2514–2527 (2005)

12. Kido, A., Wakata, Y.: Multiple equilibrium states appearing in a Venus-like atmospheric general circulation model. J. Meteor. Soc. Japan. 86(6), 969–979 (2008)

A Conservative Front-Tracking Method
for Scalar Conservation Laws in One Space Dimension
with Nonconvex Flux

Jingting Hu[1] and Dekang Mao[2]

[1] School of Mathematical Sciences, University of Jinan, Jinan, Shandong 250022, China
ss_hujt@ujn.edu.cn
[2] Department of Mathematics, Shanghai University, Shanghai, 200444, China

Abstract. The second author of this paper has designed a conservative front-tracking method. The method tracks discontinuities by using the conservation property of the hyperbolic conservation laws rather than the Hugoniot condition. We compute the numerical solution on each side of a discontinuity using information only from the same side. In this paper, we develop the method for one-dimensional scalar conservation laws with nonconvex flux. Numerical examples are presented to show the robustness and accuracy of the method.

Keywords: conservation laws, nonconvex flux, front-tracking, discontinuity cell.

1   Introduction

In this paper we develop the conservative front-tracking method for the scalar conservation law equation in one space dimension

$$u_t + f(u)_x = 0 \tag{1}$$

where the flux-function $f(u)$ is non-convex.

The second author of this paper has designed a conservative front-tracking method (see [1, 2]). We have designed the method for hyperbolic system of conservation laws in one space dimension (see [3]) and for one dimension scalar conservation laws with convex flux (see [13]). In this paper, we develop the method for one-dimensional scalar conservation laws with nonconvex flux. Our method uses the conservation property of the hyperbolic conservation laws to track discontinuities rather than the Hugoniot condition. The method works on Cartesian grid and gets rid of the small-cell problem.

Harten's subcell method ([4]) also tracks the discontinuity position by the conservation property of the solution. However, Harten's subcell method is in a capturing fashion. Some early front-tracking methods are mostly not conservative and are all first-order accurate. Chern and Colella [5], LeVeque and Shyue [6, 7]

T. Xiao, L. Zhang, and S. Ma (Eds.): ICSC 2012, Part II, CCIS 327, pp. 79–86, 2012.

developed conservative front-tracking methods. However, they do not use the conservation to locate discontinuity positions, and the adaptive grid is employed. Glimm et al. designed a conservative front-tracking method with second order accuracy (see [10]), but it also used adaptive grid. Aslam [8, 9] used a level set formulation to track discontinuities.

The paper is organized as follows. In Section 2, we describe the tracking method algorithm in four steps. In Section 3, we present some numerical examples to show the efficiency of the method. Finally, section 4 is the conclusion.

2   Algorithm of the Front-Tracking Method

In this paper, we denote the numerical and exact solution by u_j^n and $\bar{u}_j^n$ at the grid point (x_j, t_n). For describing our simply, we suppose that we are tracking one discontinuity in a grid cell $[x_{j_1-1/2}, x_{j_1+1/2}]$ at the n th time level. The cell containing discontinuity is called a discontinuity cell, the other grid cells in which the solution is smooth are called ordinary grid cells. In this discontinuity cell, besides the ordinary cell-average $u_{j_1}^n$, we also define two other cell-averages, $u_{j_1}^{n,-}$ and $u_{j_1}^{n,+}$, which are computed by the smooth part of the solution on the left and right sides of the discontinuity, respectively.

We use a finite volume scheme

$$u_j^{n+1} = u_j^n - \lambda(\hat{f}_{j+1/2}^n - \hat{f}_{j-1/2}^n) \tag{2}$$

as the underlying scheme, where u_j^n is the cell-average approximation to the exact solution

$$u_j^n \simeq \bar{u}_j^n = \frac{1}{h} \int_{x_{j-1/2}}^{x_{j+1/2}} u(x, t_n)dx, \tag{3}$$

$\hat{f}_{j+1/2}^n$ is the flux average approximation to $f(u)$ on the cell boundary at $x_{j+1/2}$

$$\hat{f}_{j+1/2}^n \simeq \frac{1}{\tau} \int_{t_n}^{t_{n+1}} f(u(x_{j+1/2}, t))dt. \tag{4}$$

And $\lambda = \tau / h$ is the grid ratio with τ and h being the time and the space step. We use second-order accuracy ENO scheme (see [11]) as the underlying scheme which ensures second-order accuracy of our method. We take five-point scheme. The numerical flux function is

$$\hat{f}_{j+1/2}^n = \hat{f}(u_{j-1}^n, u_j^n, u_{j+1}^n, u_{j+2}^n,). \tag{5}$$

Now we will give four steps to describe how to get the numerical solution at the next time level u^{n+1} from u^n.

Step 1. First we compute the numerical solution in the smooth grid on the two sides of the discontinuity using information only from the same sides, i.e.,

$$u_j^{n+1} = u_j^n - \lambda(\hat{f}_{j+1/2}^{n,-} - \hat{f}_{j-1/2}^{n,-}), \tag{6}$$

where

$$\hat{f}_{j+1/2}^{n,-} = \begin{cases} \hat{f}(u_{j_1-2}^n, u_{j_1-1}^n, u_{j_1}^{n,-}, u_{j_1+1}^{n,-}) & j = j_1 - 1 \\ \hat{f}(u_{j_1-3}^n, u_{j_1-2}^n, u_{j_1-1}^n, u_{j_1}^{n,-}) & j = j_1 - 2 \\ \hat{f}(u_{j-1}^n, u_j^n, u_{j+1}^n, u_{j+2}^n) & j < j_1 - 2 \end{cases} \tag{7}$$

with $j < j_1$, and $u_{j_1}^{n,-}$, $u_{j_1+1}^{n,-}$ being the left cell-averages in the discontinuity cell or the second-order Lagrangian extrapolation data of the cell-averages from the left side to the right side;
and

$$u_j^{n+1} = u_j^n - \lambda(\hat{f}_{j+1/2}^{n,+} - \hat{f}_{j-1/2}^{n,+}), \tag{8}$$

where

$$\hat{f}_{j-1/2}^{n,+} = \begin{cases} \hat{f}(u_{j_1-1}^{n,+}, u_{j_1}^{n,+}, u_{j_1+1}^n, u_{j_1+2}^n) & j = j_1 + 1 \\ \hat{f}(u_{j_1}^{n,+}, u_{j_1+1}^n, u_{j_1+2}^n, u_{j_1+3}^n) & j = j_1 + 2 \\ \hat{f}(u_{j-2}^n, u_{j-1}^n, u_j^n, u_{j+1}^n) & j > j_1 + 2 \end{cases} \tag{9}$$

with $j > j_1$, and $u_{j_1}^{n,+}$, $u_{j_1-1}^{n,+}$ being the right cell-averages in the discontinuity cell or the second-order Lagrangian extrapolation data of the cell-averages from the right side to the left side.

Next we compute the cell-averages in the discontinuity cell. The left and right cell-averages in the discontinuity cell are computed using information only from the same side in the same way as above, i.e.,

$$u_{j_1}^{n+1,\pm} = u_{j_1}^{n,\pm} - \lambda(\hat{f}_{j_1+1/2}^{n,\pm} - \hat{f}_{j_1-1/2}^{n,\pm}). \tag{10}$$

The ordinary cell-average $u_{j_1}^{n+1}$ in the discontinuity cell is then computed as

$$u_{j_1}^{n+1} = u_{j_1}^n - \lambda(\hat{f}_{j_1+1/2}^{n,+} - \hat{f}_{j_1-1/2}^{n,-}), \tag{11}$$

considering that the two cell boundaries are in the flows on the two sides of the discontinuity.

Step 2. In this step we use the conservation property of the solution to get the discontinuity position ξ^{n+1} at t_{n+1}. We use the following piecewise constant function

$$R(x;u^{n+1}) = \begin{cases} u_{j_1}^{n+1,-} & x < \xi^{n+1} \\ u_{j_1}^{n+1,+} & x \geq \xi^{n+1} \end{cases} \tag{12}$$

to reconstruct the solution in the discontinuity cell. $R(x;u^{n+1})$ is an approximation to the exact solution in the discontinuity cell.

The numerical discontinuity position ξ_{n+1} is computed by solving the following equation

$$\frac{1}{h}\left(\int_{x_{j_1-1/2}}^{\xi^{n+1}} u_{j_1}^{n+1,-}\, dx + \int_{\xi^{n+1}}^{x_{j_1+1/2}} u_{j_1}^{n+1,+}\, dx\right) = u_{j_1}^{n+1}, \tag{13}$$

then ξ_{n+1} is computed as

$$\xi_{n+1} = x_{j_1-1/2} + h\frac{u_{j_1}^{n+1} - u_{j_1}^{n+1,+}}{u_{j_1}^{n+1,-} - u_{j_1}^{n+1,+}}. \tag{14}$$

Step 3. For opening rarefaction waves in the vicinities of tracked discontinuities, we modify the left and right cell-average $u_{j_1}^{n+1,\pm}$ computed in the first step.

First in the discontinuity cell at time t_{n+1}, we reconstruct two pieces of solution $R(x;u^{n+1,-})$ and $R(x;u^{n+1,+})$ using information only from the same sides. They are all second-order polynomial. That is, we reconstruct $R(x;u^{n+1,-})$ by using the cell-averages in grid cells on the left of the tracked discontinuity, the left cell-averages in the discontinuity cell, and their second-order Lagrangian extrapolation on the right side; and so is $R(x;u^{n+1,+})$. We take $Rie(u_l,u_r)$ to denote the Riemann problem with u_l and u_r as its left and right states. We solve the Riemann problem $Rie(R(\xi^{n+1};u^{n+1,-}),R(\xi^{n+1};u^{n+1,+}))$ and get u_l^* and u_r^*, the two constant states separated by the tracked discontinuity. Unlike $R(\xi^{n+1};u^{n+1,-})$ and $R(\xi^{n+1};u^{n+1,+})$, state u_l^* and u_r^* contain the information of the rarefaction waves.

Next we reconstruct the solution again on the two sides of discontinuity position ξ^{n+1} using u_l^*, u_r^* and the pointwise values of $R(x;u^{n+1,-})$ and $R(x;u^{n+1,+})$, respectively. For example, we reconstruct the left solution $L(x;u^{n+1,-})$ via Lagrange

interpolation   on   a   stencil $\{x_0 = \xi^{n+1}, x_1 = \xi^{n+1} - h, x_2 = \xi^{n+1} - 2h\}$ with   data
$\{u_l^*, R(x_1; u^{n+1,-}), R(x_2; u^{n+1,-})\}$;   and so is the right solution $L(x; u^{n+1,+})$.

Finally, the left and right cell-averages are updated as the cell-averages of
$L(x; u^{n+1,-})$ and $L(x; u^{n+1,+})$ over the discontinuity cell, respectively, i.e.,

$$u_{j_1}^{n+1,\pm} := \frac{1}{h} \int_{x_{j_1-1/2}}^{x_{j_1+1/2}} L(x; u^{n+1,\pm}) dx . \tag{15}$$

Step 4. We complete the computation if the discontinuity position ξ^{n+1} is still in the
original discontinuity cell. But if it moves to either the left or right neighboring grid
cell, we must modify again the numerical solution (see [1, 3, 13] for the details). Thus
we complete the computation. If we are tracking several discontinuities which may be
very close to and even interact with each other, we design some skills to handle the
situations (see [1, 3]).

3   Numerical Examples

We take second-order ENO scheme ([11]) as the underlying scheme. In the numerical
results, circles represent the numerical solution computed by our front-tracking
method and solid lines represent the exact solution obtained by the second -order
ENO scheme with 2000 points. We used the space step of 0.02, and the Courant
number τ / h of 0.5. The number of mesh points is 100 by our calculations.

Example 1. We find the Riemann solution for the equation (1) with

$$f(u) = \frac{1}{4}(u^2 - 1)(u^2 - 4), \tag{16}$$

and the following Riemann initial value

$$u(x,0) = \begin{cases} 2 & x \leq 0, \\ -2 & x > 0. \end{cases} \tag{17}$$

The exact solution is a shock followed by a rarefaction wave followed by another
shock. The results are displayed in Figure 1 at $t = 1.0$ and $x \in [-1,1]$. The results
show that the rarefaction wave is opened gradually and the discontinuity position is
precise.

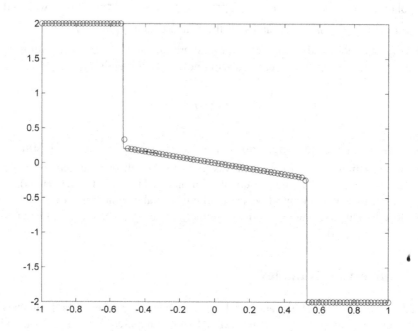

Fig. 1. Example 1: Numerical solution with 100 cells at $t=1.0$ and $x \in [-1,1]$

Example 2. We find the Riemann solution for the equation (1) with

$$f(u) = u^3,\tag{18}$$

and the following initial data

$$u(x,0) = \begin{cases} -1 & -1 \le x \le -0.8, \\ 1 & -0.8 < x \le -0.4, \\ -2 & -0.4 < x \le 1. \end{cases}\tag{19}$$

This example contains two Riemann problems, each Riemann solver is a shock wave followed by a rarefaction wave. The right shock wave and the left rarefaction wave interact gradually, and this rarefaction wave is absorbed gradually by this shock wave. Finally, the left rarefaction wave is absorbed completely by the right shock wave. After the left shock wave interacts with the right shock wave, a new shock is generated. The numerical results are computed at time $t=0.1$ and $t=1.2$ (see Fig.2, Fig.3). The results show that the discontinuity position is still precise. And our scheme can handle collisions of discontinuities.

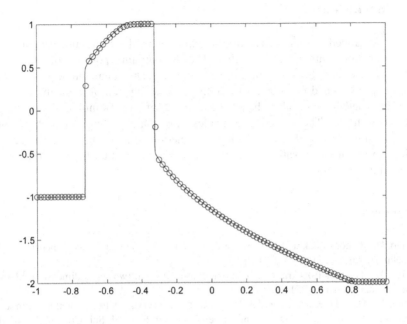

Fig. 2. Example 2: Numerical solution with 100 cells at $t = 0.1$ and $x \in [-1,1]$

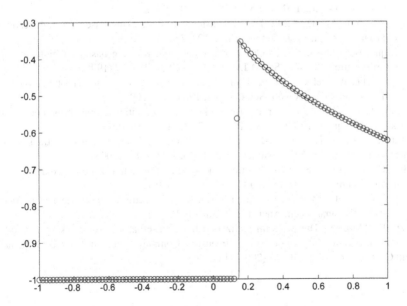

Fig. 3. Example 2: Numerical solution with 100 cells at $t = 1.2$ and $x \in [-1,1]$

4   Conclusion

We have developed a conservative front-tracking method for one-dimensional scalar conservation laws with nonconvex flux. The discontinuity position of the tracked shock is precise, and the rarefaction wave is opened. The computation proceeds still on the regular grid and this makes the coding and application of the technique quite easy. The method can also handle collisions of discontinuities and capture spontaneous shocks. The numerical examples show that the algorithm is the second-order precision. We will also develop the method for the nonclassical entropy solutions to scalar conservation laws with concave-convex flux-function ([12]). We will report it in due time.

References

1. Mao, D.: A shock tracking technique based on conservation in one space dimension. SIAM J. Numer. Anal. 32, 1677–1703 (1995)
2. Mao, D.: Towards front tracking based on conservation in two space dimension. SIAM J. Sci. Comput. 22, 113–151 (2000)
3. Yan, L., Dao, D.-K.: Further development of a conservative front-tracking method for systems of conservation laws in one space dimension. SIAM J. Sci. Comput. 28, 85–119 (2006)
4. Harten, A.: ENO schemes with subcell resolution. J. Comput. Phys. 83, 148–184 (1989)
5. Chern, I.-L., Colella, P.: A conservative front tracking method for hyperbolic system of conservation laws, LLNL Rep. No. UCRL-97200 (1987)
6. LeVeque, R.J., Shyue, K.M.: Two dimensional front tracking based on high resolution wave progation methods. J. Comput. Phys. 123, 354–368 (1996)
7. LeVeque, R.J., Shyue, K.M.: One dimensional front tracking based on high resolution wave propogation methods. SIAM J. Sci. Comput. 16, 348–377 (1995)
8. Aslam, T.D.: A level set algorithm for tracking discontinuities in hyperbolic conservation laws II: system of equations. J. Sci. Comput. 19, 37–62 (2003)
9. Aslam, T.D.: A level set algorithm for tracking discontinuities in hyperbolic conservation laws I: scalar equations. J. Comput. Phys. 167(2), 413–438 (2001)
10. Glimm, J., Li, X.-L., Liu, Y.-J., Xu, Z.-L., Zhao, N.: Conservative front-tracking with improved accuracy. SIAM J. Numer. Anal. 41(5), 1926–1947 (2003)
11. Shu, C.-W., Osher, S.: Efficient implementation of essentially non-oscillatory shock-capturing schemes, II. J. Comput. Phys. 83, 32–78 (1989)
12. Hayes, B.T., LeFloch, P.G.: Nonclassical shocks and kinetic relations: scalar conservation laws. Arch. Rational Mech. Anal. 139, 1–56 (1997)
13. Yan, L., Mao, D.: The program realization of a conservative front-tracking method for scalar conservation laws in one space dimension. Communication on Applied Mathematics and Computation 15(1), 10–18 (2001) (in Chinese)

A Retrieving Algorithm for Unfolded Sheet Metal Parts Based on the Features Relationship

Dawei Wang and Dongyun Ge[*]

Beijing Aeronautical Science & Technology Research Institute (BASTR),
COMAC, Beijing 102211, China
wdw@me.buaa.edu.cn, gedongyun@comac.cc

Abstract. This paper presents a new retrieval algorithm for unfolded sheet metal parts. The primary idea of this novel algorithm is based on the relative position relationships of features in sheet metal parts. After analyzing the data structure of sheet metal parts, some kinds of key features are abstracted and the relative position model is described to express the difference of features' relative position. Further, detailed information about the position model and the formula of similarity developed for difficult sheet metal parts is given and described. Also an example is given at the last of paper to verify the validity of our algorithm. Obviously, our new algorithm meets the requirements of searching unfolded sheet metal parts.

Keywords: feature, retrieval algorithm, sheet metal, CAD.

1 Introduction

Nowadays, growing quantities of CAD models are created in industries. Quickly and easily finding the part desired has become a big challenge of enterprises [1]. Many algorithms and methods have been proposed for model retrieval. They can be classified into two major categories according to the difference of the research objectives. One is ordinary retrieval algorithms using STL, STEP 3D file formats as the research objectives [2]. The other is particular retrieval algorithms using one or more special CAD software file formats as the research objectives such as CATIA's CATPart file format, Pro/E's PRT file format and so on [3].

However, most of the existing methods do not work well for sheet metal parts, especially the unfolded sheet metal part. An approach for feature-based retrieval of unfolded sheet metal parts is presented in the paper. It is an extended research based on [4], which focuses on retrieval algorithm for unfold sheet metal parts. In Ref 4, a feature-based retrieval method was proposed and a similarity definition was given. But the method and the definition are worked not very well. In real application, some small difference between sheet metals cannot be distinguished. It leads to the number of result in one retrieval calculation is too large. Users cannot find the desired part at

---

[*] Corresponding author.

T. Xiao, L. Zhang, and S. Ma (Eds.): ICSC 2012, Part II, CCIS 327, pp. 87–94, 2012.

first time. The main purpose of this paper is to improve the retrieval algorithm and redefine the similarity in order to solve the problems just expressed above.

2   Data Structure of Research Object

In the paper, we use ICS file format as the research object. ICS files are designed using the software CAXA Solid View 2011. CAXA Solid provides a feature-based design method to create sheet metal parts. It also provides a feature library of sheet metal parts. Designers can easily reuse these features in their design. The features which are reused in the part can be extracted by CAXA API. Here, we use some of the features as the key features, use the position difference of the key features to calculate the similarity of the sheet metal parts. In practice application, any number of key features is allowed.

More details about the sheet metal design method and the data structure of CAXA Solid can be found in Ref.[4] and Ref.[5].

3   Relative Position Model

This section discusses the method to build relative position model for unfold sheet metal part.

3.1   Relative Positions of Two Features

As we discussed in Ref. [4], the relationship of two features has only three results: Disjoint, Adjacent and Include. Suppose that there are two features named A, B, the three relationships can be expressed as: $A \notin B$, $A \cap B$ and $A \subset B$ (or $A \supset B$). Here, we define a set, named Relationships Operation Set to express the four results above. Denote as: $X = \{x | \notin, \cap, \subset, \supset\}$.

3.2   Relative Positions of Three Features

In a plane, any three features can determine a circle, named "Feature Position Circle (FPC)", as shown in Fig.1(a). Obviously, the three features contained in FPC can also determine a triangle. It is called "Feature Relative Triangle (FRT)". In FPC, the three feature and center of the circle make up three angles: ∠AOB, ∠AOC and∠BOC, as shown in Fig.1(b).

Suppose that there is a sheet metal part contains three features, named F1, F2 and F3. The centres of three features defines a FPC marked as P and a FRT also are defined marked as S. Using G to record the apex name of S's obtuse angle or right angle. If the triangle S is an acute triangle, G will be marked as empty. The three angles: ∠AOB, ∠AOC and∠BOC have a value range $(0, 2\pi)$. J1, J2 and J3 are used to denote the three angles separately. The three angles of FRT: ∠BAC, ∠ABC and ∠ACB are denoted as A1, A2 and A3.

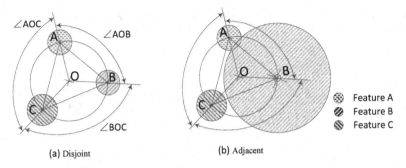

Fig. 1. Relative positions of three features

Using "×" denotes relation and "•"as delimiter between relations. The relative position relationship of three features can be defined by the following expression:

$$W = E_1 \times E_2 \cdot E_1 \times E_3 \cdot E_2 \times E_3 \cdot A_1 \cdot A_2 \cdot A_3 \cdot J_1 \cdot J_2 \cdot J_3 \cdot G$$

Where, W means the relative position relationship of three features. $\times \in X = \{x \not\subset, \cap, \subset, \supset\}$, and $G \in \{E_1, E_2, E_3, \emptyset\}$.With above definition, the two relative positions of three features in Fig.3 can be described by the following two expressions.

$$W_a = A \not\subset B \cdot A \not\subset C \cdot B \not\subset C \cdot \pi/3 \cdot \pi/3 \cdot \pi/3 \cdot 2\pi/3 \cdot 2\pi/3 \cdot 2\pi/3 \cdot \emptyset$$

$$W_b = A \cap B \cdot A \not\subset C \cdot B \not\subset C \cdot \pi/3 \cdot \pi/3 \cdot \pi/3 \cdot 2\pi/3 \cdot 2\pi/3 \cdot 2\pi/3 \cdot \emptyset$$

Use $\pi/3$ as a standard value to express these angles. If the angle's value range is $(0, \pi/3]$, marks the value with "1",if in range $(\pi/3, 2\pi/3]$ marks the value with "2". Analogously, if the value is in range $(5\pi/3, 2\pi)$ Ai or Ji $(1 \leq i \leq 3)$ will be marked as "6". Above relation changes to the following expression:

$$W_a = A \not\subset B \cdot A \not\subset C \cdot B \not\subset C \cdot 2 \cdot 2 \cdot 2 \cdot 3 \cdot 3 \cdot 3 \cdot \emptyset$$

$$W_b = A \cap B \cdot A \not\subset C \cdot B \not\subset C \cdot 2 \cdot 2 \cdot 2 \cdot 3 \cdot 3 \cdot 3 \cdot \emptyset$$

3.3 Relative Positions of Four Features

The relative positions of four features are built based on the three features' relative position expression. Fig.4 shows four features, selecting any three features of them can form a triangle. There are totally $C_4^3 = 4$ combinations as illustrated in Fig.4 (b)-(e).

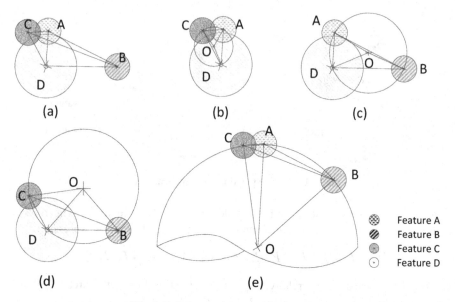

Fig. 2. Relative positions of four features

The relative position relationships of four features can be described by the following expression:

$$W_4 = W_{4b} + W_{4c} + W_{4d} + W_{4e}$$

Where, M4 means the relative position relations of four features.

$$W_{4b} = A \cap C \cdot A \cap D \cdot C \cap D \cdot 2 \cdot 2 \cdot 1 \cdot 2 \cdot 3 \cdot 3 \cdot \varnothing$$

$$W_{4b} = A \notin B \cdot A \cap D \cdot B \notin D \cdot 2 \cdot 1 \cdot 2 \cdot 3 \cdot 1 \cdot 2 \cdot \varnothing$$

$$W_{4c} = B \notin C \cdot B \notin D \cdot C \cap D \cdot 1 \cdot 1 \cdot 2 \cdot 4 \cdot 2 \cdot 1 \cdot D$$

$$W_{4b} = A \notin B \cdot A \cap C \cdot B \notin C \cdot 2 \cdot 1 \cdot 1 \cdot 1 \cdot 1 \cdot 6 \cdot A$$

3.4   Relative Positions of Five and More Features

The relative position relationships of five and more features can be built by using the above method. For example, using $C_5^3 = 10$ FRTs can express the relationships of five features relationships. Suppose that there are R features, the relationships of them can be expressed by $r = C_R^3$ FRTs.

The general expression for features' relationships can be expressed by the following summarily.

Suppose that there are R(R≥2) key features in a sheet metal part, all of these features constitute a set, named F ={f1,f2,f3,...,fR}, f∈K. Their relative position relationship is marked as WR, and can be expressed by the following:

$$W_R = \begin{cases} E_1 \times E_2 & R = 2 \\ E_1 \times E_2 \cdot E_1 \times E_3 \cdot E_2 \times E_3 \cdot A_1 \cdot A_2 \cdot A_3 \cdot J_1 \cdot J_2 \cdot J_3 \cdot G & R = 3 \\ W_1 + W_2 + ... + W_r & R \geq 3 \end{cases}$$

Where $W_r = E_{r1} \times E_{r2} \bullet E_{r1} \times E_{r3} \bullet E_{r2} \times E_{r3} \bullet A_{r1} \bullet A_{r2} \bullet A_{r3} \bullet J_{r1} \bullet J_{r2} \bullet J_{r3} \bullet G_r$. $E_i \in F$.
Using above method, the relative position relationships of any number of key features can be described.

4   Retrieval Algorithm

4.1   Location Description Matrix

Suppose that there are R(R≥2) features in a sheet metal part, all these feature triangles constitutes a set of FRT, using T to express. $T = \{T_1, T_2, T_3, ...T_i, ...T_r\}$, $i \in N$, $T_i \in F$, where Ti is a FRT constituted by three key features marked as $E_{T_i}^1$, $E_{T_i}^2$, and $E_{T_i}^3$. Denote $T_i = \{E_{T_i}^1, E_{T_i}^2, E_{T_i}^3\}$, Ti also has the six angles, marked as $A_{T_i}^1$, $A_{T_i}^2$ and $A_{T_i}^3$, Denote $A_{T_i} = \{A_{T_i}^1, A_{T_i}^2, A_{T_i}^3\}$, Similarly $J_{T_i} = \{J_{T_i}^1, J_{T_i}^2, J_{T_i}^3\}$. The feature relative position relationship of Ti can be expressed as:

$$W_{T_i} = E_{T_i 1} \times_{T_i 1} E_{T_i 2} \bullet E_{T_i 1} \times_{T_i 2} E_{T_i 3} \bullet E_{T_i 2} \times_{T_i 3} E_{T_i 3} \bullet A_{T_i 1} \bullet A_{T_i 2} \bullet A_{T_i 3} \bullet J_{T_i 1} \bullet J_{T_i 2} \bullet J_{T_i 3} \bullet G_{T_i}$$

Denote a new set P, named "relation expression set (RES)", it has four elements: $\times_{T_i 1}, \times_{T_i 2}, \times_{T_i 3}$ and G_{T_i} . $P_{T_i} = \{\times_{T_i 1}, \times_{T_i 2}, \times_{T_i 3}, G_{T_i}\}$. Then the W_{T_i} expression above can also be expressed by the following:

$$W_{T_i} = (E_{T_i 1}, E_{T_i 2}, E_{T_i 3}) \cup (A_{T_i 1}, A_{T_i 2}, A_{T_i 3}) \cup (J_{T_i 1}, J_{T_i 2}, J_{T_i 3}) \cup (\times_{T_i 1}, \times_{T_i 2}, \times_{T_i 3}, G_{T_i})$$
$$= T_i \cup A_{T_i} \cup J_{T_i} \cup P_{T_i}$$

Form above expression we can conclude that all of the features' relative position relationships can be expressed by the four sets: T, A, J, and P. Named T as "feature matrix (FM)", A as "inside angle matrix (IAM)", J as "outside angle matrix (OAM)". The four matrices are the location description matrices.

4.2   Formula of Retrieval Algorithm

The similarity definition of two groups of features is given in this section.

Let $B = \{b_1, b_2, ...b_i\}$ and $H = \{h_1, h_2, ..., h_j\}$ be two sets of features in unfold sheet metal parts, where $b_i \in K$, $h_j \in K$, $i \in N$ and $j \in N$. T_B and T_H are the FM of B and H respectively. The IAM of them can be expressed by A_B and A_H . J_B and J_H are their OAM, Set $T_B = \{T_{B1}, T_{B2}, T_{B3}, ..., T_{Bm}\}$, $T_H = \{T_{H1}, T_{H2}, T_{H3}, ..., T_{Hn}\}$, similarly $A_B = \{A_{BT_1}, A_{BT_2}, A_{BT_3}, ..., A_{BT_m}\}$. In AB each element can be expressed as $A_{BT_m} = \{A_{BT_m 1}, A_{BT_m 2}, A_{BT_m 3}\}$. $A_H = \{A_{HT_1}, A_{HT_2}, A_{HT_3}, ..., A_{HT_n}\}$, and $A_{HT_n} = \{A_{HT_n 1}, A_{HT_n 2}, A_{HT_n 3}\}$. Analogously, $J_B = \{J_{BT_1}, J_{BT_2}, J_{BT_3}, ..., J_{BT_m}\}$, $J_{BT_m} = \{J_{BT_m 1}, J_{BT_m 2}, J_{BT_m 3}\}$ and $J_H = \{J_{HT_1}, J_{HT_2}, J_{HT_3}, ..., J_{HT_n}\}$, $J_{HT_n} = \{J_{HT_n 1}, J_{HT_n 2}, J_{HT_n 3}\}$. P_B and P_H are RES of their. $P_B = \{P_{BT_1}, P_{BT_2}, P_{BT_3}, ..., P_{BT_m}\}$. In PB each element can be expressed as $P_{BT_m} = \{\times_{BT_m 1}, \times_{BT_m 2}, \times_{BT_m 3}, G_{T_m}\}$. $P_H = \{P_{HT_1}, P_{HT_2}, P_{HT_3}, ..., P_{HT_n}\}$, the same as P_{BT_m} , $P_{HT_n} = \{\times_{HT_n 1}, \times_{HT_n 2}, \times_{HT_n 3}, G_{T_n}\}$. And $m = C_i^3$ and $n = C_j^3$.

From above definition all of the relative position information of the two groups is given. If the two relative position relationships corresponding to B and H are equal, B and H should completely satisfy the following rules:

(a) $B \subseteq H$ and $H \subseteq B$;

(b) $\forall T_{Bm} \in T_B$, $\exists T_{Hn} \in T_H$ let $T_{Bm} = T_{Hn}$

(c) when $T_{Bm} = T_{Hn}$ $\forall A_{BT_m} = A_{HT_n}$, $J_{BT_m} = J_{HT_n}$ and $P_{BT_m} = P_{HT_n}$

If B and H completely satisfy the rules, denote $B \cong H(1)$. Otherwise, if B and H partially satisfy the rules, we consider that the relationships are similar to each other. Set $B \cong H(\varepsilon)$, ε is the match coefficient of the two groups. And $\varepsilon \in [0,1]$. Define a new parameter " ω " to describe the difference of user awareness of the four matrices, named "weight coefficient".

Based on above definition, now we give the formula of retrieval algorithm"

$$\begin{cases} U(t,s) = \begin{cases} 0 & t \neq s \\ 1 & t = s \end{cases} \\ \omega_1 + \omega_2 + \omega_3 + \omega_4 = 1 \\ 3\omega_4^1 + \omega_4^2 = 1 \\ \varepsilon = \sum_{i \in N, 1 \leq 4} \omega_i \varepsilon_i \end{cases}$$

The last formula in the above equations is equivalent to the following formula:

$$\varepsilon = \sum_{i \in N, i \le 4} \omega_i \varepsilon_i = \frac{1}{m} \sum_{i=1}^{m} \left\{ \sum_{i=1}^{m} \sum_{j=1}^{n} \omega_1 U\left(T_{Bi}, T_{Hj}\right) + U\left(T_{Bi}, T_{Hj}\right) \left[\frac{1}{3} \sum_{u=1}^{3} \omega_2 U\left(A_{Biu}, A_{Hju}\right) + \right. \right.$$

$$\left. \left. \frac{1}{3} \sum_{u=1}^{3} \omega_3 U\left(J_{Biu}, J_{Hju}\right) + \omega_4 \left(\sum_{u=1}^{3} \omega_4^1 U\left(P_{Biu}, P_{Hju}\right) + \sum_{u=1}^{1} \omega_4^2 U\left(P_{Biu}, P_{Hju}\right) \right) \right] \right\}$$

ω_1, ω_2, ω_3, ω_4^1 and ω_4^2 are the weight coefficient of FM, IAM, OAM , the relationships of each features and G in RES.

5   Implementation

The experiment is used to test the performance of the retrieval algorithm in calculating the similarity of unfolded sheet metal parts. Set $\omega_1 = 0.40$, $\omega_2 = 0.25$, $\omega_3 = 0.15$, $\omega_4 = 0.20$, $\omega_4^1 = 0.20$ and $\omega_4^2 = 0.40$. A query part and the retrieval results are shown in Table 1.

As seen from the experiment, our relative position model can express the difference of the position. It can be used to calculate the similarity for unfolded sheet metal part. The formula of retrieval algorithm the paper given meets the requirements of similarity calculation of unfolded sheet metal parts.

Table 1 Experiment and results

Query part	Examples and their similarity		
	$\varepsilon = 1.00000$	$\varepsilon = 0.92650$	$\varepsilon = 0.84750$
	$\varepsilon = 0.81650$	$\varepsilon = 0.77350$	$\varepsilon = 0.70550$
	$\varepsilon = 0.68650$		

6   Conclusions and Future Work

A semantic-based approach to part retrieval of CAD models for unfolded sheet metal parts is presented. Some features are chosen as the key features and a relative position model is built to express the difference between two unfolded sheet metal parts. The relative model is built based on the geometry information of the feature triangle and can be indicated by four matrices: FM, IAM, OAM, and RES. Then the paper gave the formula of the retrieval algorithm to calculate the similarity of two unfolded sheet metal parts in terms of the difference of four matrices. The method requires a high performance computer. How to reduce the calculation times is a further research direction.

References

1. Bai, J., Gao, S., Tang, W., Liu, Y., Guo, S.: Design reuse oriented partial retrieval of CAD models. Computer-Aided Design 42, 1069–1084 (2010)
2. Tao, S., Wang, S., Zheng, T., Huang, Z.: CAD model retrieval based on inexact graph matching. Journal of Computer-Aided Design and Computer Graphics 22(3), 545–552 (2010)
3. Wang, D., Yan, G., Lei, Y., Zhang, J.: A retrieval algorithm of sheet metal parts based on feature relative position. Journal of Computer-Aided Design & Computer Graphics 23(2), 314–322 (2011)
4. Wang, D., Yan, G., Lei, Y., Zhang, J.: A Retrieval Algorithm of Sheet metal Parts Based on Relationships of Features. Chinese Journal of Aeronautics 25(3), 453–472 (2012)
5. Gao, Y., Wang, M., Shen, J., Dai, Q., Zhang, N.-Y.: Intelligent Query: Open Another Door to 3D Object Retrieval. In: ACM Conference on Multimedia, pp. 1711–1714 (2010)

Finite Difference Methods for Space Fractional Advection-Diffusion Equations with Variable Coefficients[*]

Weiping Bu[1,**], Aiguo Xiao[1], and Yifa Tang[2]

[1] School of Mathematics and Computational Science,
Xiangtan University, Hunan 411105, China
weipingbu@163.com, xag@xtu.edu.cn
[2] LSEC, ICMSEC, Academy of Mathematics and System Sciences,
Academia Sinica, P.O. Box 2719, Beijing 100080, China
tyf@lsec.cc.ac.cn

Abstract. In this paper, the implicit difference scheme is presented to solve a class of space fractional advection-diffusion equations with variable coefficients. The stability and convergence of this method is discussed respectively. Finally, we give several numerical examples to confirm our theoretical analysis.

MSC 2010: 34A08, 26A33

Keywords: Space fractional differential equations, stability, convergence, variable coefficient, advection diffusion, finite difference method.

1 Introduction

Fractional advection-diffusion equations are mainly used to describe the transportation problems (cf.[1,10]). In [6,14], some authors have done a detail study on the theoretical solution of the fractional advection-diffusion equations. As everyone knows, it is important and necessary to develop efficient numerical methods to solve fractional differential equations. At present, there have been some numerical methods for fractional advection-diffusion equations, for example, the finite difference methods (cf.[2,7,9]), the finite element methods (cf.[4,5]) and the spectral methods (cf.[15]). Besides the above numerical methods, there are some approximately-analytical methods for solving fractional advection diffusion equations, for example, the Adomain's decomposition methods (cf.[3]), the

---

[*] This work is supported by projects NSF of China (10971175), Program for Changjiang Scholars and Innovative Research Team in University of China(IRT1179), the Aid Program for Science and Technology Innovative Research Team in Higher Educational Institutions of Hunan Province of China. This work is partially supported by an open project of LSEC, AMSS, Academia Sinica.

[**] Corresponding author.

T. Xiao, L. Zhang, and S. Ma (Eds.): ICSC 2012, Part II, CCIS 327, pp. 95–104, 2012.
© Springer-Verlag Berlin Heidelberg 2012

variational iteration methods (cf.[8]) and the homotopy perturbation methods (cf.[11]).

In this paper, we use finite difference methods to solve the following space fractional advection-diffusion equation with variable coefficients

$$\frac{\partial u}{\partial t} = -_0D_x^\alpha[A(x,t)u(x,t)] + _0D_x^\beta[B(x,t)u(x,t)] + f(x,t),$$
$$0 < t \le T,\ 0 < x < L \tag{1}$$

with the initial and boundary conditions given by

$$u(x,0) = \varphi(x),\ 0 \le x \le L,$$
$$u(0,t) = \psi_1(t),\ u(L,t) = \psi_2(t),\ 0 < t \le T, \tag{2}$$

where $0 < \alpha < 1$, $1 < \beta < 2$, $A(x,t) \ge 0$, $B(x,t) \ge 0$ and $_0D_x^\gamma h(x,t)$ is the Riemman-Liouville derivative defined as

$$_0D_x^\gamma h(x,t) = \frac{1}{\Gamma(n-\gamma)} \left(\frac{d}{dx}\right)^n \int_0^x (x-\tau)^{n-\gamma-1} h(\tau,t)d\tau,\ 0 \le n-1 < \gamma < n,$$

where n is a positive integer.

In particular, when $\beta = 2\alpha$, we find that equation (1) is equivalent to the model equation mentioned in [8]; when $f(x,t) = 0$, $A(x,t) = A(x)$, $B(x,t) = B(x)$ and $\alpha = \beta - 1$, we find that equation (1) is equivalent to the model 3 mentioned in [13].

The rest of the paper is constructed as follows. In Section 2, the implicit difference method is developed to solve space fractional advection-diffusion equations with variable coefficients. The stability and convergence of the implicit difference method is studied in Section 3. In Section 4, some numerical examples are taken to confirm the theoretical results derived in the above section. Finally, we draw our conclusions in Section 5.

2   Numerical Scheme

Let $\tau = \frac{T}{N}$, $h = \frac{L}{M}$ be the time and space stepsizes, respectively. Let $t_n = n\tau$, $n = 0, 1, 2, \cdots, N$; $x_i = ih$, $i = 0, 1, 2, \cdots, M$; $\Omega = [0,T] \times [0,L]$.

For $\frac{\partial u}{\partial t}$, by the backward difference method, we have

$$\frac{\partial u(x_i,t_n)}{\partial t} = \frac{u(x_i,t_n) - u(x_i,t_{n-1})}{\tau} + O(\tau).$$

For $_0D_x^\alpha[A(x,t)u(x,t)]$ and $_0D_x^\beta[B(x,t)u(x,t)]$, we take the standard Grünwald approximation and shifted Grünwald approximation, respectively, then we have

$$_0D_x^\alpha[A(x_i,t_n)u(x_i,t_n)] = h^{-\alpha} \sum_{j=0}^{i} g_j A(x_{i-j},t_n)u(x_{i-j},t_n) + O(h),$$
$$_0D_x^\beta[B(x_i,t_n)u(x_i,t_n)] = h^{-\beta} \sum_{j=0}^{i+1} l_j B(x_{i-j+1},t_n)u(x_{i-j+1},t_n) + O(h), \tag{3}$$

where

$$g_0 = 1, \ g_j = (-1)^j \frac{\alpha(\alpha-1)\cdots(\alpha-j+1)}{j!}, \ j = 1, 2, \cdots;$$

$$l_0 = 1, \ l_j = (-1)^j \frac{\beta(\beta-1)\cdots(\beta-j+1)}{j!}, \ j = 1, 2, \cdots.$$

By (3), using the backward difference method in time direction leads to

$$
\begin{aligned}
\tau h^{-\alpha} \sum_{j=0}^{i} & g_j A(x_{i-j}, t_{n+1}) u(x_{i-j}, t_{n+1}) \\
& + u(x_i, t_{n+1}) - \tau h^{-\beta} \sum_{j=0}^{i+1} l_j B(x_{i-j+1}, t_{n+1}) u(x_{i-j+1}, t_{n+1}) \\
& = u(x_i, t_n) + \tau f(x_i, t_{n+1}) + R_i^n,
\end{aligned}
\tag{4}
$$

where $|R_i^n| \leq C\tau(\tau + h)$, C is a positive constant.

Let $r_1 = \tau h^{-\alpha}$, $r_2 = \tau h^{-\beta}$, $A_i^n = A(x_i, t_n)$, $B_i^n = B(x_i, t_n)$, $F_i^n = \tau f(x_i, t_n)$, and u_i^n be the numerical approximation to the solution $u(x_i, t_n)$.

By (4), we can obtain the implicit difference scheme

$$u_i^{n+1} + r_1 \sum_{j=0}^{i} g_j A_{i-j}^{n+1} u_{i-j}^{n+1} - r_2 \sum_{j=0}^{i+1} l_j B_{i-j+1}^{n+1} u_{i-j+1}^{n+1} = u_i^n + F_i^{n+1}, \tag{5}$$

where $i = 1, 2, \cdots, M-1$; $n = 0, 1, \cdots, N-1$.

Discreting the initial and boundary conditions, leads to

$$
\begin{aligned}
u_i^0 &= \varphi(ih), \\
u_0^n &= \psi_1(n\tau), \ u_M^n = \psi_2(n\tau),
\end{aligned}
\tag{6}
$$

where $i = 0, 1, 2, \cdots, M$; $n = 1, 2, \cdots, N$.

To prove the stability and convergence of the above difference scheme, we introduce the following two lemmas.

Lemma 1. *(cf.[7])* (1) If $0 < \alpha < 1$, then $g_0 = 1$, $g_j < 0 \ (j \geq 1)$, $\sum_{j=0}^{\infty} g_j = 0$;

(2) If $1 < \beta < 2$, then $l_0 = 1$, $l_1 = -\beta$, $l_j > 0 \ (j \geq 2)$, $\sum_{j=0}^{\infty} l_j = 0$.

Remark 1. From the above lemma, we can show easily that $\{a_i = \sum_{j=0}^{i} g_j\}_{i=0}^{\infty}$ is a monotone decreasing sequence and $a_i > 0 \ (i \geq 0)$ and $\{b_i = \sum_{j=0}^{i} l_j\}_{i=1}^{\infty}$ is a monotone increasing sequence and $b_i < 0 \ (i \geq 1)$.

Lemma 2. *(1) If $A(x,t) \geq 0$, $A(x,t)$ is monotone increasing on x in Ω, then for all $\alpha \in (0,1)$, the Grünwald approximation of $_0D_x^\alpha A(x_i, t_n)$ satisfies*

$$h^{-\alpha} \sum_{j=0}^{i} g_j A(x_{i-j}, t_n) \geq 0.$$

(2) If $B(x,t) \geq 0$, $B(x,t)$ is a monotone decreasing and convex function on x in Ω, then for all $\beta \in (1,2)$, the shifted Grünwald approximation of $_0D_x^\beta B(x_i, t_n)$ satisfies

$$h^{-\beta} \sum_{j=0}^{i+1} l_j B(x_{i-j+1}, t_n) \leq 0.$$

Proof. (1) The known conditions that $g_j < 0$ $(j \geq 1)$, $A(x,t) \geq 0$ is monotone increasing on x yield

$$\sum_{j=0}^{i} g_j A(x_{i-j}, t_n) \geq \sum_{j=0}^{i} g_j A(x_i, t_n).$$

By Remark 1 and $A(x,t) \geq 0$, we have

$$\sum_{j=0}^{i} g_j A(x_i, t_n) = \left(\sum_{j=0}^{i} g_j \right) A(x_i, t_n) \geq 0,$$

thus

$$\sum_{j=0}^{i} g_j A(x_{i-j}, t_n) \geq 0, \quad i.e. \quad h^{-\alpha} \sum_{j=0}^{i} g_j A(x_{i-j}, t_n) \geq 0.$$

(2) Let $T_{i+1} = \sum\limits_{j=0}^{i+1} l_j B(x_{i-j+1}, t_n)$, $S_k = \sum\limits_{j=0}^{k} l_j$, $S_{-1} = 0$. By the Abel transformation, we have

$$\begin{aligned} T_{i+1} = \sum_{k=0}^{i+1} l_j B(x_{i-k+1}, t_n) &= \sum_{k=0}^{i+1} (S_k - S_{k-1}) B(x_{i-k+1}, t_n) \\ &= \sum_{k=0}^{i+1} S_k B(x_{i-k+1}, t_n) - \sum_{k=0}^{i} S_k B(x_{i-k}, t_n) \\ &= S_{i+1} B(x_0, t_n) + \sum_{k=0}^{i} S_k \left(B(x_{i-k+1}, t_n) - B(x_{i-j}, t_n) \right). \end{aligned}$$

$$(7)$$

To prove $T_{i+1} \leq 0$ $(i \geq 0)$, that is, to prove

$$\sum_{k=1}^{i} S_k \left(B(x_{i-j+1}, t_n) - B(x_{i-j}, t_n) \right) \leq B(x_i, t_n) - B(x_{i+1}, t_n) - S_{i+1} B(x_0, t_n).$$

$$(8)$$

Now we prove (8).

When $1 < \beta < 2$, $\{S_k\}_{k=1}^{\infty}$ is a monotone increasing sequence, $S_k < 0$ $(k \geq 1)$ and $l_0 = 1$, $l_j > 0$ $(j \geq 2)$. When $k \geq 1$, we have

$$S_k = \frac{1}{k!} \prod_{i=1}^{k} (i - \beta),$$

in fact,

$$S_k = \sum_{j=0}^{k} l_j = 1 - \beta + (-1)^2 \frac{\beta(\beta-1)}{2!} + \cdots + (-1)^k \frac{\beta(\beta-1)\cdots(\beta-j+1)}{k!}$$

$$= \frac{(1-\beta)(2-\beta)}{2!} + (-1)^3 \frac{\beta(\beta-1)(\beta-2)}{3!} + \cdots + (-1)^k \frac{\beta(\beta-1)\cdots(\beta-k+1)}{k!}$$

$$= \frac{(1-\beta)(2-\beta)(3-\beta)}{3!} + \cdots + (-1)^k \frac{\beta(\beta-1)\cdots(\beta-k+1)}{k!}$$

$$\cdots$$

$$= \frac{1}{k!} \prod_{i=1}^{k} (i - \beta).$$

$B(x,t)$ is a monotone decreasing and convex function on x in Ω, thus $B(x_{i-1}, t_n) - B(x_i, t_n)$ is monotone decreasing on i, that is

$$0 \le B(x_{i-1}, t_n) - B(x_i, t_n) \le B(x_i, t_n) - B(x_{i+1}, t_n),$$

and

$$\sum_{k=1}^{i} S_k \left(B(x_{i-k+1}, t_n) - B(x_{i-k}, t_n) \right) \le M_i \left(B(x_{i-1}, t_n) - B(x_i, t_n) \right), \tag{9}$$

where $M_i = - \sum_{k=1}^{i} S_k$. Moreover,

$$0 < M_i < 1, \quad i = 1, 2, 3, \cdots. \tag{10}$$

In fact, obviously $M_i > 0$ and

$$1 - M_i = 1 + \sum_{k=1}^{i} S_k = 1 + S_1 + S_2 + S_3 + \cdots + S_i$$

$$= 1 + (1 - \beta) + \frac{(1-\beta)(2-\beta)}{2!} + \cdots + \frac{1}{i!} \prod_{j=1}^{i} (j - \beta)$$

$$= \frac{(2-\beta)(3-\beta)}{2!} + \frac{(1-\beta)(2-\beta)(3-\beta)}{3!} + \cdots + \frac{1}{i!} \prod_{j=1}^{i} (j - \beta)$$

$$\cdots$$

$$= \frac{(2-\beta)(3-\beta)\cdots(i+1-\beta)}{i!}$$

$$> 0.$$

Moreover

$$M_i \left(B(x_{i-1}, t_n) - B(x_i, t_n) \right) \le B(x_i, t_n) - B(x_{i+1}, t_n), \tag{11}$$

that is

$$\frac{M_i B(x_{i-1}, t_n) + B(x_{i+1}, t_n)}{M_i + 1} \le B(x_i, t_n),$$

in fact, it follows from the convexity of $B(x,t)$ that

$$\frac{M_i B(x_{i-1}, t_n) + B(x_{i+1}, t_n)}{M_i + 1} \le B \left(\frac{M_i}{M_i + 1}(i - 1)h + \frac{1}{M_i + 1}(i + 1)h, t_n \right),$$

and by (10), we have

$$\frac{M_i}{M_i+1}(i-1) + \frac{1}{M_i+1}(i+1) > i.$$

Moreover, we have (11) because $B(x,t)$ is a monotone decreasing and convex function on x in Ω. By (9), (11), $S_i < 0$ and $B(x_0, t_n) \geq 0$, we have

$$\sum_{k=1}^{i} S_k \left(B(x_{i-k+1}, t_n) - B(x_{i-k}, t_n) \right) \leq M_i \left(B(x_{i-1}, t_n) - B(x_i, t_n) \right)$$
$$\leq B(x_i, t_n) - B(x_{i+1}, t_n)$$
$$\leq B(x_i, t_n) - B(x_{i+1}, t_n) - S_{i+1} B(x_0, t_n),$$

These leads to the inequality (8), thus $T_{i+1} \leq 0 \ (i \geq 0)$. $\qquad \square$

In the following text, let v_i^n be another solution of the difference method (5) and (6), $\varepsilon_i^n = v_i^n - u_i^n$, $E^n = (\varepsilon_1^n, \varepsilon_2^n, \cdots, \varepsilon_{M-1}^n)^T$, $\|E^n\|_\infty = \max\limits_{1 \leq i \leq M-1} |\varepsilon_i^n|$; let $u(x_i, t_n)$ be the exact solution of (1) and (2) at point (x_i, t_n), $e_i^n = u(x_i, t_n) - u_i^n$, $e^n = (e_1^n, e_2^n, \cdots, e_{M-1}^n)^T$, $\|e^n\|_\infty = \max\limits_{1 \leq i \leq M-1} |e_i^n|$, where $i = 0, 1, 2, \cdots, M$; $n = 0, 1, 2, \cdots, N$.

3   Stability and Convergence of Implicit Difference Method

For the implicit difference scheme (5) and (6), $\varepsilon_i^n = v_i^n - u_i^n$ satisfies

$$\varepsilon_i^{n+1} + r_1 \sum_{j=1}^{i} g_j A_{i-j}^{n+1} \varepsilon_{i-j}^{n+1} - r_2 \sum_{j=0}^{i+1} l_j B_{i-j+1}^{n+1} \varepsilon_{i-j+1}^{n+1} = \varepsilon_i^n, \qquad (12)$$

where $i = 1, 2, \cdots, M-1$; $n = 0, 1, 2, \cdots, N-1$. We can obtain the following theorem.

Theorem 1. *If $A(x,t)$ is monotone increasing on x in Ω, $B(x,t)$ is a monotone decreasing and convex function on x in Ω, then the implicit difference scheme determined by (5) and (6) is unconditionally stable.*

Proof. Let $|\varepsilon_l^1| = \max\limits_{1 \leq i \leq M-1} |\varepsilon_i^1|$. By Lemmas 1 and 2, we have

$$|\varepsilon_l^1| \leq \left(1 + r_1 \sum_{j=0}^{l} g_j A_{l-j}^1 - r_2 \sum_{j=0}^{l+1} l_j B_{l-j+1}^1 \right) |\varepsilon_l^1|$$
$$\leq \left(1 + r_1 A_l^1 + r_2 \beta B_l^1 \right) |\varepsilon_l^1| + r_1 \sum_{j=1}^{l} g_j A_{l-j}^1 |\varepsilon_l^1| - r_2 \sum_{j=0, j\neq1}^{l+1} l_j B_{l-j+1}^1 |\varepsilon_l^1|$$
$$\leq \left(1 + r_1 A_l^1 + r_2 \beta B_l^1 \right) |\varepsilon_l^1| + r_1 \sum_{j=1}^{l} g_j A_{l-j}^1 |\varepsilon_{l-j}^1| - r_2 \sum_{j=0, j\neq1}^{l+1} l_j B_{l-j+1}^1 |\varepsilon_{l-j+1}^1|$$
$$\leq \left| \varepsilon_l^1 + r_1 \sum_{j=0}^{l} g_j A_{l-j}^1 \varepsilon_{l-j}^1 - r_2 \sum_{j=0}^{l+1} l_j B_{l-j+1}^1 \varepsilon_{l-j+1}^1 \right|$$
$$= |\varepsilon_l^0| \leq \|E^0\|_\infty.$$

Suppose $\|E^j\|_\infty \le \|E^0\|_\infty$, $j = 1, 2, \cdots, n$. Now we prove $\|E^{n+1}\|_\infty \le \|E^0\|_\infty$. Take $|\varepsilon_l^{n+1}| = \max_{1 \le i \le M-1} |\varepsilon_i^{n+1}|$. By Lemma 2, we have

$$
\begin{aligned}
|\varepsilon_l^{n+1}| &\le \left(1 + r_1 \sum_{j=0}^{l} g_j A_{l-j}^{n+1} - r_2 \sum_{j=0}^{l+1} l_j B_{l-j+1}^{n+1}\right) |\varepsilon_l^{n+1}| \\
&\le \left(1 + r_1 A_l^{n+1} + r_2 \beta B_l^{n+1}\right) |\varepsilon_l^{n+1}| \\
&\quad + r_1 \sum_{j=1}^{l} g_j A_{l-j}^{n+1} |\varepsilon_{l-j}^{n+1}| - r_2 \sum_{j=0, j\ne1}^{l+1} l_j B_{l-j+1}^{n+1} |\varepsilon_{l-j+1}^{n+1}| \\
&\le \left| \varepsilon_l^{n+1} + r_1 \sum_{j=0}^{l} g_j A_{l-j}^{n+1} \varepsilon_{l-j}^{n+1} - r_2 \sum_{j=0}^{l+1} l_j B_{l-j+1}^{n+1} \varepsilon_{l-j+1}^{n+1} \right| \\
&= |\varepsilon_l^n| \le \|E^n\|_\infty.
\end{aligned}
\tag{13}
$$

Thus $\|E^{n+1}\|_\infty \le \|E^0\|_\infty$. $\qquad\square$

From (4) and (5), we have

$$
e_i^{n+1} + r_1 \sum_{j=1}^{i} g_j A_{i-j}^{n+1} e_{i-j}^{n+1} - r_2 \sum_{j=0}^{i+1} l_j B_{i-j+1}^{n+1} e_{i-j+1}^{n+1} = e_i^n + R_i^n.
\tag{14}
$$

We can obtain the convergence result of the implicit difference scheme.

Theorem 2. *If $A(x, t)$ is monotone increasing on x in Ω, $B(x, t)$ is a monotone decreasing and convex function on x in Ω, then the implicit difference scheme determined by (5) and (6) satisfies*

$$
|u(x_i, t_n) - u_i^n| \le C_1(\tau + h),
$$

where $i = 1, 2, \cdots, M-1$; $n = 0, 1, 2, \cdots, N$, C_1 is a positive constant.

Proof. Take $|e_l^{n+1}| = \max_{1 \le i \le M-1} |e_i^{n+1}|$. By Lemmas 1 and 2, we have

$$
\begin{aligned}
|e_l^{n+1}| &\le \left(1 + r_1 \sum_{j=0}^{l} g_j A_{l-j}^{n+1} - r_2 \sum_{j=0}^{l+1} l_j B_{l-j+1}^{n+1}\right) |e_l^{n+1}| \\
&\le \left(1 + r_1 A_l^{n+1} + r_2 \beta B_l^{n+1}\right) |e_l^{n+1}| \\
&\quad + r_1 \sum_{j=1}^{l} g_j A_{l-j}^{n+1} |e_{l-j}^{n+1}| - r_2 \sum_{j=0, j\ne1}^{l+1} l_j B_{l-j+1}^{n+1} |e_{l-j+1}^{n+1}| \\
&\le \left| e_l^{n+1} + r_1 \sum_{j=0}^{l} g_j A_{l-j}^{n+1} e_{l-j}^{n+1} - r_2 \sum_{j=0}^{l+1} l_j B_{l-j+1}^{n+1} e_{l-j+1}^{n+1} \right| \\
&= |e_l^n + R_l^n| \le |e_l^n| + |R_l^n|,
\end{aligned}
\tag{15}
$$

and

$$
\|e^{n+1}\|_\infty \le \|e^n\|_\infty + |R_l^n|.
$$

Repeating to use the above inequality, we have

$$\|e^{n+1}\|_\infty \leq \|e^0\|_\infty + |R_l^n| + |R_l^{n-1}| + \cdots + |R_l^0|.$$

And $\|e^0\|_\infty = 0$, $|R_l^j| \leq C\tau(\tau + h)$, $j = 0, 1, \cdots, N - 1$. Therefore,

$$\begin{aligned}
\|e^{n+1}\|_\infty &\leq (n+1)C\tau(\tau + h) \\
&\leq CT(\tau + h) \\
&= C_1(\tau + h) \qquad (C_1 = CT),
\end{aligned}$$

thus we have $|u(x_i, t_n) - u_i^n| \leq C_1(\tau + h)$, C_1 is a positive constant.   □

4   Numerical Experiments

In this section, we give some numerical examples on a finite domain to show that the unconditional stability results of the implicit difference scheme.

Example 1. Consider the fractional advection-diffusion equation with variable coefficients

$$\frac{\partial u}{\partial t} = -{}_0D_x^\alpha[A(x,t)u(x,t)] + {}_0D_x^\beta[B(x,t)u(x,t)] + f(x,t),$$
$$0 < x < 1, \ 0 < t \leq 1, \tag{16}$$

where

$$\alpha = 0.5, \quad \beta = 1.5, \quad A(x,t) = x, \quad B(x,t) = -x^2 + 1,$$

$$f(x,t) = \left[\frac{\Gamma(7/2) + \Gamma(9/2)}{2}x^2 - \Gamma(5/2) - x^{3/2}\right]e^{-t},$$

and the initial and boundary conditions are given by

$$\begin{aligned}
u(x,0) &= x^{3/2}, 0 \leq x \leq 1, \\
u(0,t) &= 0, \quad u(1,t) = e^{-t}, 0 < t \leq 1.
\end{aligned} \tag{17}$$

The exact solution of (16) and (17) is $u(x,t) = xe^{-t}$.

The following Table 1 show that the relationship between the numerical solutions given by the implicit difference scheme and the exact solution. Let the maximum error between the numerical solutions and the exact solutions be $\max\limits_{1 \leq i \leq M-1, 0 \leq n \leq N} |u_i^n - u(x_i, t_n)|$.

Table 1. The implicit difference method

time step	space step	maximum error
0.1	0.1	0.0205
0.1	0.01	0.0033
0.01	0.1	0.0275
0.01	0.01	0.0022

Example 2. Consider the following fractional advection-diffusion equation with variable coefficients

$$\frac{\partial u}{\partial t} = -{_0}D_x^\alpha[A(x,t)u(x,t)] + {_0}D_x^\beta[B(x,t)u(x,t)] + f(x,t),$$
$$0 < x < 1, 0 < t \le 1, \tag{18}$$

where

$$\alpha = 0.75, \quad \beta = 1.5, \quad A(x,t) = x^2 t, \quad B(x,t) = -x^2 + 1,$$

$$f(x,t) = \left[\frac{\Gamma(5)}{\Gamma(17/4)}x^{13/4}t + \frac{\Gamma(5)}{\Gamma(7/2)}x^{5/2} - \frac{\Gamma(3)}{\Gamma(3/2)}x^{1/2} - x^2\right]e^{-t},$$

the initial and boundary conditions satisfy

$$u(x,0) = x^2, 0 \le x \le 1,$$
$$u(0,t) = 0, \quad u(1,t) = e^{-t}, 0 < t \le 1. \tag{19}$$

The exact solution of (18) and (19) is $u(x,t) = x^2 e^{-t}$.

The Fig.1 can compare the numerical solution of the implicit difference scheme with the exact solution on the domain $[0,1] \times [0,1]$ by taking the time and space step size 0.02.

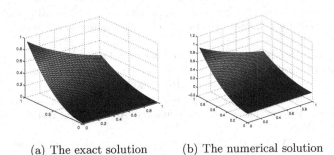

(a) The exact solution   (b) The numerical solution

Fig. 1.

5   Conclusion

In this paper, we discuss the numerical solution of the implicit difference method for space fractional advection-diffusion equations with variable coefficients. For this numerical scheme, we examine the stability and convergence, meanwhile, by some numerical experiments, we prove the correctness of our theoretical analysis. For the space fractional advection-diffusion equations with variable coefficients, moreover, based on Lemmas 1 and 2, we can discuss similarly the stability and convergence of the explicit difference methods and Crank-Nicholson methods applied to these equations. Although we construct some effective numerical schemes, the following deficiencies still exist: (1) there are the restrictions "monotone" to $A(x,t)$ and $B(x,t)$; (2) the convergence order of the constructed difference schemes are still not high.

References

1. Benson, D.A., Wheatcraft, S.W., Meerschaert, M.M.: Application of a fractional advection-dispersion equation. Water Resources Research 36(6), 1403–1412 (2000)
2. Ding, Z., Xiao, A., Li, M.: Weighted finite difference methods for a class of space fractional partial differential equations with variable coefficient. Journal of Computational and Applied Mathematics 233, 1905–1914 (2010)
3. El-Sayed, A.M.A., Behiry, S.H., Raslan, W.E.: Adomain's decomposition method for solving an intermediate fractional advection-dispersion equation. Computers and Mathematics with Application 59, 1759–1765 (2010)
4. Ervin, V.J., Roop, J.P.: Variational solution of fractional advection dispersion equations on bounded domains in ℝ. Numerical Methods for Partial Differential Equations 23(2), 256–281 (2007)
5. Huang, Q., Huang, G., Zhan, H.: A finite element for the fractional advection-dispersion equation. Advances in Water Resources 31, 1578–1589 (2008)
6. Huang, F., Liu, F.: The fundamental solution of the space-time fractional advection-dispersion equation. J. Appl. Math. and Computing. 18, 339–350 (2005)
7. Liu, F., Zhuang, P., Anh, V., Turner, I., Burrage, K.: Stability and convergence of the difference methods for the space-time fractional advection-diffusion equation. Applied Mathematics and Computation 191, 12–20 (2007)
8. Odibat, Z., Momani, S.: Numerical solution of Fokker-Planck equation with space- and time-fractional derivatives. Physics Letters A 369, 349–358 (2007)
9. Shen, S., Liu, F., Anh, V.: Numerical approximations and solution techniques for the space-time Riesz-Caputo fractional advection-diffusion equation. Numer. Algor. 56, 383–403 (2011)
10. Schumer, R., Meerschaert, M.M., Baeumer, B.: Fractional advection-dispersion equations for modeling transport at the Earth surface. Journal of Geophysical Research 114, F00A07 (2009), doi:10.1029/2008JF001246
11. Yildirim, A., Kocak, H.: Homoyopy perturbation method for solving the space-time fractional advection-dispersion equation. Advances in Water Resources 32, 1711–1716 (2009)
12. Yang, S., Xiao, A., Su, H.: Convergence of the variational iteration method for solving multi-order fractional differential equations. Computers and Mathematics with Applications 60, 2871–2879 (2010)
13. Zhang, Y., Benson, D.A., Meerschaert, M.M., LaBolle, E.M.: Space-fractional advection-dispersion equations with variable parameters: Diverse formulas, numerical solutions, and application to the Macrodispersion Experiment site data. Water Resources Research 43, W05439 (2007), doi:10.1029/2006WR004912
14. Zhang, Y., Benson, D.A., Meerschaert, M.M., Scheffler, H.P.: On using random walks to solve the space-fractional advection-dispersion equations. Journal of Statistical Physics 123(1), 89–110 (2006)
15. Zheng, G.H., Wei, T.: Spectral regularization method for a Cauchy problem of the time fractional advection-dispersion equation. Journal of Computational and Applied Mathematics 223, 2631–2640 (2010)

Review of the Power Grid Model Vulnerability Based on Complex Network Theory

Zhiguo Ding[1,2] and Minrui Fei[1]

[1]School of Mechatronics Engineering and Automation,
Shanghai University, Shanghai, 200072 China
[2]College of Mathematics, Physics and Information Engineering,
Zhejiang Normal University, Jinhua, Zhejiang, 321004,China
mrfei@staff.shu.edu.cn, dingzhiguo@shu.edu.cn

Abstract. Topology structure of power grid has intrinsic and substantial characteristics which if once ascertained in the build of the power grid will have crucial impact on its performance. Therefore, in this paper, some network models commonly used in power grid are introduced and analyzed byreference of the domestic and overseasresearches which are based on the complex theory. There exist some key transmissionlines and/or vulnerable nodesin thepower grid,and if either of them breaksdown, itmay result in wide-area blackoutsand even the cascading failures. Since smart grid is the trend of the current power grid, cyber-physical network structure model as well as some current researches on smart grid has been introduced. At last, some thoughts about how to better develop smart gridare proposed.

Keywords: Complex Network Theory, Network Topology, Vulnerability, Smart Grid.

1   Introduction

The power grid is so far the most complicated man-made physical system. With the development of the modern power grid, this system has gradually becomemuch more large-scale and more complex. However, the increasing importance of the security problem, reliability problem and some others brings great difficulty for the power grid to monitor and find the hidden failures as early as possible. In the recent years there happened more than ten large-scale blackouts all over the world, such as America and Canada blackout in 2003, 18 states in Brazil and neighboring Paraguay blackouts in 2009, Queensland blackouts in Australia in 2010 and so on, those power outages have brought considerableharm to people's work and daily life[1]. In order to alleviate the damage and loss in the power outage, many researchers at home and aboard have devoted much attention and done a lot ofwork.

Topology structure of power grid has intrinsic and substantial characteristic which once ascertained in the build of the power grid will have a crucial impact on the performance of power grid.The high frequency of the power grid blackouts has drawn great attentionto the fault transmission mechanism and network structure vulnerability

T. Xiao, L. Zhang, and S. Ma (Eds.): ICSC 2012, Part II, CCIS 327, pp. 105–113, 2012.
© Springer-Verlag Berlin Heidelberg 2012

in the power utility[2][3]. For example, the complex network theory, which mainly focuses on the awareness of blackouts occurrence mechanism and analysis from the perspective of topology structure, is applied to study the complexity of the large-scale power grid andbecomes a hot topic.The analysis and awareness ofpower grid mechanism,protection of the vulnerable nodes are significant to improve the reliability of power grid and to reduce the large-scale blackouts [4], Therefore, this paper mainly reviews the study of the structure vulnerability of the power grid based on the complex theory in recent years.

The remainder of the paper is organized as follows: section 2 presents a few important feature parameters of network topology; section 3 describes several kinds of network models commonly used in the power grid system and analyzes their advantages and disadvantages; Section 4 introduces Cyber-physical networkstructure for the smart gridand present some current study result; The last section points out some limits and the future work.

2   Topological Feature Parameters of Complex Network

Power grid is always described as an abstract topology structure, which has N nodes and K edges. Node represents power plant, generator or substation, while edge stands for transmission lines or transformer branch. There are some concepts and waysproposed byresearchers to analyze and describe the complex statistical property of power grid, the four basic parameters enumerated belowregarded as the most important.

2.1   Length of Characteristic Path

The distance between nodes$i$ and j in the topology structure, denoted by d_{ij},is defined as the shortest number of edges. The average value of distance of all node pairs in the network is the length of characteristic path, which is defined as:

$$L = \frac{1}{N(N-1)}\sum_{i \neq j} d_{i,j} \tag{1}$$

Where N represents the number of nodes

2.2   Clustering Coefficient

Specially, the clustering coefficient C is an important parameter specialized to measure the aggregation degree of network nodes, node clustering coefficient and network clustering coefficient is described respectively. Node clustering coefficient is defined as $C_i = a_i/b_i$, where$a_i$represents the number of triangle formed by the nodes and edges which one vertex is node i,b_i represents the number oftriple formed by the nodes. The network clustering coefficient is defined as:

$$C = \frac{1}{N}\sum_{i=1}^{n} C_i \tag{2}$$

2.3   Degree and Degree Distribution

Degree is a simple and important concept which describes the characteristic of single nodes in the network.The degree of node i,denoted as k_i, is defined as the number of the nodes which is connected with itself. The bigger the degree of the node is,the more important the node is in some sense in the network. The average degree of the network nodes, denoted as $<k>$, is defined as the average value of all nodes degree. The degree distribution of nodes in the network can be described by the distribution function $p(k)$, the one which represents the probability of the randomly selected node which degreejust equals k.

2.4   Betweenness

The concept of betweenness is always categorized as node betweenness and edge betweenness, the formerdefined as the proportion of the number of the shortest path by way of this node to the number of the shortest path in the network, while the latterdefined as the proportion of the number of shortest path by way of this edge to the number of the shortest path in the network.Betweenness reflects the important pole of the corresponding node and edge played in the network.

Complex network is composed of numerous nodes and edges whichconnects with two adjacent nodes. The four parameters described above reflect the characteristic of network topological structure. The length of characteristic path in power grid shows the speed of fault propagation in some sense, while the clustering coefficient, degree distribution and betweenness indicate the scope and degree of fault propogation.All above mentioned parameters exert great importance in the fault propogation.

3   Topology Model of Power Grid

Using the complex theory to study the structural inherent vulnerability of power grid is an important method for the exploration of the fault occurrence mechanism and evolution law. The research field of the theory mainly covers network structure model, generative mechanism and evolution law. Since the study has attracted much attention and has gained plentiful results, this paper will make a brief introduction of some in this section.

3.1   Simple and Regular Network Model

Small-scale power grid in the past usually used the tree model, quadrilateral model, hexagon model and so no to describe the network topology structure and analyze the network characteristic[5][6]. Those models are easy to build, but too simple to describe the complexity of the modern power grid structure. Additionally, there are other network models based on the mutual connection character to build, such as nearest neighbornetwork model and globally coupled network model which are often adopted by the researchers. But all above mentioned models are incapable to describe the complexity of large-scale power network structure.

3.2   ER Random Network Model

In order to express and explain therandom characteristic during the evolution of complex power grid, some researchers began to incorporate the random characteristicinto the study of complex network theory and proposed the method of probability statistics, which is a big breakthrough in the study of the complex theory. In 1959, Hungarian mathematicians Paul Erdös and Alfred Rényi built a completely random network model which subsequently was regarded as the classical ER random modelto describe the communication network and gained good performance[7].

The random characteristics of ER random network model fit in with some connection characters of complex network in reality and easy to build, which laid the foundation for the advanced study in the complex power grid. Many researchers carried out their study in the power grid model based on this theory. Although ER random network model has itsirreplaceable virtue in expressing random characteristic, it is incapable to express some characteristics during the process of the network dynamic revolution, such as the Matthew effect. With the development of the modern smart grid, the ER random model theory may be used in this field, for the new energy resource and electric car are randomly inserted into the power grid[8].

3.3   WS Small World Network Model

Small world network model was proposed originally by doctoral student Watts and his tutor Strogatz,in Cornell University, who worked together and published jointly the paper titled*Collective dynamics of 'small world' networks*in journal of*Nature*in 1998. It was for the first time to reveal the characteristics of small world network of power grid network of the western United States[9]. Consequently, this model was named the classical WS-Small-World-Networks model by the following researchers.

The characteristic of small world model indicates that complex networks usually have the higher clustering coefficient C similar to the regular networks' and meanwhile have shorter length of characteristic path L similar to the random networks', which spread the information, energy, breakdown quickly.

In the small world power grid, if one node breaks down it not only affects the adjacent nodes but also affects other non-adjacent nodes failureresulting in cascading failure and eventually makethe whole power grid blackouts.In this sense, the small world networks characteristic of the shorter L and the higher C aggravates the fault spread. There are a few nodes or circuit lines with the higher betweenness than other nodes or circuit lines, so if one node or circuit line has breakdowns or loss, the shortest characteristic paths between nodes would redistribute and energy between nodes would transfer, causing the cascading failure disastrous eventually[4].

3.4   BA Scale-Free Network Model

The professor Barabási along with his doctoral student Albert, in Madonna University, USA, constructed jointly a network model which has the characteristic of power law distribution. They published the paper titled*Emergence of scaling in random networks*in journal of*Science*in 1999 and discovered firstly the characteristics of scale-free network model in western United State power grid[10], which was named famous BA Scale-free network model consequently. This network model indicates that the degree distribution of many complex networks in reality has the power law distribution characteristics, formulated by $P(k)=k-r$, rather than the Poisson distribution characteristics.

Mostnodes in scale-free networkalways only has few connection,which means when these nodes in power grid suffers attack or fault, it would have a little effect on the whole networks connection. However, there exist a few nodes in networks which have a high degree and connection with many other nodes, so they are the central pivot nodes and hub nodesaffecting the connectivity and some important topological characteristic of networks.

Complex networks may suffer two kinds of attack, namely, random attack and hostile attack. The former refers to the assault done by randomly-selected nodes, for example, the bad weather would cause the short circuit in power grid; the latter refers to the attack intentionally on those nodes which have the high degree nodes (important nodes) in the network.For example, terroristsdestroy maliciously electric power infrastructure. Though scale-free network has good robustness for the random attack, and some low degree nodes missing or suffering attack would not have serious effect on the performance of the whole network[11][12],it has the inherent vulnerability to the hostile intentionally attack, which means some high degree nodes missing or suffering attack would destroythe network connectivity. This heterogeneity of topological structure needs further study inpower gird application.

3.5   OPA Model

OPA model is proposed jointly by researchers of the Oak Ridge national Laboratory of the United State (ORNL), Power System Engineering Research Center of theWisconsinUniversity(PSERC) and the University of Alaska. Themain line of research is described as follows: With the development of the power system, the power generation capacity and load level is continuously ascending which consequently results in the increase of line power flower and improvement of the line load factor. The line with heavy load capacity is break in a certain probability, which leads to the power flow transferring and changes other lines into heavy load lines and finally evolves into the cascading failure.

OPA model simulates the running of the power system by introducing the sand-pile model with the self-organization characteristics, the core content of which is to explore the whole dynamics behaviorcharacteristic of cascading failure and blackouts in power system based on the study of vary of the load capacity, generator,linetransmission capacity. When the OPA model is used to simulate the real power grid, the computation complexity is the same as the linear programming problem which will cause a quick computation speed suitable for the study of the complex characteristic of large-scale mutual connection power grid and mechanism of cascading failure especially[13][14].

Researchers proposed many improved OPA model based on the basic OPA models[15][16]. However, the original OPA modes and improved modes all didn't take into account the topological evolution of power grid. Additionally, in the environment of smart grid, OPA model does not have the efficient methods to improve power grid load and insert new energy generation randomly.

3.6   CASCADE Model

The main idea of the cascade failure model is to suppose that there are N same transmission lines withrandom initial load[17]. According to the predefined load distribution principle, when the initial disturbance makes one or some components failure, the load on those fault components will transfer to other components which don't have any failure, which will consequently causethe corresponding line over-load. If it happens again and again,the outages would spread the whole power grid.

CASCADE model can analyze and stimulate in a qualitative way the cascading accidents of large-scale blackouts which may be caused by transmission line and generator breakdown, but it has the obviousshortcomings. For one thing, this model supposesinteraction of among transmission line is equal, but thiswill not happen in the real world. What's more, under the over-load circumstance it doesn't take into account the network structure for load redistribution, which does not reflect the variation of generate electricity side and failure situation, etc.

4   Complex Network Model of Smart Grid

Smart grid, which integrates the power grid, communication network and computer network as a whole, will be the trend of the existing power grid, for it has a much more complex network structure than any other models. Take the small-world network model and scale-free network model for example, although they can reflect some power grid characteristics, one node breakdown in the power grid will not only impact the neighboring nodes but also result in non-adjacent nodes failure and cascading failure, leading to the whole power system blackouts eventually. The scale-free characteristic of power grid has the striking robustness for the stochastic fault, but it has its intrinsic vulnerability for the smart attack to the power grid. The target of smart grid is to develop the new generation power grid, which has the performance of robustness, reliability and self-healing. Some researchersregardthat the future smart grid as the dual compound network composed of the physical power network and cyber-network[18][19]. The mainly content below is to introduce the CPPG (Cyber-Physical Power Grid) network model.

Ref. [19] studied the security problem of cyber network and physical power network for the future smart grid from the perspective of complex network theory,and moreover, it studied the network modeling, feature extraction of topological structure, mechanism of cascading failure and so on. smart grid is regarded as the whole super large-scale dual compound network composed of the cyber network, physical power network, and is expected to build the dual compound complex network theory based on the CPPG.

In general, Cyber network and physical power grid in GPPC are entirely different in structure characteristics. It is indicated by some research that cyber network appears some scale-free characteristic[10], while some practical power grid appears some small-world characteristics[20]. In this context, CPPG would be regarded as theinterdependent evolution dual component heterogeneous network which is composed ofcyber network and physical power network. For this reason, the attack in the CPPG would come either from physical power grid or from cyber network, which can be described by Fig. 1[19].

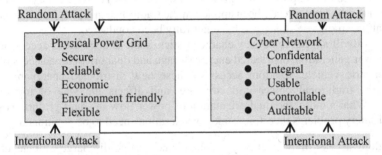

Fig. 1. Schematic diagram of cyber-physical power grid

With reference to CPPG vulnerability, there already have some studies for the cascading fault modeling of cyber network and physical power grid[21].Although to some extent people have known about the procedure of cascading failure of single network, the occurrence and transmission procedure of cascading failure in CPPG might be very different.To study the occurrence and transmission procedure of cascading failure, it needs to take the mutual independency of cyber network and physical power grid into account so as to acquire a comprehensive analysis of the fault occurrence and transmission mechanism in these two kinds of network.Then, on the basis of the integrated CPPG network model mentioned above, the influence of occurrence and development process of cascading failure for the physical equipment, data acquisition equipment, computation equipment also needs considering. In this sense, the details about how to analyze the cascading failure characteristics of CPPG network will be described as follows.

(1) Construct the CPPG cascading fault model based on the cyber network and physical power network;
(2) Identify the critical factor which results in the occurrence of cascading failure;
(3) Analyze in quantitative way the cascading failure which occurs in CPPG network; analyze the disaster risk by in view of value at risk and value indicator at risk[21]; Compare the similarity and difference between CPPG network and traditional physical power grid; highlight the analysis of the effect of cyber network on cascading failure of CPPG network;

(4) Constructtheindex system of vulnerability evaluation for CPPG network;
(5) With the help of cascading failure model, simulate the probable procedure of cascading failure occurrence and development when CPPG network suffers the random attack or intentionalattack; evaluate the variation of system performance under different attack circumstance and identify the attack pattern of impact performance and system vulnerable section.

5   Conclusions

This paper reviews the power grid topological model and analyzes its vulnerability on the basis of the complex network theory, thenintroduces the recent development of this field.It finds that the previous studies have analyzed the fault mechanism and fault occurrence rules of complex power grid based on complex network theory, and some theoretical results have already been applied in the traditional grid, but it also should be noted that the studies on smart grid have not fully been conducted.

Smart gridwill appear some new characteristics, such as continuous access of new energy power generation, distributed energy storage and dual orientation access of new hybrid electric vehicle. Random access of these new distributed energy resources changes the traditional power grid structure, and affects the way of topological modeling. What's more, the dual orientation of power flow in smart gridbrings some potential safety problems,therefore,some considerations need to be mentioned.

(1) Random access of new energy resource and charge-discharge storage energy devices may cause the stability problem of smart grid.In addition, the dual orientation of power flowposes some challenge to analyze the new network topological structure.
(2) No matter how complexthe existing power network is, it can't satisfy the development demand of multi-element and heterogeneous network in smart grid, for it is tailored only to the single complex network. Therefore, a more advanced complex network theory is urgently needed.
(3) The cyber network has much more running risk than physical power grid, the current analysis methodis only designed for the physical power grid. Therefore, how to improve the whole running performance and offer some useful reference to the security and stability of network structureis also an important issue.

Acknowledgments. This work is supported by the National Natural Science Foundation of China under Grant No. 61074032, and the Project of Science and Technology Commission of Shanghai Municipality under Grant No. 10JC1405000.

References

1. Xu, L.X., Yang, J.M., Yao, C.Z., et al.: Analysis of cascading failure in power grids based on weighted network model. J. Control Theory & Applications 28(11), 1012–1067 (2011)
2. US-Canada Power System Outage Task Force. Final report on the August 14th blackout in the United States and Canada: causes and recommendations,
   https://reports.energy.gov

3. Yin, Y.H., Guo, J.B., Zhao, J.J., et al.: Preliminary analysis of large scale blackout in interconnected North American power grid on August 14 and lessons to be drawn. J. Power System Technology 27(10), 8–11 (2003)
4. Cao, Y.J., Chen, X.G., Sun, K.: Identification of vulnerable lines in power grid based on complex network theory. J. Electric Power Automation Equipment. 26(12), 1–5 (2006)
5. Carreras, B.A., Lynch, V.E., Dobson, I., et al.: Dynamics criticality and self-organization in a model for blackouts in Power transmission systems. In: Hawaii International Conference on System Science, Hawaii (2002)
6. Carreras, B.A., Lynch, V.E., Dobson, I., et al.: Complex dynamic of blackouts in power transmission system. J. Chaos. 14(3), 643–652 (2004)
7. Erdös, P., Rényi, A.: On the evolution of random graphs. Publ. Math. Inst. Hung. Acad. Sci. 5, 17–61 (1960)
8. Baek, S.J., Kim, D., Oh, S.-J.: Modeling of Electric Vehicle Charging Systems in Communications Enabled Smart Grids. J. IEICE Transactions on Information and System, 1708–1711 (2011)
9. Watts, D.J., Strogatz, S.H.: Collective dynamics of 'small world' networks. J. Nature 393, 400–442 (1998)
10. Barabási, A.L., Albert, R.: Emergence of scaling in random networks. J. Science 286, 509–512 (1999)
11. Albert, R., Jeong, H., Barabási, A.L.: Error and attack tolerance of complex network. J. Nature 406, 378–382 (2000)
12. Zhao, L., Kwangho, P., Lai, Y.C.: Attack vulnerability of scale-free network due to cascading breakdown. J. Phys. Rev. 70, 035101(R) (2004)
13. Dobson, I., Carreras, B.A., Lynch, V.E., et al.: An initial model for complex dynamics in electric power system blackouts. In: 34th Hawaii International Conference on System Science, Hawaii, pp. 710–718 (2011)
14. He, F., Mei, S.W., Xue, A.C., et al.: Blackouts Distribution and Self-Organized Criticality of Power System Based on DC Power Flow. J. Power System Technology. 30(14), 7–12 (2006)
15. Ren, H., Dobson, I., Carreras, B.A.: Long-Term Effect of the N-1 Criterion on Cascading Line Outages in an Evolving Power Transmission Grid. J. IEEE Transactions on Power System 23(3), 1217–1225 (2008)
16. Mei, S.W., Weng, X.F., Xue, A.C., et al.: Blackout Model Based on OPF and Its Self-organized Criticality. J. Automation of Electric Power System 30(13), 1–5 (2006)
17. Dobson, I., Carreras, B.A., Lynch, V.E., et al.: Complex systems analysis of series of blackouts: cascading failure, criticality, and self-organization. Bulk Power System Dynamics and Control-VI, Italy (2004)
18. Buldyrev, S.V., Parshani, R., Paul, G., et al.: Catastrophic cascade of failure in interdependent networks. J. Nature 464(7291), 1025–1028 (2010)
19. Mei, S.W., Wang, Y.Y., Chen, L.J.: Overviews and prospects of the Cyber Security of Smart Grid from the view of Complex Network Theory. J. High Voltage Engineering. 37(3), 672–679 (2011)
20. Meng, Z.W., Lu, Z.X., Song, J.Y.: Comparison analysis of the small world topology model of Chinese and American power grid. J. Automation of Electric Power System 28(15), 21–24 (2004)
21. Mei, S., Zhang, X., Cao, M.: Power grid complexity. Springer-Tsinghua Press, Beijing (2011)

Extraction of Vortices and Exploration of the Ocean Data by Visualization System

Chi Zhang, Takashi Uenaka, Naohisa Sakamoto, and Koji Koyamada

Graduate School of Engineering, Kyoto University, Japan
zhang.chi.24e@st.kyoto-u.ac.jp

Abstract. Naturally, fishery highly depends on the environment in the ocean. To increase fishing hauls, the analysis of the ocean is of great significance. In this paper, we proposed some visualization tools which help to filter and analyze the ocean data such as temperatures and currents velocities. Sea currents are visualized as streamlines and vortices can be detected and extracted. We constructed a system environment in which we can analyze the relationship between the vortices and the distribution of temperatures, which is visualized by volume rendering.

Keywords: ocean data, volume rendering, streamline, vortices extraction.

1 Introduction

According to the existing theories, the fishing hauls have a relationship with the distribution of temperatures and vortices. When warm currents meet cold currents, warm currents lift the nutrients in cold currents up to the shallow part of sea, which makes a favorable environment for the reproduction of plankton, and thus the plankton-eating fish will be attracted. Besides, many kinds of fish move with currents, hence the fish density may be relatively higher at the confluence of warm currents and cold currents. Vortices also help to gather nutrients and fish. To find the relationship between these factors, some visualization methods need to be applied to our system. In this paper, we propose a system which is composed of overall and detailed visualization tools in order to verify the relationship between these factors. As for the visualization tools, we develop a parallel coordinates plot to show the overview of the high-dimensional ocean data, a streamline tool to show sea currents and a volume rendering tool to show the distribution of temperatures.

In the streamline tool, the 3-dimensional currents velocity field is visualized by streamlines with the starting points very close to vortices. Therefore, the features of these vortices are illustrated intuitively and we can find some typical vortices by comparison. The volume rendering tool is used for visualizing the overall distribution of temperatures. In the volume rendering view, a powerful tool is developed for user to customize the transfer function so as to emphasize some significant information and ignore the minor part. By ortho-slices, the 2-dimensional distribution of temperatures with different depths can be shown respectively as 2D plots, which is useful for us to understand the details of the internal distribution.

T. Xiao, L. Zhang, and S. Ma (Eds.): ICSC 2012, Part II, CCIS 327, pp. 114–123, 2012.
© Springer-Verlag Berlin Heidelberg 2012

2   Related Works

The study on the relationships between the fishing hauls of squids in the sea area in Japan and the hydro-graphic conditions was first proposed by Suzuki in 1963[3]. This study explains why squids tend to migrate to "boundary zones" where different water masses meet each other and create prolific fishing areas. We try to get the same results as this study but using modern techniques of visualization to make a system allowing users to view and select the useful information in the data conveniently. Not only the fluid visualization, but also the flow visualization has been a primordial subject for researchers in a wide range of scientific fields. A lot of different rendering techniques has been developed[1]. From all those techniques, we use the volume rendering to visualize the distribution of temperatures in the ocean. Vortices are important features in flow research and visualization. Studies concerning vortices detection have been introduced by Sadarjoen et al.[2] and the scale calculation method for vortices proposed by Guo et al.[4] is applied to our system. Parallel coordinates plot is used in our system for providing an overview about the high-dimensional ocean data. To solve the cluttering problem, the k-means algorithm, which is introduced by Hartigan [5] and improved by Hamerly [6], is utilized to partition the input data into a number of partitions.

3   Proposed System

3.1   Overall Exploration of Data

Parallel coordinates plot is widely used for visualizing and analyzing multivariate data. In a parallel coordinates plot, each dimension of the input data is plotted as a vertical axis. Different with the Cartesian coordinate system, all of the axes are parallel with each other and a data point is plotted as a polyline connecting the corresponding positions on these axes so that it is possible to show more than three dimensions in a 2D plane. Therefore, parallel coordinates plot is a good way to provide the overview of the ocean data. Users can pick up the data points that they want to pay attention to by simply select the relative range on one or more axes. For example, if users tend to view the data with relatively high temperatures, they can select the corresponding range on the axis representing for temperatures and only the data points with the temperatures in this range will be shown. Therefore, they can know the ranges of latitude, longitude, depth or current velocities of these data points from other axes. Thus it is very useful to explore the relevance of the data in different dimensions. Furthermore, when the size of the input data is extremely large and the whole data can not be read into the main memory, the out-of-core feature can be utilized to process every part of the data sequentially. Only a part of the data is loaded at a time and after the calculation, the present data will be deleted from the memory and the next part of data will be loaded and processed. This procedure will be repeated until all of the data is processed. The high-speed k-means clustering method[6] can be used to solve the cluttering problem that when the number of data points is very large and it is difficult for users to discern so many lines. The input data is partitioned to a number of clusters and each cluster is plotted as a polygon in parallel coordinates, which accelerates the rendering as well.

3.2   Extraction of Vortices

Types of Vortices   In our system, the types of vortices are determined by the directions of vortices. In a horizontal plane, the directions of vortices can be divided into two cases: the direction of the currents in a vortex points toward to its center or far away from it. Similarly, in vertical direction, we can also divide the direction of currents into two cases. Therefore, there are four types of vortices in our system, which are detected by checking the real parts and imaginary parts of the eigenvalues of the Jacobian matrix calculated from the vector field of the currents in a vortex region as shown in Figure 1(a), Figure 1(b), Figure 1(c) and Figure 1(d). The details of the calculation will be introduced in the next part.

Only the types of vortices in the cases of Figure 1(a) and (b) are extracted because the currents go toward to the center of vortices so that it can gather nutrients and attract fish.

Detection of Vortices   To detect vortices form a vector field, firstly the position of a vortex (x', y', z') is calculated by the Newton-Raphson method by solving the equation:

$$(u', v', w') = 0 \tag{1}$$

where u', v' and w' are the current velocities in the direction of x, y and z at the point of (x', y', z'). The calculated position is defined as a critical point, which can be a source, a sink, a saddle, or a vortex center. To confirm that the critical point is categorized into a vortex center, the Jacobian matrix J is calculated as follows:

$$J = \begin{pmatrix} \dfrac{\partial u}{\partial x} & \dfrac{\partial u}{\partial y} & \dfrac{\partial u}{\partial z} \\ \dfrac{\partial v}{\partial x} & \dfrac{\partial v}{\partial y} & \dfrac{\partial v}{\partial z} \\ \dfrac{\partial w}{\partial x} & \dfrac{\partial w}{\partial y} & \dfrac{\partial w}{\partial z} \end{pmatrix} \tag{2}$$

where u, v and w are the current velocities in the directions of x, y and z respectively.

Then the eigenvalue λ of the matrix J is calculated with the equation as follows:

$$\det(J - \lambda I) = 0 \tag{3}$$

where I is the 3×3 identity matrix. The Newton-Raphson method is used for solving this equation and calculating the eigenvalue. After the eigenvalue being figured out, the eigenvector x can be calculated by the equation as follows:

$$(J - \lambda I)x = 0 \tag{4}$$

If there are two conjugate complex eigenvalues, we can get a vortex in the cell. Vieta's formulas is utilized to check it:

$$D_3(T) = Q^2 P^2 - 4RP^3 - 4Q^3 + 18P \text{ OR} - 27R^2 \tag{5}$$

(a) $\mathrm{Re}(\lambda_1) > 0$, $\mathrm{Im}(\lambda_1) = 0$, $\mathrm{Re}(\lambda_2) < 0$, (b) $\mathrm{Re}(\lambda_1) < 0$, $\mathrm{Im}(\lambda_1) = 0$, $\mathrm{Re}(\lambda_2) < 0$, $\mathrm{Im}(\lambda_2) = 0$,
$\mathrm{Im}(\lambda_2) = 0$, $\mathrm{Re}(\lambda_3) < 0$, $\mathrm{Im}(\lambda_3) = 0$ $\mathrm{Re}(\lambda_3) < 0$, $\mathrm{Im}(\lambda_3) = 0$

(c) $\mathrm{Re}(\lambda_1) > 0$, $\mathrm{Im}(\lambda_1) = 0$, $\mathrm{Re}(\lambda_2) > 0$, $\mathrm{Im}(\lambda_2) = 0$, (d) $\mathrm{Re}(\lambda_1) < 0$, $\mathrm{Im}(\lambda_1) = 0$, $\mathrm{Re}(\lambda_2) > 0$, $\mathrm{Im}(\lambda_2) = 0$,
$\mathrm{Re}(\lambda_3) > 0$, $\mathrm{Im}(\lambda_3) = 0$ $\mathrm{Re}(\lambda_3) > 0$, $\mathrm{Im}(\lambda_3) = 0$

Fig. 1. Types of Vortices

where P , Q and R are defined as

$$
\begin{aligned}
P &= \alpha_0 + \alpha_1 + \alpha_2 \\
Q &= \alpha_1\,\alpha_2 + \alpha_2\,\alpha_0 + \alpha_0\,\alpha_1 \\
R &= \alpha_0\,\alpha_1\,\alpha_2
\end{aligned}
\tag{6}
$$

Here α_0 , α_1 and α_2 can be calculated by

$$
\begin{aligned}
\alpha_0 &= -\det(J) \\
\alpha_1 &= \det(A) + \det(B) + \det(C) \\
\alpha_2 &= -\mathrm{tr}(J)
\end{aligned}
\tag{7}
$$

And the matrix A, B and C are calculated by

$$
A = \begin{pmatrix} \dfrac{\partial u}{\partial x} & \dfrac{\partial u}{\partial y} \\ \dfrac{\partial v}{\partial x} & \dfrac{\partial v}{\partial y} \end{pmatrix}
\tag{8}
$$

$$B = \begin{pmatrix} \dfrac{\partial v}{\partial y} & \dfrac{\partial v}{\partial z} \\ \dfrac{\partial w}{\partial y} & \dfrac{\partial w}{\partial z} \end{pmatrix} \qquad (9)$$

$$C = \begin{pmatrix} \dfrac{\partial u}{\partial x} & \dfrac{\partial u}{\partial z} \\ \dfrac{\partial w}{\partial x} & \dfrac{\partial w}{\partial z} \end{pmatrix} \qquad (10)$$

If $D_3 (T) < 0$, there will be two conjugate complex eigenvalues, indicating that the critical point can be categorized into a vortex center.

Visualization of Vortices Streamlines are used for visualizing sea currents in our system, especially the sea currents around vortices. By streamlines plot, we view and analyze the shape and the range of vortices.

It is necessary to set a suitable starting point before drawing a streamline. Since we have calculated the eigenvalues and eigenvectors of vortices, an option is to set starting points near vortices. First we figure out two vectors as follows:

$$\begin{cases} m = \eta \times e_z \\ n = m \times \eta \end{cases} \qquad (11)$$

where η is the eigenvector and $e_z = (0, 0, 1)$. Because the range of each cell is set to $1 \times 1 \times 1$, the two vectors m and n are normalized and we get two new vectors m_0 and n_0. Finally we set four starting points around a vortex with their positions being calculated by

$$\begin{cases} s_0 = m_0 \cdot \beta \\ s_1 = -m_0 \cdot \beta \\ s_2 = n_0 \cdot \beta \\ s_3 = -n_0 \cdot \beta \end{cases} \qquad (12)$$

where β is the scale coefficient, which is set to 0.1 in our system to make the starting points close to their vortex centers. Beginning with the starting points, new points will be figured out based on the vector field of currents velocity at the previous points and streamlines through these points will be plotted.

Scale of Vortices In our system, the scale of a vortex is mainly determined by the range. The cross method[4] is used for detecting the range of a vortex, which is illustrated as Figure 2. The center of a vortex is set as the origin and the Cartesian coordinates is set as shown. If the direction of currents points toward to the center of the vortex, the streamlines will go through the four quadrants in the order of Quadrants III, IV, I and II. Suppose there are two neighbouring intersection points A and B, which are the crossing points of the streamline and the x axis. And the distance between the two points | AB | can be figured out. Then we compare this distance with a specified threshold value d. If | AB |> d, we consider that the vortex ends at A and the distance between the origin O and the point A is the radius of the vortex. By specifying the threshold value of the radius, our system can pick up the vortices above a certain scale.

3.3   Distribution of Temperatures

Volume rendering is used to visualize three dimensional data without imposing any geometric structure on it. It is applied to our system to show the distribution of temperatures. Because the temperature data is converted from the volume data with uniform grids, it is appropriate to use volume rendering to render the input data.

By adjusting the transfer function, it is possible to view the internal struc-ture of the 3D object rendered by volume rendering. Besides, another method named ortho-slice is also utilized in our system to visualize the distribution of temperatures at a certain depth. In our system, the proportion of depth can be specified by users. A proportionality factor $k \in [0, 1]$ is used for representing the proportion of the height from the bottom of the sample ocean data. Assume that D is the total depth of the ocean and d is the depth from the ocean surface, the equation used to calculate the depth d will be

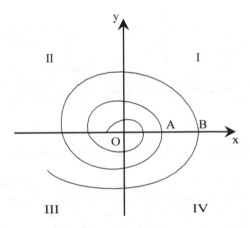

Fig. 2. Scale of a Vortex

$$d = (1 - k)D \tag{13}$$

To show the distribution of temperatures and the streamlines simultaneously in one window, we utilize the ortho-slice and streamlines together to visualize the two types of data in two dimensional case or the volume rendering and streamlines in three dimensional case. The transfer function of volume is able to be adjusted intuitively through the transfer function editor and be applied to the present rendering result in real time.By modifying the transfer function, we can change the colors and the opacity values which are used for indicating a certain range of values. For instance, if we specify a very low opacity value to relatively low temperatures and high opacity values to high temperatures, the corresponding parts of low temperatures will become nearly transparent in the volume rendering image and only the parts of high temperatures are left. Besides, since the temperature of the shallow part of the sea is usually higher than that of the deep sea, we can rotate the volume dataset in order to see the internal structure if the opacity of the deep part is very low.

4   Experimental Results and Discussion

We select the ocean data near Aomori in Japan as the sample data, for the sea area near Aomori abounds with neon flying squids. The overview of the input data is visualized as clustered parallel coordinates, which is shown in Figure 3. The data points can also be plotted as polylines to provide more details, which costs much more rendering time especially there are a lot of data points in the input data. Because data points are plotted as polylines in parallel coordinates or polygons in clustered parallel coordinates, users are able to view the relationships between dimensions. The preliminary understanding of the data will help them plan their work about the further processing of the data at the next stage. In the figure, the range representing for lower temperatures are selected and two clusters satisfying the condition are picked up. It is possible to view the corresponding range such as latitude, longitude, depth and current velocity of each cluster on other axes conveniently.

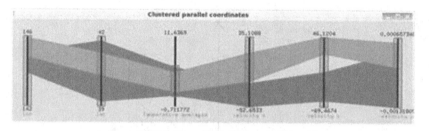

Fig. 3. Overview by Clustered Parallel Coordinates

The vortices with radii over 50 kilometers have been extracted and the result is illustrated as Figure 4. In this figure, vortices are plotted as streamlines and the small arrows show the direction of the sea currents. The background is the ortho-slice used for visualizing the distribution of temperatures. As mentioned in the previous section, the proportionality factor k is customizable to set the proportion of depth. A smaller value of k makes the slice close to the sea surface, while a larger value of k makes the slice close to the bottom of the sea. We set the value to 0.99 here to show the temperatures distribution near the sea surface. In ortho-slice, the rainbow color map is utilized, meaning that the sea areas with higher temperatures are colored in red while the sea areas with lower temperatures are colored in blue. Therefore, the areas in yellow or green are considered as the areas where warm currents meet cold currents. According to the figure, there are many vortices located at the confluence of warm currents and cold currents. If the temperature changes dramatically, there will be more likely a vortex. The temperature in the range of a vortex can be higher or lower than the area around the vortex.

Figure 5. illustrates the distribution of temperatures by volume rendering. The color map of volume rendering is the same as that of ortho-slice in Figure 4. The transfer function has been adjusted to set lower opacity values to the areas with lower temperatures and higher opacity values to the areas with higher temperatures so that only the areas with higher temperatures are emphasized and the internal structure of rendered volume object can be viewed. From the figure we can see that the cold currents from the northern part of the sea and the warm currents from the southern part of the sea meet in the sea area near Aomori in Japan. The seawater with higher temperatures in the warm currents can reach to the depth of hundreds of meters and as the depth increasing, the temperature will become lower and lower.

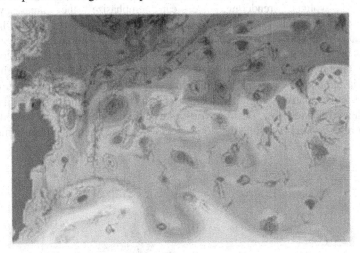

Fig. 4. Extraction of Vortices

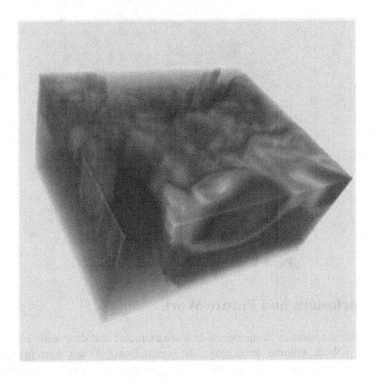

Fig. 5. Temperatures Distribution by Volume Rendering

The volume rendering and streamlines can also be shown together in one window as Figure 6. Different with the rendering result in Figure 4, both of the volume rendering view and streamlines are three dimensional. By adjusting the transfer function   of   volume   rendering,   we   can   emphasize   the   areas   with the temperatures in a certain range and explore the vortices there. The figure illustrates that the shapes of vortices in three dimensions are more complex. Therefore, other algorithms need to be utilized to calculate the scale of vortices in three dimensional case. Since the rainbow color map applied to streamlines shows the part of high current velocities in red and low current velocities in blue, we can find that the warm currents from south have relatively higher velocities and the current velocities of cold currents from north are relatively low. Besides, vortices usually have higher flow velocities than the sea currents around them and the flow velocities change dramatically in vortices.

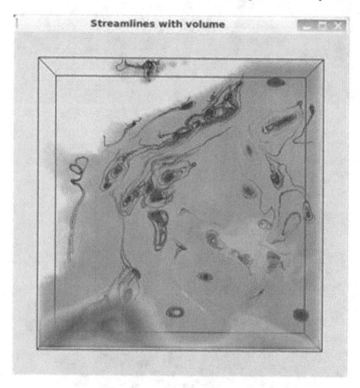

Fig. 6. Volume Rendering with Streamlines

5   Conclusions and Future Work

In our system, the vortices in the ocean data are extracted and their scale is able to be figured out. With volume rendering, the streamlines of sea currents and the distribution of temperatures can be displayed together in a window so that users can analyze the temperatures and vortices conveniently. For the parallel coordinates plot, it is necessary to get a balance between information details and rendering speed. Generally, clustered parallel coordinates can be used if the scale of the input data is large, which requires faster clustering algorithms and smarter methods to determine the number of clusters. The integration of ortho-slice and streamlines has done well in providing a combined view about temperatures distribution and vortices. In three dimensional case, since the shapes of vortices are more complex, other algorithms need to be used for calculating the scale of vortices. Upwelling is an oceanographic phenomenon that involves wind-driven motion of dense, cooler, and usually nutrient-rich water towards the ocean surface, replacing the warmer, usually nutrient-depleted surface water. Based on the analysis of the vectors' direction of sea currents in three dimensions, we are trying to find a way to detect upwelling currents. The movements and changes of vortices are also very important and the program used for tracing the vortices in time varying data is planning to be developed in the near future.

Acknowledgements. This research was partially supported by the Ministry of Education, Culture, Sports, Science and Technology (MEXT), Grant-in-Aid for Research Program on Climate Change Adaptation (RECCA), and by Japan and France JST-ANR joint Grand-in-Aid for PetaFlow project.

References

1. Post, F.H., Vrolijk, B., Hauser, H., Laramee, R.S., Doleisch, H.: The State of the Art in Flow Visualisation: Feature Extraction and Tracking. Computer Graphics, 775–792 (2003)
2. Sadarjoen, I.A., Post, F.H., Ma, B., Banks, D.C., Pagendarm, H.-G.: Selective Visualization of Vortices in Hydrodynamic Flows. In: Visualization 1998, pp. 419–422 (1998)
3. Suzuki, T.: Studies on the relationship between current boundary zones in waters to the southeast of Hokkaido and migration of the squid, Ommastrephes sloani pacificus (steenstrup). Memories of the Faculty of Fisheries Hokkaido University, 75–153 (1963)
4. Guo, D., Evangelinos, C., Patrikalakis, N.M.: Flow Feature Extraction in Oceanographic Visualization. In: Proceedings of Computer Graphics International, pp. 162–173 (2004)
5. Hartigan, J.A., Wong, M.A.: A K -Means Clustering Algorithm. Journal of the Royal Statistical Society Series C (Applied Statistics), 100–108 (1979)
6. Hamerly, G.: Making k-means Even Faster. In: SIAM International Conference on Data Mining, pp. 130–140 (2010)

Modeling and Simulation of Partial Shaded PV Modules

Zhou Diqing, Chunhua Wu, and Zhihua Li

Shanghai Key Laboratory of Power Station Automation Technology,
Department of Automation, Shanghai University, Shanghai 200072, China
{Dq1@live.cn,154809693}@qq.com, lzh_sh@staff.shu.edu.cn

Abstract. Partial shading instances are very common in photovoltaic (PV) systems. The mismatch losses and hot spot effects caused by partial shading can not only affect the output power of solar system, but also can bring security and reliability problems. A mathematical model reflecting the output electrical characteristics of the partial shading PV module is put forward in this paper. Compared with the traditional model, it is able to show the variation of the output electrical characteristics of the PV module by adjusting the irradiance, temperature and the area of partial shading. The model is used to analyze the power losses of the partial shaded PV model with different number of bypass diodes. The simulation results show that a PV model under partial shading with 6 bypass diodes is the best configuration to minimize the mismatch power loss. It has an important meaning for practical engineering application.

Keywords: PV module, Partial shading, Bypass diode, Output electrical characteristics.

1 Introductions

Photovoltaic (PV) module is the central part to convert solar energy to electrical energy in PV power system. Up to now, the conversion efficiency is still low because of the complex characteristics of the device. The output of PV module is nonlinearity and affected by many external environment parameters such as irradiance, temperature, load, and parasitic resistance. Nonuniform irradiance caused by clouds, leaves, buildings, poles, even bird droppings will lead to partial shading of PV module. The PV cells in PV modules are connected in series. If one PV cell is shaded, the currents of the non-shaded cells will be higher than the current of the shaded cell. Based on Kirchhoff's voltage law, the shaded cell will be reverse biased by the other cells in the series connection. In this case, the reverse biased cell acts as a load, which will cause power losses and reduce the power production of the PV module. It is very important to study the output electrical characteristic of partial shaded PV cell.

Due to the complexity of the output electrical characteristic of partial shaded PV module, there is not a precise mathematical model for PV cell in such condition. Literature [2-6] set up a PV module or array simulation model under Matlab/Simulink environment, but did not analysis the partial shading problems in-depth. In this paper, we set up an improved PV module simulation model in Matlab/Simulink. Compared

T. Xiao, L. Zhang, and S. Ma (Eds.): ICSC 2012, Part II, CCIS 327, pp. 124–134, 2012.
© Springer-Verlag Berlin Heidelberg 2012

with the traditional model, it is able to show the variation of the output electrical characteristics of the PV module by adjusting the irradiance, temperature and the area of partial shading. In order to prevent PV cells from being damaged caused by mismatch losses and hot spots, manufacturers of PV modules have connected bypass diodes in antiparallel with PV cells. This paper analyzes the power losses of the partial shaded PV model with different number of bypass diodes, and puts forward a PV Module configuration.

2   Mathematical Simulation Model of Partial Shaded PV Cell

2.1   Equivalent Model of PV Cell

PV cells convert solar energy to electrical energy by the photovoltaic effect of the P-N junction. The equivalent circuit shows in fig.1, where I_{ph} is the photoemissive current, I_d is the reverse saturation current of the diode, R_s is the equivalent series resistance, and R_{sh} is the equivalent parallel resistance. The current equivalent equation of a PV cell is given as follow.

$$I = I_{ph} - I_0 \left[\exp\left(\frac{V + IR_s}{nV_{th}} \right) - 1 \right] - \frac{V + IR_s}{R_{sh}} \tag{1}$$

$$I_0 = I_{or} \left[\frac{T}{T_r} \right]^3 \exp\left[\frac{qE_G}{Bk} \left(\frac{1}{T_r} - \frac{1}{T} \right) \right] \tag{2}$$

$$I_{ph} = [I_{SCR} + K_I(T - 25)]\lambda/100 \tag{3}$$

Where I is the PV cell output current, U is the PV cell output voltage, I_{ph} and I_0 is the photoemissive and dark saturation currents respectively, n is the diode ideality factor, T (in Kelvin) is the temperature, k is the Boltzmann constant ($1.3806503 \times 10^{-23} J/k$), q is the electron charge ($1.60217646 \times 10^{-19} J/k$), $K_I = 0.0017 A/^\circ C$ is the short circuit current temperature coefficient, λ is the sunlight intensity, I_{SCK} is the short circuit current under 25°C and 1000 W/m², E_G is the Silicon forbidden band width, B is the ideal parameter, which is between 1 and 2, $T_r = 301.18K$ is the referenced temperature, I_{or} is the PV cell saturation current under the reference temperature T_r.

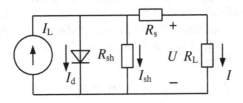

Fig. 1. The PV cell equivalent circuit

2.2   Simulation Model of Partial Shaded PV Cell

Traditional PV cell model is based on equation (1), but it is not suitable for simulating PV cells under partial shading. An improved mathematical model should be established.

2.2.1   Types of Shading

Building integrated photovoltaic system is easy to be covered by surrounding buildings, trees, street lamp, utility poles, clouds, fowls, and leaves. Because of the refraction of sunlight, partial shading will reduce the intensity of irradiance on PV module..

PV cells can be divided into three categories, as shown in Fig.2, The first category is PV cells under uniform irradiance; The second category is PV cells in completely shading; The third category is PV cells in partial shading.

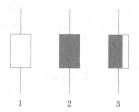

Fig. 2. Classification of PV cells

The area of the partial shading caused by surrounding objects is much larger than the area of the commonly used monocrystalline silicon PV cell. The probability of three kinds of sun irradiances appears on one PV cell at the same time is negligible. Supposing there are two kinds of sun irradiances on one PV cell at most, we begin to model partial shading PV cell.

2.2.2   Modeling of Partial Shaded PV Cell

If the irradiance and temperature are stable, the area and the light-generated and the dark saturation currents can be expressed as following:

$$I_{ph} = AJ_{ph} \; ; \; I_0 = AJ_0 \qquad (4)$$

Where the current density J_{ph}, J_0 can be calculated by the irradiance, temperature and the internal parameters of the PV model.

The cell can be separated into different parts according to the irradiance. If the area of the partial shading is A_1, the irradiance is G_1, the light-generated and the dark saturation currents can be expressed as:

$$I_{ph1} = A_1 J_{ph1} \; ; \; I_{01} = A_1 J_{01} \qquad (5)$$

If the area under uniform lighting is A_2, the irradiance is G_2, the light-generated and the dark saturation currents can be expressed as :

$$I_{ph2} = A_2 J_{ph2} \; ; \; I_{02} = A_2 J_{02} \tag{6}$$

According to the literature [7], the total light-generated current and the dark saturation current can be expressed as:

$$I_{ph} = A_1 J_{ph1} + A_2 J_{ph2}, \quad I_0 = A_1 J_{01} + A_2 J_{01} \tag{7}$$

The change of the internal resistance caused by partial shading is negligible. The current equation of partial shaded PV cell is given as following.

$$
\begin{aligned}
I = {} & A_1 J_{ph1} - A_1 J_{01} \left[\exp\left(\frac{V + IR_s}{n V_{th}} \right) - 1 \right] \\
& + A_2 J_{ph2} - A_2 J_{02} \left[\exp\left(\frac{V + IR_s}{n V_{th}} \right) - 1 \right] - \frac{V + IR_s}{R_{sh}}
\end{aligned}
\tag{8}
$$

Where the A_1 is the partial shading area, J_{ph1} is the corresponding light-generated current, J_{01} is the corresponding dark saturation current. A_2 is the area under uniform lighting conditions, J_{ph2} is the corresponding light-generated current, J_{02} is the corresponding dark saturation current.

Simulating model of partial shaded PV cell is set up based on equation (8) in Matlab/Simulink.

3   Simulation of Partial Shaded PV Module

PV cells are usually connected in series to form PV modules. The most widely used PV module consists of 72 PV cells. The traditional mathematical model is combined with the improved mathematical model to simulate PV module with partial shading.

Suppose the number of the cells in series connection is M, the current of the series circuits is I. The total voltage the sum of all cells voltage, $V = \sum_{i=1}^{M} V_i$, the relation between the parameters of the series cells and a single cell can be expressed as following [8]:

$$
\begin{cases}
I_{PH} = I_{ph} \\
I_O = I_o \\
R_S = M R_s \\
R_{SH} = M R_{sh} \\
n_s = M n
\end{cases}
\tag{9}
$$

Where I_{PH} is the series cells total photoemissive current, I_O is the total reverse saturation current of the diode, R_S is the total series resistance, and R_{SH} is the total parallel resistance.

Therefore, the proposed method is that: the cells belong to the same bypass diode and under the uniform lighting conditions can be integrated into one module, and simulated based on the traditional PV cell model current equivalent equation (1), the others that under partial shading conditions are simulated based on the improved mathematical model equation (8). This simulation can worked on most of the partial shading conditions.

4   Simulation of PV Module with Different Structures

In order to prevent PV cells from damaging due to the power losses and hot spots, PV manufacturers have connected bypass diodes in antiparallel with PV cells. When reverse biased cell appears, the corresponding bypass diode conducts to bypass the reverse biased cell. Power losses can be decreased by increasing the number of bypass diodes. The cost of PV module will rise at the same time. It is important to find out the appropriate number of bypass diodes in a 72 cells connected PV module.

Suppose the number of the bypass diodes is x. Power loss of partial shaded PV model is analyzed separately when $x=0$, $x=3$ and $x=4$.

Fig.3 shows partial shading pattern of PV module, where shaded parts of the cells are shown with gray color. Shading of the cells has been supposed one by one, and one string protected by one diode is completely shaded before shading another string. The amount of shaded cells varies from 0 to 72 (0 to 100%).

The main variables are the relative portion of shaded PV cells in the PV module (system shading) and the attenuation of irradiance due to the shading (shading strength). Shading strength is the percent of the amount of lost irradiance to the total irradiance. We consider typical shading with a shading strength of around 85%.

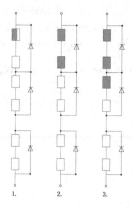

Fig. 3. Partial shading pattern of PV module

4.1 Simulation Results of Normal Uniform Radiation

Fig.4 shows the output P-V curves under three different sunlight radiations.

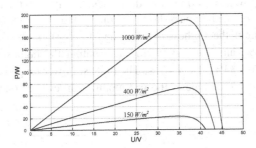

Fig. 4. The output P-V curves under three different operating conditions

4.2 Relation between the Global MPP and System Shading

Fig.5 shows the output P-V curve under partial shading. It has multiple peaks because of the bypass diode, where P_{GMPP} is the global MPP and P_{LMPP} is the local MPP. The purpose of the MPPT is to make the PV module operating at the point of P_{GMPP} and output its maximum power.

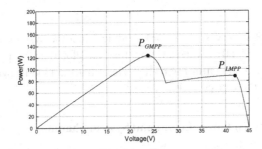

Fig. 5. Output P-V curve of PV module under partial shading

The power of the global MPP has been shown as a function of system shading.

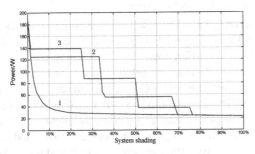

Fig. 6. Global MPP power and system shading when the shading strengths is 85%

Fig.6 shows the relative curves of the global MPP power and the system shading when the shading strength is 85%.The curves 1, 2, 3 represent such configurations as the bypass diodes number $x=0$, $x=3$, $x=4$.

The global MPP power of $x=0$ module decreases rapidly with the increasing system shading. But the module with bypass diode can output the power more effectively. The $x=4$ module can output the highest power when the system shading is 2%-25%、 33%-50%、 67%-75%, and the $x=3$ module can output the highest power when the system shading is 25%-33%、 50%-67%. The highest power range of the $x=4$ module curve is 23% more than the range of the $x=3$ module curve. The concrete P-V curve is shown in the Fig.7.

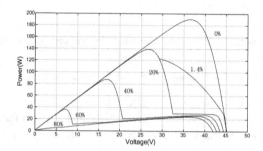

Fig. 7. P-V curves of the x=4 module with increasing system shading under 85% shading strength

Fig.7 shows the P-V curves of the $x=4$ module when the system shading is 1.4%, 20%, 40%, 60%, and 80%, we can find that its global MPP power values are correspond to curve 3 shown in Fig.6. It is clear that the module with more bypass diodes output power more effectively.

4.3   Relation between Power Losses and System Shading

According to the actual situation, the global MPP is not suitable for the PV system sometimes. For example, as shown in Fig. 7, when the system shading is larger than 60%, the voltage of global MPP is too low for the DC/DC converter to trace. We have to make the PV module operate at its local MPP. Operating at the local MPP will cause power loss compared with the global MPP.

The power difference of local MPPs for the studied PV modules at shading strength of 85% is shown in Fig.8. The relative power difference is calculated by using the absolute value of the power difference.

In the fig.8, the curves 1 shows the relative power differences of local MPPs as a function of system shading for $x=3$ module, the curves 2 shows the relative power differences of local MPPs as a function of system shading for $x=4$ module. The power losses of the $x=4$ module is less than $x=3$ module as shown in fig.8. When the system shading is 25%-33% and 50%-67%, the output power of $x=3$ module is larger than $x=4$ module, but the relative power differences for the $x=4$ module is less.

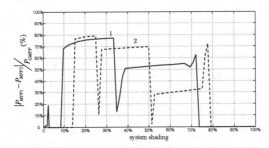

Fig. 8. Relation power differences of local MPPs as a function of system shading for different modules and shading strength of 85%

So the x=4 module performances better on the power production point of view in case of partial shading conditions than the x=3 module.

The simulation results demonstrate that the PV model with more bypass diodes output the power more effectively and reduce the mismatch losses under partial shading.

5   The Effects of Bypass Diodes on PV Module Output Power

It has been proved that losses produced by shadows are dependent on the bypass diodes configuration of the PV modules. This paper analyzes the power losses of the partial shaded PV model with different number of bypass diodes in two aspects.

5.1   Global MPP Power

Based on the relative curves of the global MPP power and the system shading, this paper compares the global MPP power and area of the different x module from the view of mathematics.

Suppose there are two PV module: x model, and x-1 module($x\geq3$),   the higher power range of x module is A_x, the higher power range of x-1 module is A_{x-1}, the difference of the power range $A=A_x-A_{x-1}$.

The x, x-1 modules' highest power appears staggered emergence. To facilitate the analysis, the big-slope part of power curve can be approximated to be vertical curve ignoring the effect of slash. The range A can be expressed by

$$A = \sum_{n}^{x-2}[(\frac{n}{x}-\frac{n-1}{x-1})-(\frac{n}{x-1}-\frac{n}{x})]+\frac{x-1}{x}-\frac{x-2}{x-1}=\frac{1}{x}\times100\% \tag{10}$$

Fig.9 shows that the power range difference curve decreases gradually and weakens with the increasing of the diode numbers x. When the value of x is more than 6, the decrement of A is less than 3%. When x=9, the higher power range difference A is 11.1%. Compared to the x=8 module, the decrement of A is less than 1.5%. Taking into account the cost and manufacturing process, as x increased to 6, continue to increase x is meaningless.

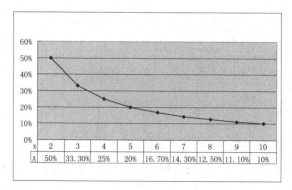

Fig. 9. The range A for different x module

5.2   The Average Maximum Power

Due to changes in the global MPP power, this paper studies the variation of average maximum power.

Suppose the number of the cells is N, the diode number is x, the power of cell under uniform lighting conditions is p, the shading strength is 100%. To facilitate the analysis, the big-slope part of power curve can be approximated to vertical curve and ignore the effect of the slash. The average maximum power P can be calculate by the equation (11)

$$P = \frac{p}{X}\left[\sum_{n}^{x-1}\frac{N}{X}\times(X-n)\right] = \frac{Np(X-1)}{2X} \tag{11}$$

When N is 72, p=2.64W, the average maximum power with the change in value of x as shown in fig.10, The module consists of 72 single cells does not exist the case that x=5 and x=7.

The average maximum power P can be calculate by the equation (11), the average maximum power as shown in fig.10. When x=6, compared to the x=4 module, the increment of the average maximum power is 11%. The average maximum power of

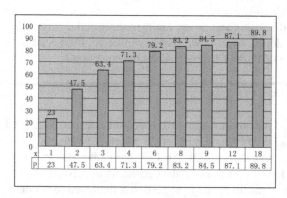

Fig. 10. The average maximum power or different x module

x=8 module increase only 5% compared with the x=6 module and only 1.5% compared with the x=9 module.

In summary, when the diode number x increased to 6, it is meaningless to increase the diode numbers. The increment of the x=6 module average maximum power is 11% compared to the x=4 module, and 25% to the x=3 module. So the PV model with 6 bypass diodes is the best generator configuration to minimize the mismatch power losses under partial shading conditions.

6   Conclusions

The physical model of PV cell was analyzed and an improved mathematical model reflecting the output characteristics of partial shaded PV module was put forward. Compared with the traditional model, it is able to show the variation of the output electrical characteristics of the PV module by adjusting the irradiance, temperature and the area of partial shading. A study on the behaviors of PV modules with different number of bypass diode has been carried out. It has been proved that power losses produced by shadows are dependent on the bypass diodes configuration. The simulation results show that a PV model under partial shading with 6 bypass diodes is the best configuration to minimize the mismatch power losses. It has an important meaning for practical engineering application.

Acknowledgment. This Project was supported by the National Natural Science Foundation of China (No.51107079) and "11th Five-Year Plan" 211 Construction Project of Shanghai University.

References

1. Duhui, Lin, Y., Zhang, S.: The Analysis of Output Features and the Simulation Research of Solar Energy Photovoltaic Cell. Press of University of Science and Technology of China, Taiyuan Shanxi (2008)
2. Xue, Y., Hang, J.-D.: Simulation Modeling and Analysis of Photovoltaic Array under Partial Shading. East China Electric Power 36(6), 949–952 (2011)
3. Li, D., Chen, R., Cui, Y.: A research of hot spot on PV module with Pspic. Journal of Harbin Institute of Technology 38(11), 1888–1897 (2006)
4. Liu, B.-Y., Duan, S.-X., Kang, Y.: Modeling and analysis of characteristics of PV module with partial shading. Acta Energiae Solaris Sinica 29(2), 188–192 (2008)
5. Patel, H., Agarwal, V.: Matlab-based modeling to study the effects of partial shading on PV array characteristics. IEEE Transactions on Energy Conversion 23(1), 302–310 (2008)
6. Zhou, D.-J., Zhao, Z.-M., Wu, L.-B., et al.: Simulation model based on features of solar photovoltaic cell array. Tsinghua Science and Technology 47(7), 1109–1112 (2007)
7. Castañer, L., Silvestre, S.: Modelling PhotoVoltaic Systems using PSpice, March 8, pp. 23–53. Universidad Politecnica de Caraluña, Barcelona (2006)
8. Di, Z.: The output electrical characteristic Predicting of PV Array in Arbitrary Condition. The University of Science and Technology of China, Hefei (2008)

9. Maki, A., Valkealahti, S.: Power Losses in Long String and Parallel-Connected Short Strings of Series-Connected Silicon-Based Photovoltaic Modules Due to Partial Shading Conditions. IEEE Transactions on Energy Conversion 27(1), 173–183 (2012)
10. Chen, R.: A Research on PV Hot Spot and MPPT under Non-uniform Insolation. Shantou University (2007)
11. Silvestre, S., Boronat, A., Chouder, A.: Study of bypass diodes configuration on PV modules. Applied Energy 86(9), 1632–1640 (2009)

Research on Run-Time Atmosphere Environment Database Based on Berkeley DB

Jinzhan Zhang, Guanghong Gong, Jiangyun Wang, and Dongdong Gao

Aviation Key Laboratory for Advanced Simulation Technology,
School of Automation Science and Electrical Engineering,
Beihang University, 100191 Beijing, P.R. China
spiderman0502@126.com

Abstract. Synthetic Natural Environment is an important support for modern simulation systems. Atmosphere data is one special kind of SNE. To fulfill the performance requirements of atmosphere environment data storage and access during simulation, we need to build an efficient run-time atmosphere database. This paper mainly analyses the characteristics of atmosphere data and run-time atmosphere database, then introduces a famous embedded database Berkeley DB and analyses the feasibility of building run-time atmosphere database based on it.

Keywords: Run-time Atmosphere Database, Berkeley DB, SNE.

1 Introduction

Synthetic Natural Environment (SNE) is an important support for many modern simulation systems. For example, in distributed battle simulation, SNE provide the whole natural environment (including atmosphere, terrain, oceans, space, etc.) that needed for a real world environment simulation for the other components in the system. Modern high-tech weapon experiment also needs typical environment for the evaluation of the weapon model.

An SNE service system usually contains two major parts: the development part and the simulation run-time part. In the development part, we collect raw environment data from historical data, observational data and forecast data, then transform and store them in the standard environment database. Also we can use data of other standard such as SEDRIS as our data source. Beside the standard database, the development part also contains an environment simulation scenario generator to generate specific simulation-requirement-oriented data for the run-time part of the SNE service system. In the simulation run-time part, we can build a run-time environment database to store specific data generated from the scenario generator, fuse the data with dynamical environment data models, and then provide it for the specific simulation systems.

So run-time environment database is on the top of the SNE service system and provide data service for the simulation system directly. This requires run-time environment database high access performance.

T. Xiao, L. Zhang, and S. Ma (Eds.): ICSC 2012, Part II, CCIS 327, pp. 135–143, 2012.

In this paper, we mainly focus on the research of run-time atmosphere environment database based on one famous embedded database Berkeley DB. Because of the huge time and space span of battle simulation and the feature of atmosphere data, the run-time atmosphere database can usually be huge. We will study on the features and performance optimization of Berkeley DB and discuss how to build an efficient run-time database to manage atmosphere data to reach the requirement of a specific simulation system.

2   Analysis of Run-Time Atmosphere Environment Database

2.1   Main Characteristics of Atmosphere Data

Time and Space Relative. Atmosphere data changes with time and space.

$$Atmos\_3D\_Data = F(long, lati, alti, time)$$

$$Atmos\_2D\_Data = F(long, lati, time)$$

For example, temperature reduces with height rising and wind speed changes at different space point and different time point. This characteristic usually makes volume of atmosphere data very large, which can vary from hundreds of MBs to several TBs[1].

Grid-Based and Non-relational.   The data of run-time atmosphere database is derived from the standard environment database. Atmosphere data is usually presented on grids. It can be rectangular grid, orthogonal curvilinear grid or others. For example, high altitude atmosphere data is usually presented on rectangular grid, while low sea atmosphere data can be presented on specially designed grid such as UPS to implement high resolution ratio.

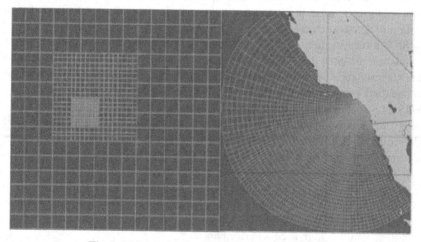

Fig. 1. Different kinds of grids for Atmosphere data

No matter what kind of grid it is, atmosphere data is a non-relational data model and can be indexed by longitude, latitude, altitude and time. So it is better to use a No-relational database such as Berkeley DB to establish a run-time atmosphere environment database. Because by eliminating the complexity of relational model, the database can be more efficient and flexible.

Read-Only. Read-only is an important characteristic of run-time atmosphere database. First, because run-time database is designed by the specific simulation requirements, once it is established before the simulation, it usually won't change. Second, unlike other data like terrain data which can be affected by the entities in simulation system, atmosphere data only changes by time and space as defined when the run-time database is established.

2.2 Data Organization Structure

Run-time atmosphere database is simulation-system-oriented, so we should design the database structure as the specific simulation system requires. Usually, we divide the whole data set by time, data types and resolution ratios to independent tables. As presented above, atmosphere data is indexed by space and time, so we use longitude, latitude, altitude and time as key, and the attributes of certain data types as fields. Since Berkeley DB is a key/value database, we serialize the key and fields separately to key/data pairs. We should design tables as small as possible so that we can separate the data queries into different tables at the table router to search data in smaller tables to save time.

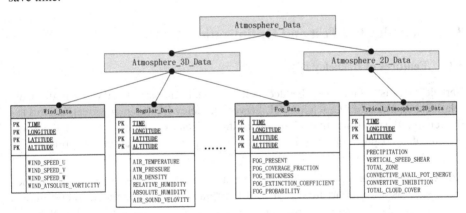

Fig. 2. Data organization of atmosphere environment runtime database

2.3 Performance Discussion

Storing a huge volume of atmosphere data, it is a challenge for the run-time atmosphere database to have a good performance of concurrency accesses. We can use a memory cache or in memory database to achieve a high access speed.

Memory Cache. The memory pool subsystem of Berkeley DB can let us put the data into a memory cache so that all database operation can be done in the main memory which is much faster than the disk. Though Berkeley DB is not a pure main memory database, it can provide a main-memory-database-like performance through this memory pool mechanism.

Notice that the atmosphere data is often too large for the main memory size. And when it is stored in the database, we have to take extra space to manage database related information such as region and mutex information. What's more, when using access method such as B-tree, there will be unused space in the tree nodes because of the data structure's intrinsic feature. So the database file size will be larger than the data itself. When build a run-time atmosphere database, we need to consider how to make the database file's size as small as possible to make sure most database operation can be done in the memory.

Concurrency Access. In distributed simulation system like battle simulation system, run-time atmosphere database will need to handle multiple entities accessing it concurrently. For example, in an HLA/RTI based battle simulation, there can be dozens of federate members and hundreds of instances. These instances all need require environment data constantly. Run-time atmosphere database must have a high data throughput capacity to meet the simulation system's real time requirement. Though the run-time atmosphere database is read only, which makes the concurrency access much easier, it is still a challenge because of the high simultaneous access volume. Heavy traditional database like Oracle can't meet the requirement because of its essential low performance, so we turned to Berkeley DB – a high-performance embedded database.

3   Berkeley DB Test and Optimization

3.1   Features of Berkeley DB

Berkeley DB is a famous embedded non-relational database. Unlike the traditional relational database like Oracle or SQL Server, Berkeley DB has many great features to fit scenario like run-time atmosphere environment database which needs to handle a big volume of atmosphere data and keep a high access performance at the same time.

Embedded. The term *embedded* here means Berkeley DB is embedded into the application as a third part library. It uses the same address space as the application, which makes the database a significant improvement at performance. The Berkeley DB library itself is only about 1 MB in size, but it can provide almost all the functions that traditional databases normally have and its database file can be up to 256TB in size.

NoSQL. *NoSQL* is a new popular buzzword in the database world today. As a historical database itself, Berkeley DB has many features to meet the virtues of *NoSQL*. First, it is a non-relational database which uses a key/value store. As we discussed above, atmosphere data is a non-relational data model with a space and time point corresponding with a set of attributes. Different kinds of atmosphere data have no relationships with each other. It is more appropriate to manage atmosphere data with a non-relational database. What's more, Berkeley DB is very flexible on structure and data durability. With five relatively independent subsystems (access method subsystem, memory pool subsystem, transaction subsystem, log subsystem and lock subsystem), Berkeley DB let user to custom the functions and data durability of their database. Since the data of run-time atmosphere database is derived from the standard environment database and stay constant during the simulation process, it needs zero data durability. This can be used to significant reduce the complexity of the run-time database and improve its performance.

Memory Pool Subsystem. Memory pool subsystem is a very important mechanism that makes Berkeley DB a high-performance database. Berkeley DB manages data with pages. We can set up a memory cache with a max size of 4GB on 32-bit systems and 10TB on 64-bit systems to cache the atmosphere data into memory in pages. By setting the cache size, we can put all the data into memory so that all database operation can be done in memory. This gives out run-time database a main-memory-database-like performance.

3.2   Performance Test and Optimization

Berkeley DB provides four kinds of access methods, memory pool and two kinds of concurrency mechanisms. As shown below, we have done a series of performance test of Berkeley DB aiming at atmosphere data management and summarized some performance optimization   methods that are referential for run-time atmosphere database establishment.

All the tests are run on the following hardware configuration.

Table 1. Hardware configuration

PROCESSOR	OPERATING SYSTEM	RAM	STORAGE	FILE SYSTEM
Intel E8400 3GHz	Windows XP SP3	2GB	SATA, 7200RPM	NTFS

To simulate the atmosphere data, we use a 32 bytes key to present the longitude, latitude, altitude and time, and a 64 bytes value to present the attributes of one atmosphere table. Since it is a read-only application, we only test the performance of fetch operation.

Memory Pool and Access Methods Test
We first set the memory cache size (from 0 to 80 MB) and put 500,000 records into one Berkeley DB database (table), then did a 500,000 times' random fetch operations, recorded the time used and calculated the quantity of fetch operations per microsecond. The database file size was about 78MB. The access method was B-tree and the page-size is 4KB.

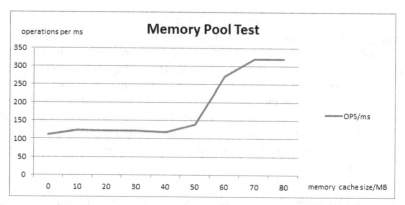

Fig. 3. This shows how fetch operation performance (operations per microsecond) improves as the memory cache increases

The fetch performance shown in figure 1 shows that the memory cache can significant improve Berkeley DB's fetch performance. At the earlier stage when the cache is not big enough, it doesn't help with the performance because the fetch operations are totally random, and the exchanges of data pages between memory and disk will reduce the performance. So when we build run-time atmosphere database, we must set big enough memory cache.

Berkeley DB provides four access method as B-tree, Hash, Queue and Recno. Usually we choose between B-tree and Hash, and between Queue and Recno. Hash is for random access and can't do range query. Considering the operating feature of atmosphere data and data locality, B-tree is more suitable for us. Queue and Recno are both for data management based on logical record numbers. Compared with Queue, Recno is based on a B-tree and can store variable-length records, which makes it more space wasting and less efficient, while Queue is a simple and efficient structure provide fixed-length records storage. Since atmosphere data is fixed-length in one specific table, we choose Queue from Recno.

When the gird of the atmosphere data is regular, we can change the longitude, latitude, altitude and time to logical record numbers so that we can use Queue access method to store it which gives us a constant level search performance because Queue search the records by calculating the offset from the top of the file using the record numbers. But when the grid is irregular, we have to use B-tree as our access method. B-tree can provide a good random search performance and better continuous search performance. Figure 2 shows a performance comparison between B-tree and Queue under large enough memory cache.

Concurrency and Throughput

Berkeley DB provides two essential concurrency mechanisms, TDS and CDS. Both of the two mechanisms involve a lock overhead, which can be avoided in a read only database like atmosphere runtime database by only use DB_THREAD flag in BDB. DB_THREAD is a flag that sets BDB's database handles thread-free and not involve locks.

On our dual-core and double-thread PC, we established one to six threads each doing 2,000,000 times of random fetch operations form one Berkeley DB database (table) with 2,000,000 records stored. The throughput is still presented   as operations per microsecond. The page-size is 4KB.

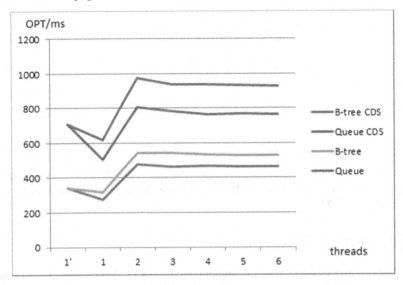

Fig. 4. This shows how throughput changes with the number of threads increases under B-tree and Queue access methods. The memory cache is large enough to hold the whole database file. CDS mean the CDS mechanism and the others are DB_THREAD only.

Read throughput is mainly subject to the CPU utilization. When there is only one thread, the database doesn't involve any overhead of locks, so the increase of throughput is not significant between one and two threads. On B-tree, it even decreases. But it still improves on Queue method. Because it is only a dual-core CPU, the throughput decreases on 3 to 6 threads. The read throughput can be significant improved in an environment that deploys multi-tasking multi-processor systems.

Page-Size
Different access methods have different space utilization. Generally, B-tree has a bad space utilization because it splits to keep the tree balance to have a good search performance. Page is Berkeley DB's minimum data access unit and one page is one node of B-tree. So the page-size, which can be set from 512B to 64KB, affects Berkeley DB's performance and the access methods' space utilization.

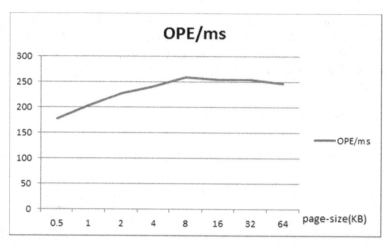

Fig. 5. This shows how read performance changes with page-size. The access method is B-tree and key-value are 32bytes and 64bytes. We can see that under this situation, the best page-size that should be set is 8KB.

4   Application System

After all these analysis and test, we implemented an AST Atmosphere Environment Runtime Database System based on RTI and Berkeley DB. The main user interface of the software is as follow(Fig 6).

The system stores certain atmosphere data retrieved from a standard database of environment and join the RTI as an atmosphere runtime database federate. The other entities can subscribe the interaction class and require atmosphere data from it.

We had a test with four simulation entities to require from the database federate. The result shows that the average data query time is stable between 60 to 70 microseconds. And each simulation step takes about 20 milliseconds. So we can see that the performance of the atmosphere runtime database is good enough to match general simulation applications.

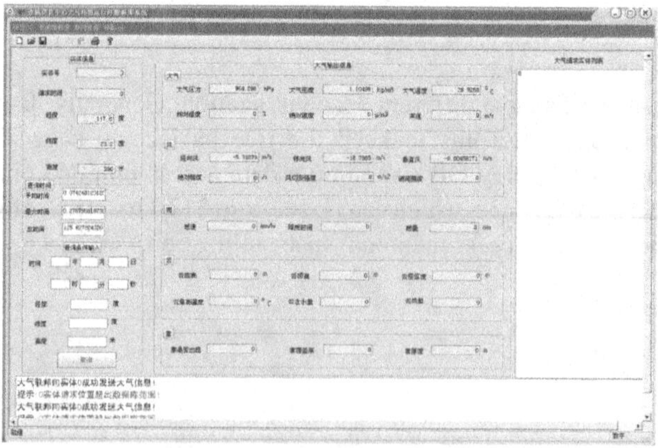

Fig. 6. The main interface of AST Atmosphere Environment Runtime Database System

5   Conclusion

This paper analyses the characteristics of run-time atmosphere environment database, including the features of atmosphere data and the functionalities and performance requirements for it. Then we introduce a famous embedded database Berkeley DB and talks about the performance test and optimization methods oriented building run-time atmosphere environment database. At last, we use Berkeley DB to implement a run-time atmosphere environment database system and have a test on it, which shows the performance of BDB can fit the requirements of general simulation applications well.

Acknowledgement. This work was supported by the National Natural Science Foundation of China (Grant No.6117414807277).

References

1. Wang, J., Dong, D., Wang, X.: Research on Database Technologies of Synthetic Natural Environment. In: 2008 Asia Simulation Conference, pp. 1329–1333 (2008)
2. Xiao, S., Lijun, X.: Research on Key Technologies of Standard Atmosphere Database. In: 2008 Asia Simulation Conference, pp. 1497–1550 (2008)
3. Guo, S., Wang, J.: Representation and Storage Model of Ocean and Atmosphere Environmental Data. Journal of System Simulation 22(11) (2010)
4. Yadava, H.: The Berkeley DB Bookp. APRESS, USA (2007)
5. Zhang, P., Gong, G.-H.: Atmosphere Environment Simulation Scenario Generator for Distributed Simulation System. Journal of System Simulation 20(19) (2008)

Expert System Application in Simulation Tutoring for Weapon Utilization

Danhua Peng, Xiaohong Shi, and Ge Li

College of Mechatronics Engineering and Automation,
National University of Defense Technology, Changsha, China, 410073
pengdanhua26@126.com, redsxh@hotmail.com, geli@nudt.edu.cn

Abstract. According to the characteristics and requirements of simulation tutoring system for weapon utilization, a hybrid rule-based expert system was designed to offer intelligent assists during the teaching process. The architecture and function of the simulation tutoring system were introduced firstly. Then with the disadvantages of production system analyzed, a kind of XML-based production knowledge representation was presented. Combining the object-orient method and XML technology, the rule-based expert system can make rules flexible-defined, intuitionistic and easy to access. In order to reason conveniently, fact base was also built in the form of XML, which leads to efficient inference. With examples given, the detail of knowledge representation was interpreted, the design of rule base and fact base were described, and the process of inference was illustrated. The implementation proved that the expert system can reason on students' operations according to rules and return inference results, which met the requirements well.

Keywords: simulation tutoring system, weapon utilization, rule-based expert system, XML.

1 Introduction

With the fast development of military technology, information-based weapons play a more and more important role in modern wars. And the requirement for commanders' ability of weapon utilization becomes higher. Thus the tutoring for weapon utilization also faces more challenge. However, traditional tutoring methods have obvious disadvantage: a great deal of weapons' characteristics are difficult to be mastered only through class teaching. In order to improve the efficiency of tutoring, building a simulation tutoring system for weapon utilization was put forward. Through employing visual simulation technology, the system offers 3-dimension display and friendly interaction with human, which gives students a feeling of immersion, so as to achieve intuitionistic and visual teaching. On the other hand, considering the knowledge of weapon utilization is numerous, better effect will be obtained if the system offers intelligent assist and decision when students use it to do exercises. Therefore, in this paper we applied artificial intelligence technology into the simulation tutoring. According to the reality and characteristics of weapon utilization, an expert system for simulation tutoring of weapon utilization was designed.

T. Xiao, L. Zhang, and S. Ma (Eds.): ICSC 2012, Part II, CCIS 327, pp. 144–152, 2012.

2   System Overview

2.1   System Function

This simulation tutoring system is used to offer assistant teaching for weapon utilization. Firstly, teachers set the scenarios which are related to weapon utilization, such as targets, weapons and environment. With the system, teachers assign some tasks for students to test whether the knowledge are mastered. During the process of finishing task, the expert system will provide suggestions according to students' operation after inference.

2.2   System Architecture

The architecture of the system is as shown in Figure 1. In order to reuse all kinds of resources, the system's architecture was designed as "resources + platform + applications".

1) Resources

Resources layer offers basic data support, and stores all kinds of real resources, including weapon basic information, the information used for interaction among units, and so on. It's mainly in the form of database.

2) Platform

The platform layer offers the public and common environment for the whole system. It's the crucial part. As shown in Figure 1, it consists of system management and control unit, visual simulation unit, expert system unit, knowledge management unit and the interaction interface among them.

The system management and control unit controls the overall function of the simulation tutoring system. It interacts with the other components of the whole system, calling the inference system whenever it's necessary. Furthermore, it plays a user interface role.

The visual simulation unit provides 2-dimension and 3-dimension display function for the system, including the war environment, 2D/3D maps, and 2D/3D weapon models and so on. It mainly incorporates 2-dimension visual function unit, 3-dimension visual function unit and all kinds of models for visualization.

The expert system unit is generally made up of knowledge base, inference system and facts base. When students do exercises, the expert system unit will check the rationality and validity of students' operation, and provide useful related information for decision-making.

The knowledge management unit is concerned with acquisition and update of the knowledge contained in the various knowledge bases of the system. With knowledge management unit, domain experts such as teachers can transfer the knowledge which will be tested during teaching process into the expert system knowledge in the given form, and save them into knowledge bases.

The pedagogical unit is used to transform the lesson plan into the current user model, by making decisions on the teaching strategy, the teaching concepts and the teaching material. The inference system applies to any of the knowledge bases to produce corresponding conclusions.

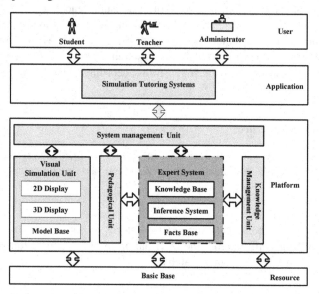

Fig. 1. Architecture of Simulation Tutoring System

3   Expert System Design

According to the method of knowledge representation, expert system can be divided into many types: rule-based expert system, case-based expert system, neural-networks-based expert system and so on [1].

Rule-based expert system is the common method which knowledge engineers use to construct expert system. It's also called production system, and its rule is also called production rule. The form of production rule is "IF premise THEN conclusion". This natural express form which is close to human language makes rule-based expert system intuitionistic, easy to understand and convenient for inference. Meanwhile, rules are independent, andmodularized. But it also has the following disadvantages [2]:

● Exact match

Production system matches the obtained facts and rules' premise to draw conclusions. Only the process of match is exact can it be useful. And this leads to strict coding.

● Low efficiency

It exists a repeat process of "Knowledge match-Conflict clear-Execute result" in production system. When the number of rules is huge, the match can be time consuming, which means low efficiency.

In recent years, object-oriented knowledge representation has become one of active domains in artificial intelligent [3]. And the XML-based (eXtensible Markup Language) object-orient knowledge representation is a popular method. Because XML has good characteristics: extensibility, self-definition and heterogeneity. First of all, XML guarantees the reliability from the aspects of logic, grammar and completeness [4]. Secondly, the information included in XML is tree-structured, so it can define any types of data structure and nesting structure. Besides, the extensibility if XML provides simple ways for knowledge maintenance [5]. Above all, the tree structure of XML makes information search easy and efficient.

If combine the production system with XML technology, we can make the best of their advantages.   According to the characteristics of the simulation tutoring system, XML-based production knowledge representation was presented in this paper. With object-orient method employed, production rules were represented with XML.

3.1   The Rule Base Design

Initially, all weapons were divided into some classes on the basis of their function: land forces weapons, navy weapons, air force weapons and so on. As the number of weapons and targets is not large in a particular application, rule base was built for every weapon upon database based on their classes.

After acquiring knowledge from domain experts, rules were abstracted from the reality and then classified. The whole rule base can be viewed as a class, and it has different attributes, such as target match rule, characteristics constraint rule, environment match and so on. Every particular class of weapon rule can be viewed as a subclass of the whole rule base class, as shown in Figure 2.

3.2   Rule Representation

As mentioned before, XML-based knowledge representation can integrate many kinds of traditional knowledge representation methods. It provides open architecture and allows users to define certain semantic signs. For that reason, rules in this paper can be designed as shown in Figure 3.

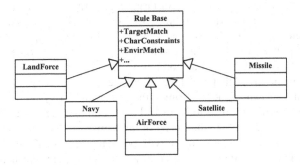

Fig. 2. Architecture of Rule Base

The core of hybrid rule designed in this paper is to express a rule in the form of XML. As the basic form of a rule is "IF premise THEN conclusion", we seperated it into different parts which are different items in a XML-based rule, such as the rule shown in Fig.3. Every rule consists of five parts: <RuleID> is rule's ID number; <RuleName> is rule's name; <If> includes the precision part of the rule; when the premise part is satisfied <Then> is the conclusion and <Else> will be used if it's not. It can be represented as a five-tuple array: <RuleID, RuleName, If, Then, Else>. In one rule there can be one or more <If> parts, and the <If> part is made up of one or more <Pre>. The content of <Pre> will be explained latter. Elements of <Then> and <Else> part are the same, which are <RetMessage> and <RetValue>. <RetMessage> contains the result message in the form of text, and <RetValue> gives the information about whether the rule is satisfied or not in the form of numerical value:'1' means satisfied and '0' means unsatisfied.

The <Pre> part is essential to rule representation. It represents premise and its structure is designed as variable according to the type of rule. There is a five-tuple array in <Pre> part as shown in Figure 3,<Mode, Object, ObjAttribute, Relation, Value>. In this paper, we define some objects and their attributes. According to the system requirement, we need to inference on the users' operation, which includes the targets, the weapons, and the time they want to use the weapons and so on. We divided the facts information into three kinds of classes: Target, Weapon, and Operation. Target class gives the information about targets; Weapon class describes weapons; and Operation class is used to represent other operation information, such as time information. Every class has some attributes, which can be set by teachers, as shown in Figure 4. Considering that one kind of weapon may be used in several different ways, we define <Mode> as the usage ways to identify it, such as recce, attack. Thus, in the five-tuple array of <Pre>, <Mode, Object, ObjAttribute, Relation, Value>, <Object> represents one object of one class from the three classes, and also <ObjAttribute> means one attribute of that object. <Relation> can be 'E' (equal), 'NE' (not equal), 'L' (larger), 'EL' (equal or larger), 'S' (smaller), 'ES' (equal or smaller) and so on. And <Value> can be the expect value related to <ObjAttribute>. The left part of the relation signs is always the element before <Relation>.

Thus, the message shown in Figure 3 includes a rule of one weapon that RuleID is 01, RuleName is 'TargetMatch', and the content is that under the mode of recce, if the ID attribute of Target is 01, then the target matches the weapon and return value is 1; else the weapon cannot be used on the target and return value is 0.

The five-tuple array discussed above is for target match rule. As to other type rules, it can be other arrays, such as<Mode, Object, ObjAttribute, Relation, Attribute>, in which the <Attribute> refers to the weapon's attribute. Besides simple relation comparation among attributes of objects and given value, there may be some simple mathematical computation needed, such as computing the distance of two weapons. It's not so convenient to describe that in <Pre>. Because this expert system is not designed as universal, we can predefine something according to system requirement. Therefore, we predefined some methods to deal with complex computation. An example is shown in Figure 5. The method used in the <Pre> is DistanceCompute (Target, Weapon), and the return value of it will be compared with the 'FightArea' attribute of the weapon. The method is predefined in the system and it returns the distance with input parameters. There can be other methods if they are needed, and the usage is the same.

```
- <dataroot>
  - <Rule>
      <RuleID>01</RuleID>
      <RuleName>TargetMatch</RuleName>
    - <If>
      - <Pre>
          <Mode>Recce</Mode>
          <object>Target</object>
          <ObjAttribute>ID</ObjAttribute>
          <Relation>E</Relation>
          <Value>01</Value>
        </Pre>
      </If>
    - <If>
      + <Pre>
      + <Pre>
      </If>
    - <Then>
        <RetMessage>Target Match Succeeds</RetMessage>
        <RetValue>1</RetValue>
      </Then>
    - <Else>
        <RetMessage>Target Match Fails</RetMessage>
        <RetValue>0</RetValue>
      </Else>
    </Rule>
</dataroot>
```

Fig. 3. An Example of Rule

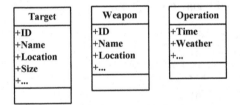

Fig. 4. Classes of Facts Information

```
- <If>
  - <Pre>
      <Mode>Attack</Mode>
    - <Method>
        <Name>DistanceCompute</Name>
        <Para>Target</Para>
        <Para>Weapon</Para>
      </Method>
      <Relation>ES</Relation>
      <Attibute>FightArea</Attibute>
    </Pre>
  </If>
```

Fig. 5. an Example of Method Use

As mentioned before, in one <If> there can be one or more <Pre> parts and in one rule there also can be one or more <If> parts. Only when all the <Pre> items in an <If> part are satisfied at the same time, can the <If> besatisfied. However, all the items of <If> make up of a rule group. In a rule group, once one <If> is satisfied, the whole group is satisfied, and then the <Then> part can be obtained.

3.3   Fact Representation and Fact Base

Besides rule re0presentation, fact representation is also important to an expert system, and it has close connection with the former. In this paper, facts actually are operation information of users. They are also described in XML. An example is shown in Figure 6. And the structure can be changed according to requirement under the form.

The fact base is also designed as a part of database. It contains facts related to the current user and learning session. And the operation information is included too.

3.4   Inference System

The inference system consists of two components: (a) inference engine and (b) explanation unit. The inference engine (IE) implements the way rules cooperate to reach conclusions. In this paper, inference engine uses backward chaining strategy that inference starts from the original facts base to get conclusions. The inference process is as following, and in order to interpret it better we will explain with an example at the same time using Figure 3 and Figure 6.

```
- <dataroot>
  - <Target>
      <ID>01</ID>
      <Name>TargetName</Name>
    </Target>
  - <Weapon>
      <ID>01</ID>
      <Name>WeaponName</Name>
      <Type>Satellite</Type>
      <Location>WeaponLocation</Location>
      <Mode>Recce</Mode>
    </Weapon>
  - <Operation>
      <Time>TimeExpress</Time>
    </Operation>
  </dataroot>
```

Fig. 6. An Example of Fact Representation

(a). Get operation information from fact base, and find weapon item to obtain related information. In Figure 6, we get the weapon information that ID is 01 and type is satellite.

(b). Search the weapon in rule base and get its rules. As the weapon type is satellite, search the satellite rule base and find the weapon whose ID is 01, and get its rules.

(c). Reason according to all types of rules one by one. For every type get its rule at first, as shown in Figure 3.

(d). For every rule, get the <If> part firstly. Then find the <Pre> parts and start from the first one in sequence. For every <Pre>, search the items in fact and get related information from basic bases. If all the <Pre> parts are satisfied, then go to <Then> part.

(e). If there are more than one <If> part, start from the first in sequence until one satisfied. If no <If> part is satisfied, then go to <Else> part.

Suppose that the weapon's target match rule is as shown in Figure 3 and the facts are as shown in Figure 6. In the rule, we firstly get the first <If> part. In the first <If> part, there is only one <Pre>, and we get the five-tuple array <Mode, Object, ObjAttribute, Relation, Value>. In this <Pre>, we can get <Mode> is recce. Then we search the <Mode> part in facts and find it matches with the rule. From other items of the five-tuple array, the information we can obtain is that the target's ID attribute equals 01. So we search target information in facts and find the target's ID is 01. Thus, the <Pre> part and <If> part are both satisfied. Then we can go to the <Then> part, and inference for this type of rules is finished.

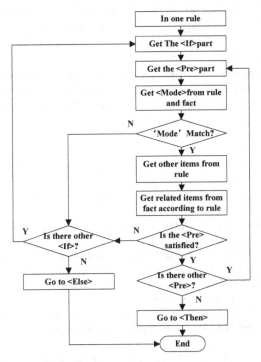

Fig. 7. Process of Rule Match

As to the explanation unit, we simplified it in this paper. According to the system design, only when users' operation makes rules unsatisfied does the expert system return explanation message. Therefore, in one rule if the <If> part is unsatisfied, it goes to the <Else> part. And the <RetMessage> which gives an explanation of operation will be fed back to users through the system supervisor.

4   Implementation

The expert system in this paper was developed upon C++ DLL (dynamic link library) and SQL Server. The tutoring system operates as following: users do operations on the system interface, and then the system supervisor writes down the information as facts and calls the expert system DLL with interface parameters transferred when necessary. With facts information and basic base, the expert system makes inference and draws conclusions. After that the conclusions will be returned to system supervisor and be fed back to users in the end.

5   Conclusions and Future Work

In this paper, we built an expert system for simulation tutoring of weapon utilization. The architecture of expert system and the process of inference were represented. According to the requirements and characteristics of the tutoring system, we used a hybrid rule-based formalism to represent knowledge, which combines XML and production rule. Also we employed object-orient method to simplify knowledge representation and inference. The combination of them leads to easy knowledge representation and fast inference.

This expert system was established for the certain tutoring system of weapon utilization. Thus it has some limitations: the explanation unit can only offer limited explanation; the knowledge representation is not so complete as to need some predefine methods, and so on. Those are the work we need to do in the future.

References

1. An, L.-N., Zhang, S.: Progress and prospects of expert system. Application Research of Computers 24(12), 1–5 (2007)
2. Zixing, C., Durkin, J., Tao, G.: Advanced Expert Systems: Principles, Design and Applications. Science Publication, Beijing (2005)
3. Li, Z., He, D., Li, S., Liu, Y.: Research on Knowledge Base Construction Method for Web Expert System based on XML. Microcomputer Information 17, 299–307 (2006)
4. Chen, Y.: Knowledge Representation Technology Research of XML in Expert System. Wuhan University of Technology, Wuhan (2008)
5. Yang, J., Xiong, Q., Tao, Q.: Research on the Mapping between XML Document Framework and Relational Data Model. Computer Engineering and Applications 27, 168–172 (2004)
6. Hatzilygeroudis, I., Prentzas, J.: Using a hybrid rule-based approach in developing an intelligent tutoring system with knowledge acquisition and update capabilities. Expert Systems with Applications 26, 477–492 (2004)

Design of the Teaching Demonstration Platform of Missile Control System

Tao Yang, Xiaofei Chang, Wenxing Fu, and Jie Yan

College of Astronautics, Northwestern Polytechnical University, Xi'an 710072, China

Abstract. According to the lacking of teaching experiments in design of missile control system course, a teaching demonstration platform is built. In this paper, the general scheme of the design is completed, and the system is departed to teacher-control-terminal and student-design-node based on client/server model. The simulation is demonstrated vividly through the steering engine, 3D visual simulation, and trajectory of the missile. Some pieces of the software including Matlab, RT-lab and Vega are integrated to design the frame of software, and the running flow of the software is given. Finally, the contents of the experiment are introduced. The teaching experiment shows that this system is useful to help students understand the composition and design methods of typical control system. The operation of the system is simple, intuitive and vivid.

Keywords: design of control system, teaching demonstration, simulation, client/server.

1   Introduction

Missile control system design is a required course to train the guidance weapon control system designer, and is an important part of Navigation Guidance and Control engineering[1]. In the current teaching activities, students understand and grasp the course contents through textbooks, blackboards and multimedia courseware. Teaching form is relatively single that only written introduction and explanation make the communication between students and teachers very limited. Because of the lack of practice in the curriculum design and experimental contents, students' interest in learning and understanding is not high, to some extent students' understanding of missile control system and knowledge application are hindered[2,3]. While in Europe and the United States or other aerospace power, in this course, a large number of experimental equipment is provided. It ensures that the course combines classroom teaching with student experiments[4].

In this paper, based on the server/client model, we design a missile control system design teaching demonstration platform. The system can be used in undergraduate and postgraduate teaching experiment with rich experimental contents and simple operation. Using the material object and image to display the experimental results, the process is intuitive vivid, thus students' understand and use of the curriculum contents of flight control system design can be deepen.

T. Xiao, L. Zhang, and S. Ma (Eds.): ICSC 2012, Part II, CCIS 327, pp. 153–159, 2012.
© Springer-Verlag Berlin Heidelberg 2012

2   The Platform Overall Scheme Design

In order to achieve the needs of the classroom experimental teaching, based on the client/server mode, this paper completed the overall design scheme. It is convenient for teachers in the experiment teaching management and the students' operation to the experimental course. In order to improve the students' learning interest, the visual animation, physical model and real rudder actuators are brought into the system, it largely improves the experimental teaching intuitive.

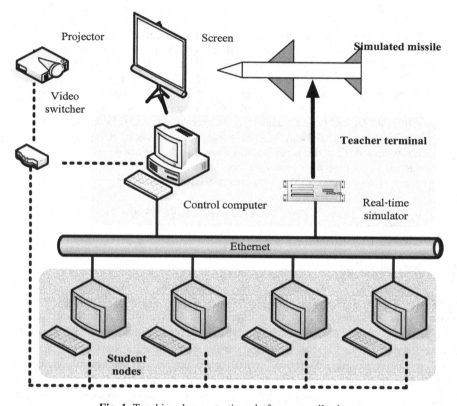

Fig. 1. Teaching demonstration platform overall scheme

Teaching demonstration platform overall scheme can be seen from the Fig 1 that the whole system includes teacher control terminal, more students design nodes and the auxiliary equipment.

Students choose missile control system structure in the student nodes, design the control parameters step by step, obtain the time domain and the frequency domain analysis results and upload the design parameters to teacher terminal through the net.

The teacher terminal includes control computer and real-time simulator, including control system design function, network data receiving function, and can make the function validation of six degrees of freedom simulation through the real-time simulator.

Simulated missile is used for displaying the typical missile structure and layout, with four rubber actuators. It is convenient for teaching.

3   Teaching Demonstration Software Design

3.1   Software Framework Design

According to the overall scheme and task partitioning of various subsystems, based on the modular design principle, the design of software framework is completed.

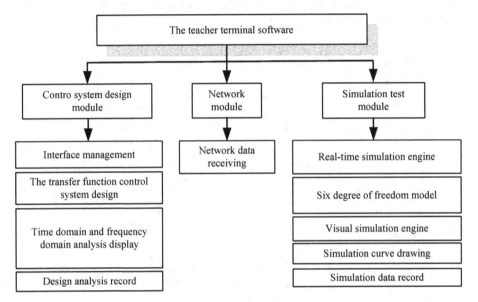

Fig. 2. The teacher terminal software framework diagram

The teacher terminal software includes the following several parts:

1. Control system design

This part uses the Vc and Matlab mixed programming[5] to achieve the choice of the missile transfer function and control system, the analysis and display of the time domain and the frequency domain, analysis results record and software management etc.

2. Network module

This module mainly uses the TCP / IP protocol, receives the design results of the students via Ethernet, and makes the appropriate display and record.

3. Simulation test module

The simulation verification is to use the control system to design parameters for six degrees of freedom simulation verification and real-time displays the simulation results.

This module contains six degrees of freedom simulation model, real-time simulation platform RT-LAB engine, three dimension visual simulation Vega engine, simulation curve drawing and data record part.

The student nodes are similar, but only contain the former two parts.

3.2   Software Running Flow

According to the teacher terminal software design framework, the flow chart of software running is given. After teacher starting the software, through the software operation, control system design, data reception, teaching tasks such as the real-time simulation can be completed.

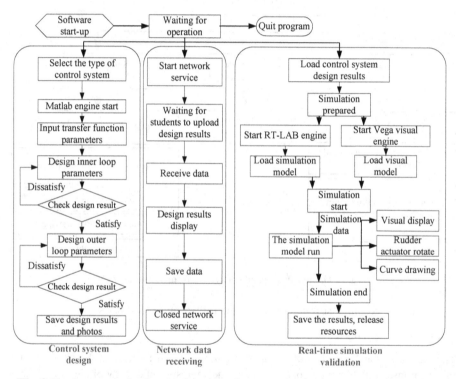

Fig. 3. Teacher terminal software of teaching demonstration platform operation flow chart

In the control system design, first control system type would be selected. This platform offers six different control system structures including pitch, yaw and roll three channels, so that it's easy to carry out various types of teaching experiments. After inputting the missile transfer function, gradually the missile control system design is completed from inside to outside by calling the Matlab calculation engine.

After completing the control system design based on the linear function, it's needed to assess the design results through the nonlinear model. By calling the RT-Lab simulation platform[6], the software completes the compilation of the simulation model, loads to the real-time simulator for real-time solution, obtains the simulation data during the simulation process via Ethernet, draws the trajectory curve. In order to let the students can be more effective to understand the process and mechanism of the missile flight, by calling the Vega visual simulation engine, the missile attitude change can be shown vivid. At the same time, serial communication control modules are added to the simulation model to control four electromechanical actuators rotation, so that students can have a clear intuitive understanding about the missile during flight and the design results.

3.3   Software Running Interface

According to the software framework and design flow , the software development work is completed. Software running interface is shown below:

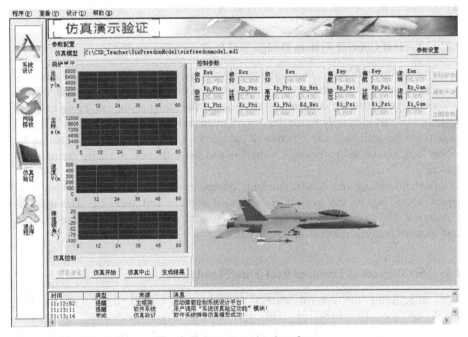

Fig. 4. Software running interface

4   Teaching Experimental Design

To enable students to grasp more knowledge in the experimental curriculum, but also for designing homework, the demonstration system designs a variety of teaching experiments.

4.1   The Missile Transfer Function Calculation

The space motion of the missile is described by a set of nonlinear differential equations, there is no general analytical method for solving in mathematics. Therefore it's needed to build the linear model of the missile during the missile control system design. According to the missile aerodynamic data and ballistic characteristic point, using the small disturbance linearization method, the missile transfer function coefficients can be got[7].

In the classroom, explain the meaning and calculation method of the missile transfer function, then arrange the different characteristic points aerodynamic data to students as their homework to calculate solution. In classroom experiment, students can compare results calculated by their own with the software built-in missile transfer function parameters to check their calculation.

By experiment, students can master the linearized missile aerodynamic data and lay the foundation for the design of the control system.

4.2   Typical Control System Design and Performance Analysis

In the experimental class, the students choose the typical type of missile control systems, to understand the block diagram and system composition. The control system design starts after determining the transfer function parameters. From inside to outside, students gradually finish the time domain and the frequency domain analysis, understand the influence and function of each control parameters, and can change the rubber actuator model parameters to understand the influence of rubber actuator on system.

After completing the design, students complete the design analysis experiment report according to the generated analytical reports and pictures. Through the experiment, the students can master the structure of control system, design process, performance analysis method and quality index.

4.3   Six Degrees of Freedom Real-Time Simulation

After completing the control system design, based on six degree of freedom simulation model, combining with the missile flight mechanics, a detailed introduction about simulation modeling method and matters needing attention are given, so that students can master and understand missile simulation model structure and create procedure.

By calling the RT-Lab environment, the system achieves real-time simulation, and controls four rubber actuators to rotate real-time. The teaching introduces the hardware-in-the-loop simulation contents including the concept, composition and function, and lets students have a clear understanding of hardware-in-the-loop simulation.

Through this experiment, students can master the general approach of the missile 6-DOF modeling, and do a comprehensive assessment to the designed control system quality.

5   Conclusions

The teaching demonstration system can be used for completing teaching experiment task of the missile control system design course. According to the needs, the client/server system framework design is completed, and the software framework design and software running process are given. Software platform achieves the simulation model real-time operation by calling the RT-Lab engine, and shows the simulation results through the physical rudder actuator, 3D visual display, ballistic curve and other forms. The system has a variety of experimental contents to facilitate the teaching and learning activities. The software is simple, vivid, and will help to deepen students' understanding of the missile control system design concepts and processes.

References

1. Yang, J., Yang, C.: Modern Missile Guidance Control System Design. Aviation Industry Press, Beijing (2005)
2. Liu, X.-X., Li, G.-Y., Zhang, W.-G.: An Exploration on Teaching Innovation of Flight Control Systems Curriculum. Higher Education Forum (1), 47–49 (2009)
3. Liu, J.-X., Tang, Q.-G., Li, J.-T.: Teaching Reform and Practice of Graduate Course "Missile Overall Design and Analysis". Journal of Higher Education Research 29(3), 54–55 (2006)
4. Zeng, Q.-H., Zhang, W.-H.: Flight Control System Experimental Course. National University of Defense Technology Press, Changsha (2011)
5. Dong, Z.-H.: MATLAB Compiler and External Interface. National Defense Industry Press, Beijing (2010)
6. RT-LAB Version 8.1 User Guide. OPAL-RT Inc. (2005)
7. Liang, X.-G., Wang, B.-R., Yu, Z.-F.: Missile Guidance and Control System Design. National Defense Industry Press, Beijing (2006)

The Study on Integration between General Mobile Device and Desktop Virtual Reality System

Meng Wang, Binjie Xu, Zhenggong Han, and Dekun Chen

School of Mechatronic Engineering and Automation, Shanghai University,
Shanghai Key Laboratory of Manufacturing Automation and Robotics 1, China

Abstract. This paper presented a lightweight, low cost, quasi-real-time distributed virtual reality system to verify the feasibility of the idea of college freshmen navigation. Desktop virtual reality system with Virtools was achieved with the real size of the Web-3D scenes and virtual 3D character behavior. Based on iOS and Android, mobile platform was achieved a custom Google Map Web-2D scenes and characters of 2D. Through the VR shared database and mobile terminal local VR library, data synchronization was realized in the system.

Keywords: General Mobile Device, DVR, Web-3D, Integration.

1 Introduction

Virtual reality (VR) is a kind of technology, which makes use of computer graphics systems and a variety of display and control interface devices. It can provide immersed senses in the three dimensional interacted environment which generated by computer. Virtual reality can be exempted from the restrictions of time and space to experience the events of the world already or does not occur, the observation and study of the occurrence and development of the same event in a variety of hypothetical conditions; Virtual reality is divided into three categories: the imitation of reality, imitation of virtual reality, and the imitation of a dynamic reality. The implement of the imitation of a dynamic reality is relative difficult. Virtual reality technology has shown its huge economic and social benefits in many areas, such as military, manufacturing, urban planning, architecture, geography, entertainment and so on.

Web-3D is virtual reality technology applications on the Internet. At present, the build in Web-3D distributed virtual environment was divided into two aspects, the development of Web-3D virtual space and the Web-3D network service platform. There are a lot of popular Web-3D virtual environment development tools, such as Virtools, VRML, Quest3d and domestic VRP etc. Domestic and international institutions made use of the Web -3D to develop a virtual environment, such as virtual Olympic Village, a virtual National Stadium, Nanjing Ming Xiao ling, and the virtual Forbidden City. Web-3D network services platform and virtual environment were combined to build a Web-3D distributed virtual environment. But VR also has many drawbacks, such as complex system equipments, real-time data acquisition requires more expensive equipment.

T. Xiao, L. Zhang, and S. Ma (Eds.): ICSC 2012, Part II, CCIS 327, pp. 160–167, 2012.

The development of mobile devices and wireless networks can partially compensate for the above shortcomings. In less demanding situations, we used the ordinary universal mobile equipment to complete the virtual simulation system for real-time data acquisition. This paper presented the concept of the portable mobile virtual simulation system to verify the feasibility of the idea of college freshmen navigation. Smartphone which is carried a variety of sensors, can simply access the user's state and the state of the environment around. In addition, it is equipped with the operating system which is able to be continuously expand the functionality of the phone by third-party software, through a variety of mobile communication network, wireless network access. It can also realize the wireless network access through a variety of mobile communication network. In the integration between mobile device and the desktop VR system, the main problems needed to be solved include integrated framework, application system mutual operation semantics, syntax, and interactive sequence.

2 The Overall Design of the Distributed Quasi-Real-Time Virtual Reality System

This paper presented a lightweight, low cost, quasi-real-time distributed virtual reality system. This system realized the real-time system for mobile and desktop virtual reality system of quasi-real-time interaction. Base on the Virtools, desktop virtual reality system was achieved with the real size of the Web-3D scenes and virtual 3D character behavior. Based on iOS and Android, mobile platform was achieved a custom Google Map Web-2D scenes and characters of 2D. Through the VR shared database and mobile terminal local VR library, data synchronization was realized in the system.

2.1 The Integrated Logical Framework for Mobile Devices and VR Virtual Simulation System

Program specific technical framework was designed as follows:

1. Access control layer of virtual reality:

In a distributed virtual reality system design, network topology design was mainly based on client / server mode. Network topology was usually the two layers of B / S mode. As a result of the two layers structure, it was difficult to meet the dynamic interaction created by large number of users, therefore this paper had an access control layer. It not only implemented for multiple user access control, but also helped to improving the system flexibility and scalability.

2. Access layer of virtual reality:

- The implementation of Desktop virtual reality system and VR data shared interface

Desktop virtual reality system using ASP technology achieved the synchronization of the simulation data.

- The implementation of Mobile terminal simulation system and VR data shared interface

The synchronization between the local VR library in the mobile terminal and VR library state data was realized by Web Service technology. Mobile terminal read the VR library state data and updated the interface position and action of other users.

3. Application layer of virtual reality:

Different from general virtual reality system, this system added a mobile front-end. In the mobile front-end, there were Web applications and applications based on the Platform SDK. The former development was simple and can be deployed to a variety of mobile devices. The latter can access local resources, such as a variety of sensors and local databases. This system made use of the offline features to improve the best user experience and enriched interface design.

In this paper, the mobile platform application was integrated with the web page based on Google Maps Javascript API and the application based on the Platform SDK, which reduced the workload of the multi-platform development.

The key technologies to be solved as follows:

- The implementation of Desktop virtual reality system and VR data shared interface
- The implementation of Mobile terminal simulation system and VR data shared interface
- The design of VR Shared database
- The conversion of Geographical coordinates and virtual reality coordinate

2.2   The Design of Interoperable Process for Mobile Devices and VR Virtual Simulation System

When Desktop client and mobile device client logged on, a role, the role name, role position, role behavior, and other shared information would be registered to the shared database. By testing shared database information regularly, the appropriate substitute was created if the user online information had been detected. People in the same scene interact with others through codes of conduct and the latitude and longitude conversion module.

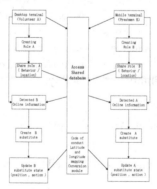

Fig. 1. Web-3D and VR shared database for data transmission schematic diagram

2.3   The Integrated Shared Database of Mobile Device System and VR System

Nowadays, in the virtual reality environment, the interaction of each platform can be divided into centralized and peer-to-peer system. The centralized system exchanges synchronous data through shared database and the peer-to-peer system does it by IM(Instant Messaging). The implementation of centralized system is easier, more low-cost and quicker than the peer-to-peer. This paper designed the following database structure:

Device Table: DeviceID,   DeviceName,   DeviceDescription,   Class

Role Table: RoleID, RoleName, RoleDescription, Class

Scene Table: SceneID, SceneName, SceneDescription, Class

State Table: ID, UserID, RoleID, DeviceID, SceneID, UserGroupID, Latitude, Longtitude, Virtual location,Action, Data

User Table: UserID, UserName, UserUnit, UserEmail,Class

UserGroup Table: UserGroupID, UserGroupName, UserGroupDescription, Class

3   The Implementation of the Interface between Web-3D VR System and VR Shared Database

In our system, the appropriate URL was entered in the browser. When the browser send http request to Web Server, the html and cmo files were downloaded to the local and were run. The BB module, "Web Get Data", in the cmo file in the browser would send post request to the Web Server. ASP read the parameters from the request by the function of Request.from and connected to the Access database by the function of ADO.Connection. The query result was returned to the client by the function of Response.Write. At last, cmo file will update the local state table(Array) by the BB module, "Set Cell" in the browser.

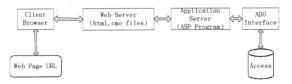

Fig. 2. The framework of the interface between Web-3D VR System and VR Shared Database

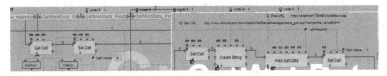

Fig. 3. Access to shared data module

	0. CopyaID	1. CopyerStatus	2. ActorName	3. location	4. CopyLocation	5. Action
0	2	TRUE	jack1	208,-3.5,-350	6,1,0	A
1	3	FALSE	jack2	210,-4,-350	8,1,0	B
2	4	FALSE	jack3	212,-4.5,-350	3,1,0	C
3	5	FALSE	jack4	212,-5,-350	4,1,0	A

Fig. 4. Local state table

3.1   The Loading of a Substitute

A character was built when desktop client or mobile device client logged on, and the shared information include name, location, and action wrote in shared database. The BB module-"Web Get Data" gained other users' information and updated the local state table. The loading of a substitute was implemented by using Object Copy module to load and rename it by Object Rename module where the state was "TRUE" when continuing to traverse the local state table.

3.2   The Implementation of Substitute Behavior

The key problem with the expression of mobile user's behavior was as follows: the interactive operation from mobile device resolved to the Web-3D interactive command. In this paper, the customize behaviors of the mobile device were mapped onto Web-3D behavior with VR standard format data. The change of the interactive command was implemented by the BB module "Test".

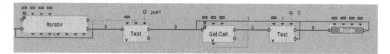

Fig. 5. Substitute behavior realize module

3.3   The Implementation of Substitute Location

In this system, the movement of substitute was realized by the Navigation Tips method, then the substitute location was quasi-real-time updated by the distance and calculated by the "Get Radius" module and direction identified by "Character Go To" module.

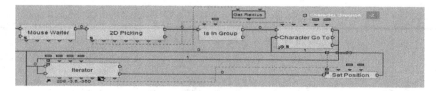

Fig. 6. Substitute behavior module

4   The Implementation of the Interface between Simulation System of the Mobile Terminal and the VR Shared Database

4.1   The Process Design of Mobile Terminal to Access the VR Shared Database

The mobile device with iOS or Android platform that provided with a variety of sensors and interactive techniques not only is very suitable for virtual reality system as an input device, but also can be enhanced to the interactivity of the whole system. In addition, according to own characteristics and limitations, the mobile terminal that was regarded as one of display subsystems in the whole simulation system adopted the self-defined Google Map and user avatar as the primary output content.

As an input device, the mobile terminal acquired, filtered, converted and updated all kinds of sensor signals.

- **Acquisition:** Acquire the measured value of position sensor, acceleration sensor and angle acceleration sensor on the device.
- **Filtering:** The measured values with little change or error would be filtered in consequence of the real-time performance of sensor signal which would produce a large number of measured values in the running process.
- **Conversion:** A few measured values (such as three axial acceleration values acquired through acceleration sensor) cannot be reflected in the simulation system so as to convert motion commands with algorithm.
- **Update:** After the above three steps, the data management module updated the virtual reality local database when the user's position or behavior changed. Besides, the user status records in status table of virtual reality shared database would be updated through calling virtual reality state update module on the mobile application server. And the user's position or behavior would be updated by calling interface update module.

As a display subsystem, the mobile terminal read the state table of virtual reality local database through starting up regularly virtual reality state synchronous module and interface update module. Then, other users' positions or behaviors were updated by interface update module.

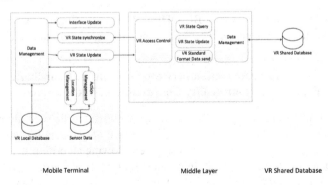

Fig. 7. The interface between mobile system and VR shared database

The middle layer was composed of the following modules:

● Virtual reality access control module

Workflow technology allowed the users' access to run in accordance with the process templates, which it was convenient for administrator to analyze reasonableness of process design according to workflow running records in order to modify the program process expediently and timely. In addition, workflow can easily combine multiple services to meet the complex application.

● Virtual reality state data query model and virtual reality state data update module

After the module read mobile client or desktop client requests and determined the reasonableness and accuracy, it called the data management module to query or update the shared VR database.

The main code of the virtual reality state data update module was as follows:

```
//get parameters from accelerometer
double ax=accelerometerData.acceleration.x;
double ay=accelerometerData.acceleration.y;
double az=accelerometerData.acceleration.z;
            //determine the action mode
NSString *state_motion = [self check_Shake:ax ay:ay
                az:az];
        if (state_motion == @"shake") {
    // virtual reality state data update
        [selfperformSelectorOnMainThread:@select
        or(updataAction:) withObject:myself
                waitUntilDone:NO];
                }
```

● VSirtual reality standard format data sending module

The module was a general messages-sending module in the middle layer, which packages returned message of a variety of requests as virtual reality standard format XML message.

● Data management module

Data management module used JDBC-ODBC Bridge to define the basic operation for the database, such as database connection, query, update, insert and delete etc.

4.2   Coordinate Transformation between Geographic Coordinates of Mobile Terminal and Virtual Reality Coordinates of VR Terminal

Coordinate transformation is indispensable to be converted through algorithm due to the complete differences between frame of reference of geographical coordinates and virtual reality coordinates. The system used the following algorithm:

Geographic coordinates (Longitude and Latitude) of three points would be measured at the campus perimeter, and marked as A(Alng, Alat), B(Blng,Blat),

C(Clng,Clat). Meanwhile, geographic coordinates of the same points would be measured in virtual reality environment, marked as A(Ax,Ay), B(Bx,By), C(Cx,Cy). As shown in the following figure, it was coordinate transformation of point E between geographical coordinates and virtual reality coordinates. Formula was shown as follows:

$$\frac{Elng - Alng}{Blng - Alng} = \frac{Ex - Ax}{Bx - Ax},$$
$$\frac{Elat - Alat}{Clat - Alat} = \frac{Ey - Ay}{Cy - Ay} \qquad (1)$$

4.3   The Actual Effect of the Foreground

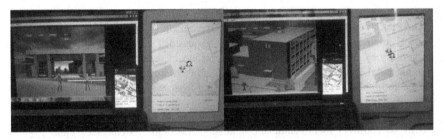

Fig. 8. The renderings of Desktop client, mobile client based on iOS and Android platform

5   Conclusion

This paper did deeply research into the key technology of distributed virtual reality system, which was a lightweight, low-cost, quasi-real-time system on the basis of an in-depth analysis of its architecture. Simultaneously, the system prototype was developed, and the quasi-real-time interaction of position and behavior between the mobile real-time system and virtual reality system was realized.

References

1. Luo, X., Sun, Z.Q., Guo, G.Q.: Hypersonic vehicle simulation system based on distributed virtual reality. Journal of University of Science and Technology 34(1) (2012)
2. Nan, N.: The Web-3d Based Interactive Virtual Community Research and Implementation. Southwest Jiaotong University, Sichuan (2011)
3. Li, J.: Research and implemention of universal mobile office platform. Yanshan University (2011)
4. Yu, Z., Zheng, M., Chen, X.: Android SDK development case. Post & Telecom Press, Beijing (2009)

An Improved DES Anti-DPA Algorithm and Its Automatic Simulation System

Jingjing Liu, Shiwei Ma[*], Guanghua Chen, Hui Tao, Long Qin, and Weimin Zeng

School of Mechatronic Engineering & Automation,
Shanghai Key Laboratory of Power Station Automation Technology,
Shanghai University, NO.149,Yanchang Rd.,
200072 Shanghai, China
masw@shu.edu.cn

Abstract. Based on the analysis of DES cryptographic algorithms and anti-attack strategy, this paper proposes an advanced DES anti-DPA attack algorithm by further improving the Mask method in the power consumption points and the simplicity of working codes. And then, we focus on establishing the algorithm and the validation model by using SystemC, after completing the circuit design of such a DES cryptographic coprocessor that meets the requirement of NFC applications. In order to reduce the development time and costs, we construct a set of automatic simulation system for SystemC model and the RTL circuit. Results of the simulation of this experiment procedure are given to prove the proposed algorithm and design effective.

Keywords: DES algorithms, anti-DPA attack, automatic simulation.

1 Introduction

During the past decade, the technology of NFC[1] (Near Field Communication) deduced from the contactless RFID and interoperability technology is used for near field communication, which has been widely applied in such service sectors as contactless payment, traffic ticket booking, and consumption discount feedback. The most important security mechanism of the NFC internal chip is the integrated modules of encryption/decryption algorithms which have existed some familiar algorithms nowadays, such as RSA(Rivest, Shamir, Adleman), ECC(Elliptic Curve Cryptosystem), AES(Advanced Encryption Standard), DES[2] (Data Encryption Standard).

With the development and widespread applications of the NFC chips, it is neither realistic nor economic that we rely on the method of artificial analysis and routine testing tools to figure out the fault of NFC cryptographic coprocessor circuit, which has gradually exposed their weaknesses. So the automatic simulation system of cryptographic algorithms is becoming the favor of industry. According to this situation, an automatic simulation system based on the improved DES anti-DPA [3] (differential power analysis) attack algorithm is presented.

---

[*] Corresponding author.

T. Xiao, L. Zhang, and S. Ma (Eds.): ICSC 2012, Part II, CCIS 327, pp. 168–174, 2012.

2   Improved DES Anti-DPA algorithm

2.1   DES Algorithm Introduction

DES algorithm is Secret-key cryptography, which can provide its users with unconditional security on condition that the users share a sufficiently long secret key beforehand. DES was developed by IBM in 1975 and it was adopted as a standard two years later. It employs very simple arithmetic operations and therefore it can easily be implemented in hardware, where it can reach very high speeds of encryption. However, because it consists of an initial and final permutation and 16 rounds of main processing with each round transforming the input bits via a "mix and mash" process, the power signal has some evident characters during the period of operation, and the attacker could get the hardware power consumption easily. During the DPA attack, the attackers collect the power signal firstly, and then analyze the information of DES power curves. So DPA is a fearful threat for currently crypt-system, and designing a kind of secure DES algorithm module anti-DPA is importantly meaningful to NFC information security fields.

2.2   The Improved DES Anti-DPA Algorithm

Based on the section 2.1, the main object of DPA attack is a kind of crypt-system using the fixed key, so the metabolic sub-key is the main idea to solving DPA problem, which made the relativity between the key value and power curve to zero almost. And Mask is the bridge to finish this function.

Mask [4] is a technology that masking the input or output data of the encryption algorithm by using the random x. Since the x is unknown, the result that is obtained by the DPA is the untrue ending. For logic circuit: $y' = y \oplus x$, for arithmetic circuit: $y' = y + x$. In which, y is the unmasked data, y' is the masked data, x is the random number generating by hardware. As is shown in figure 1, S box is nonlinear in DES anti-DPA algorithm module, so we should modify the original S box in order to adapt to the mask method and make sure the output data from the S box that can eliminate the random number X and get the decrypted data. We can see that,

$$S'\_BOX(A) = S\_BOX(A \oplus E(IP(X)_{(31,0)})) \oplus IP(X \oplus M)_{(31,0)} \qquad (1)$$

So, the input signal of the modified S box is masked by $E(R0')$, and the DES anti-DPA algorithm under this model is described as follows.

1) First, the random number generator produces a 64bit random number X, XOR with the 64bit plaintext M.
2) At the first round of DES encryption operation, $L1 = R0 \oplus (L0' \oplus R0')$, and $R1 = P(S'\_BOX(C)) \oplus L0R0' \oplus L0' \oplus P(L0R0')$.
3) At the last round, exchange the right-left data, XOR with $L0'$ and $R0'$ respectively, and then export the results of the actual encryption after IP inverse permutation.

Compared with ordinary Mask methods [5], the improved algorithm masks the plaintext by adding a random number both in the beginning and the end, which divides the medial variables into multiple variables, so it is not easy to be forecasted. Because of the randomness, the ability of anti-DPA attack is greatly enhanced, which strengthens the security of the system application. In comparison with the literature [6], the improved algorithm can achieve the completely shielded key, and also defense high-order DPA attack by adding the modified S box. Compared with the literature [7,8], it won't only include 83 power consumption points in the flow of algorithm but also doesn't need to import another new constructed function P^{-1}, which can make the entire code simple and feasible, so that the resource utilization rate of the circuit design is reduced and the encryption speed will be increased. So Mask is effective to against DPA attacks.

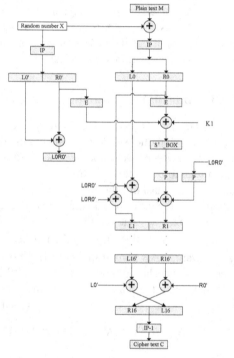

Fig. 1. Procedure of improved DES anti-DPA algorithm

3   Algorithm Model and Circuit Structure

Based on the section 2, we establish the bottom hardware modules of improved DES anti-DPA algorithm on the SystemC platform. The system will generate six 64bit input data randomly, and then compare the improved algorithm with the original algorithm and the literatures [6, 7, 8]. If the comparison is consistent, the final results of encryption/decryption are exported; otherwise, the system will display error data and address and stop comparing. After testing, the results of these algorithms are completely consistent, which manifests that the improved algorithm is correct.

In view of the above improved DES anti-DPA algorithm and the SystemC algorithm model, we complete the DES cryptographic coprocessor which can be embedded into the NFC security system as an independent IP core. During the circuit design, area and speed is always a pair of contradictions. The method of this paper adopts a time-sharing circuit structure, which makes a reasonable compromise between speed and area for the requirements of NFC application. In the time-sharing circuit, the results will be temporarily stored in the registers after the completion of the operation and will be called to complete the current operation at the next cycle. After working out the basic circuits, we just need a set of basic circuit and temporary registers to complete the circuit operations at 16 clock cycles. Thus it can reduce the area of the chips effectively. The circuit structure of cryptographic coprocessor is shown in figure 2.

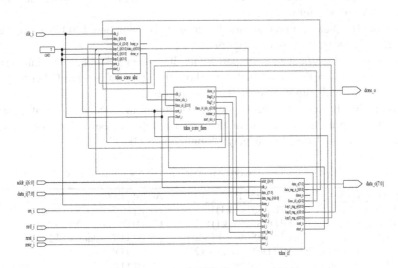

Fig. 2. The circuit structure of DES Cryptographic Coprocessor

4   Automatic Simulation System Based on SystemC and RTL

Considering the typical design, require a lot of critical data and random tests to verify the functionality and performance of circuit at the same time, usually take up about 2/3 of the entire design cycle time, therefore, we need an authentication method that is efficient and accurate to improve the efficiency of verification as soon as possible. Many complex processes, unfortunately, do not yield to this design procedure and have, therefore, not yet been automated. On basis of the above, we are considering designing an automatic simulation system based on the modularity. Each module can be tested separately and the testing result is different and also can be tested with superposition combination and can't affect the result of each module. However, if we input the test data and view the waveform manually, it makes the entire validation process at lower degree and difficult to achieve the requirements of the validation quickly. So, automatic simulation is necessary.

This paper establishes a set of automatic simulation system between SystemC algorithm model and RTL (Register Transfer Level) circuit. By defining the Read/ Write communication transactions to exchange the data in order to ensure synchronous operation, it has nothing to do with the protocol, and usually does not involve the bus timing and other details. Using this authentication method, it can compare a number of dynamic test data at any time as needed, which the chip development cycle can be shorten and the human and material cost can be saved. The described function of the bottom hardware in the automatic simulation system is given in Table 1. The automatic simulation steps are as follows:

1) First, run the SystemC algorithm model, generate six 64-bit input data randomly, then output the value of F0~Fb when the Timer=1, and then write the value to the DAT files in turn.

2) In the Test bench, initialize the Timer=0, Loop Number=1000 (the number of cycles=1000), then run the script of Test bench.

3) Read the value of.dat file, compared with the value of F0~Fb, if the data result is consistent, then the Test bench will show the value of F0~Fb; Otherwise, stop comparing and output the error data and address.

4) In the Test bench, set Timer+1, begin to compare the second round of algorithm results, repeat steps 1,2,3 until the Timer=Loop Number=1000, then stop the automatic simulation and display: "Simulation is OK!!"

Table 1.   The described function of the bottom hardware

Function description	Not added rand	Added rand
ECB_DES Encrypt	F0: E{DES(data,k1)}	F0: E{DES(data, k1,rand)}
ECB_DES Decrypt	F1: D{DES(data, k1)}	F1: D{DES(data, k1,rand)}
ECB_TDES Encrypt	F2: E{TDES(data, k1,k2)}	F2: E{TDES(data, k1,k2,rand)}
ECB_TDES Decrypt	F3: D{TDES(data, k1,k2)}	F3: D{TDES(data, k1,k2,rand)}
ECB_TDES Encrypt	F4: E{TDES(data, k1,k2,k3)}	F4: E{TDES(data, k1,k2,k3,rand)}
ECB_TDES Decrypt	F5: D{TDES(data, k1,k2,k3)}	F5: D{TDES(data, k1,k2,k3,rand)}
CBC_DES Encrypt	F6: E{DES(data,k1)}	F6: E{DES(data, k1,rand)}
CBC_DES Decrypt	F7: D{DES(data, k1)}	F7: D{DES(data, k1,rand)}
CBC_TDES Encrypt	F8: E{TDES(data, k1,k2)}	F8: E{TDES(data, k1,k2,,rand)}
CBC_TDES Decrypt	F9: D{TDES(data, k1,k2)}	F9: D{TDES(data, k1,k2,rand)}
CBC_TDES Encrypt	Fa: E{TDES(data, k1,k2,k3)}	Fa: E{TDES(data, k1,k2,k3,rand)}
CBC_TDES Decrypt	Fb: D{TDES(data, k1,k2,k3)}	Fb: D{TDES(data, k1,k2,k3,rand)}

5   Simulation Results

After the design is completed, we use the simulation tool, Modelsim, to simulate the design circuit. The simulation waveforms are shown in figure 3 for DES anti-DPA algorithm, and its work principle is: under the control signal, 64 bits plaintexts and 56 bits key are inputted in turn, then the control flag word for encrypt/decrypt is inputted, in which 1 means decrypt and 0 means encrypt. When the read signal is 1, the contents of control register are read out, and encrypt/decrypt don't end unless the low order bit for control word is 0. And the simulation results with the Mask X are the same as ones without X, which shows that the mask algorithm is correct. Meanwhile, it is obvious that the attackers will only get the wrong key during the DPA attack.

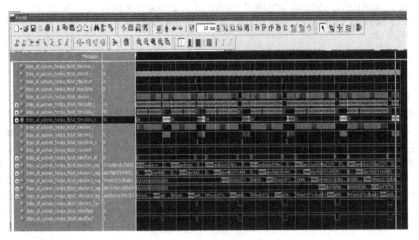

Fig. 3. The simulation waveforms of DES Cryptographic Coprocessor

Fig. 4. The automatic simulation results between SystemC and RTL

The Automatic simulation of comparison results between SystemC algorithm model and RTL circuit are shown in Figure 4, in which Timer shows the number of compare times, and this figure only gives the value of 98th automatic simulation results. It shows that the results of improved DES algorithm model under 1000 sets of random automated testing process are consistent. So the improved algorithm is correct. Automation simulation test makes the process which has required several weeks or several months reduce to only a few hours or days.

6   Conclusions

In this paper, the advanced DES algorithm is given according to DPA principal, and its effectiveness is illuminated in simply mathematics. Furthermore, in order to take efficient and precise verification measures to improve test efficiency and find out the design flaw as soon as possible, we establish the automatic simulation system between SystemC algorithm model and RTL circuits, which we can proceed the dynamic matching of test times and test results as required, shorten the development cycle of the NFC chip and save manpower and material costs. This paper indicates that the design of the anti-DPA attack DES algorithm can satisfy the design requirements of NFC application.

References

1. Ortiz Jr., S.: Is Near-Field Communication Close to Success, 18–20. IEEE Computer Society (March 2006)
2. Data Encryption Standard. Federal Information Processing Standard (FIPS) Publication 46, National Bureau of Standards. US Department of Commerce, Washington, DC (1977)
3. Kocher, P., Jaffe, J., Jun, B.: Differential Power Analysis. In: Proceedings of Advances in Cryptography, California, USA, August 15-19, pp. 388–397 (1999)
4. Chari, S., Jutla, C.S., Rao, J.R., Rohatgi, P.: Towards Sound Approaches to Counteract Power-Analysis Attacks. In: Wiener, M. (ed.) CRYPTO 1999. LNCS, vol. 1666, pp. 398–412. Springer, Heidelberg (1999)
5. Messerges, T.S.: Securing the AES Finalists Against Power Analysis Attacks. In: Schneier, B. (ed.) FSE 2000. LNCS, vol. 1978, pp. 150–162. Springer, Heidelberg (2001)
6. Jiang, H., Mao, Z.: Advanced DES Algorithm against Differential Power Analysis and its Hardware Implementation. Journal of Computer 27(3), 334–338 (2004)
7. Li, H., Zhou, Y.: Advanced DES Algorithm against Differential Power Analysis. Communications Technology 40(11), 277–279 (2007)
8. Han, J., Zeng, X., Tang, T.: VLSI Design of Anti-Attack DES Circuits. Chinese Journal of Semiconductors 26(8), 1646–1652 (2005)

The Model of Target Value Judgment
Based on Fuzzy Logic Illation System

Wei Chen, Haiyang Zhu, Feng Qiu, Bo Sun, and Mingqi Guan

Department of Logistics Command, Air Force Logistic College, Xuzhou, 221000, China
13775989848@139.com

Abstract. By applying the theory of fuzzy logic illation system into the model of target value judgment, this paper implements the model by fuzzy logic toolbox of Matlab. This model can full utilize the experience of specialist and target information of target value element. It can offer a scientific and effective support for commander.

Keywords: Fuzzy logic, Expert system, target value judgment, Mamdani fuzzy inference process.

1   Introduction

Target value judgment is also called target value evaluation. Main elements include that base on collecting the target information and the target analytical method; we can conclude the target value judgment. It can provide basis for decision-maker assigning force and firepower. Target value judgment can direct impact the firepower's distribution and use; it can direct impact the battle effectiveness and the weapon efficiency exertion. Base on joint operations of informationization, it is a lot of troop, information and target. So if we want to get the efficiency in process of joint operations, we need evaluate target value judgment and assign force and firepower in reason. Zadeh introduced fuzzy logic theory since 1965. It used for many domains in many situations successfully. It models human thinking process and natural language enabling decision making [1-4]. The fuzzy logic theory can full utilize the experience of specialist and target information of target value element. It can offer a scientific and effective support for operation decision-maker.

2   The Structure of Target Value Judgment's Model

Firstly, base on joint operations characteristic, both sides operation situation and weapon efficiency, we need establish the target value judgment's rules as a knowledge repository. Secondly, we need gain some target information and treat it with integration information. Lastly, the model can utilize the target value judgment's rules and integration information and gain the result that we want to. Furthermore if some target value judgment's rules are out of place, we can change it in time and accord with the fact.

T. Xiao, L. Zhang, and S. Ma (Eds.): ICSC 2012, Part II, CCIS 327, pp. 175–180, 2012.

3   The Structure of the Knowledge Repository and Illation System

The information repository is a hardcore of system. It makes up of two parts: the factual knowledge and the illation knowledge. It is the primary condition that comes into being the target value judgment's rules. As to target value judgment's model, the factual knowledge refer to the sanction in joint operations; the illation knowledge refer to the chief factors in target value judgment.

3.1   The Sanction in the Joint Operations

It makes up of three parts: the material sanction, the space sanction and the time sanction. The material sanction refer to all kinds of weapons must be in normal preparedness. If NO. I Weapon is in normal preparedness, we record $K_i = 1$, otherwise $K_i = 0$.

The space sanction refer to the target locates the space area. If NO.I Weapon can shoot the NO.J target, it must satisfy that distance locates $d_{min} \leq d_{ij} \leq d_{max}$ and height locates $h_{min} \leq h_{ij} \leq h_{min}$. If NO.I Weapon is can shoot the NO. J target, we record $P_{ij} = 1$ otherwise $P_{ij} = 0$.

The time sanction refer to there is relation between the time that target stays in shooting range and the minimal period that weapons shoot. If NO.I Weapon can shoot the NO.J target, the time that target stays in shooting range must satisfy that $t_{ij} \geq T_{min}$. We record $T_i = 1$, otherwise $T_i = 0$.

3.2   The Main Factors of Target Value Judgment

Fuzzy logic system consists of few inputs, outputs, set of inference rules and a defuzzification method with respect to the selected fuzzy inference system. The main factors of target value judgment makes up of four parts: the target's significance, the target's menace, the target's destructibility and the target's informative credibility.

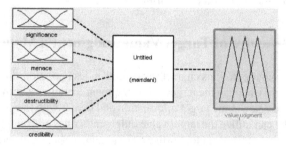

Fig. 1. The main factors of target value judgment

The target's significance refers to the target's station and function in joint operations. It's range from 0 to 1. The bigger number implies the more importance scale of the target's significance. Mathematics formula accord with gauss distribution [5]:

$$f(x) = \begin{cases} e^{-x^2}, & 0 \leq x \leq 0.7 \\ e^{-(x-5)^2}, & 0.2 \leq x \leq 0.8 \\ e^{-(x-1)^2}, & 0.3 \leq x \leq 1 \end{cases} \tag{1}$$

The image of Mathematics formula is Gaussian curve:

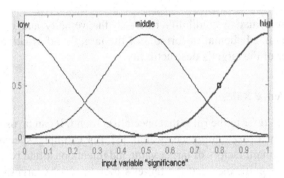

Fig. 2. The Gaussian curve of the target's significance

The target's menace refers to the target's threaten our troop in joint operations. It's range from 0 to 1. The bigger number implies the more danger scale of the target's menace. Mathematics formula resembles the Mathematics formula of the target's significance.

The target's destructibility refers to the target's quality of being capable of destruction. It relate to the structure, shape, key position and the ammunition power. We can describe the target's destructibility as bigness or smallness. Mathematics formula accord with trapezoidal membership function[6-7]:

$$gh(x) = \begin{cases} 1, & 0 \leq x \leq 0.3 \\ \dfrac{0.7 - x}{4}, & 0.3 \leq x \leq 0.7 \\ 0, & x \geq 0.7 \end{cases} \tag{2}$$

$$gl(x) = \begin{cases} 0, & 0 \leq x \leq 0.3 \\ \dfrac{x}{4}, & 0.3 \leq x \leq 0.7 \\ 1, & x \geq 0.7 \end{cases} \tag{3}$$

The image of Mathematics formula is trapezium:

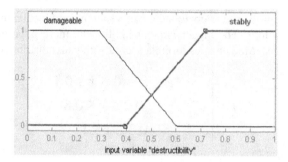

Fig. 3. The trapezium of the target's destructibility

The target's informative credibility refers to the veracity and opportunity about target's information. Mathematics formula of the target's informative credibility has similarity number of the target's destructibility.

3.3   The Inference Rules

The inference rules refer to the rules that specialists found. It can be used to inspect the rules being used by a fuzzy inference system. [8]. For example, specialists found one inference rule: the main factors of target value judgment constitute two parts. It makes up of the target's significance and the target's menace. If the target's significance is high and the target's menace, the target value judgment must be high. This inference rule can describe as:

IF the target's significance is high and the target's menace is high Then the target value judgment is high.

IF we want to acquire the inference rules, we can exert the specialist's consultant theory. We can implements the inference rules refer by fuzzy logic toolbox of Matlab.To uses this editor to create rules, we must first have all of the input and output variables we want to use defined with the FIS editor. We can create the rules using the list box and check. The inference rules of fuzzy expert system make use of 36 fuzzy rules which are adaptive to give decisions for different situation.

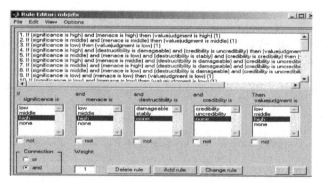

Fig. 4. The inference rules

3.4   The Fuzzy Logic Mechanism

Let $X_i = [E_{\max i}, E_{\min i}] (i = 1,2,...n)$ be the universe of input variable $x_i = (1.2....n)$ and let $Y = [U_{\max}, U_{\min}]$ be the universe of output variable y. $\Psi_i = \{A_{ij}\}(j = 1,2,...m)$ stand for the fuzzy sets X_i and $\Phi_j = \{B_j\}$ stand for the fuzzy logic setting Y. The inference rule is formed as follows [9]:

R : IF x is A THEN y is B

Fuzzy relation formula Rc is formed as follows:

$$Rc = A \times B = \int_{X \times Y} \mu_A(x) \wedge \mu_B(y) \quad f(x, y)$$

If x is A' and the arithmetic is the Mamdani of fuzzy inference process. The Mamdani fuzzy inference is based on an implication function minimum (Min) and aggregation function maximum (Max). Therefore, it is also known as Min-Max rule. the fuzzy logic system formula is formed as follows:

$$B' = A' \circ R$$
$$= \int \vee (\mu_A(x) \wedge (\mu_A(x) \wedge \mu_B(y)))$$

4   Calculation Results

By applying the theory of fuzzy logic illation system into the model of target value judgment, this paper implements the model by fuzzy logic toolbox of Matlab. In case of target appear and parameter appeases all sanctions in the joint operations. The main factors of target value judgment compose four parts: the target's significance, the target's menace, the target's destructibility and the target's informative credibility. Its parameters show the Fig.5:

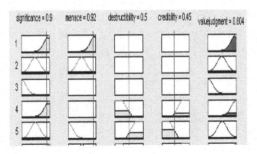

Fig. 5. The parameters and result

We can draw the conclusion that the target value is 0.804.

5   Conclusions

The fuzzy logic illation system provides a greater flexibility to the model of target value judgment by acquiring military expert knowledge. The rules in the fuzzy expert system describe the relationship between the target's significance, the target's menace, the target's destructibility and the target's informative credibility. According as requirement, we can add and reduce the inference rules at any moment. In practice, the system obtains obvious effects.

References

1. Meitzler, T., Reynolds, T., Sharma, V., Singh, H., Dixit, A.M., Mekki, A.: Fuzzy Logic for Determination of Crack Severity in Defense Applications. ADA528479 (2010)
2. Zadeh, L.: Fuzzy sets. Inform. Control 8(3), 338–353 (1965)
3. Mondel, J.: Fuzzy logic systems for engineering: A tutorial. Proc. IEEE 83, 345–377 (1995)
4. Das, H.C., Parhi, D.R.: Online fuzzy logic crack detection of a cantilever beam. International Journal of Knowledge-Based and Intelligent Engineering Systems, 157–171 (December 2008)
5. Kamthan, S., Singh, H., Dixit, A.M.: Fuzzy Logic Approach for Impact Source Identification in Ceramic Plates. ADA525952 (2009)
6. Wang, L.: Model Predictive Control System Design and Implementation Using MATLAB. Springer-Verlag London Limited (2009)
7. Li, R.J.: Fuzzy method in group decision making. Computers and Mathematics with Applications 38(1), 91–101 (1999)
8. Chen, W., He, H.: Application of fuzzy logical inference system in target damage analysis. Electronics and Control 11(15), 63–65 (2008) (in Chinese)
9. Cao, D.-Y., Zeng, S.-P., Li, J.-H.: Variable universe fuzzy expert system for aluminum electrolysis. Transactions of Nonferrous Metals Society of China 02(4), 429–436 (2011)
10. Wen, X., Zhou, L.: The Analysis and Application of MATLAB Fuzzy Logic Tool Box. The Science Publishing Company, Beijing (December 2002) (in Chinese)

Research of Quick Processing Mechanism for Massive Battlefield Situation Data in Combat Simulation

Wei Shao, Xiying Huang, and Dinghai Zhao

Academy of Armored Force Engineering, Beijing 100072

Abstract. In the combat simulation, the battlefield situation data need be stored and visualized, but battlefield situation data volume is becoming larger, it is difficult to handle, we build compression and decompression mechanism to solve the problem, we also improve the visualization mechanism, the situation information is divided into static type and dynamic type, in the simulation process the dynamic information need be handled from the beginning to the end. Through the two kinds of mechanisms the situation data is handled effectively.

Keywords: combat simulation, battlefield situation dat, visualization, compression, decompression.

1   Introduction

The battlefield simulation data is mainly used to record the changes of battlefield simulation in Combat Simulation, simulation system shows the situation data to users by visualization tools. The situation data comprises the maneuver and combat state of combat unit, if the simulation process and small changes in the battlefield can be mastered by users, the battlefield situation data should be recorded in detail.

The battlefield situation data volume has greatly increased, along with the expansion of the simulation scale and the improvement of simulation accuracy, so it's difficult to process situation data, for example the burthen of visualization for battlefield simulation is increasing, the storage space for situation data is becoming more and more large. In order to solve this problem, we design the real-time data compression and decompression mechanism, also improve the battlefield situation visualization mechanism according to the large data volume, we only process the changes of battlefield situation. The storage space of situation data can be reduced using the two mechanisms, efficiency of situation visualization can also be improved.

2   The Compression and Decompression Mechanism of Battlefield Situation Data in Combat Simulation

If you want to effectively compress or decompress the battlefield situation data, you should explicitly understand the transformation process of simulation data, then you

T. Xiao, L. Zhang, and S. Ma (Eds.): ICSC 2012, Part II, CCIS 327, pp. 181–186, 2012.

can determine the time when the situation data is compressed or decompressed. If the time you selected is reasonable, the compression or decompression can be achieved easily, on the other hand the execution of other modules will not be affected, if the time you selected isn't reasonable, the system may not run normally.

2.1   The Research of Information Transformation in Combat Simulation

The transformation process of information is shown below:

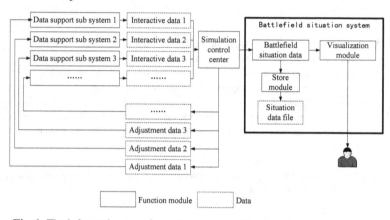

Fig. 1. The information transformation graphs of Combat simulation system

The each data support system interact one another through simulation control center, then they can achieve synchronization. For example a command post issues command to reconnaissance units, the command should be issued through simulation control center, then the control center generates adjustment data, the each data support system can continue to run according to the adjustment data. The control center also generates the nowaday battlefield situation data and provides the data to the situation system, the situation data is showed to the user by the situation system, also is stored as file.

You should understand the generation process and transformation process of various information, then you can clearly understand the mechanism of compression and decompression.

2.2   The Treatment Process of Battlefield Situation Data

The battlefield situation data volume is large, so the treatment of situation data will cost a lot computer resources including computation time of CPU and memory space. In order to take advantage of computer hardware performance, we design the multithreading mechanism to process situation data, in the real time simulation the treatment process of battlefield situation data is shown below:

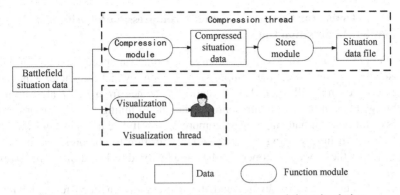

Fig. 2. The treatment process of situation data in real time simulation

After the situation data is built in real time simulation, we start two threads to deal with the data, the compression thread is mainly responsible for compressing and preserving the data, the visualization thread is mainly responsible for showing battlefield situation. The two threads can keep synchronization by reading synchronization information, then the situation data can't be missing.

In the simulation playback the treatment process of situation data is shown below:

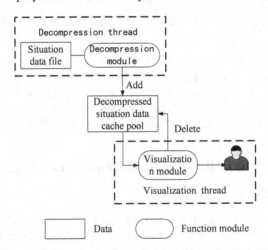

Fig. 3. The treatment process of situation data in the simulation playback

In the simulation playback, the decompression thread is responsible for decompressing data file, and transferring the data to cache pool, the visualization thread is responsible for read situation data from cache pool and showing situation, the visualization thread will delete the situation data from cache pool after showing completely.

2.3   The Selection for Compression and Decompression Algorithm of Battlefield Situation Data

The battlefield situation data volume is large and renewal speed of situation data is very fast, so we should select the compression algorithm which is efficient, then other modules can run normally. DEFLATE algorithm comes from LZ77 algorithm, the algorithm will cost a little system resources when it is running, and the algorithm can compress a lot types of data, now many compression software use this algorithm[1].

We select zlib library using the DEFLATE algorithm to compress the battlefield situation data, the library is open, it has gradually developed into the industry standard.

We mainly use the compression and decompression functions to deal with the situation data[2]:

Compression:

Function: int compress (Bytef *dest, uLongf *destLen, const Bytef *source, uLong sourceLen);

Action: Compressing the source buffer to aim buffer.

Decompression:

Fuction: int uncompress (Bytef *dest,uLongf *destLen,const Bytef *source, uLong sourceLen);

Action: Decompressing the source buffer to aim buffer.

The compression and decompression can be achieved using the function. After we do experiment, we find that the compression ratio is high, and other modules can't be affected. For example, before compressing the size of situation data file is 40GB, after compressing the size is 1.5GB,   compression ratio is 0.0375:1.

3   The Research of Battlefield Situation Visualization Mechanism

Battlefield situation visualization is a type of dynamic view, its basic principle is the same as animation building, the time axis is scattered into sequence, there is a picture of the battlefield situation at every moment, we show the seriate picture according to the time sequence, then the dynamic situation view is built. This can reflect the change and development trend of battlefield situation[3].

In order to show the situation map of every time, we should deal with the situation data of every time, the situation data volume is large, if we do not distinguish the situation data, the burden of visualization will increase. So we should distinguish the situation data, after the initial situation is loaded, we only deal with the variational information, it will greatly reduce the computer burden.

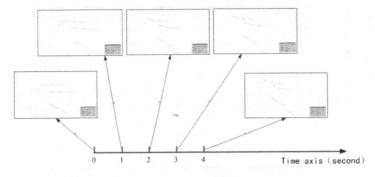

(second 0 is XXXX(year):X(month):X(day) X(hour):X(minute):X(second))

Fig. 4. Situation visualization diagram

According to the change, we can divide the situation information into static information and dynamic information[4], static information mainly includes mark information, such as name, dynamic information includes the current position, damage state and other information. The construction of battlefield situation system is different, the type of situation information is different, but we can distinguish the information as change.

4 The Visualization Example of Battlefield Situation Visualization

The showing of battlefield situation can be fluent using above-mentioned treatment. In this paper, we construct the battlefield situation system using two-dimension military geographic information system (MGIS) as frame, the effect is shown below:

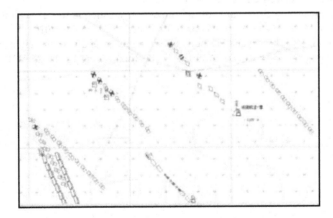

Fig. 5. Damage state

Fig. 6. Fire situation

5   Conclusions

We compress and decompress battlefield situation data using multithreading mechanism, we also improve the showing mechanism, the showing of situation is fluent, on the other hand we can sufficiently use the computer advantage. Combining with many experiments, if the scale of simulation is becoming large, two threads are not enough, we can rely on high-powered computer, for example the blade computer, start multiple threads to deal with, the efficiency will be greatly increased.

References

1. Zhu, G.: The development and present situation of image's compression technology. Journal of Chongqing Communication Academy 3, 43–45 (1997)
2. Wei, L., Zhu, W.: The research and application of data compression technology. Flight Control and Photoelectric Detection 2, 45–47 (2011)
3. Wei, S.: Research on aggregation of two dimension situation in war game system of army tactics corps. Academy of Armored Forces Engineering 12, 35–36 (2010)
4. Huang, X.: Research on situation building in command and control system with tactics level of army corps. Academy of Armored Forces Engineering 12, 23–25 (2010)

The Study of Three-Dimensional Virtual Battlefield Large Terrain Dynamically Generated

Fanfan Yao[1], Qiang Liang[1], Pei Long[2], and Gaige Huang[3]

[1] Department of Equipment Command and Management of AAFE, Beijing, 100072
[2] Military Representation Department of 127 Factory, Qiqihaer Heilongjiang Province, 110015
[3] Logistics Academy, Beijing, 100858

Abstract. Large terrain three-dimensional visualization immediacy impact third dimension immersion and of virtual battlefield and cover area of warfare simulation mission .Aim at the characteristic of virtual battlefield large terrain visualization, emphasize the study large area terrain visualization technic, and take Digital Elevation Model and satellite photograph of northwest area of China as source data, use multilayer LOD and Virtual Texture, predigest grid and terrain division technic, and use three-dimensional modeling software Creator Terrain studio made a block of large terrain of area about 400X400km2 ,and fulfill the demand of three-dimensional virtual battlefield of warfare simulation.

Keywords: Large Terrain, Dynamic scheduling, Virtual Texture, CTS, Virtual Battlefield.

1 Introduction

With the development of simulation technic, more and more three-dimensional virtual battlefield visualization simulation technic has been used in the research of battlefield circumstance. The modern war has been cooperate with multi Force joint operations, and this made the space and depth of battlefield unprecedented extend, and also the range of battlefield has become a integrative area which include sea, land, air and out space area. So, it is ineluctability that display and disposal large area three-dimensional virtual battlefield in battlefield circumstance visualization simulation and large area visualization simulation has been a hot point of battlefield circumstance three-dimensional visualization simulation research. In application of large terrain three-dimensional virtual battlefield, because of the limit of large area there should been disposal a great deal of terrain data model and terrain texture data, so we should take use of special new technic and method to conquer the physical limit of graphics hardware when disposal large terrain visualization data base.

In this paper, combine with development of three-dimensional virtual battlefield warfare simulation system, based on modeling software of CTS (Creator Terrain studio), the key technic of large terrain simulation has been studied which include virtual texture technic, protract of multi LOD and division block attemper technic and

T. Xiao, L. Zhang, and S. Ma (Eds.): ICSC 2012, Part II, CCIS 327, pp. 187–194, 2012.
© Springer-Verlag Berlin Heidelberg 2012

arithmetic, and last use three-dimensional modeling software Creator Terrain studio made a block of large terrain of area about 400X400km^2 of northwest of China.

2   Synopsis of CTS Software

As so far, more and more visualization simulation and training need combine with high definition satellite photograph, and at same time equality precision Digital Elevation Model are also needed, and thousands upon thousands culture characteristic were distributed in it. It needs which covered terrain area from larger to larger, sometimes it exceed 100Km x 100Km, and summation of data need GB to weigh. Creator Terrain Studio (CTS) was specially design for this , and it was the most advanced large terrain generation tool which belongs MPI Co., main characteristic of CTS as follow[1][2]:

1) Data management and expansively
2) work flow management
3) State management
4) antetype design and iterative
5) Preview 3D and MetaFligh format
6) CTS support more format of data and this reduce demand of data source
7) Though the management of work flow improves the intuitionistic and real time of task management
8) Use grid stack manage data make data predigest and display become easier.

At the same time, CTS afford a powerfully work flow and data management tool, assistant user establish precisely and dependability large terrain database more efficiency in short time. Chart1 is main interface of CTS [3].

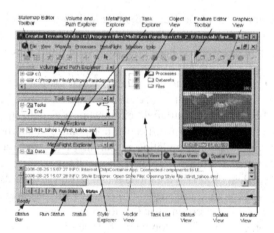

Fig. 1. Main interface of CTS

3   Key Technic of Large Terrain Simulation

3.1   Virtual Texture Technic

The basic idea of large area and high definition texture Real-time display is that divided large texture into small blocks and only takes in the part which near view point. and also the near view point part take in the high definition texture , the parts far away view point take in low precisely texture[2]. In this paper we take use of virtual texture technic to divided large texture.

The root of virtual texture technic is Clipmapping technic under platform of SGI. The framework of this technic is Level + Tile, as chart 2. The level starts from 1×1 texture and doubly increases level after level until the highest level. And every level covers the all area of terrain. From level 1 to level 9 are only one texture cover the entire terrain, size from 1×1 to 512×512₀ From the level 10 it has 2×2 blocks of 512×512 texture, and the level 11 has 4×4 blocks of 512×512 texture, till the highest level.

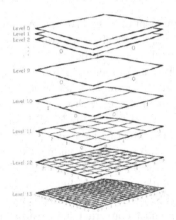

Fig. 2. The architecture virtual texture

When we run terrain database real time the Vega Prime selected a virtual texture from level of VT base on the position of view point automatically, and this is key of optimization. So the calculate of theoretically usage of texture memory as follow:

$$SizeX \times SizeY \times (R+G+B+A) \times ColorDepth \times (N+1.3)/8192000[2] \tag{1}$$

There into, N was the number from the highest level to the level 10.

3.2   Multilayer LOD（Level Of Detail）

The level of detail (LOD) is what the premise does not affect the actual simulation results, by successive simplify the details of the model to reduce the complexity of the model, thereby improving the efficiency of the scene rendering. To hierarchical structure of the virtual texture, 3D terrain generation also need to be reasonable hierarchical / processing by blocks, and in the corresponding layer, the size of terrain block must be less than or equal to the size of texture block, so as to show corresponding layer of high-precision texture. In addition, the hierarchical of the terrain and VT layered, there is no need to so as VT divided into ten to twenty layers, in general, in accordance with the LOD stratified set, divided into 4 to 6 layers to meet the application requirements[4]. In this paper, taking into account the 30m definition texture display, the terrain is divided into four layers the LOD, and in accordance with limit of the parameters of the polygon and the number of view frustum, set of LOD distance and polygon structure each LOD

In the process of CTS generate virtual textures and terrain LOD, based on level of hierarchical terrain / hierarchical texture level, automatically generate a file directory structure, and generate a specific the file of MetaFlight format , notice Vega Prime how match and call these block file.

3.3   Hierarchical Scheduling and Algorithm of Large Terrain

Large Area Database Management of Vega Prime, (LADBM) is specifically designed to meet a very large and complex database scheduling needs, in particular, a huge database in a dynamic scene scheduling of tiles and data set loading and organization. With combination of LADBM and MetaFlight format, collaboration between large data sets become more effective, hierarchical data structure of MetaFlight in real-time scene optimization also be maintained. In short, core feature of the Vega Prime s, including double-precision, multi-threaded, the MetaFlight and LADBM provides an optimal solution of virtual simulation of a large area [4].

Paging strategy is divided into two, one is taking scheduling in all the data set of the entire in one time which   for small data set; another is to define a location for the center to this location chosen tiles in the coordinates of the scene graph this is called the Paging strategy point (PSP). If the scene graph and the grid is not the same coordinate system, the PSP must converted the position coordinates of the scene graph to grid coordinates, while to determine which cells of each floor grid scheduling within range of the Strategy's Position Point , and only taking those tiles into the scene. When the strategic position of the point move, who are no longer scheduling within the tiles will be transferred out of the scene, and transferred to the new tile into the policy range. The dispatch central point of LADBM attachment to any object on the VP (as long as it is vpPositon or its derived class objects on the line). PSP does not necessarily follow the point of view; it can be moved to the scene at any point. Vega Prime supports multiple scheduling policies used in a scene, such as in the scene to set up two channels, each channel can have its own scheduling policy. The only restriction is that all data sets which attachment to the scene has the same coordinate system.

The following summarizes is the LADBM workflow in Vega Prime [6]:

(1) If the grid coordinate system and the data coordinate system are inconsistent, transform the strategic position of the coordinate to the coordinates of the grid;

(2) Starting from the lowest level of the LOD, find out which tiles contain the strategic position of the point (or closest to the strategic position of points). Tiles closest to the strategic position of points is not the scope of the strategy, then there will be no paging, contrary to submit a dispatch of the request of the tiles;

(3) Check all adjacent tiles meet the scheduling range until beyond the range of transferred submit the request to dispatch all meet the conditions of tile;

(4) submit a request to tune out those who no longer meet the scheduling range of tiles;

(5) Into the next level of the LOD, repeat steps 2 to 4 until all levels have been processed.

4 Three-Dimensional Virtual Battlefield Large Terrain Generation Based on CTS

4.1 Workflow of CTS

Creator Terrain studio is dedicated terrain-production software, the software which in the production of terrain easily and quickly generates a wide range of terrain and standardized management of topographic data. The picture shows the CTS generate a model of the process:

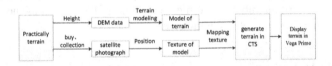

Fig. 3. CTS work flow of terrain generate

The terrain simulation process is what based on flow to produce terrain data, and then publish the MFT final file which called in the Vega Prime terrain management module (LADBM). Use CTS to generate a terrain model data, the main process steps, create texture → create terrain →publish MFT database, the production of each data are based on the process.

4.2 Create Texture Data

In CTS texture creation process is divided into five steps: the List the Dataset Selection → the Grid Dataset Selection →Earth, Selection→the Workflow the Name Prefix→ the Workflow Generation.

Production of the virtual texture need to go through a number of steps can be roughly divided into as shown: the image segmentation, building the structure of the virtual texture grid, fusion, and format conversion, as shown in Figure:

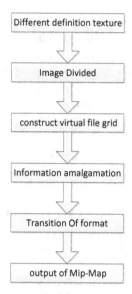

Fig. 4. Process of texture created

Segmentation of the input picture, based on the definition of their image and display precision, respectively, split into im×ik a tile. Each tile corresponds to a file format; sizes of file are 768K bytes. CTS file generated according to a certain format, rules such as the serial number of the tiles where the LOD, as well as the location of the LOD, line number and column number.

4.3   Create Terrain Data

CTS is commonly used Polymesh to generate the grid divided and this is more evenly in a large area of terrain. And as create textures; this process also requires more than one parameter setting process. Design Pattern→Elevation→the Coverage and coordinate system→Terrain design→to Culture projection.

(1) According to the actual need to select terrain types, to facilitate simulation of observe.
(2) Select an information of digital elevation data (DEM data of 160,000 square kilometers of the Northwest China) to create terrain features, in order to build the altitude of the surface, undulating state.
(3) Set Coverage of terrain and the coordinate system. Such as before the texture set, you can choose the existing data and thus provides a good coverage, both basically the same scope and coordinate system settings compared with the previous texture coverage.
(4) Select the default data coordinate system coordinate projection MPI a flat the earth project.

(5) Set the observer perspective for terrain LOD conversion and data dynamic scheduling, field of view for the observer decided to once amount of data of terrain transferred to memory.
(6) Select texture mapping, the final terrain texture and terrain matching mapping.
(7) Add cultural identity.
(8) Select the output path.

After the start of the workflow generation, generate workflow will appear in task and data. To select terrain mesh and start work flow, after a period of time to generate the terrain file.

4.4   Publish MFT File

MFT file is description of the data structure, to facilitate the organization and management of topographic data, and can generally choose to publish certain of the data, including texture and terrain data, including feature information data can also choose to publish. The Publish MetaFlight following the specific location of the Insert→the process→utilities→the Publish. MetaFlight will appear in Figure window after release, select the dataset, and each MFT file containing up to 20 Datasets.

4.5   Display of Large Terrain in Vega Prime

Vega Prime is responsible for managing the MFT file dynamically changer function is the VP LADBM the Paging Strategy. Vega Prime LADBM module in accordance with observer location, take the visual range of the terrain and texture LOD in-out as a reference systemic , refer to the observer coordinate calculation should show the terrain of the terrain area transferred to the remaining area of the memory is not displayed. With the transfer of the observer point of view, the system is about to show the area transferred to the background loaded and ready to display, the before terrain area is out of memory to free up space, this dynamic process of the changer is the actual hard disk and memory and exchange of data between memory and graphics. Determine the dynamic changer will have to refer to the relationship between the Hierarchical terrain data and texture LOD level. Figure 5 show large terrain generated in the VP.

Fig. 5. Large terrain in Vega Prime

5   Conclusion

In combination with the application of three-dimensional terrain of a region of northwest China, to explore the methods to generate large-scale terrain with CTS (Creator Terrain studio), discuss the key technologies of the three-dimensional terrain visualization, for the characteristics of the three-dimensional virtual battlefield warfare simulation effective technical measures has been put forward, with a certain value.

References

1. Yang, J., Li, C., Fei, L.-F.: Simulation applications based on the CTS large terrain. Surveying and Mapping 33(1), 185–187 (2008)
2. Wang, S., Liu, H., Li, Z.: Large terrain modeling and simulation based on CTS. In: 2007 System Simulation Technology and its Applications Conference Proceedings, vol. III, pp. 165–169 (2007)
3. Tong, X., Luo, T., Li, W.: Vega Prime rendering its simulation. Computer and Digital Engineering 36(2), 610–613 (2008)
4. Huang, J., Mao, F.: Based on Vega Prime the large river basins in 3D management system. Journal of System Simulation 18(10), 2819–2824 (2006)
5. Creator Terrain Studio User's Guide (Version 2.0). Multi Gen-Paradigm Inc. (2006)
6. Yao, B., Zhao, H.: Flight visual simulation 3D terrain generation. Journal of System Simulation 3(6), 48–51 (2009)
7. Gao, Y., Yang, H., Di, C., Zhou, Z.: Based on CTS and Vega Prime scene simulation study. Journal of System Simulation 3(6), 38–41 (2008)
8. Vega Prime Options Guide (Version 2.0). Multi Gen-Paradigm, Inc. (2005)
9. Yan, B.: Based on Vega Prime terrain of visual simulation technology, Xi'an University of Electronic Science and Technology

Simulation and Analysis of Space Object Visibility Based on Space-Based Optics Surveillance

Xiangchun Liu[*], Ying Liao, Yuanlan Wen, and Zhi Zhang

College of Astronautics and Material Engineering, National University of Defense Technology,
Changsha, Hunan Province, China
xiaoniu_lxch@163.com

Abstract. The visibility analysis model of space object based on space-based optics surveillance is derived from constraints including the earth masking, the earth shadow, the sunlight and the field of view. According to the orbit distribution character of space objects, we analyzed the visibility of some typical space objects using three groups of observation platform which has low, middle and high orbits respectively. Three helpful results are derived from the simulation experiments. Firstly, the visibility of low orbit space objects is poor, the total time of visible arcs is less than 1 hour in the 24 hours observation. Secondly, there is extremely little influence made by restraints of the earth masking and the earth shadow for the visibility of middle and high orbit space objects. Finally, the visibility of space objects using middle or high orbit observation platform is beneficial than using low orbit observation platform.

Keywords: Space-based Optics Surveillance, Space Object, Visibility.

1 Introduction

Along with the rapid developments of space Science and technology, the capability of dominating the space is increasingly important for the national strategic interest, and many countries have been developing space surveillance system[1] against each other. For the purpose of improving the capability of space surveillance and building the integrated space surveillance system of ground-based and space-based, some great countries such as America and Canada have been developing space-based space surveillance system. America has launched the Midcourse Space Experiment satellite[2] with a Space-Based Visible (SBV[3]) on board in 1996 into an 898-km altitude, near sun-synchronous orbit, which has demonstrated the key technologies of space-based surveillance[4] and has done important job on GEO objects detecting. Six years later, America Military started the Space-Based Space Surveillance

---

[*] This work is partially supported by the Aerospace science and technology innovation fund of China under Grant #CASC201101 to Yuanlan Wen and the National High Technology Research and Development Program of China (863) under Grant #2007AA12Z308 to Liao Ying.

T. Xiao, L. Zhang, and S. Ma (Eds.): ICSC 2012, Part II, CCIS 327, pp. 195–203, 2012.

System(SBSS[5, 6]), a low orbit optics remote sensing satellite constellation, and the first satellite has launched in 2010 into an 630-km altitude, on which fixed an optics detector with a double axis universal foundation support to improve the observation maneuverability and mission adaptability. Besides, For the purpose of improving the tracking capability of space-based surveillance system America plans to deploy an Orbit Deep Space Imager (ODSI) composed by a geostationary orbit satellite constellation.

The space-based optics surveillance system[7-9] is a valuable style of surveillance system owing to its advantages which are integrated from both space-based platform and optics sensor, including wide coverage, low energy cost, high measure accuracy, upstanding concealment and without limit of terrain and weather. However, Space-based optics surveillance system has some inherent restrictions as the earth masking, the earth shadow, the sunlight and the field of view, and the Analysis of Space object visibility based on space-based optics surveillance is significance, moreover, effective surveillance strategies should be made to provide advantages for the next step work of space object orbit determination.

Some profitable works have been done on visibility study of space-based surveillance[10], Lei Liu[11] analyzed the visibility of space-based constellation observation and the influences of visibility induced by the observation equipment. Chaozhen Lan[12, 13] derived an optics visibility determination model from taking into account of the earth masking, the earth light, the earth shadow, the sunlight and the moonlight, and put forward a visibility prediction method of space-based optics observation. Yan Zhao[14] discussed the geometry visibility, optics visibility and equipment visibility by a single surveillance satellite. Huafei Diao[15] studied the pointing strategy of the space-based surveillance for the purpose of improving the efficiency of the GEO objects visibility. According to the orbit distribution character of space objects, the visibility of three typical space objects is simulated and analyzed using three groups of observation platform, the space objects including low earth orbit, sun synchronous orbit and earth synchronous orbit while the observation platform has low, middle and high orbit respectively. Further discussions on observation strategy of space objects with different orbit type are also included in this paper.

2   Constraint Conditions

2.1   The Constraint of the Earth Masking

The constraint of the earth masking is induced by the relative movement between the observation platform, the space object and the earth. As the earth move to the middle of the link line between the observation platform and the space object, the space object is invisible for the observation platform. Actually, the effect of the earth atmosphere should be took into account as to the performance of optical observation equipment. The visibility of space object under the constraint of the earth masking can be calculated by Eq.(1) according to the space geometry relation of the observation platform, the space object and the earth (as fig.1 shows).

$$f = \sqrt{\left|\vec{r}_G^I\right|^2 - \left(R_e + h\right)^2} + \sqrt{\left|\vec{r}_M^I\right|^2 - \left(R_e + h\right)^2} - \left|\vec{r}_M^I - \vec{r}_G^I\right| < 0. \tag{1}$$

where R_e is the average radius of the earth, h is the thickness of the earth atmosphere, $\vec{r}_G^I$ is the position vector of observation platform in J2000 (an initial coordinate system), $\vec{r}_M^I$ is the position vector of space object in J2000.

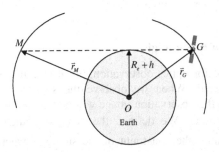

Fig. 1. The constraint of the earth masking

2.2   The Constraint of the Earth Shadow

The constraint of the earth shadow should be considered for the reason that the space object only can be seen on condition of lighted by the sunlight as to optics observation. We defined the factor C_{OD} and C_{DM} to estimate whether the space object is visible under the constraint of the earth shadow.

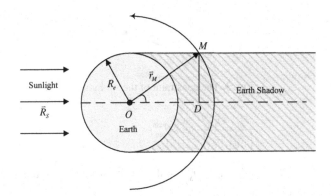

Fig. 2. The constraint of the earth shadow

$$C_{OD} = \vec{r}_M^I \cdot \vec{R}_S^I. \tag{2}$$

$$C_{DM} = \sqrt{\left|\vec{r}_M^I\right|^2 - C_{OD}^{\;2}}. \tag{3}$$

We assume the sunlight is parallel and the earth shadow is columnar, as show in Fig.2. Where "O" represents the earth center and $\bar{R}_S^I$ is the unit position vector of observation platform in J2000. The visibility model of space-based surveillance considering the constraint of the earth shadow can be depicted as

  i.   If $C_{OD} \leq 0$, visible;

  ii.   If $C_{OD} > 0$ and $C_{DM} \geq R_e$, visible;

  iii. If $C_{OD} > 0$ and $C_{DM} < R_e$, invisible.

2.3   The Constraint of the Sunlight

Sunlight is a requirement for optics observation, but it is a disadvantage as to optics imaging on the other hand. When we observe the space object on the negative direction of the sunlight, the observation image will be ambiguous and useless caused by the powerful background. We defined the constraint angle of sunlight θ_{Sun} to analysis the visibility under the constraint of the sunlight, where θ_{Sun} is the angle between the line connecting observation platform and the space object and the line connecting observation platform and the sun (Fig.3). Eq.(4) shows the visibility model of space-based surveillance considering the constraint of the sunlight.

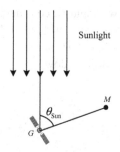

Fig. 3. The constraint of the sunlight

$$\frac{\vec{r}_{GM}^I}{\left|\vec{r}_{GM}^I\right|} \cdot \frac{\vec{r}_{GS}^I}{\left|\vec{r}_{GS}^I\right|} - \cos\theta_{sun}^{min} < 0. \tag{4}$$

where $\vec{r}_{GM}^I = \vec{r}_M^I - \vec{r}_G^I$, $\vec{r}_{GS}^I = \vec{r}_S^I - \vec{r}_G^I$, $\vec{r}_S^I$ is the position vector of the sun in J2000, θ_{sun}^{min} is the critical value of θ_{Sun}.

2.4   The Constraint of the Field of View

2.4.1   The Visibility Model

The field of view, which is limited by the technology of observation equipment and space-based platform, should also take into account for the visibility analysis of space-based optics surveillance. In this instance, we can obtain the visibility of space-based surveillance according to Eq. (5).

$$\frac{\vec{r}_{GM}^{G}}{\left|\vec{r}_{GM}^{G}\right|} \cdot \vec{R}_{O}^{G} - \cos\theta_{fov}^{max} > 0 . \tag{5}$$

where $\vec{r}_{GM}^{G} = M_{GB} \cdot M_{BO} \cdot M_{OI}\vec{r}_{GM}^{I}$, θ_{fov}^{max} (Fig.4)is the critical value of the field of the view, here we define θ_{fov}^{max} as an equivalent angle that including the maneuverability of the observation equipment and the attitude control capability of the platform. M_{GB} is the coordinate transformation matrix from the body coordinate system of observation platform to the observation equipment coordinate system, while M_{BO} is from the orbit coordinate system of observation platform to the body coordinate system of observation platform and M_{OI} is from the J2000 initial coordinate system to the orbit coordinate system of observation platform.

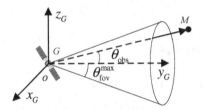

Fig. 4. The constraint of the field of view

2.4.2   Coordinate Transformation

The coordinate system of observation platform is defined as RTN, where "R" represents the radial direction, "T" represents the track direction, "N" represents the normal direction. A new coordinate system that paralleled the RTN coordinate system of the observation platform could be gained by rotating the angle of Ω_{G} , i_{G} and $\omega_{G} + f_{G}$ in the sequence of "3-1-3" from the J2000 initial coordinate system. So M_{OI} can be calculated by Eq.(6).

$$M_{OI} = M_{3}\left(\omega_{G} + f_{G}\right) \cdot M_{1}\left(i_{G}\right) \cdot M_{3}\left(\Omega_{G}\right) . \tag{6}$$

where Ω_{G} , i_{G} , ω_{G} and f_{G} are the right ascension of ascending node, the orbit inclination angle, the argument of perigee and the true anomaly of the observation platform in sequence.

The body coordinate system of observation platform could be gained by rotating the attitude angle of pitch(θ), yaw(ψ) and roll(φ) in the sequence of "3-1-2" from the RTN coordinate system of the observation platform. Similarly, M_{BO} can be calculated by Eq.(7).

$$M_{BO} = M_{2}\left(\varphi\right) \cdot M_{1}\left(\psi\right) \cdot M_{3}\left(\theta\right) . \tag{7}$$

As an example, the transformation matrix can be calculated by Eq.(8) to Eq.(10) with the rotate angle α .

$$M_1(\alpha) = \begin{bmatrix} 1 & 0 & 0 \\ 0 & \cos(\alpha) & \sin(\alpha) \\ 0 & -\sin(\alpha) & \cos(\alpha) \end{bmatrix}. \tag{8}$$

$$M_2(\alpha) = \begin{bmatrix} \cos(\alpha) & 0 & -\sin(\alpha) \\ 0 & 1 & 0 \\ \sin(\alpha) & 0 & \cos(\alpha) \end{bmatrix}. \tag{9}$$

$$M_3(\alpha) = \begin{bmatrix} \cos(\alpha) & \sin(\alpha) & 0 \\ -\sin(\alpha) & \cos(\alpha) & 0 \\ 0 & 0 & 1 \end{bmatrix}. \tag{10}$$

3   Surveillance Strategies

3.1   Orbit Distribution of Space Objects

The orbit distribution of space objects based on the statistic analysis of the catalogue space objects is shown in Table 1. Particularly, most low orbit objects including earth observation satellites and reconnaissance satellites are near-circular orbit, while the middle and high orbit objects are distributed mainly in near-circular orbit and ellipse orbit with big eccentricity.

Table 1. Orbit Distribution of Space Objects

Orbital Elements	Distribution	Percentage
Semimajor Axis	1.15, 4.15 and 6.55(define the earth radius as 1.0)	>90%
Eccentricity	$e < 0.1$, $0.6 < e < 0.75$	About 85%
Inclination	$100°$, $65° \sim 85°$, $0° \sim 15°$	>80%

3.2   Surveillance Strategies

Four groups of observation objects (M1, M2, M3 and M4) are selected according to the orbit distribution of the catalogue space objects. For the purpose of researching the effects of visibility caused by the orbit altitude of the observation platform, we chose three groups of observation platforms (G1, G2 and G3) in the simulation experiments. The orbital elements of both space objects and observation platforms are listed in Table 2.

Table 2. Orbital Elements of Space Objects and Observation Platforms

object	a (km)	e	i (deg)	Ω (deg)	ω (deg)	f (deg)
G1	7078.137	1e-4	98	0	0	0
G2	26469.27	1e-4	98	0	0	0
G3	42164.17	1e-4	98	0	0	0
M1	7334.858	5e-3	98	0	0	0
M2	26469.27	1e-3	2	0	0	0
M3	26469.27	0.7	70	0	0	0
M4	42164.17	0	1e-4	0	0	0

4   Simulation and Analysis

4.1   Simulation Parameters

In all simulations of this paper, the total simulation time span is 24-hours, the simulation step is 5-seconds, and we assumed all of the attitude angles as 0, $R_e = 6378.137$ km, $h = 150$ km, $\theta_{sun}^{min} = 80$ degree, $\theta_{fov}^{max} = 85$ degree.

4.2   Results and Analysis

The simulation results are shown in Fig.5 to Fig.8 according to the surveillance in section 3. In these figures, "Fov" indicates the visibility under the constraint of the field of view, while "Sun" indicates sunlight, "ES" indicates the earth shadow, "EM" indicates the earth masking and "All" indicates the visibility under all of the above constraints.

Three helpful facts can be found as follows by comparing all of the simulation results.

(1) The visibility of low orbit space object(M1) is the worst one in all of the four groups by comparing the average time span of visible arcs.
(2) According to the total time and the number of visible arcs, the visibility of all space objects is the worst by low orbit observation platform.
(3) Little effect is caused by the constraint of the earth shadow and the earth masking for middle and high orbit space objects.

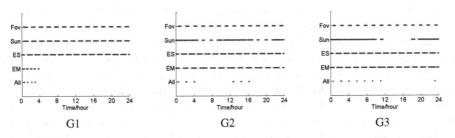

Fig. 5. The Visibility of M1

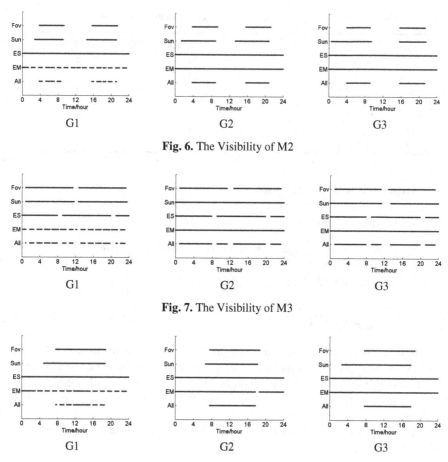

Fig. 6. The Visibility of M2

Fig. 7. The Visibility of M3

Fig. 8. The Visibility of M4

5   Conclusion

According to the orbit distribution character of space objects, the visibility of four groups of classical space objects, which are observed by three observation platforms separately, is studied considering constraints including the earth masking, the earth shadow, the sunlight and the field of view. Several helpful results are derived from the simulation experiments. Firstly, the visibility of low orbit space objects is poor, the total time of visible arcs is less than 1 hour in the 24 hours observation. Secondly, extremely little influence from restraints of the earth masking and the earth shadow is exist in the visibility of middle and high orbit space objects .Finally, the visibility of space objects using middle or high orbit observation platform is beneficial than using low orbit observation platform. Besides, some further ideas of this work are suggested in the future studies: First, the influence of the sunlight reflected by the earth should take into account as the altitude of observation platform orbit is higher than the space object orbit. Second, the influence of the distance between the observation platform and the space object should be considered for the performance limitation of observation equipment. Third, the visibility analysis of space object observed by constellation is an attractive work.

References

1. Musci, R., Flohrer, T., Flury, W.: Monitoring the space debris environment at high altitudes using data from the ESA optical surveys (2006)
2. Stokes, G.H., Von Braun, C., Sridharan, R., et al.: The Space-Based Visible Program. Lincoln Laboratory Journal 11(2), 205–238 (1998)
3. Harrison, D.C., Chow, J.C.: The Space-Based Visible Sensor. Johns Hopkins Apl Technical Digest 17(2), 226–236 (1996)
4. Sharma, J., Stokes, G.H.: Toward Operational Space-Based Space Surveillance. Lincoln Laboratory Journal (2), 309–334 (2002)
5. Xiu-Yun, C., Hui, L.: The Development of America Space surveillance System. Aerospace China (2), 31–33 (2011)
6. Xiao-Xiao, C.: Survey of America Space-based Space objects surveillance System. Space International (7), 37–43 (2011)
7. Gaposchkin, E.M., Von Braun, C., Sharma, J.: Space-Based Space Surveillance with SBV, 73–86 (1997)
8. Jun, L.: Research on Key Technologies of Space Objects Surveillance and Tracking in Space-based Optical Surveillance. National University of Defense Technology (2009)
9. Weidong, S.: Research on Target Tracking Technologies for Space-based Optical Surveillance System. National University of Defense Technology (2011)
10. Jing, W., Bo, W., Jun, L., et al.: Observability Analysis on Space Object Tracking in Space-based Optical Surveillance. Journal of Hunan University (Natural Sciences) 36(11), 32–37 (2009)
11. Lei, L.: Study on the Initial Orbit Determination of Space Targets with Space-based Surveillance. National University of Defense Technology (2010)
12. Chao-Zhen, L.: Modeling and Detecting Capability Analysis of Space-based Space Object Optical Observation System. PLA Information Engineering University (2009)
13. Chao-Zhen, L., Jian-Sheng, L., Sai-Jin, M., et al.: Prediction and Analysis of Orbital Target's Visibility Based on Space-based Optics Observation. Opto-Electronic Engineering 35(12), 23–27 (2008)
14. Yan, Z., Dong-Yun, Y., Xiao-Gang, P., et al.: Analysis of Spaceobject's Visibility Based on Space-based Optics Observation. Journal of Spacecraft TT&C Technology 26(3), 5–12 (2007)
15. Hua-Fei, D., Zhi, L.: The Research on Pointing Strategy of Space-based Visible Space Surveillance. Aerospace Control 29(6), 39–43 (2011)

Feature Separability Evaluation for Advanced Radar Emitter Signals

Bin Zhu[1,2], Weidong Jin[1], Zhibin Yu[1], and Meijun Duan[1]

[1] School of Electrical Engineering, Southwest Jiaotong University, Chengdu 610031, China
[2] School of Electron Engineering, Yangtze Normal University, Chongqing 408100, China
zb8132002@163.com, wdjin@home.swjtu.edu.cn

Abstract. For the realization of feature separability evaluation for advanced radar emitter signals (RES), the evaluation methods of feature separability of advanced radar emitter signals were proposed based on four kinds of measure. It reflects the within-class aggregation and class separation of the feature clustering through the maximum of within-class Euclidean distance, the sum of within-class Euclidean distance, the variance of within-class Euclidean distance and the sum of Euclidean distance between classes. The corresponding measures were calculated by using six typical advanced radar emitter signals. The results show that this method is effective and feasible, and can implement the feature separability evaluation for advanced radar emitter signals.

Keywords: Radar emitter signals, Feature separability, Feature evaluation, Euclidean distance.

1 Introduction

The recognition for advanced radar emitter signal (RES) is an important part of electronic intelligence (ELINT) systems, electronic support measure (ESM) systems, and radar warning receiver (RWR) systems in electronic warfare. With the radar electronic warfare is becoming increasingly fierce, stealth and anti-jamming ability of the new complex system radar gradually dominate, the new advanced radar with good stealth and anti-interference ability gradually dominate [1],[2],[3], and the traditional signal separation method based on five parameters(carrier frequency, time of arrival, pulse amplitude, pulse width, pulse direction of arrival) is difficult to achieve satisfactory recognition results, To this end, domestic and international scholars have conducted a large number of in-depth studies to explore new RES characteristic parameters, such as the resemblance coefficient characteristics which was proposed in literature [4], the wavelet ridge frequency cascade characteristics which was proposed in literature [5], the instantaneous frequency derived characteristics which was proposed in literature [6], and the empirical mode decomposition (EMD) energy entropy characteristics which was proposed in literature [7], etc. However, the separability of these new excavation RES characteristics is still lack of systematic research. There is urgent need to establish the feature separability evaluation method for advanced radar emitter signals.

T. Xiao, L. Zhang, and S. Ma (Eds.): ICSC 2012, Part II, CCIS 327, pp. 204–212, 2012.

At present, the researches of RES feature extraction are mostly concentrated in the within-class feature selection. That is to say that they were in their respective platforms, and used the mathematical methods to achieve the dimensionality reduction of high-dimensional RES characteristics. There is the lack of effective method which can assess advantages and weaknesses of the feature performance between each various characteristics in unified platform. Therefore, this article proposes a feature separability evaluation method for advanced radar emitter signals based on four kinds of measure, and realized the feature separability evaluation for advanced radar emitter signals through large quantification calculation of the each measure value.

2   RES Feature Extractions

2.1   Derived Features of Instantaneous Frequency

The main difference between the RES of different modulation types is performance in different modulation function, the difference of the modulation function cause the instantaneous frequency differences of the RES. Signals of different modulation types have different instantaneous frequency characteristics. The algorithm is first to extract the instantaneous frequency characteristics of RES through the improvement of instantaneous self-correlation algorithm, which was processed by no ambiguity phase expansion and moving average. Then extract secondary features of the instantaneous frequency through the cascade normalized feature extraction algorithm. The extraction algorithm of derived characteristics of instantaneous frequency (IF) as follows:

2.2   Resemblance Coefficient Features

The spectrum shape of RES with different pulse modulation laws is quite different. The differences in spectral shape contains the change of frequency, phase and amplitude information of the pulse signal, it will can distinguish the radar emitter pulse signal with different pulse modulation mode by measuring the extent of the differences of the different RES spectrum shape. Resemblance coefficient is effectively portrayed on the radar emitter signal spectrum shape; it can be used as effective features to distinguish the radar emitter signals which have different pulse modulation modes, Resemblance coefficient features (RC) extraction algorithm is as follows[9].

2.3   Wavelet Ridge Frequency Cascade Features

The main difference of the different modulation types RES embody only on different time-frequency variation, while the instantaneous frequency response the changes of signal frequency in every moment. The wavelet ridge reflects the instantaneous frequency of the signal. Therefore, a new wavelet atom has been proposed to improve the detection probability of the signal ridge characteristics and anti-noise performance. It improves the detection efficiency of the ridge line features through a new definition of the ridge line detection strategies. Wavelet ridge frequency cascade characteristics (WRFCCF) extraction algorithm is as follows [10].

2.4   EMD Energy Entropy Features

EMD method can divided non-stationary signal into the sum of several IMF components, the algorithm's aim is to decompose the poor performance signal into a better performance of the IMF. As the frequency components that the intrinsic mode function contains are related with the sampling frequency, and they also change with the change of the signal itself. Therefore, EMD signal analysis method has a strong adaptability which makes it possible to break through the limitations of Fourier transform in fundamental, extraction algorithm of EMD energy entropy feature (WPEMD) is as follows.

3   Separability Measurements

The distribution of RES features in the feature space is critical to the radar emitter signal recognition, if some characteristics of different radar emitter signals in the feature space overlap the less or no overlap, then the feature is more favorable to the recognition of radar emitter signals. For some sort of feature extraction methods, the characteristics of different radar emitter signal distribution different. We can determine whether the feature is conducive to the classification though the analysis of characteristics of the feature distribution. In order to compare the separability of RES features in different feature extraction methods and to know the separability of what kind features is more effective, this article does not discuss this problem that how to choose effective low-dimensional features from high-dimensional feature, only studies the separability problem of radar emitter signal features. This paper describes the distribution measure of RES features by using Euclidean distance [11],[12],[13].

Assume that $\alpha(x_1, x_2, \cdots, x_n)$ and $\beta(y_1, y_2, \cdots, y_n)$ are the two feature points in the n-dimensional feature space, then the Euclidean distance between α and β is as follow.

$$D(\alpha, \beta) = \left(\sum_{i=1}^{n} (x_i - y_i)^2 \right)^{1/2} \tag{1}$$

It uses the following measure to describe the separability of RES features.

1) It compares the maximum distance between the feature points which located in the feature distribution of the same radar emitter signals in some kind of feature extraction methods. This value reflects to some extent the within-class aggregation degree of certain features. The value is smaller, the aggregation degree of the feature distribution is better.

$$D_{max} = \max_{i,j=1}^{n}(D(\alpha_i, \alpha_j)), \quad i, j = 1, 2, \cdots, n \tag{2}$$

Where, α_i, α_j are the two feature points in the feature distribution of a RES in the same feature extraction method.

2) It compares the sum of the distance between the feature points which located in the feature distribution of the same radar emitter signals in some kind of feature extraction methods. This value reflects to some extent the within-class aggregation degree of certain features. The value is smaller, the aggregation degree of the feature distribution is better.

$$D_{sum} = \sum_{i,j=1}^{n}(D(\alpha_i, \alpha_j)), \quad i, j = 1, 2, \cdots, n \tag{3}$$

3) It compares the Euclidean distance variance of the same RES feature in some kind of feature extraction methods. This value reflects the uniformity of the feature distribution in the state space. Distribution of the feature is more uniform, the quality is the better.

$$D_{var} = (n \cdot \sum_{i,j=1}^{n}(D(\alpha_i, \alpha_j))^2 - (\sum_{i,j=1}^{n} D(\alpha_i, \alpha_j))^2)/(n \cdot (n-1)), \quad i, j = 1, 2, \cdots, n \tag{4}$$

4) To account for the case of the characteristic distribution overlap, the minimum distance between single feature points of the different RES does not reflect the dispersion degree of the different feature clustering. To this end, it uses the sum of the distance between all feature points in the feature distribution of different RES to reflect the dispersion degree of the different RES feature clustering in the same feature extraction method.

$$D_{mutualsum} = \sum_{i,j=1}^{n}(D(\alpha_i, \beta_j)), \quad i, j = 1, 2, \cdots, n \tag{5}$$

Where α_i, β_j are the two feature points in the feature distribution of different RES in the same feature extraction method.

4   Calculations and Analysis

The calculation and analysis is completed on the platform of Lenovo E46L. The processor speed is 2.3GHz and the memory capacity is 2GB. It selected six typical radar emitter signals in BPSK, QPSK, LFM, NLFM, FSK, and CSF and added 10db noise to all RES. 50 feature vectors were extracted by using the aforementioned four kinds of feature extraction methods, these feature vectors were used to measure calculation.

4.1   Maximum Within-Class Euclidean Distance Measure

Within-class Euclidean distance was calculated by using the extracted feature vector and Equation (8), and to extract the maximum value of within-class Euclidean distance. We will get the within-class Euclidean Distance maximum value of the different RES in different feature extraction methods, the calculation results shown in Figure 1 as below. In order to see the figure clearly, the maximum value of within-class Euclidean distance of WFCCF feature was reduced 10 times.

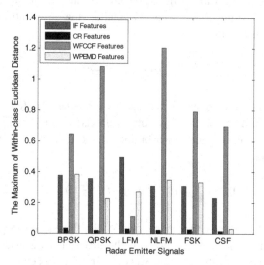

Fig. 1. Maximum within-class Euclidean distance map of RES features

It can be seen from figure 1 that the maximum within-class Euclidean distance of RC feature is the smallest in all radar emitter signals. It can also be seen that the maximum within-class Euclidean distance of BPSK、 NLFM、 FSK of IF feature is smaller than that of WPEMD feature. However, the maximum within-class Euclidean distance of QPSK、 LFM、 CSF of WPEMD feature is smaller than that of IF feature. The maximum within-class Euclidean distance of WFCCF feature is the largest.

4.2   Measure of the Within-Class Euclidean Distance Sum

Calculated results of the measure of the within-class Euclidean distance sum were shown in figure 2. In order to see the figure clearly, the sum of within-class Euclidean distance of the WFCCF feature was reduced 10 times. We can see that the sum of the within-class Euclidean distance of the RC features is most minimal in all RES. Secondly, the sum of the within-class Euclidean distance of the IF feature is smaller than the sum of the within-class Euclidean distance of the WPEMD feature on NLFM signal. Accordingly, the sum of the within-class Euclidean distance of the WPEMD feature are smaller than the sum of the within-class Euclidean distance of the IF feature on BPSK, QPSK, LFM, CSF and FSK signals.

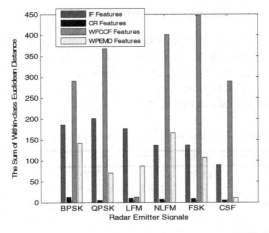

Fig. 2. Within-class Euclidean distance sum map of RES features

4.3   Variance Measure of Within-Class Euclidean Distance

The variance calculation results of within-class Euclidean distance of the RES were shown in figure 3 as below.

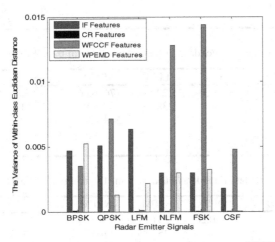

Fig. 3. Within-class Euclidean distance variance map of RES features

To see the figure clearly, the within-class Euclidean distance variance of WFCCF feature was reduced 400 times. It's not difficult to see that the variance of within-class Euclidean distance of RC feature is the minimum, and the WFCCF feature is the largest. On BPSK and FSK, the within-class Euclidean distance variance of IF is smaller than WPEMD. The within-class Euclidean distance variances of WPEMD feature are smaller than that of IF feature on QPSK、 LFM、 NLFM and CSF signals.

4.4   Between-Class Euclidean Distance Sum Measure

The feature vectors of different radar emitter signals were extracted by the same method and the sum of the Euclidean distance between all feature points of any two feature vectors were calculated. Then, the between-class Euclidean distance sum is taken as the measure. Calculation results of the sum of between-class Euclidean distance (SBCED) were shown in table 1-4.

Table 1. Between-class Euclidean Distance Sum Table of The IF Features

The SBCED	QPSK	LFM	NLFM	FSK	CSF
BPSK	413.90	459.01	457.39	457.39	765.65
QPSK	--	478.82	557.89	557.89	736.41
LFM		--	521.34	521.34	822.55
NLFM			--	272.41	921.70
FSK				--	921.70

Table 2. Between-class Euclidean Distance Sum Table of the RC Features

The SBCED	QPSK	LFM	NLFM	FSK	CSF
BPSK	1162.18	207.72	485.60	454.58	2692.84
QPSK	--	1369.91	676.57	707.59	3855.02
LFM		--	693.33	662.31	2485.11
NLFM			--	31.44	2692.84
FSK				--	3147.43

Table 3. Between-class Euclidean Distance Sum Table of the WFCCF Features

The SBCED	QPSK	LFM	NLFM	FSK	CSF
BPSK	6744.37	22227.91	17676.60	13650.56	26507.12
QPSK	--	22389.33	18643.94	14428.51	27282.05
LFM		--	24869.61	14941.37	18213.17
NLFM			--	14323.33	17281.56
FSK				--	16829.95

Table 4. Between-class Euclidean Distance Sum Table of the WPEMD Features

The SBCED	QPSK	LFM	NLFM	FSK	CSF
BPSK	300.20	241.21	1510.54	432.16	2493.32
QPSK	--	257.35	1705.17	264.35	2493.87
LFM		--	1546.33	417.68	2492.15
NLFM			--	1691.00	2490.95
FSK				--	2497.35

From the results we can see, in IF features, the sum of the Euclidean distance between all feature points of NLFM and FSK are 272.41, it is the minimum. In RC features, the sum of the Euclidean distance between all feature points of NLFM and FSK is 31.44; it is the minimum in RC features. In WFCCF features, the sum of the Euclidean distance between all feature points of BPSK and QPSK is 300.20; it is the minimum in WFCCF features. In WPEMD features, the sum of the Euclidean distance between all feature points of BPSK and LFM is 241.21; it is the minimum in WPEMD features. Through comparison of the minimum, we find that the WFCCF is the best, followed by the IF features, the WPEMD characteristics and RC features.

In pattern recognition, we all hope that the within-class aggregation of a feature class is small, the distribution of features is relatively uniform, and the separation degree between different feature classes is larger, which is conducive to the classification and identification. In other words, the measure of maximum within-class Euclidean distance, the measure of the within-class Euclidean distance sum and the measure of within-class Euclidean distance variance is as small as possible. If the minimum value of the between-class Euclidean distance sum is greater, it indicates that the distance of different feature classes is greater, and the classification and recognition would be more easily achieved. The calculated results show that the features that meet all of the above conditions do not exist. Therefore, the different measures were given the same weights. The feature separability evaluation is implemented by rank-sum method. The calculation results were shown in figure 4. Comprehensive separability evaluation result of the RC feature is the best among the four kinds of RES features, followed by the WPEMD feature, the IF feature and the WFCCF feature.

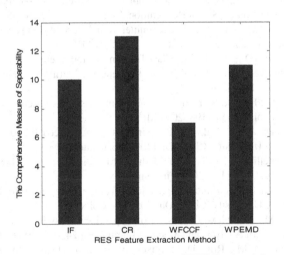

Fig. 4. Comprehensive Evaluation Map of RES Features' Separability

5   Conclusions

Separability evaluation of RES features is an important content of its performance assessment. On the basis of four kinds measure definition of the RES features' separability, this paper analyzes the pros and cons of RES feature separability in different measure through a large number of quantitative calculations, and the separability of different RES features were evaluated by using the rank-sum method.

Calculation and evaluation results have important practical significance on the establishment and improvement of the advanced RES feature index system.

Acknowledgments. This work is supported by the national natural science foundation of China (No. 60971103) and the science research project of Chongqing city board of education (No. KJ121322) and science & technology project of Fuling district of Chongqing city (No. FLKJ2012ABA1037). The authors thank the editors and reviewers for their valuable comments and good suggestions.

References

1. Jin, W.-D., Zhang, G.-X., Hu, L.-Z.: Radar Emitter Signal Recognition Using Wavelet Packet Transform and Support Vector Machines. Journal of Southwest Jiaotong University 14, 15–22 (2006)
2. Zhang, G.-Z., Huang, K.-S., Jiang, W.-L., et al.: Emitter feature extract method based on signal envelope. Systems Engineering and Electronics 28, 795–797 (2006)
3. Zhu, M., Jin, W.-D., Hu, L.-Z.: A Novel Method for Radar Emitter Signals Recognition Based on Spectrum Atoms. Journal of Electronics & Information Technology 31, 188–191 (2009)
4. Zhang, G.-X., Jin, W.-D., Hu, L.-Z.: Resemblance Coefficient Based Feature Selection Algorithm for Radar Emitter Signal Recognition. Signal Processing 21, 663–667 (2005)
5. Yu, Z.-B., Jin, W.-D., Chen, C.-X.: Radar Emitter Signal Recognition Based on WRFCCF. Journal of Southwest Jiaotong University 45, 290–295 (2010)
6. Pu, Y.-W., Jin, W.-D., Hu, L.-Z.: Classification of radar emitter signals using the characteristics derived from instantaneous frequencies. Journal of Harbin Institute of Technology 41, 136–140 (2009)
7. Zhu, B., Jin, W.-D.: Feature Extraction of Radar Emitter Signal Based on Wavelet Packet and EMD. LNEE, vol. 100, pp. 198–205 (2012)
8. Pu, Y.-W.: Deinterleaving Models and Algorithms for Advanced Radar Emitter Signals. Southwest Jiaotong University, Cheng Du (2007) (in Chinese)
9. Zhang, G.-X.: Intelligent Recognition Methods for Radar Emitter Signals. Southwest Jiaotong University, Cheng Du (2005) (in Chinese)
10. Yu, Z.-B.: Study on Radar Emitter Signal Identification Based on Intra-Pulse Features. Southwest Jiaotong University, Cheng Du (2010) (in Chinese)
11. Ho, T.K., Basu, M.: Complexity Meastres of Supervised Classification Problems. IEEE Transactions on Pattern Analysis and Machine Intelligence 24, 289–300 (2001)
12. Hu, X.-P., Laura, D.-M., Roy, D.E.: Bayesian feature evaluation for visual saliency estimation. Pattern Recognition 41, 3302–3312 (2008)
13. Han, Z.-J., Ye, Q.-X., Jiao, J.-B.: Combined feature evaluation for adaptive visual object tracking. Computer Vision and Image Understanding 115, 69–80 (2011)

Research on Anti-ARM Model with Outboard Active Decoys

Yupeng Xie, Zhongjie Wang, Jiangang Yan, and Yanbo Song

Department of Command, Naval Aeronautical and Astronautical University,
264001 Yantai, China
labyrinthy@163.com

Abstract. As ship-borne radar system is composed of various types of radars, it can't be simplified as single radiation source when the warship adopts active decoy to deal with anti-radiation missile (ARM). By analyzing working characteristics of ARM, attacking models of ARM to ship-borne radars with active decoys were built. The simulation results show that burst points of ARM are in dense distribution around the ship-borne radars, which still pose a threat to ship-borne radar system.

Keywords: anti-radiation missile, active decoy, efficiency, operation, evaluation.

1 Introduction

ARM which adopts passive radar seeker to search and track radar signals and can oppress or destroy radiation source effectively plays an important role in modern war[1]. The high speed ARM destroys target by following the radar emission to its source[2]. As ship-borne radar system is composed of various types of radars which are densely distributed[3], to protect radar system from ARM's attack becomes very important. Adopting active decoys to anti-ARM is a traditional method[4], which use active decoys to compose the integrated countering system so as to protect the radar system. However, as the complexity and diversity of ship-borne radars, to simplify radar system as single radiation source is unreasonable, and whether the method is effective should be studied furthermore.

2 Countermeasure Process of ARM to Radar System

In self-guided phase, the ARM seeker searches, intercepts and tracks the target by radar signals. For those radar signals which meet acquire conditions of ARM, ARM is prior to acquire radiation source with the biggest power. To get a high acquire probability, the field angle of typical ARM has a large range, always between $\pm 30°$, and tracking angle of typical ARM is usually between $\pm 4°$ to get the high tracking accuracy[5]. On the tracking process, if the target signal was lost and the lost time

T. Xiao, L. Zhang, and S. Ma (Eds.): ICSC 2012, Part II, CCIS 327, pp. 213–220, 2012.

reaches a specified value, ARM state transfers to searching mode from tracking mode till a target is acquired.

As passive radar seeker of ARM is a passive direction locating system which finds angle tracking information by normal direction deviation of radar signal wavefront from ARM aiming axis, the seeker may not resolve radiation resources with the same or similar working parameters at the long distance, and will treat these radiation resources as single resource. If outboard decoys were configured around ship-borne radar and compose the integrated countering system, tracking process of ARM is:

(1) At the beginning of tracking stage, distance of ARM and warship is much further than distance of warship and decoys, and line of sight angle difference in any 2 radiation resources is much smaller than a specified threshold φ, ARM will track the geometric center of these radiation resources.

(2) When ARM approaches the warship, distances between ARM and each radiation resource decreases, and line of sight angle difference increases. If the angle difference is bigger than φ but smaller than resolution angle θR, ARM will track power centre of radiation resources.

(3) If line of sight angle difference increases to θR, a radiation resource can be recognized from the other. With approaching of ARM, more and more radiation resources are recognized. At last only one radiation resource is tracked by ARM.

(4) For those ship-borne radars adopting rotating antennas, such as searching radars, ARM may lose the target intermittently. The lost time threshold is defined as *tlost*, and ARM will search and lock a target again, and make a trajectory correction, the hitting process was shown in figure 1.

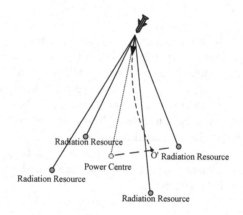

Fig. 1. Trajectory correction process of ARM

3   Characteristics of Radiation Resources

3.1   Conditions to Compose an Integrated Countering System

To compose an integrated countering system, it should meet some conditions. These conditions are:

(1) Radiation resources are in field angle of ARM;

(2) Carrier frequency difference of radiation resources is smaller than frequency resolution of ARM;

(3) Pulse period of each radiation resource is similar;

(4) Amplitude ratio should be smaller than a certain value, and the value is always 1.25.

From these conditions, it's important to guarantee radiation resources to work synchronously so as to get the similar power and waveform. As scanning mode of the ship-borne guidance radar is steady compared to searching radars, the decoying conditions are easier to meet.

3.2   Calculation of Total Electric Field

For the ith (i=1,2,...) radiation resource, the average power is given by[6]

$$P_i = P_{fi} \cdot f_{ri} \cdot \tau_i.$$ (1)

Where P_{fi} is peak power, f_{ri} is pulse repetition frequency, and τ_i is pulse width.

Then the received power density is

$$S_i = \left[\frac{P_i G_{i0} G_i\left(\alpha,\beta;t\right) A_e}{4\pi L_t} \right]^{\frac{1}{2}} \frac{1}{R_i}.$$ (2)

Where G_{i0} is the maximum gain of the ith radar antenna, $G_i(\alpha,\beta,t)$ is antenna directivity, R_i is distance between the ith radiation resource and ARM, A_e is antenna aperture of ARM seeker, and L_t is transmission loss.

If coordinate of the ith radar is (x_i,y_i,z_i), and coordinate of ARM is (x_a,y_a,z_a), then

$$R_i = \sqrt{\left(x_i - x_a\right)^2 + \left(y_i - y_a\right)^2 + \left(z_i - z_a\right)^2}.$$ (3)

Where P_{fi} is peak power, f_{ri} is pulse repetition frequency, and τ_i is pulse width.

Then the received power density is

$$E_i\left(t\right) = E_i \cos\left(\omega_i t - 2\pi R_i / \lambda_i + \phi_i\right).$$ (4)

Where ω_i is angular frequency, λ_i is wavelength, and ϕ_i is the initial phase. Then the detected phase and amplitude of the ith radiation resource is defined by

$$\begin{cases} \phi = \arctan\left(\sum_{i=0}^{n} E_i \sin\phi_i \Big/ \sum_{i=0}^{n} E_i \cos\phi_i \right) \\ E = \left[\left(\sum_{i=0}^{n} E_i \sin\phi_i \right)^2 + \left(\sum_{i=0}^{n} E_i \cos\phi_i \right)^2 \right]^{1/2} \end{cases}.$$ (5)

4   Hitting Model of ARM

With distance decreasing and line of sight angle difference increasing when ARM approaches warship, more and more radiation resources are recognized. Suppose that radiation j^{th} resource was the first recognized radiation resource. As the remained radiation resources can't be recognized at this time but have the bigger total electric field, ARM will track the remained radiation resources. On the analogy of this, with the decreasing of distance between ARM and radiation resources, more radiation resources are separated. At last, all the radiation resources were recognized by ARM seeker, and ARM may lock one of these targets randomly. However, as the distance at this time (defined as D_s) is so short that no enough time left for a trajectory correction, hitting error is so big that ARM may not destroy any one of them.

For ARM, there is a stall distance where the distance is so short and the received power is so strong that ARM even can't locate the target and can't control itself. Define the stall distance as D_{min}. D_s and D_{min} determine the hitting point of ARM together.

(1) If D_s is bigger than D_{min}, ARM can recognize all the radiation resources on the terminal trajectory.

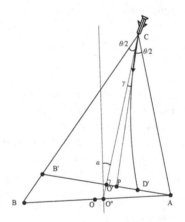

Fig. 2. Errors of ARM confronting active decoys

Figure 2 shows the hitting process at the terminal trajectory of ARM, where O is power centre of radiation resource A and radiation resource B, C is position of ARM, θ is resolution angle of ARM, CO" is angular bisector of θ, γ is angle measuring error, α is angle of normal plane and ARM aiming axis, and D' is hitting point of ARM.

Suppose that ARM chose radiation resource A. Considering the angle measuring error, distance between A and D' is given by[7]

$$AD' = \frac{1}{2}L' - \frac{L'}{2tg\left(\dfrac{\Delta\theta}{2}\right)} \cdot tg\gamma - \frac{-b_1 - \sqrt{b_1^2 - 4a_1c_1}}{2a_1}\cos\gamma. \tag{6}$$

Where

$$\begin{cases} L' = L \cdot \left[\cos\alpha - \sin\alpha \cdot tg\left(\dfrac{\theta}{2}\right) \right] \\ \alpha_1 = 1 + tg^2\gamma \\ b_1 = -2\left(R - \dfrac{L' \cdot tg\gamma}{\cos\gamma} \right) \\ c_1 = \left(\dfrac{L'^2}{2 \cdot tg\dfrac{\theta}{2} \cdot \cos\gamma} \right) \end{cases}$$

(7)

Where L is distance between A and B, R is the maximum turning radius.

Coordinates of radiation resource A and radiation resource B are denoted as (x_a, y_a, z_a) and (x_b, y_b, z_b), distances between A and ARM, B and ARM are given by

$$\begin{cases} r_{AC} = \sqrt{(x_a - x_c)^2 + (y_a - y_c)^2 + (z_a - z_c)^2} \\ r_{BC} = \sqrt{(x_b - x_c)^2 + (y_b - y_c)^2 + (z_b - z_c)^2} \end{cases}$$

(8)

Coordinate of B' is given by

$$(x_{b'}, y_{b'}, z_{b'}) = \left(1 - \frac{r_{AC}}{r_{BC}}\right)(x_c, y_c, z_c) + \frac{r_{AC}}{r_{BC}}(x_b, y_b, z_b).$$

(9)

Distance between B' and A is

$$\begin{cases} x_{d'} = \left(1 - \dfrac{AD'}{r_{B'C}}\right)x_a + \dfrac{AD'}{r_{B'C}}x_{b'} \\ y_{d'} = \left(1 - \dfrac{AD'}{r_{B'C}}\right)y_a + \dfrac{AD'}{r_{B'C}}y_{b'} \\ z_{d'} = \left(1 - \dfrac{AD'}{r_{B'C}}\right)z_a + \dfrac{AD'}{r_{B'C}}z_{b'} \end{cases}$$

(10)

(2) If D_s is not bigger than D_{min}, ARM can't separate all the radiation resources effectively. On this condition, ARM flies on the wavefront normal direction, which is given by

$$\frac{x - x_A}{\partial\phi/\partial x_A} = \frac{y - y_A}{\partial\phi/\partial y_A} = \frac{z - z_A}{\partial\phi/\partial z_A}.$$

(11)

Where xA, yA, and zA are stall coordinates of ARM.

Intersection point of the wavefront normal direction and plane $z=h$ is

$$\begin{cases} x' = \left[\sum_{i=0}^{n}\sum_{k=0}^{n} E_i E_k \frac{x_k z_A - x_A z_k + h(x_A - x_k)}{R_k \lambda_k} \cos(\phi_i - \phi_k) \right] \Big/ \left[\sum_{i=0}^{n}\sum_{k=0}^{n} E_i E_k \frac{z_A - z_k}{R_k \lambda_k} \cos(\phi_i - \phi_k) \right] \\ y' = \left[\sum_{i=0}^{n}\sum_{k=0}^{n} E_i E_k \frac{y_k z_A - y_A z_k + h(y_A - y_k)}{R_k \lambda_k} \cos(\phi_i - \phi_k) \right] \Big/ \left[\sum_{i=0}^{n}\sum_{k=0}^{n} E_i E_k \frac{z_A - z_k}{R_k \lambda_k} \cos(\phi_i - \phi_k) \right] \end{cases} \quad (12)$$

Coordinate of D' is given by

$$\begin{cases} x_{d'} = x' \\ y_{d'} = y' \\ z_{d'} = z' \end{cases} . \quad (13)$$

We then have

$$R_{di} = \sqrt{(x' - x_i)^2 + (y' - y_i)^2 + (z' - z_i)^2} . \quad (14)$$

Where R_{di} is distance between D' and radiation resource i. If R_{di} is smaller than damage radius of ARM, the ith radiation resource will be destroyed.

5   Numerical Example

5.1   Initial Conditions

When the ARM with proximity fuze is lunched, the distance of ARM and warship is 50km, the altitude is 6km, the speed is 3Ma, and guide itself by proportional guidance law. The azimuth angle of ARM is a random uniform number in omni-direction. The ship-borne radar system on the target warship includes a guidance radar and 2 searching radars which work normally and can be acquired by ARM. Decoys which have the similar parameters with the guidance radar were allocated around the warship already, the distance of decoys and warship is 200m.

5.2   Analysis

Simulate the countermeasure models with Monte Carlo. Figure 3 and figure 4 show the bust points of ARM in vertical plane and horizontal plane.

In figure 3, as ARM may acquire any ship-borne radar and positions of ship-borne radar are not the same, the burst points are in various altitudes. From these results we can find that burst points are in dense distribution around warship, the reason is that the ship-borne radars are densely distributed on warship, and decoys can't achieve expected effect.

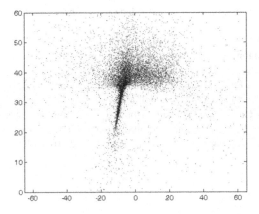

Fig. 3. Burst points in vertical plane

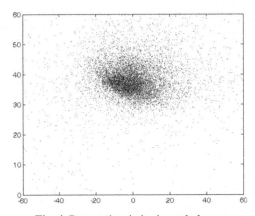

Fig. 4. Burst points in horizontal plane

6   Conclusions

Basing on countermeasure process of ARM and decoys, radiation characteristics of radiation resources were analyzed and hitting models of ARM were built. Simulation results show that as the complexity of ship-borne radars, adopting outboard active decoys to anti-ARM is not an effective method, and new anti-ARM methods to protect ship-borne radars system should be studied furthermore.

References

1. Wang, F., He, R., Sha, X.: Anti-ARM technique: distributed general-purpose decoy series (DGPD). In: IEEE CIE International Conference, pp. 306–309. IEEE Press, China (2001)
2. Farrokh, A., Krishnamurthy, V.: Optimal threshold policies for hard-kill of enemy radars with high speed anti-radiation missiles (HARMS). In: IEEE Acoustics, Speech and Signal Processing, pp. 1–8. IEEE Press, England (2006)

3. Commodore Stephen Sauders, R.N. (ed.): Jane's Fighting ships. Jane's Information group, London (2005)
4. Wang, Z., Lu, X., Wu, X., Ni, C., Hu, J.: Analysis of scheme of decoy and its operation efficiency in antagonizing anti-radiation missile. Journal of PLA University of Science and Technology 8, 270–273 (2007)
5. Xie, Y., Wang, G., Reng, D., Li, F.: Research on the damage model of ARM against shipborne 3-d radar. Tactical Missile Technology 2, 43–46 (2010)
6. Merrill, I.: Radar Handbook. Publishing House of Electronics Industry, Beijing (2004)
7. Mu, F., Zhou, J., Luo, P.: Further Discussion on Error Distance of ARM Disturbed by Dual Point-source. Journal of System Simulation 7, 1665–1668 (2008)

Research on Anti Saturation Attack Model of SAM to ARM

Jiayou Zeng, Yupeng Xie, Hongfei Bian, and Cao Lv

Department of Command, Naval Aeronautical and Astronautical University,
264001 Yantai, China
zengjiayou@sohu.com

Abstract. By establishing efficiency indexes of ship-to-air missiles (SAM) weapon system, serving process of SAM for anti-radar missile (ARM) were quantitatively derived. Basing on countermeasure process of SAM operation, the anti saturation model of SAM to ARM was built on Monte Carlo, which includes numerical characteristic of shooting stream, threat estimation, firepower distribution, interception and effectiveness estimation. Simulation results demonstrate the effectiveness of this model, which lay a foundation for further quantitative research on operations of SAM.

Keywords: air defense missile, anti-radar missile, efficiency, operation, evaluation.

1 Introduction

Currently, saturation attack of missiles poses a threat to warship seriously. The definition of saturation attack is that the intensity of missile's attacking stream is so strong that weapon channels of air-defense system can't serve each incoming missile[1]. Saturation models of anti-ship missile (ASM) were studied by many references. Reference [2] deduced description method of saturation attack stream, and further descriptions of intensity of saturation attack were given by [3-4]. As working principles of anti-radar missile (ARM) varies from ASM greatly, attacking process and trajectory of ARM are very different from ASM. ASM adopts active radar seeker and most of the time flies in low-altitude[5], while ARM adopts passive radar seeker and flies in mid-high altitude to search, intercept and track radar signals[6]. Therefore, it's important to study on anti saturation attack models of warship to ARM basing on the countermeasure process.

2 Attacking Model of ARM to Warship

Figure 1 shows the detection area of ARM to ship-borne radars, where φ is field angle of ARM. According to the numbers of detectable radars, detection coverage of ARM can be divided into several intervals, and O_1, O_2, ..., O_n are tracing points of ARM where the numbers of detectable radars are 1, 2, ..., n.

T. Xiao, L. Zhang, and S. Ma (Eds.): ICSC 2012, Part II, CCIS 327, pp. 221–228, 2012.

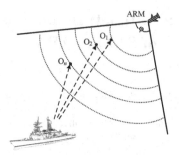

Fig. 1. Detection area of ARM to ship-borne radars

In the vertical plane, ARM always adopts proportional guiding law subject to terminal angular constraint to get a better impact angle

$$\theta_c = k_1 \dot{q} + k_2 (q - \beta). \tag{1}$$

Where θ_c is trajectory inclination angle rate, q is pitching line-of-sight angle, β is expectation impact angle, and k_1, k_2 are guidance coefficients.

Compared to ARM, speed of the ship is very low, so the value of $\dot{q}$ approaches 0, and (1) can be simplified as

$$\theta_c = k_2 (q - \beta). \tag{2}$$

The azimuth angle rate of ARM is considered to be subject to proportional guidance law

$$\psi_{vc} = k_3 \dot{\sigma}_f. \tag{3}$$

Where ψ_{vc} is trajectory declination angle rate, σ_f is azimuth line-of-sight angle, and k_3 are guidance coefficient.

3   Service Process of SAM Weapon System

3.1   Shooting Stream of ARM

ARM which works reliably and acquires the ship-borne radars is believed to threat the warship, and will be intercepted by the ship-borne weapons system. As each of these incoming ARMs which threats the target is lethal, the threat grade can be defined by the range between ARM and the warship, the nearer the higher. Then, the attack intensity of ARM can be defined by the time interval of nearby incoming missiles. The interval (δ_t) of nearby incoming missile is a type of uniform distribution for an organized saturation attack salvo.

3.2   Distribution of Weapon Channels

ARM which works reliably and acquires the ship-borne radars is believed to threat the warship, and will be intercepted by the ship-borne weapons system. As each of these incoming ARMs which threats the target is lethal, the threat grade can be defined by the range between ARM and the warship, the nearer the higher. Then, the attack intensity of ARM can be defined by the time interval of nearby incoming missiles. The interval (δ_t) of nearby incoming missile is a type of uniform distribution for an organized saturation attack salvo.

4   Interception Model of SAM to ARM

4.1   Interception Trajectory Model of SAM

The most important condition of SAM to intercept target effectively is that the target should be in emitter region of SAM. Emitter region is always described as internal boundary, outer boundary and lateral boundary, which were determined by performances of the target as well as SAM. Define R_{max}, R_{min}, q_{max}, ε_{max}, H_{max}, H_{min} as far range, near range, the maximum azimuth angle, the maximum elevation angle, upper boundary and lower boundary of SAM weapon system.

Thus the emitter region can be defined as

$$D = f_D \left(R_{max}, R_{min}, q_{max}, \varepsilon_{max}, H_{max}, H_{min} \right). \tag{3}$$

The relative position of SAM and ARM is determined by distance and direction of SAM and ARM, which can be described by

$$\begin{cases} \dfrac{dD}{dt} = V_m \cos(\theta_m - q) - V_s \cos(\theta_i - q) \\ D \cdot \dfrac{dq}{dt} = V_m \sin(\theta_m - q) - V_s \sin(\theta_i - q) \end{cases}. \tag{5}$$

Where D is the range between ARM and SAM, V_m, V_s are velocities of ARM and SAM, θ_m, θ_i are azimuth angles of ARM and SAM, q is line-of-sight angle.

Define K as guidance coefficient, according to proportional guiding law, and we then have

$$\frac{d\theta_i}{dt} = K \cdot \frac{dq}{dt}. \tag{6}$$

Integrating on the both sides of (6), we then have

$$\theta_i = K \cdot q + C. \tag{7}$$

By (6) and (7), trajectory equations of SAM can be deduced

$$\begin{cases} \dfrac{dD}{dt} = V_m \cos(\theta_m - q) - V_s \cos[(K-1)q + (\theta_i - K \cdot q_0)] \\ D \cdot \dfrac{dq}{dt} = V_m \sin(\theta_m - q) - V_s \sin[(K-1)q + (\theta_i - K \cdot q_0)] \end{cases}. \tag{8}$$

4.2   Interception Model to Single Target

Suppose that the initial coordinate position of ARM is S_{fa} when SAM was the first time launched to intercept this specified target. After this interception, we then have

$$\begin{cases} S_1 = S_{fa} - V_m(k-1)\Delta t \\ S_1 = S_{z,1} + V_m(t_{qf} + t_{df,1}) \\ t_{df,1} = \sqrt{S_{z,1}^2 + H^2 + P^2} \big/ V_d \end{cases} \quad . \tag{9}$$

Where S_1 is projection coordinate of the launching point along axis S when SAM was firstly launched to intercept this specified target, $S_{z,1}$ is projection coordinate of the meeting point of SAM and ARM along axis S, Δt is time interval, $t_{df,1}$ is flight time of SAM, P is shortcut course of ARM, and H is flight altitude.

Consuming time of the first interception is

$$t_1 = t_{qf} + t_{df,1} + t_{pg} + (k-1)\Delta t . \tag{10}$$

On the analogy of this, when the nth interception was finished for the specified target, we then have

$$\begin{cases} S_n = S_{n-1} - V_m[t_{n-1} + (k-1)\Delta t] \\ S_n = S_{z,n} + V_m(t_{qf} + t_{df,n}) \\ t_{df,n} = \sqrt{S_{1z,n}^2 + H^2 + P^2} \big/ V_d \end{cases} \quad . \tag{11}$$

Where S_n is projection coordinate of the nth interception launching point at axis S, $S_{z,n}$ is projection coordinate of the nth interception meeting point of SAM and ARM on axis S, and $t_{df,n}$ is flight time of SAM.

Consuming time of the nth interception is

$$t_n = t_{qf} + t_{df,n} + t_{pg} + (k-1)\Delta t . \tag{12}$$

Suppose that the maximum interception times of SAM to this target is n. If the nth interception is carried out, the target may be destroyed or flies out of the emitter region, the total consumed time (t_{toal}) is defined as

$$t_{total} = \sum_{j=1}^{n} t_j . \tag{13}$$

4.3   Interception Model to Multi Target

The overall performance of air-defense weapon system is determined by the air-defense missiles as well as the radars. For an optimization, in the design of air-defense weapon system, performance of air-defense radars should match performance of missiles. That means

$$S_{mb1} = S_{fy} . \tag{14}$$

When the first target reaches emitter region far boundary of SAM, a weapon channel has been already distributed to intercept this target. If there are total m weapon channels, the preparation time of the $j^{th}(j=1,2,\ldots,m)$ weapon channel is defined as T_{fs1j}. For the first target, as all the weapon channels were ready and available, it means no preparation time is needed and T_{fs1j} is 0. Therefore, a weapon channel was randomly allocated to intercept the first target.

Suppose that a^{th} weapon channel was allocated to intercept the first target. For the first target, the total interception time $t_{total,1}$ can be calculated by the single target interception model. When the second target reaches emitter region far boundary of SAM, preparation time of the jth weapon channel T_{fs2a} is

$$T_{fs2a} = [(T_{fs1a} + |T_{fs1a}|)/2] + t_{zong,1} + t_f - \delta t_1. \tag{15}$$

Where t_f is shift time of SAM weapon channel.

Preparation time of the other $(m-1)$ weapon channels is

$$T_{fs2j} = [(T_{fs1j} + |T_{fs1j}|)/2] - \delta t_1 \quad j = 1,2\cdots m(j \neq a). \tag{16}$$

We then have

$$T_2 = \min\{T_{fs2j}\} \quad j = 1,2\cdots m. \tag{17}$$

If prepare time of only one weapon channel is T_2, it's allocated to intercept the target. If there are multi weapon channels, a weapon channel was randomly allocated to intercept the second target.

When the allocated weapon channel was ready for the second target, position (S_{mb2}) of the target is

$$S_{mb2} = S_{fy} - V_m[(T_2 + |T_2|)/2]. \tag{18}$$

Suppose that the bth weapon channel was allocated for the $(n-1)^{th}$ target. By the single target interception model, interception time $t_{z,n-1}$ can be calculated. Then when the nth target reaches the far boundary, prepare time of the bth weapon channel (T_{fsb}) is

$$T_{fsnb} = [(T_{fsn-1b} + |T_{fsn-1b}|)/2] + t_{z,n-1} + t_f - \delta t_{n-1}. \tag{19}$$

Preparation time of the other $(m-1)$ weapon channels for the nth target is

$$T_{fsnj} = [(T_{fsn-1j} + |T_{fsn-1j}|)/2] - \delta t_{n-1} \quad j = 1,2\cdots m(j \neq b). \tag{20}$$

We then have

$$T_n = \min\{T_{fsnj}\} \quad j = 1,2\cdots m. \tag{21}$$

If prepare time of only one weapon channel is T_n, it's allocated to intercept the target. If there are multi weapon channels, a weapon channel was randomly allocated to intercept the second target.

When the allocated weapon channel was ready for the nth target, position (S_{mbn}) of the nth target is

$$R_{di} = \sqrt{(x'-x_i)^2 + (y'-y_i)^2 + (z'-z_i)^2} \ . \tag{22}$$

4.4   Interception Efficiency Assessment

The destroy probability of each interception is

$$P_l = 1 - (1 - P_d)^k \ . \tag{23}$$

Where P_d is the destroy probability of each SAM successfully intercepts one ARM. If

$$P_l \geq \eta_2 \ . \tag{24}$$

Where η_2 is the random uniform number in (0, 1), ARM is considered to be destroyed. If ARM is destroyed, firepower shift is possible. Otherwise, this interception is a failure; the target needs to be intercepted again.

5   Anti Saturation Attack Capability of SAM

For the nth incoming target, if $S_{mbn} < S_{fj}$, the nth incoming target flies out of the emitter region and penetrates successfully. When the saturation attack is formed, the number of the total target intercepted (F) is

$$F = n - 1 \ . \tag{25}$$

Mathematical expectation of the number of ARM intercepted successfully (M_f) is

$$M_f = \sum_{b=1}^{n-1} M_{fb} \ . \tag{26}$$

Where the value of M_{fb} is 0 if the interception is failed, otherwise the value is 1.
   Mathematical expectation of consumed SAM is

$$M_k = \sum_{b=1}^{n-1} M_{kb} \ . \tag{27}$$

Where M_{kb} is the number of SAM consumed for the bth target.

6   Numerical Example

6.1   Initial Conditions

The parameters of stand-off ARM: $\varphi = 120°$, $H = 5000m$. Parameters of SAM system: $H_{max} = 12km$, $H_{min} = 20m$, $\varepsilon_{max} = 60°$, $q_{max} = 60°$, $D_{sy} = 40km$, $D_{sjmin} = 300m$, $t_{pg} = 2s$, $t_{qf} = 3s$, $t_f = 2s$, $P_k = 0.7$, $V_d = 1000m/s$. Regarding V_m (speed of ARM) , m (weapon channel number), δ_t (time interval) as variables. Simulate this model with Monte Carlo. The result shows in figure 2 and table 1.

6.2 Analysis

Figure 2 shows interception trajectory of SAM to a ARM target. The first and second interception was failed, and an interception was carried out once more.

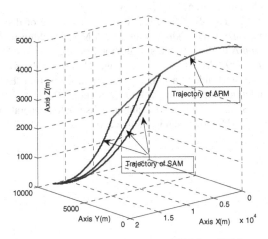

Fig. 1. Interception trajectory of SAM to ARM

Table 1. Anti saturation attack capability of SAM

		$\delta_t=1s$	$\delta_t=2s$	$\delta_t=3s$	$\delta_t=4s$	$\delta_t=5s$
$m=1$	$V_m=2Ma$	4.5	5.5	5.8	6.6	7.1
	$V_m=3Ma$	3.8	4.0	4.6	4.9	5.5
$m=2$	$V_m=2Ma$	10.5	11.7	14.5	21.4	24.2
	$V_m=3Ma$	6.7	8.0	10.7	16.4	19.1
$m=3$	$V_m=2Ma$	14.7	22.5	25.1	28.4	31.6
	$V_m=3Ma$	11.1	12.6	19.6	20.6	24.0

In table 1, anti saturation attack capability of SAM is depicted in terms of ARM speed, weapon channel number and time interval of the attacking stream. From the result we can find that the intensity of ARM shooting stream is stronger, the anti saturation attack capability of SAM is weaker. The intensity of ARM shooting stream is determined by speed of ARM as well as the time interval. If weapon channels can't intercept each of the incoming missiles, the saturation attack is formed.

7   Conclusion

Basing on countermeasure process of SAM to ARM, service process and interception models were derived, by which the anti saturation attack capability of SAM can be quantitatively analyzed. The numerical example shows the influence of ARM shooting stream intensity, which provides the useful reference for further operation of SAM.

References

1. Wang, G., Sun, X., Yan, J., Xie, Y.: Study on the model of anti-ship missile saturation attack. Journal of China Ordnance 6, 10–15 (2010)
2. Wu, S., Jiang, Z., Zhang, M.: Nonlinear Correction of Terminal Guidance Signal for an Antiship Missile. Acta Aeronautica Et Astronautica Sinica 16, 555–558 (2003)
3. Zeng, J., Jiang, Q., Yan, J.: Measures in improve the penetration capability of anti-ship missile. Winged Missile Journal 11, 22–25 (2006)
4. Yang, G., Wang, G., Yan, J., Wang, R.: Analysis of scheme of decoy and its operation efficiency in antagonizing anti-radiation missile. A Model of Ship-to-Air Missile Weapon System Intercepting Ant-Ship Missile's Saturation Striking 7, 8–12 (2003)
5. Ristic, B., Hernandez, M., Farina, A., Ong, H.-T.: Analysis of radar allocation requirements for an IRST aided tracking of anti-ship missiles. In: IEEE Information Fusion International Conference, pp. 1–8. IEEE Press, Florence (2006)
6. Wang, F., He, R., Sha, X.: Anti-ARM technique: distributed general-purpose decoy series (DGPD). In: IEEE CIE International Conference, pp. 306–309. IEEE Press, China (2001)

Design and Integration of Hardware-in-the-Loop Simulation System for Certain Missile

Xiaofei Chang, Tao Yang, Jie Yan, and Mingang Wang

College of Astronautics, Northwestern Polytechnical University, Xi'an 710072, China

Abstract. Hardware-in-the-loop simulation is generally large distributed heterogeneous real-time system. Its overall scheme design and system integration is essential. According to the mission requirement of flight control system simulation experiment for certain missile, the frame of the distributed hardware-in-the-loop simulation system is designed. The nodes are divided into server, client and monitor. And the composition of the system is given. The stage of system integration test is divided into interface matching test, open-loop following test and closed-loop simulation test. The methods and steps are introduced in detail, and the content of bias simulation is enumerated. Finally, the contrastive results between the digital simulation and hardware-in-the-loop simulation are given, and the deviation is preliminarily analyzed. The study shows that the simulation system meets the demands of design, and the flexibility and reliability of the simulation system are enhanced.

Keywords: hardware-in-the-loop simulation, distributed heterogeneous simulation system, system integration, error analysis.

1   Introduction

Flight control system is one of the key components with complicated structure and high reliability requirements in missile system. The parameters of flight control system are required to pass through calculation, design, test, and some other stages, thus only using mathematical simulation and dynamic test can't ensure the correctness of the system performances. In order to reduce the risk of developing, raise the success probability, shorten the development cycle, the hardware-in-the-loop simulation test of the flight control system appears very necessary[1].

The hardware-in-the-loop simulation will replace the corresponding mathematical model[2] with the physical components linking to the simulation loop. It can overcome the imprecise and interference factors of the mathematical model, truly reflect the actual situation of the system.

In order to link the physical components to the simulation loop, it needs to develop the corresponding physical effects simulation equipment according to the different equipment in loop. Multiple nodes form large distributed real-time system. In the development process, the simulation equipment will be provided from different vendors, so the development and operation environment can also be varied. Therefore, the quality

T. Xiao, L. Zhang, and S. Ma (Eds.): ICSC 2012, Part II, CCIS 327, pp. 229–237, 2012.

of system overall design scheme largely determines the success or failure of the system. In addition, how to accomplish the linked test and integration of such a complex system also is the major problem faced in the development of the hardware-in-the-loop simulation system.

In view of the hardware-in-the-loop simulation test requirements of certain missile flight control system, this paper completes the system overall design scheme. Finally the simulation results and the bias analysis are given.

2   Simulation System Overall Design Scheme

The certain missile uses program control guidance scheme[3]. Flight control system includes flight control computer, gyro, Inertial Measurement Unit consisting of accelerometer, and actuator consisting of four rudder actuators.

2.1   System Task Analysis

The hardware-in-the-loop simulation runs through the whole development process of the certain missile flight control system[4]. The mission includes the following points:

- Run the performance simulation of flight control system and check whether the actual performance reaching the system index for providing simulation reference conditions to the control system parameters design and overall error distribution;
- Investigate the harmony and matching attribute among the Inertial Measurement Components, navigation software, control algorithm, actuator, and other partial systems;
- Run the bias test in variable situations, assess the anti-disturbance performance and stable performance of system, and check the effect of all cross coupling interference to optimize the system design, improve the system reliability, and lay a foundation for the success of flight test.

The goal of construction of the system is to construct a distributed, real-time, and hardware-in-the-loop simulation system, which has good openness and expansibility, so that the join of subsequent simulation equipment and components of the test would be convenient.

2.2   Simulation Framework Design

In the simulation system, because of the requirements of each node's heterogeneity and the synchronicity of the data, the simulation framework becomes very complex.

In order to ensure that the whole system can coordinate and orderly complete simulation task, considering the requirements of adaptability maintenance extensibility of the system, the distributed design scheme is adopted. Based on the VMIC real-time fiber network communication, absorbing the message and event driven advanced thought, referencing the mechanism of Server/Client, the nodes are divided into Server, Client and Monitor three types[5].

1. Server

The main task of Server is the management of the whole system simulation data, task scheduling and control of the system, generating real-time synchronous signal in simulation, monitoring the status of the rest of nodes, maintenance the system refresh and data synchronization.

2. Client

Client responses the synchronizing signal of Server, and produces or uses the simulation data according to the requirements of the node task.

3. Monitor

According to the operation status and node assignment, Monitor finishes data consumption, and doesn't response system synchronized signal.

2.3   System Construction Program

According to the test mission requirements and the number of equipment taking part in the simulation, design the scheme of hardware-in-the-loop simulation system (Fig. 1). The missile flight control computer, Inertial Measurement Components and electric rudder actuators link into the simulation loop. The three-axis turntable simulates the missile space attitude. The load simulator loads the hinge moment on the rudder actuator axle, and simulates the real flight status. Inertial Measurement Unit simulates the missile line acceleration. Mathematical simulation model calculates the missile dynamics and kinematics. Production interface test completes the communication between the system and flight control computer.

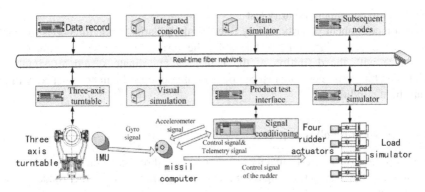

Fig. 1. Simulation system structure diagram

In this simulation system, the simulation console is Server node, the visual simulation is Monitor node, and the rest are Client nodes.

3   The Simulation System Integration Test Process

After each subsystem completing the development task, in order to prevent improper operation causing damage to the product, and ensure smooth completion of the test, the integration test according to the certain steps is necessary. Integration process shall follow the basic principles that from the components to the system, from the open-loop to the closed-loop[6].

3.1   Interface Matching Test

Interface matching test mainly includes the following contents:

1. Electrical interface suitability test
Mainly assess the adaptation of interface electrical characteristics between flight control computer and simulation system, including the flight control computer discrete input/output signal, rudder control analog signals, etc. Inspect the power supply lines of product and simulation equipment.

2. Communication interface correctness test
Communication interface testing mainly includes two aspects: Data transmission among the simulation nodes, namely real-time fiber network communication correctness; Correctness of serial communication between flight control computer and simulation system, including the signal transmission, data decoding, etc.

3. Inertial Measurement Unit simulator performance test
Mainly check for the simulation performance of Inertial Measurement Unit simulator performance relative to the real Inertial Measurement Unit, including the simulation of electrical characteristics, accelerometer model and the accuracy of the gyroscope model.

4. Simulation equipment polarity test
Simulation equipment polarity mainly refers to the polarity of the three-axis turntable and load simulators. As for the turntable, the turntable rotation axes must be in accordance with the definition of the launching coordinate system of simulation model; The hinge moments loaded by load simulators must be in accordance with the actual flight condition.

3.2   Open-Loop Follow-Up Test

Open-loop follow-up test mainly assesses the three-axis turntable follow-up performance, the navigation algorithm and the correctness of the rudder mixed strategies, etc.

1. Three-axis turntable follow-up test
The gyro of Inertial Measurement Unit gets the missile flight attitude by turntable movement. Therefore, the performance of the turntable following instructions will affect the system simulation precision.

Run mathematical closed-loop simulation, let the turntable follow the attitude of the missile. Through the comparison of the turntable instructions and actual position, inspect the follow-up performance of turntable.

2. Assessment of navigation algorithm

According to the information of Inertial Measurement Unit, the navigation algorithm of flight control system calculates the current attitude and position of missile, used for the calculation of the control system. Therefore, we must assess the precision of the navigation algorithm.

For the open-loop simulation, flight control computer and Inertial Measurement Unit simulator will link into the simulation loop. Through the comparison of the remote navigation information and simulation ballistic data, assess the navigation algorithm of flight control system.

3. Rudder mixed strategy examination

During the missile flight process, according to the current attitude and task requires, the control system calculates three-channel rudder control instructions, controls four rudder rotation after the rudder distribution. The load simulators acquire four rudder angles and three equivalent rudder angles after rudder mixed, provides to model for aerodynamic interpolation. Therefore, the correctness of the rudder mixed strategy must be assessed.

Link the flight control computer and rudder actuator into the simulation loop, still make the open-loop follow-up test. After the end of the simulation, compare three rudder control instructions in telemetry data and three rudder angles after the rudder mixed strategy, check the correctness of the rudder mixed strategy.

4. Preliminary validation of flight control law

Finally, it's the whole system open-loop follow simulation test. Compare the acquired rudder deviation curves and rudder deviation curves of mathematical simulation. Compare the rudder control output between flight control computer and mathematics model under the same flight status, prove the correctness of the flight control computer control law preliminarily.

3.3   Closed-Loop Test

When the interface matching and the open-loop follow-up test are finished, after ensuring the hardware circuit and the correctness of the flight control system, closed-loop simulation can be started.

Through the standard trajectory test, verify the effectiveness and correctness of the whole system. During the test the components should be added step by step. First, run the flight control in the loop closed-loop simulation. Then the three-axis turntable and Inertial Measurement Unit are linked to the simulation. Finally, link the load simulators and rudder actuator to the loop, and complete the whole system integration and test.

4   The Bias Test

In missile manufacturing assembly, there will some deviation in the mounting of airframe and engine system. And in the actual flight process, missiles will be affected by the atmospheric environment, wind field interference, etc. These deviations can make the deviations from the scheduled ballistic missiles, and even lead to the failure of mission. Therefore, in the process of simulation, the error, disturbance and fault factors influencing on control system must be considered. Main contents are as follows:

1. Launch conditions
Assess the launch flight trajectories under different conditions, including the longitude and latitude of launching point, the initial attitude and speed.

2. Aerodynamic coefficient bias
The aerodynamic coefficients of airframe dynamics model come from wind tunnel data. And in the aerodynamic blowing process and the process of data processing, the data error that aerodynamic data degree of confidence is inevitable. Therefore, it is necessary to implement the aerodynamic coefficients bias test, to check the control performance under aerodynamic calculation deviation.

3. Engine parameters bias
Engine parameters bias includes the engine installation angle, thrust point and the thrust bias, etc.

4. Airframe parameters bias
The airframe parameters bias mainly includes the airframe quality, the rotation inertia, and the centroid installation position, etc.

5. Wind field environment bias
Test the flight status in the wind field conditions, including steady wind field, atmospheric turbulence and shear wind, etc.

6. Impact interference bias
Assess the missile control system performance under the disturbances of various impacts, including the shock of separation, the engine ignition shock, etc.

5   The Simulation System Commissioning Test Process

The following are the comparison between the hardware-in-the-loop simulation and the mathematical simulation under a certain simulation status, and the preliminary analysis of bias factor.

5.1   Simulation Results

The following are parts of the simulation results contrast curves.

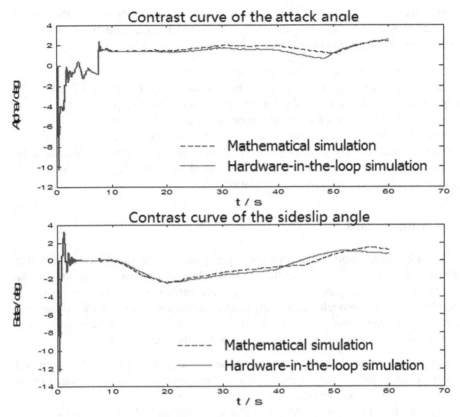

Fig. 2. Simulation results contrast curves

As we can see from the graph, the simulation curves of the mathematical simulation and hardware-in-the-loop simulation are basically the same. It shows that the system reaches the design requirements.

5.2   Bias Analysis

Through the primary qualitative analysis, the differences of the hardware-in-the-loop simulation and the mathematical simulation are mainly caused by the following parts[7]:

1. Electrical noise
Because the existing of the system zero potential and electrical signals noise will cause the differences of the hardware-in-the-loop simulation and mathematical simulation, it may be improved through improving the conditioning circuit.

2. Turntable follow-up and inertial navigation drift
In simulation, the follow-up bias and the Inertial Measurement Unit drift will cause the difference of attitude and position information between the calculating of flight

control, navigation algorithms and trajectory simulation. Then the bias of the control instructions will exist. The bias can reduce by improving the turntable performance and revising inertial navigation model.

3. Performance decline under rudder actuators loaded

Because the real rudder actuators are subjected to the load simulators loading the hinge moment in the process of simulation, the rudder actuators performance downs. So that actual rudder angles and rudder control instructions exist bias.

According to the preliminary analysis on the simulation bias, several factors causing the bias are only given qualitatively. If you want to quantitative determine the factors resulting in the magnitude of bias, you need for each component test, as well as more in-depth data analysis and calculation.

6   Conclusions

Based on the simulation task analysis, this paper designs the simulation system, and presents the overall scheme of the system; Then a detailed description of the simulation system integrated method and steps are introduced, and the bias test is also introduced. Finally through closed-loop system simulation results the validity and the correctness of the system are proved. At present, the system has been put to use. Through the experiment, this system can reach the following conclusions:

- Certain missile hardware-in-loop test is the effective means to test flight control components and assess control performance. After acceptance testing, system functions and indexes reach the design requirements.
- The simulation framework design of Server, Client and Monitor form makes the whole system easy to upgrade and maintain, facilitate subsequent simulation node to join in.
- The method and procedure of large distributed real-time simulation system integration and test are given. For the establishment of similar simulation system, this paper has some reference value for engineering.

References

1. Fu, W.-X., Yu, Y.-F., Huang, Y., Wei, J.-L.: Precision Guided Missile Control System Simulation. Northwestern Polytechnical University Press, Xi'an (2010)
2. James, B., John, P., Bernard, V.: Design of the Ballistic Missile Defense System Hardware-in-the-Loop. ITEA Journal 29(1), 23–28 (2008)
3. Fu, W.-X., Peng, Q.-S.: Program Controlled Missile Hardware-in-loop Simulation System Research. Journal of Solid Rocket Technology 32(2), 127–130 (2009)
4. Chan, J.-Y., Meng, X.-Y., Ding, Y.: Hardware-in-loop Simulation. National Defence Industry Press, Beijing (2008)
5. Wu, Z.-F.: Distributed Flight Simulation Research. Northwestern Polytechnical University, Xi'an (2003)

6. Su, J.-G., Fu, Y.-M.: Design of Hardware-in-the-loop Simulation System for Laser End-Guided Shell. Journal of System Simulation 18(9), 2469–2472 (2006)
7. Bi, Y.: Error Analysis of Missile Hardware-in-the-loop Simulation System. Northwestern Polytechnical University, Xi'an (2006)

Design of the Virtual Training Platform for Carrier Aircrafts Approach and Landing

Xianjian Chen[1], Gang Liu[2], and Guanxin Hong[1]

[1] School of Aeronautic Science and Engineering, Beihang University, Beijing 100191, China
[2] National Laboratory for Aeronautics and Astronautics,
Beihang University, Beijing 100191, China
`xianjian97@sina.com`, `{LG,honggx}@buaa.edu.cn`

Abstract. A virtual training platform for carrier aircrafts approach and landing is designed based on virtual reality technology. Distributed framework is adopted, and every node of the system is introduced in detail. Then it gives a method of real-time communication using Reflective Memory technology in this paper. And it introduces the logical relation and integration of dynamic modules of three types of landing. The environmental library of training platform of approach and landing is built with 3d graphics engine. The 3d visual models are built using DOF and texture mapping technology. And the scheme of voice communication between LSO and pilots is proposed. Then it analyses the problems of collision detection. Finally the global visualization is given.

Keywords: carrier aircraft, approach and landing, virtual training platform, distributed framework.

1   Introduction

The technology of carrier-based aircraft approach and landing is very important. It decides success of the task finished by carrier aircrafts. Because of large scale of the dynamical system of carrier aircraft landing and numbers of subsystems which are high degree coupling and various internal and external factors, it is very hard for us to study about the whole system. For the pilot it also quite difficult to center the deck, capture and keep the glide path, finally arrest and land on the short narrow runway of the carrier.

Virtual reality is a kind of technology which makes people immerse in virtual environment that people can use associated equipment to interact. Recent years virtual reality has achieved rapid development in model building, performance form, human interface devices, developing platform and run-time infrastructure [1]. All these have given a direction for the research of the carrier aircraft approach and landing. The references [2, 3] are visual simulations for the landing of carrier-based aircraft using distributed system. It is helpful for people to learn the landing system and for the further research of the system. But most of simulations before adopted a man-out-of-loop way, which couldn't be used for the training of relevant personnel. So it can't

T. Xiao, L. Zhang, and S. Ma (Eds.): ICSC 2012, Part II, CCIS 327, pp. 238–247, 2012.

improve the proficiency of the operator including pilot and LSO[1] . If we take real landing training, it will cost a large amount of money. And it may bring accidents because of the immature technology. So design of the virtual training platform of carrier aircraft landing is especially important.

Based on the work of previous people, this paper adopts distributed framework to build training platform of carrier aircrafts approach and landing, applies various model building technology to building the 3d visual models, and gives the method of the voice communication. It makes a comprehensive design for the training platform.

2   Basic Framework of the Virtual Training Platform

Because of large number of subsystems and heavy load of calculation in the training platform, we adopt distributed framework as Fig. 1 shows.

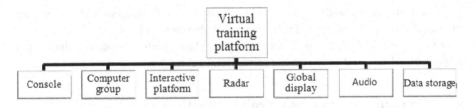

Fig. 1. Composition of the Training Platform

The console is the control center of the whole training system. It can initialize the system, dynamically manage the process of training, such as freezing, thawing and resetting, etc. when the system runs, the console will monitor the exceptions and synchronize the nodes.

A group of computers are used to solve the dynamic equations because one computer may not fit for the work.

The interactive training platform which consists of a group of carrier-based aircraft simulators and an LSO platform is the core of the system. Each carrier based aircraft simulator which can be transformed from land-based aircraft simulator has a console. Through it we can set the parameters of the carrier aircraft simulator including type, camp, dynamic parameters and the states of the aircraft. The console coordinates not only the internal communications between the subsystems of carrier aircraft simulator but also the network communications with the other nodes of the system. LSO simulation platform includes a data helmet and data gloves and other interactive device. The sight tracking device inside the helmet can make the scene changed with the sight of LSO training personnel. Thus the training people can keep watch on environment of the sea and situation of the aircraft landing, and operate on the virtual instruments with the data gloves which also can produce sense of touch to interact

---

[1] LSO: Land Signal Officer.

with the virtual scene. Each console of carrier aircraft simulators and LSO platform has a respective dynamical model, through which the whole system can show the aircraft landing in a man-out -of-loop way without the simulators.

Radar system displays the position information of carrier and aircrafts. When the aircrafts are far from the carrier, LSO trainer uses radar to track them. If some aircraft simulators are set to enemy side by their consoles, the radar is able to show the side of every aircraft.

Global display system consists of dual-channel 3D projectors and cylindrical screen. It displays the entire scene of the carrier aircraft approach and landing. According to special requirement, it makes view focus on any aircraft to track it by operation on computer of this subsystem. When the aircraft takes important actions such as extending and retracting of the landing gears or tail hook, it can display the actions in close-up. In addition the scene can be switched to that from LSO or pilot's view, thus we can watch the situation of carrier aircraft landing from their eyes.

The quality of the audio system also affects sense of immersion of the virtual training platform, so realistic 3D audio system is also an important part.

Data storage computer is used for storing the data which is generated during the training, and draws real-time curves for important parameters.

3   Communication of the Training Platform

3.1   Type of Connection

Most Aircrafts today are adopted jet engines and the flight speed is very high. So dozens of milliseconds of jitter can make a considerable deviation. It will result in failure for decision-making mistakes. So the Ethernet the traditional method of communication can't make sure of reliability of this platform. Now we try to adopt a method of communication based on hardware. That is Reflective Memory technology. It realizes communication between nodes via fiber-optic cables and Reflective Memory Cards. This method is stable and rapid [4]. It doesn't consume CPU resources and the jitter it generates is predictable. Here we use star configuration. In this way, single node failure will not affect the operation of the entire system. Nodes are connected as shown in Fig. 2.

3.2   Time Synchronization

In order to make the time of all nodes the same, we can create the standard time to console by GPS timing or define it by ourselves. Then the console computer writes the standard time to the special memory space in its Reflective Memory Card. And other nodes read this standard time in the same memory space in respective Reflective Memory Card to correct of their time.

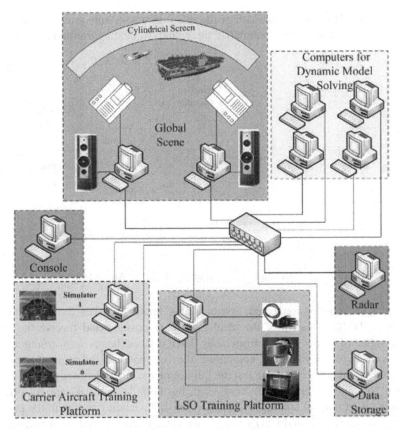

Fig. 2. Framework of the Virtual Training Platform for Carrier Aircrafts Approach and Landing

4   Key Issues of the Virtual Training Platform

4.1   Dynamic Models of Carrier Aircraft Landing

Dynamics is the theoretical basis of this training platform. There are a number of subsystems participating in the process of carrier aircraft approach and landing. So the workload of model build is heavy. Control system includes DMC[2] model, autopilot system model, throttle control strategy and bolting judgment model. Landing aid system includes FLOLS[3] model. Environment system involves prediction model of the ship motion and perturbation model of wind field. Full motion equations of aircraft, landing gear and arrest model are in the ontological system. If the system can turn into a man-out-of-loop validated simulation, LSO and pilot dynamic models are required. But it is not enough to build these subsystem models. We also have to

---

[2] DMC: Deck Motion Compensation.
[3] FLOLS: Fresnel Lens Optical Landing System.

integrate them. This paper summarizes the relationships of subsystems as shown in Fig. 3. And according to it we summarize three kinds of landing training methods:

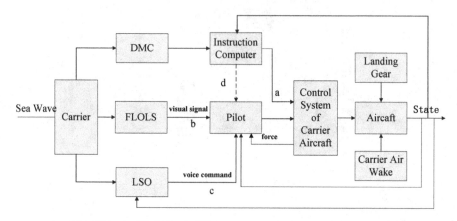

Fig. 3. Logical Relations of Subsystems of Carrier Aircraft Landing

When "a" circuit is connected, instruction computer receives the compensation signal from DMC to calculate the ideal glide path position and receive the actual position signal of carrier aircraft from radar. Then it gives the revise instruction to the control system of aircraft after comparing the two positions. And in this process people don't participate. So it can test the full-automatic landing system [5].

When "b" and "c" circuits are connected, but both "a" and "d" are cut off, this process is called manual landing. Pilot has to finish the landing task with the guide of FLOLS's visual signals and LSO's voice command. It can be used for the training of manual approach and landing of carrier aircraft.

When "b" and "c" circuits are connected, "a" is cut off, which means that instruction computer doesn't work on the aircraft control system directly. But through "d" circuit it shows the deviation to pilot by relevant instruments. And aviator can operate the control system of the aircraft to revise the deviation. This is semiautomatic landing training.

4.2   Virtual Environment Building

Because of the vagary of climate and its large effect on the process of carrier-based aircraft's approach and landing, we sort the environment into four aspects. They are the sea, the sky, the climate and special effects.

As for the sea, its wave affects the motion of carrier directly, so as to affect the ideal landing point. Here we divide the sea into seven cases according to levels of state. In fact there may be higher sea state levels. In this case, the carrier aircraft is not permitted taking off or landing, so we needn't build them. The sea state is summarized as Table 1.

Table 1. Levels of the Sea State

Sea state	Wave height(m)	Conditions	Wind speed(m/s)
0	0	Mirror-like	0-0.2
1	0-0.1	Micro wave	0.3-1.5
2	0.1-0.5	Small wave	1.6-3.3
3	0.5-1.25	Small wave	3.4-5.4
4	1.25-2.5	Moderate wave	5.5-7.9
5	2.5-4	Large wave	8.0-10.7
6	4-6	Larger wave	10.8-13.8

Vega Prime is a popular 3D graphics engine. We can directly use Vega Prime Marine to build the sea under different state [6]. It supports mirror effect, and we can call the function to set the level of the sea state.

The approach and landing of carrier aircraft is also affected by the weather. According to the height of cloud and visibility, the weather can be divided three cases as Table 2. The processes of approach and landing in different weather are not the same. In Vega Prime we can call the sky box and the function of setTimeOfDay to set the time to be day or night and use myEnvSnow and myEnvRain to describe the rain and snow. In reality sudden changes of weather often happen during the approach and landing of carrier aircraft. At this time the process of the landing has to be changed [7]. So when establishing the environmental library we should consider the cross of different weather.

Table 2. Three Kinds of Weather

Environment	Weather	Height of lower cloud	Visibility	Other
1	Good	≥3000ft	≥5nm	Flight by day
2	Bad	≥1000ft	<5nm	Flight by day
3	Very bad	<1000ft	<5nm	Flight at night

There are kinds of special effects in the process of the training, such as the smoke of the landing gears when they touching the deck, flame of the engine, even the explosion of the plane crash and so on. In virtual reality technology we usually use particle system to express the special effects. Most 3D graphics engines have particle systems. So we can achieve the special effects by simple setting and programing.

4.3   3D Objects Modeling

The quality of the objects modeling directly impacts on the immersion of the virtual platform. There are various ways of modeling [1]. We can choose the method of artificial construct to model. Creator is a modeling tool produced by MultiGen-Paradigm. It stores data based on hierarchical structure. It divides nodes into five types which are database header node, group node, object node, face node, and vertex node. The file format of OpenFlight creator generates has been the industry standard.

To model the carrier we divide the carrier model into appearance part, light part and movable part. Appearance part includes deck, body of ship, building and mast.

They are all unmovable. We just use ordinary notes to build them according to their actual sizes. Light scene includes runway edge lamps, center line lamps, abeam lamps, deck edge lights, marker lights of buildings and so on. These lights are built with light nodes. For JBD[4] and radar which are movable they can be built with DOF[5] nodes, and then we can drive them with program according to requirements.

Modeling of the carrier based aircrafts is similar to carrier. It doesn't introduce again here.

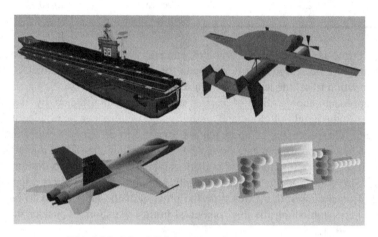

Fig. 4. Models of Carrier, Aircrafts, and FLOLS

FLOLS is an important guide facility in the stage of glide. It involves lamp array and stabilizing mechanism. It's not appropriate to build the lights using texture technique. Although it's more vivid and easier, visual range of texture is small. So we also adopt light nodes to build the lights of FLOLS. And we still need to set the light range of the lamp array. FLOLS can't be fixed on the coordinate system of carrier directly or it will move when the carrier moving, rather than form a stable glide slope.

So considering the effect of stabilizing mechanism, we set FLOLS as a DOF node of the carrier. When the carrier does a motion of pitching, heaving and rolling, the attitude of FLOLS must be real-time revised [8].

Fig. 4 shows the 3D models.

For the instruction of LSO platform, we simplify the content of it. After modeling it with GL-studio, we lead it to the right position of LSO platform in virtual scene. LSO trainer can monitor it with the data helmet. Fig. 5 shows the instrument of LSO platform we build.

4.4   Voice Communication

LSO will give an order of deviation to the pilot when the carrier-based aircraft is landing, and it also gets feedback to assure that the pilot has received the signal and

---

[4] JBD: Jet Blast Deflectors.
[5] DOF: Degree Of Freedom.

acquire condition of landing. For that, the mechanism of voice communication among system nodes should be built. Specifically, there are several of equipment such as radio transceiver, control panel, headset and microphone put in the aircraft simulator. Then the voice connection should be easily established by wired communication if only the related devices are set on the platform of LSO. Furthermore, in order to make the communication between LSO and simulator more lifelike, a noise generator should be added, which can imitate the effect of radio communication.

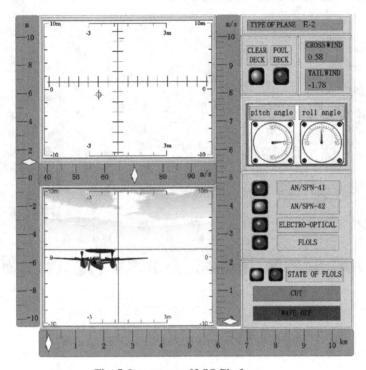

Fig. 5. Instrument of LSO Platform

4.5   Collision Detection

For the virtual platform of the approach and landing system of carrier aircraft, collision detection is an important aspect. It includes the rigid-body collision and the flexible-body collision. When the carrier aircraft is touching the ship, the rigid-body collision should be detected, but the collision detection can only examine whether the two objects collide. In order that the distortion never happens, virtual platform should be corrected afterwards to avoid the penetration. The simulation continues if the speed of carrier airplane is in the regular range, or the carrier airplane is judged to be crash if the speed exceeds the limited value. When the aircraft lands on the deck of carrier, the flexible-body collision between the tail hook and barrier cable should be detected. If the tail hook succeeds to hook the barrier cable, the course deforms the barrier cable, and the carrier airplane will decelerate and finally stop for the sake of the effect of blocking force. The vplsector class of Vega Prime provides seven modes of the collision detection. The basic principle is that some lines extend at the position of lsector. When the lines intersect the target, it is judged as collision and returns the Boolean value back.

The global view of the system has been shown as Fig. 6. We can track the scene as we need by conducting the tool bar.

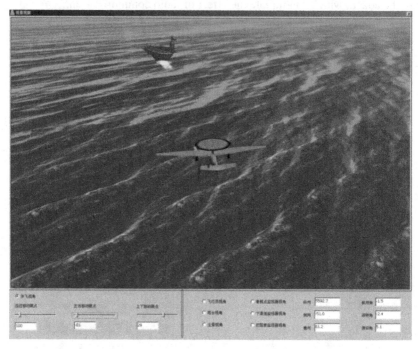

Fig. 6. An Instance for Global Scene of the System

5   Conclusions

This paper based on the virtual reality technology, gives a design of training platform for carrier aircrafts approach and landing, it meets requirement of synchronization of the system to adopt the distributed framework and the method of communication based on the hardware. And it summarizes three types of training, and builds the 3d models of the system. Finally it gives the solution of the problems voice communication and collision detection. This platform is able to give pilots and LSO a clearer understanding of the whole landing procedure and improve their operation ability. Besides, the staff can accumulate their experiences undergoing emergencies and enhance the percentage of successful landing in using this facility. Moreover, this platform also provides the practical basis for carrier aircraft landing system designs and improvements in the future.

References

1. Zhao, Q.: Summary of Virtual Reality. Science in China Series F: Information Sciences 39, 2–46 (2009)
2. Li, J., Bian, X.: Research on Visualization of Fly Simulation for Carrier Aircraft Based on HLA. Journal of System Simulation 20, 2352–2356 (2008)
3. Dong, C., Wang, J., Wang, Q.: Design and Development of Carrier Aircraft Landing Visualization Simulation System. Journal of System Simulation 20, 4626–4629 (2008)
4. Zhao, K., Xu, S., Ye, Q., Li, Y.: Design and Realization of Flight Simulation System Based on Virtual Reality Technology. In: Chinese Control and Decision Conference (2011)
5. Prickett, L., Parks, C.J.: Flight Testing of the FA-18E/F Automatic Carrier Landing System. In: IEEE Proceedings of Aerospace Conference, Big Sky, MT, vol. 5, pp. 2593–2612. IEEE USA (2001)
6. Vega Prime Options Guide, version 2.2. Multigen- Paradigm, U.S.A (2002)
7. Chen, X., Liu, G., Hong, G.: Selection and Analysis of Key Points and Factors in Carrier Aircraft Landing Process. Flight Dynamics 29, 20–24 (2011)
8. Qiao, Y., Bai, X., Xie, X., Li, Y.: Visual Simulation of Aircraft Carrier Assistant Landing System. In: IEEE Pacific-Asia Workshop on Computational Intelligence and Industrial Application, pp. 714–717 (2008)

An Experimental Approach
for BMDS Effectiveness Analysis

Hua Chai, Yangang Liang, and Guojin Tang

National University of Defense Technology, No.109, Deya Road, Kaifu District,
Changsha 410073, China
chaihuanudt@gmail.com

Abstract. The problem of ballistic missile defense system (BMDS) effectiveness analysis has been highly concerned for years. In this paper, a simulation study of BMDS is fulfilled by accomplishing large number of experiments. In order to improve the simulation efficiency, the orthogonal design methodology is adopted to arrange experiment plans. After resultant data are selected, the variance analysis method is employed to analyze the relativity between variable parameters and indexes. In the end, two demos are given to show how the approach works.

Keywords: BMDS, effectiveness analysis, orthogonal design, variance analysis.

1   Introduction

Ballistic missile defense system (BMDS) is one of the most important weapons in 21st century. A lot of investigations have been developed upon the topic of BMDS effectiveness analysis. Except few battlefield evaluation (e.g. PAC system in the Gulf War), flight tests play a significant role in analyzing BMDS effectiveness. However, the complexity and uncertainty of BMDS result in a fact that in pursuit of high reliability, a large number of flight tests should be deployed; this is unfeasible due to its high costs.

To address the preceding paradox, simulation experiments are operated as substitutes. Many people and institution have developed relevant investigation. Based on modeling and simulation technique, Mei Dan etc. evaluate the ballistic missile defense ability of multi-functional phased array radar [1]. Tommer Ender etc. employ neural network surrogate models to fulfill architecture level analysis of the BMDS, which achieve a tradeoff between model fidelity and computation rapidity [2]. QASIM Zeeshan etc. present a conceptual design architecture for boost phase ballistic missile defense, which simulates the defense process of warning, decision making, tracking, intercepting and effectiveness assessing [3].Most of the investigations focus on the improvement of the model or the architecture of simulation system; few involve the design and amelioration of simulation experiments.

T. Xiao, L. Zhang, and S. Ma (Eds.): ICSC 2012, Part II, CCIS 327, pp. 248–254, 2012.

This paper employs orthogonal design methodology to arrange ballistic missile defense simulation experiments. Based on a functional, distributed simulation system of BMDS, a large number of experiments which consider multi-parameter multi-level conditions are implemented. Many indexes that describe the BMDS effectiveness are selected from experiments output, provide data support for further analysis.

2   Indexes System

Before we start to construct a simulation system of BMDS, a problem should be answered at first: the missile defense process is a quite complex one that calls for a high level of cooperation of several subsystems, well then how to depict the effectiveness of BMDS? Focus on which kind of parameter can we hold the essence of the missile defense process? In this paper, we abstract and establish a layered BMDS effectiveness indexes system via classical ballistic missile defense process, referring to Fig.1.

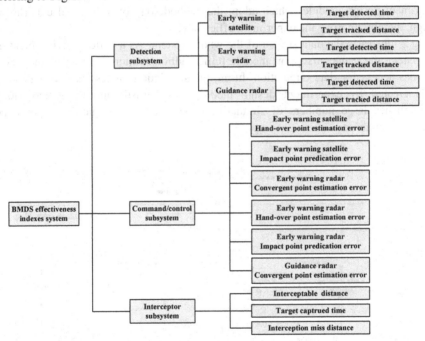

Fig. 1. BMDS effectiveness indexes system

The indexes system presented in Fig.1 contains several sets of indexes which provide a full-scale measure of the BMDS effectiveness; it is available for both flight tests and simulative experiments. However, it should be pointed out that this indexes system is available only under the single-target-attacking circumstances, i.e. discrimination between warhead and decoy are not involved in this paper.

3   Distributed Simulation System of BMDS

Contraposing the indispensable subsystems that make up of an integral BMDS, a set of functional models have been abstracted and constitute a ballistic missile defense loop which simulate the whole operation process of BMD. In addition, a manager/support module and an experiment design module are integrated to drive the loop and improve the efficiency; all the data and indexes acquired are saved in the database.

Ballistic missile defense process involves many parameters of different equipments, in order to investigate indexes' sensitivity relative to these parameters respectively, it is necessary to deploy multi-parameter multi-level experiments. As to every single experiment plan with certain initial conditions, considering the uncertainty due to environment influence, repetitious experiments should be implemented to restrain the randomicity. According to the preceding reasons, the total experiments magnitude could be egregious. To address this problem, we add an experiment design module, which adopt the methodology of orthogonal experiment design, thereby improve the experiment efficiency.

Fig.2 illustrates the data stream of the whole system. As a bottom environment of the system, the manager/support module fulfills administration and surveillance, also provides access for data circulation during the simulation process; according to the plans created by experiment design module, the ballistic missile defense loop accomplishes large numbers of simulative experiments, consequently exports the indexes to database.

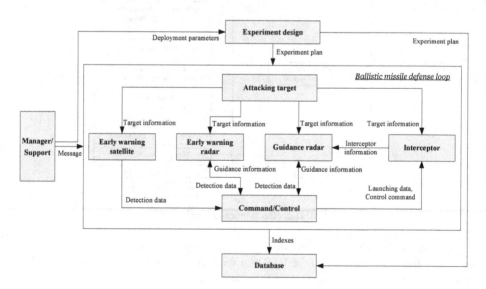

Fig. 2. Distributed simulation system of BMDS

4   Example

To witness and understand how to analyze the BMDS effectiveness based on the simulation system raised in this paper, it is best to give an example. This section fulfills a 12-parameter 2-level condition, which demands 16 experiments to be accomplished according to the orthogonal design method. Assume that every single experiment is repeated 100 times, the total number will be 1600.

The example employs a simple BMDS which consists of two early warning satellites, one early warning radar, one guidance radar, one command/control system and one interceptor. Sensor detection precision, such as range measuring deviation and angle measuring deviation of sensors, is variable while other parameters are fixed. Table.1 presents relevant parameters and their level.

Table 1. Variable parameters and their level

	Parameters	Level1	Level2
Satellite 1	Azimuth angle deviation α_{Se1} (deg)	0.01	0.001
	Elevation angle deviation β_{Se1} (deg)	0.01	0.001
Satellite 2	Azimuth angle deviation α_{Se2} (deg)	0.01	0.001
	Elevation angle deviation β_{Se2} (deg)	0.01	0.001
Early warning radar	Azimuth angle deviation α_{Re} (deg)	0.5	0.05
	Elevation angle deviation β_{Re} (deg)	0.5	0.05
	Range deviation ρ_{Re} (m)	100	30
	Range derivative deviation v_{Re} (m/s)	1	0.3
Guidance radar	Azimuth angle deviation α_{Xe} (deg)	0.1	0.01
	Elevation angle deviation β_{Xe} (deg)	0.1	0.01
	Range deviation ρ_{Xe} (m)	50	10
	Range derivative deviation v_{Xe} (m/s)	0.5	0.1

According to orthogonal table $L_{16}(2^{15})$, the initial conditions of the 16 experiments are set. After 1600 runs of the simulation system, a great deal of indexes is accumulated. Variance analysis method is used for data disposal, which can objectively tell how much influence the parameters can have on BMDS effectiveness. Two demos are shown as below.

4.1   Early Warning Radar's Target Detected Time

It is obviously that those parameters which may affect early warning radar's target detected time should be early warning satellite detection precision, but not involve radar precision because the whole system is marked by causality, which means things happened latterly cannot possibly have influence on things happened formerly. Tab.2 gives the variance analysis result about preceding question.

Table 2. Variance analysis result of demo1

Source of variance	Quadratic sum of deviation	Degrees of freedom	Mean square	F ratio	Critical value $(\alpha =0.1)$	Significance
α_{S1e}	27.56	1	27.56	0.36	3.23	×
β_{S1e}	3.80	1	3.80	0.05	3.23	×
α_{S2e}	21.62	1	21.62	0.28	3.23	×
β_{S2e}	5.60	1	5.60	0.07	3.23	×
Error	837.41	11	76.13			
Summation	895.99	15				

In Table.2 the notation "×" denotes that the change of parameter have no significant influence on the index. We can see from the table that under a significance level of 0.1, early warning satellite detection precision do not affect the target detected time of early warning radar evidently; this is because the estimative information of target state based on early warning satellite detection has a poor veracity, its function of leading posterior sensors is quite limited.

4.2   Early Warning Radar's Hand-Over Point Estimation Error

According to causality, the variance analysis in this demo involves more parameters including both early warning satellite and radar's detection precision.

Table 3. Variance analysis result of demo2

Source of variance	Quadratic sum of deviation	Degrees of freedom	Mean square	F ratio	Critical value $(\alpha =0.1)$	Significance
α_{S1e}	11901.87	1	11901.87	0.23	3.59	×
β_{S1e}	11583.95	1	11583.95	0.22	3.59	×
α_{S2e}	10051.01	1	10051.01	0.19	3.59	×
β_{S2e}	10644.37	1	10644.37	0.21	3.59	×
α_{Re}	1389892.78	1	1389892.78	26.93	3.59	√
β_{Re}	1643339.72	1	1643339.72	31.84	3.59	√
ρ_{Re}	16053.33	1	16053.33	0.31	3.59	×
ν_{Re}	10601.10	1	10601.10	0.21	3.59	×
Error	361245.62	7	51606.52			
Summation	3465313.75	15				

We can see from Table.3 that under a significance level of 0.1, the parameters which can evidently affect early warning radar's hand-over point estimation error are α_{Re} and β_{Re}, i.e. the angle detection precision of early warning radar. Fig.3 represents the filter error curve based on two sets of different angle measuring precision, which can illustrate the preceding conclusion visually.

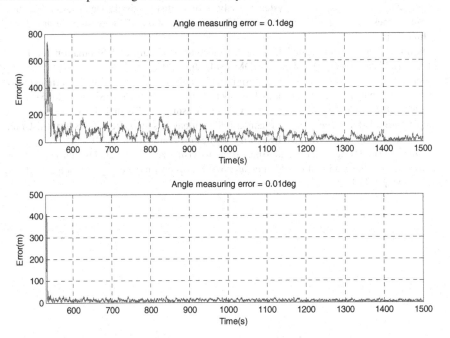

Fig. 3. Contrast of filter error curve in two different conditions

5   Conclusions

This paper utilizes distributed simulation technique to fulfill BMDS effectiveness analysis. Repetitious experiments are deployed to restrain the randomicity and complexity of the whole system. In order to improve the efficiency, methodology of orthogonal experiment design is adopted to arrange experiment plans. The resultant data are analyzed by using variance analysis method, which can objectively tell how much influence the parameters can have on BMDS effectiveness via hypothesis testing theory. The two demos given in section 4 show that the approach raised in this paper is quite feasible.

The BMDS in reality is far more complex than those in computers, thus there are many aspects of issues should be improve for the study in this paper, such as the fidelity of models, the defense process consider discrimination etc. Further investigations will be developed upon these issues.

References

1. Dan, M., et al.: Simulation and Evaluation of Phased Array Radar Ballistic Missile Defense Capability. In: Proceedings of the 2008 IEEE International Conference on Information and Automation, Zhangjiajie, China (2008)
2. Ender, T., et al.: Systems-of-Systems Analysis of Ballistic Missile Defense Architecture Effectiveness Through Surrogate Modeling and Simulation. IEEE Systems Journal 4(2) (June 2010)
3. Qasim, Z., et al.: Conceptual Design Architecture Modeling and Simulation for Boost Phase Ballistic Missile Defense. CADDM 18(4) (June 2008)
4. Jack, P.C.: An overview of the design and analysis of simulation experiments for sensitivity analysis. European Journal of Operational Research 164, 287–300 (2005)
5. Sessler, A.M., Cornwall, J.M., et al.: Countermeasures: A Technical Evaluation of the Operational Effectiveness of the Planned US National Missile Defense System. In: Union of Concerned Scientists and MIT Security Studies Program (April 2000)
6. Daniel, C.H.: Using models and simulations to visualize NMD C3: lessons learned. In: Proceedings, International Conference and Workshop on Engineering of Computer-Based Systems, pp. 139–141 (1997)

The Modeling and Simulation of Command and Control System Based on Capability Characteristics

Huijing Meng and Xiao Song

Science and Technology on Aircraft Control Laboratory, School of Automation Science and Electrical Engineering, Beihang University, 100191 Beijing, China

Abstract. Command and control are key factors in a variety of military theories. Command and control system simulation, uses computer simulation technology to examine the performance of designed command post system in a virtual environment, which has been the basis for an assessment or optimization of command post system. This paper analyzed the shortcomings and deficiencies of the current command and control system modeling, and proposed a command and control system modeling based on the entity-relationship. Combined with the Lanchester model considering efficiency of command this paper takes command and control system models for scenario analysis.

Keywords: command and control system, capability-based characteristics, Lanchester model.

1   Introduction

Command and control are key factors in a variety of military theories. The importance of command and control system to national security has been widely recognize. Command and control system represents various command posts composed of personnel and equipment. It has information reception and processing, decision support, command and control functions in the C^4ISR system.

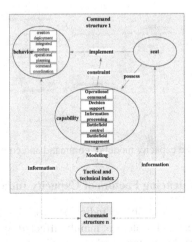

Fig. 1. The overall structure of command and control system

T. Xiao, L. Zhang, and S. Ma (Eds.): ICSC 2012, Part II, CCIS 327, pp. 255–261, 2012.
© Springer-Verlag Berlin Heidelberg 2012

So far, the main simulation outcome of command post is process-based simulation method which is process-centric. However, proposed studies still can not meet the actual requirements.

The command and control modeling method based on capability characteristics uses behavior model of command structure, capacity model of command structure and the relationship between them to model command and control system, as shown in Figure 1. This article only models part capability indexes of command and control system with Lanchester equation.

2   Command and Control System Modeling Based on Capacity Characteristics

In order to characterize and compare entity's capacities, a various of indicators usually are creates to describe them. Entity capability indices are the quantify presentation of various factors which affect entity capability.

2.1   To Extract Capability Indices

In terms of time and quality, command structures are abstracted from the capacity characteristics of creation deployment, integrated posture, operational planning, command coordination, damage reorganization and corresponding capacity indicators are extracted . as shown in Figure 2.

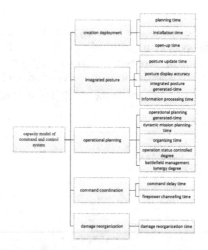

Fig. 2. The capacity model of command and control system

2.2   To Clear the Influencing Factors of Capacity Indicators

Then the factors affecting the above indicators will be analyzed in this part. In general, command and control system is mainly affected by performance parameters, operating parameters, baseline values, technique gain and training gain.

2.3   To Determine the Algorithm of Indicators

Here only discuss the algorithm of integrated posture capacity indicators, and the algorithm of other indicators will be described in subsequent articles.

(1) Posture update time
Posture update time is a period of time from changes of target information detected by intelligence reconnaissance systems to the changes shown on the figures of corresponding command post and it is measured in seconds .

The specific algorithm is: to record the current time T_{zc} , and intelligence reconnaissance systems mastering targets ;to poll $\{Track_i\}$ .If information changes at the time $Track_i$, update T_{gx}^i the   time information shown on the picture of command post. Else T_{gx}^i takes posture update cycle: $T_{gx}^i = T_{gxzq}$;to calculate posture update time T_{gx} : $T_{gx} = \max\{T_{gx}^i - T_{zc}\}$.

Table 1 gives the optimal value , the worst value and the average value of posture update time T_{gx} :

Table 1. The analysis of the value of posture update time

	The optimal value T_{gx}^{min}		The worst value T_{gx}^{max}		The average value T_{gx}^{ave}	
	The red	The blue	The red	The blue	The red	The blue
T_{gx}	10	20	60	60	35	40

Then the impact factor to posture integrated C from posture update time T_{gx} is:

$$C_1 = \frac{T_{gx}^{max} - T_{gx}^{ave}}{T_{gx}^{max} - T_{gx}^{min}}$$

(1) Posture display accuracy
Posture display accuracy means the accuracy of different posture information displayed in map. Its specific algorithm is:

$$P_{Accu} = K_4 \times (1 + K_2) \times P_{Accu}^0$$

P_{Accu}^0 represents average posture display resolution. K_2 represents technique gain and K_4 represents posture display resolution.

Table 2 shows the values of K_2 and K_4 when posture display accuracy P_{Accu} takes the optimal value, the worst value and the average value respectively:

Table 2. The analysis of the value of posture display accuracy

	The optimal value P_{Accu}^{max}		The worst value P_{Accu}^{min}		The average value P_{Accu}^{ave}	
	The red	The blue	The red	The blue	The red	The blue
K_2	0.9	0.7	0.3	0.1	0.6	0.4
K_4	0.9	0.7	0.5	0.3	0.7	0.5

Then the impact factor to posture integrated C from posture display accuracy P_{Accu} is:

$$C_2 = \frac{P_{Accu}^{ave} - P_{Accu}^{min}}{P_{Accu}^{max} - P_{Accu}^{min}}$$

(2) Integrated posture generated-time

Integrated posture generated-time is ultimately formed after command post carrying out reconnaissance of different posture information. It is mainly affected by posture distribution level, information overload, technique gain. Its specific algorithm is:

$$T_g = \frac{(1 - K_2) \times K_5}{K_6} \times T_g^{i0}$$

$i = 1,2,3,4$ denote enemy's posture, our posture, real-time air situation, battlefield environment respectively. T_g^{i0} represents baseline generation time of integrated posture information. K_5 represents information overload, $K_5 = \begin{cases} 1, N_{Load} < N_0 \\ e^{h(N_{Load} - N_0)}, N_{Load} \geq N_0 \end{cases}$, in which N_{Load} represents the number of pending messages , N_0 represents the number of messages can be processed simultaneously (information capacity), and h is coefficient could be valued between [0,1] based on experience. K_6 is posture distribution level.

Table 3 shows the values of K_2 , K_5 and K_6 when integrated posture generated-time T_g takes the optimal value, the worst value and the average value respectively:

Table 3. The analysis of the value of integrated posture generated-time

	The optimal value T_g^{min}		The worst value T_g^{max}		The average value T_g^{ave}	
	The red	The blue	The red	The red	The blue	The red
K_2	0.9	0.7	0.3	0.1	0.6	0.4
K_5	0.2	0.4	1	1	0.6	0.7
K_6	4	3	1	1	2.5	2

Then the impact factor to posture integrated C from integrated posture generated-time T_g is:

$$C_3 = \frac{T_g^{max} - T_g^{ave}}{T_g^{max} - T_g^{min}}$$

(3)   Information processing time

Information processing time is the processing time of receiving/distributing telegrams by command and control entities. It is mainly related to information processing time, personnel training time, technology gain, information processing types and information processing capacity. Its specific algorithm is:

$$T_{C2} = K_1 \times (1 - K_2) \times e^{h(N_{Load} - N_0)} \times T_{C2}^0$$

K_1 represents personnel training factor. T_{C2}^0 represents baseline information processing time .

Table 4 shows the values of K_1 , K_2 and $e^{h(N_{Load} - N_0)}$ when information processing time T_{C2} takes the optimal value, the worst value and the average value respectively:

Table 4. The analysis of the value of information processing time

	The optimal value T_{C2}^{min}		The worst value T_{C2}^{max}		The average value T_{C2}^{ave}	
	The red	The blue	The red	The red	The blue	The red
K_1	0.2	0.4	0.8	0.6	0.5	0.5
K_2	0.9	0.7	0.3	0.1	0.6	0.4
$e^{h(N_{Load} - N_0)}$	0.2	0.4	1	1	0.6	0.7

Then the impact factor to posture integrated C from information processing time T_{C2} is:

$$C_4 = \frac{T_{C2}^{max} - T_{C2}^{ave}}{T_{C2}^{max} - T_{C2}^{min}}$$

In summary, posture integrated $C = \beta_1 \times C_1 + \beta_2 \times C_2 + \beta_3 \times C_3 + \beta_4 \times C_4$, in which, $\beta_1, \beta_2, \beta_3, \beta_4$ are the impact weight of posture update time, posture display accuracy, integrated posture generated-time and information processing time respectively.

3   Scenario Analysis

In order to verify the validity of the model, we developed a simple scenario example: in a war, the average loss rates of red side and blue side are equal, $\alpha = \beta = 0.25$; both the initial forces are equal, too, $x_0 = y_0 = 200$; the command efficiency value of the red is $\varepsilon_x = \dfrac{1}{C_x}$, and the command efficiency value of the blue is $\varepsilon_y = \dfrac{1}{C_y}$. Then by Lanchester model considering efficiency of command, there is:

$$\begin{cases} \dfrac{dx}{dt} = \dfrac{-\alpha xy}{x_0 - \varepsilon_x(x_0 - x)} \\ \dfrac{dy}{dt} = \dfrac{-\beta xy}{y_0 - \varepsilon_y(y_0 - y)} \end{cases}$$

By the dates in 2.3, it is assumed that the red impact weight of posture update time, posture display accuracy, integrated posture generated-time and information processing time respectively take 0.1,0.2,0.3,0.4 and the blue impact weight of posture update time, posture display accuracy, integrated posture generated-time and information processing time respectively take 0.4,0.3,0.2,0.1. According to the algorithm of integrated posture capacity indicator , the red integrated posture capacity indicator is $C_x = 0.7157$, and the blue integrated posture capacity indicator is $C_y = 0.5565$.

Then the efficiency value of the red is $\varepsilon_x = \dfrac{1}{C_x} = 1.397$, and the efficiency value of the blue is $\varepsilon_y = \dfrac{1}{C_y} = 1.797$.

To solve the equations with iteration:

$$\begin{cases} \dfrac{dx}{dt} = \dfrac{-\alpha xy}{x_0 - \varepsilon_x(x_0 - x)} \\ \dfrac{dy}{dt} = \dfrac{-\beta xy}{y_0 - \varepsilon_y(y_0 - y)} \end{cases}$$

And to draw the curves of the forces versus time of the red and the blue:

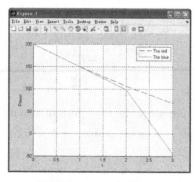

Fig. 3. The curves of the forces versus time of the red and the blue

From above figure, the red win the battle ultimately in less than three minutes. As a result , there is a conclusion that the smaller command efficiency value makes dominant position in war, that is ,the bigger integrated posture capacity indicator makes dominant position in war.

4   Conclusion

This paper analyzed the shortcomings and deficiencies of the current command and control system modeling, and proposed a command and control system modeling based on the entity-relationship. The second section maked a command and control system modeling based on capacity indicators , extracted the capacity indicators of command and control system, cleared the influencing factors of capacity indicators, analyzed the factors affecting ability index, and determined the algorithm of indicators. This paper only discuss the algorithm of integrated posture capacity indicators, and the algorithm of other indicators will be described in subsequent articles.

Acknowledgements. This research was supported by grant 61104057 and 61074144 from the Natural Science Foundation of China and Pre-research project of PLA. The authors thank the reviewers for their comments.

References

1. Andriole, S.J.: Advanced Technology for Command and Control Systems Engineering. National Defence Industry Press, Beijing (2005)
2. Hu, X.-F., Li, Z.-Q., Yang, J.-Y., Si, G.-Y., Luo, P.: Some Key Issues of War Gaming & Simulation. Journal of System Simulation 22(3), 549–553 (2010)
3. Liu, Q., Xue, H.-F.: Study of Simulation and Effect Evaluation for C2 in Air-Defense Operation Based on Multi-agent. Microelectronics & Computer 25(2), 126–128 (2008)
4. Ning, W.-H., Chen, S.-S., Tian, X.-H., Chen, Y.-G.: Analysis on the stratagems for transforming the battlefield situation based on Lanchester Equation. Electronics Optics & Control 11(4), 11–13 (2004)
5. Zhang, Y.: Combat Simulation Basis. Higher Education Press, Beijing (2004)
6. Zeng, Y.-Y., Kang, F.-J., Zhang, J.-C.: Layered Command and Control Simulation System Architecture Based on SOA. Journal of System Simulation 23(8), 1714–1718 (2011)

Based Acceleration Compound Control with Equivalent Input Disturbance Observer for Flight Simulator

Ying Liu[1], Yan Ren[2], and Zhenghua Liu[2]

[1] Beijing Changan Auto Engineering Research Co.Ltd, Beijing, China
[2] School of Automation Science and Electrical Engineering, Beihang University, Beijing, China

Abstract. Friction torque is the main factor that influences dynamic response performance of high accuracy of servo systems at low speed movement. To compensate for the friction torque and other disturbances, a compound control strategy based on backstepping and acceleration feedback with the equivalent input disturbance observer is proposed. In this control strategy, make use of the state-observer to estimate the equivalent disturbance, and obtain the acceleration estimation. The acceleration feedback controller is introduced to compensate for friction torque and disturbances; the backstepping controller with integral element is used for the position loop. The simulation results show that dynamic friction torque is inhibited more effectively, and the robustness of system for the exterior disturbance is also improved simultaneously.

Keywords: Flight simulator, Backstepping, Friction compensation, Acceleration.

1 Introduction

Friction modeling and compensation have been studied extensively, but is still full of interesting problems due to their practical significance and the complex behavior of friction. Being a highly nonlinear, the friction phenomenon causes steady-state tracking errors, limit cycles, undesired stick-slip motion, the low-speed shaking and other types of poor performance[1,2]. To achieve high performance of the system, appropriate control method should be designed. At present, two main methods—the approach based on the friction model compensation[3,4] and the non-model compensation [5,6]—are usually employed. It has been well known that to have high accuracy of motion control at low speed movement, such as flight simulator, friction cannot be simply modeled as a static nonlinear function of velocity alone, but rather a dynamic function of velocity and displacement. Moreover, nonlinearities and uncertainties existing in the flight simulator such as friction moment, motor moment fluctuation, lopsided moment and system parameter change often deteriorate the performance and robustness of the system. Therefore, it is important to select an effective means to compensate for these nonlinear factors.

With the development of sensor technology and the successful application of acceleration feedback controller in some systems[7-9], acceleration feedback gradually

T. Xiao, L. Zhang, and S. Ma (Eds.): ICSC 2012, Part II, CCIS 327, pp. 262–271, 2012.

attracts people's attention in the field of high precision servo control. Acceleration feedback is a kind of robust control method based on state feedback, and improves the stiffness of the control system without broadening the bandwidth of the position or speed loop. Consequently, the ability of suppressing all kinds of disturbances, including the friction, is strengthened [10]. As the above mentioned, few scholars has used acceleration feedback to compensate the friction and disturbance yet. This paper, taking the flight simulator as an example, applies acceleration feedback to achieve effective compensation of the nonlinear factors of the system, such as friction torque , and suppress the effect of low speed shaking of the system. Generally, varied applications of the backstepping control techniques demonstrate its superiority over classical controllers, especially in the servo system control problem. Unlike the traditional control method, it could guarantee the stability and tracking performance simultaneously [11,12]. Therefore this paper uses backstepping controller in position feedback loop.

The organization of the paper is as follows. Section 2 describes the dynamic mathematical model of flight simulator. The design of the servo control system is given in Section 3. The simulation results are introduced in Section 4. Section 5 is the conclusion.

2   Mathematical Model of Flight Simulator

Three-axis flight simulator is a high precision servo system with nonlinearities and uncertainties. The differential equation of one axis of a certain three-axis flight simulator is given by

$$J_o \ddot{\theta} = -B_o \dot{\theta} + u(t) - T_f + \Delta(x,t)$$ (1)

where θ is the angular position of the actual system, J_o is the inertia of the system and B_o is the damp; u represents control variable, T_f stands for external disturbance force, such as the friction torque , $\Delta(x,t)$ denotes unknown time-vary nonlinear dynamics. By assembling the parameters mismatch, external disturbance and unknown dynamics into an equivalent disturbance d , (1) can be rewritten as (2)

$$J_n \ddot{\theta} + B_n \dot{\theta} = u(t) + d(t)$$ (2)

where, J_n、 B_n is the nominal inertia and the nominal damping, respectively. The equivalent disturbance: $d = (J_n - J_o)\ddot{\theta} + (B_n - B_o)\dot{\theta} - T_f + \Delta(x,t)$.

The equation (2) can be written as state space equation:

$$\begin{cases} \dot{x}(t) = Ax(t) + Bu(t) + Bd(t) \\ y = Cx(t) \end{cases}$$

where $x=\begin{bmatrix} x_1 & x_2 \end{bmatrix}^T = \begin{bmatrix} \theta & \dot{\theta} \end{bmatrix}^T$, $A=\begin{bmatrix} 0 & 1 \\ 0 & B_n/J_n \end{bmatrix}$, $B=\begin{bmatrix} 0 & 1/J_n \end{bmatrix}^T$,

$C=\begin{bmatrix} 1 & 0 \end{bmatrix}$.

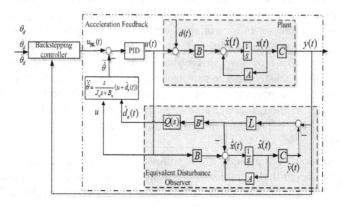

Fig. 1. The control loop structure diagram of the servo flight simulator system

3   Design of Servo Control System

In this paper, the outer loop controlle used the robust backstepping algorithm, inner loop controller applied   acceleration feedback control. Fig.1 shows the overall control scheme of servo control system, and the acceleration feedback loop is shown in the dashed box. The detailed progress is showed as below.

3.1   Backstepping Controller Design

This paper adopts the backstepping controller with integral element to realize the stable outer loop, whose design step is as follows:

Step 1:
Defining the error equation of system

$$e_1 = \theta - \theta_d \tag{4}$$

where θ_d is a command signal. Then

$$\dot{e}_1 = \dot{\theta} - \dot{\theta}_d = \omega - \dot{\theta}_d \tag{5}$$

Defining virtual control value as

$$\omega_d = -c_1 e_1 + \dot{\theta}_d - \lambda \chi \tag{6}$$

where $c_1 > 0, \lambda > 0$, $\chi = \int_0^t e_1(\tau)dt$ is an integral action of the position tracking error. It ensures tracking error converging to zero when system model and load disturbance are uncertain.

There is an error e_2 between the actual angular velocity ω and the reference signal ω_d , so the velocity error equation can be defined:

$$e_2 = \omega - \omega_d \tag{7}$$

Then

$$\dot{e}_1 = \omega - \dot{\theta}_d = \omega_d + e_2 - \dot{\theta}_d = -c_1 e_1 + e_2 - \lambda \chi \tag{8}$$

A Lyapunov function is chosen:

$$v_1 = \frac{1}{2} e_1^2 + \frac{1}{2} \lambda \chi^2 \tag{9}$$

Then

$$\dot{v}_1 = e_1 \dot{e}_1 + \lambda \chi \dot{\chi} = e_1(e_2 - c_1 e_1 - \lambda \chi) + \lambda \chi e_1 = -c_1 e_1^2 + e_1 e_2 \tag{10}$$

If $e_2 = 0$, then $\dot{v}_1 \le 0$ .Therefore, it is necessary to design the following step.

Step 2:
Defining a Lyapunov function:

$$v_2 = v_1 + \frac{1}{2} e_2^2 \tag{11}$$

The time derivative of formulae (7) can be written as:

$$\dot{e}_2 = \dot{\omega} - \dot{\omega}_d = \frac{1}{J_n} u_{BK} - \frac{B_n}{J_n} \omega - \dot{\omega}_d = \frac{1}{J_n} u_{BK} - \frac{B_n}{J_n} \omega + c_1 \dot{e}_1 - \ddot{\theta}_d + \lambda \dot{\chi} = \frac{1}{J_n} u_{BK} - \frac{B_n}{J_n} \omega + c_1 e_2 + (\lambda - c_1^2) e_1 - c_1 \lambda \chi - \ddot{\theta}_d \tag{12}$$

To make $\dot{v}_2 \le 0$, the   backtepping control law is designed as:

$$u_{BK} = [B_n - J_n(c_1 + c_2)] \omega + J_n(c_1 + c_2) \dot{\theta}_d + J_n \ddot{\theta}_d - J_n(1 + \lambda + c_1 c_2) e_1 - J_n \lambda c_1 \int_0^t e_1(\tau)d\tau \tag{13}$$

where $c_2 > 0$.Then $\dot{v}_2 = -c_1 e_1^2 - c_2 e_2^2 \le 0$

3.2   Design of Acceleration Feedback

Acceleration feedback signal, different from other traditional feedback signal, can increase the whole system dynamic stiffness while the position or velocity loop bandwidth is unchanged [13]. Generally speaking, there are three means to obtain the acceleration signal. To get the acceleration signal by the position or velocity differentiating signal is the first method. The second is measuring the acceleration signal by an acceleration sensor. The third is establishing an acceleration observer to estimate acceleration signal. In this pape , the acceleration estimation can be obtained as the below formula:

$$\ddot{\hat{\theta}} = \frac{s}{J_n s + B_n}(u+d) \tag{14}$$

3.2.1   Equivalent Input Disturbance Observer Design

According to formula (14), the equivalent input disturbance is the key factor to obtain the acceleration signal. The equivalent input disturbance estimator makes use of the state observer instead of the inverse dynamics of the plant. This is a big difference in system structure between the traditional DOB method and the one presented in this paper.

In Fig. 1, for the state observer

$$\dot{\hat{x}}(t) = A\hat{x}(t) + Bu(t) + LC(x(t) - \hat{x}(t)) \tag{15}$$

where $\hat{x}(t)$ is the estimation of the state system, L denotes the state-observer gain matrix, $L \in R^{2 \times 1}$. For a suitably designed the state-observer gain matrix L, guarantees $\hat{x}(t)$ converge to $x(t)$ quickly and $A - LC$ is stable.

Let $\Delta x = \hat{x} - x$, and substitute it into (3) yields

$$\dot{\hat{x}}(t) = A\hat{x}(t) + Bu(t) + Bd(t) + \Delta\dot{x}(t) - A\Delta\hat{x}(t) \tag{16}$$

Assume that there exists $\Delta d(t)$ that satisfies

$$\Delta\dot{x}(t) - A\Delta\hat{x}(t) = B\Delta d(t) \tag{17}$$

Substitute (17) into (16) and let the estimate of the $d(t)$ be

$$\hat{d}(t) = d(t) + \Delta d(t) \tag{18}$$

Express the plant as the below formula:

$$\dot{\hat{x}}(t) = A\hat{x}(t) + Bu(t) + B\hat{d}(t) \tag{19}$$

Equations (15) and (19) yield

$$B\hat{d}(t) = LC[x(t) - \hat{x}(t)] \tag{20}$$

If there exists $B^+ = \dfrac{B^T}{B^T B}$, then

$$\hat{d}(t) = B^+ LC[x(t) - \hat{x}(t)] \tag{21}$$

$\hat{d}(t)$ is filtered by $Q(s)$, which selects the angular- frequency band for disturbance estimation. Thus, the filtered equivalent disturbance estimate $\hat{d}_e(t)$ is given by

$$\hat{d}_e(t) = Q(s)\hat{d}(t) = \frac{1}{Ts+1}\hat{d}(t) \tag{22}$$

Substitute $\hat{d}_e(t)$ into equation (14), then it follows that

$$\ddot{\theta} = \frac{s}{J_n s + B_n}(u + \hat{d}_e(t)) \tag{23}$$

To sum up, the control structure of acceleration feedback is shown in the dashed box of Fig1.

3.2.2   The Design of Acceleration Feedback

The classical PID control is employed in the acceleration controller, as shown in figure 1; the control law is defined as:

$$u = K_i \int_{t=0}^{t} (u_{BK} - \ddot{\theta})dt + K_p(u_{BK} - \ddot{\theta}) + K_d(u_{BK} - \ddot{\theta})' \tag{24}$$

where K_i is integral factor of the controller, is proportional factor of the controller, K_d is differential factor of the controller, and they are positive real numbers. According to the design principle of acceleration feedback controller, acceleration feedback loop must be stable first. In order to verify the stability of the acceleration feedback loop, let

$$X_1 = \int_{t=0}^{t} (u_{BK} - \ddot{\theta})dt \,, X_2 = \dot{X}_1 = (u_{BK} - \ddot{\theta}) \,, \dot{X}_2 = (u_{BK} - \ddot{\theta})' \,.$$

Substitute equation (24) into (2),

$$J_n\ddot{\theta} = u - d - B_n\dot{\theta} = K_i \int_{t=0}^{t} (u_{BK} - \ddot{\theta})dt + K_p(u_{BK} - \ddot{\theta}) + K_d(u_{BK} - \ddot{\theta})' - d - B_n\dot{\theta} = K_i X_1 + K_p X_2 + K_d \dot{X}_2 - d - B_n\dot{\theta}$$

Adds $-Ju_{BK}$ to both sides of the equation, as following:

$$\dot{X}_2 = -K_i / K_d X_1 - (J_n + K_p)/K_d X_2 + (d + J_n u_{BK} + B_n \dot{\theta})$$.

Let $U = d + J_n u_{BK} + B_n \dot{\theta}$, the new state space representation can be written:

$$\begin{bmatrix} \dot{X}_1 \\ \dot{X}_2 \end{bmatrix} = \begin{bmatrix} 0 & 1 \\ -K_i / K_d & -(J + K_p)/K_d \end{bmatrix} \begin{bmatrix} X_1 \\ X_2 \end{bmatrix} + \begin{bmatrix} 0 \\ 1 \end{bmatrix} U \tag{25}$$

According to the Lyapunov stability equation, a result can be concluded as:

For any given positive definite symmetric matrix Q, if there is a unique positive definite symmetric matrix P satisfying equation (26), the system is asymptotically stable.

$$A^T P + P A^T = -Q \tag{26}$$

Let $Q = \begin{bmatrix} 1 & 0 \\ 0 & 1 \end{bmatrix}$, work out

$$P = \begin{bmatrix} \dfrac{(K_p + J_n)^2 + K_i(K_i + K_d)}{2K_i K_d (K_p + J_n)} & \dfrac{1}{2K_i} \\ \dfrac{1}{2K_i} & \dfrac{K_i + K_d}{2K_i(K_p + J_n)} \end{bmatrix}.$$

To make the matrix P a positive definite matrix, K_i, K_p, K_d must meet the condition as follows:

$$(K_p + J_n)^2 + K_i(K_i + K_d) > K_d(K_p + J_n)^2 \tag{27}$$

Therefore, it follows the Lyapunov stability theory and acceleration feedback loop is asymptotic stability. Equation (27) implies that the acceleration feedback system satisfies the stability condition when K_i, K_p, K_d select appropriate value.

4   Simulation Results

Based on the above approach for flight simulator, the parameters of actual plant and control system are shown as follows:

Table 1. Parameters

B_n	J_n	c_1	c_2	λ	K_p	K_i	K_d	T	L
0.2	0.007	350	350	5	50	10	0.6	0.01	[-5 25]

In simulation experiments, friction torque of the system use LuGre friction model[14].The form of LuGre model is

$$\begin{cases} F = \sigma_0 z + \sigma_1 \dfrac{dz}{dt} + \sigma_2 w \\[2mm] \dfrac{dz}{dt} = w - \dfrac{|w|}{g(w)} z \\[2mm] \sigma_0 g(w) = F_c + (F_s - F_c)e^{-(\frac{w}{w_s})^2} \end{cases},$$

where, the parameters are expressed as follows:

Table 2. Parameters of LuGre mode

σ_0	σ_1	σ_2	F_c	F_s	v_s
260	2.5	0.02	0.28	0.34	0.01

Still more, let the reference input signal be a triangular signal where the amplitude is 0.01 degree and frequency is 0.025Hz . In order to verify the system robustness to external disturbances, a sinusoidal interference signal whose amplitude is 0.05 degree and frequency is 1Hz is appended into the system.

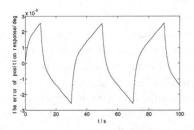
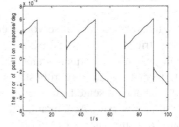

(a) position tracking error for the traditional   (b) position tracking error for the new controller

Fig. 2. Position tracking error for flight simulator

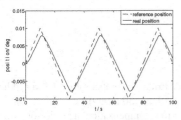
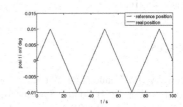

(a) position output for the traditional   (b) position output based on acceleration compound
                                                                                    controller

Fig. 3. Position tracking response for flight simulator

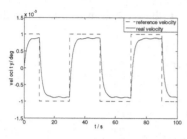

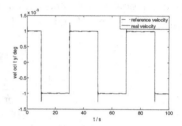

(a) velocity tracking for the traditional

(b) velocity tracking based on acceleration compound controller

Fig. 4. Velocity tracking for flight simulator

From the above simulation results, we can see that the tracking error of the system under the novel controller is evidently smaller than that under the traditional backstepping controller. By using the novel backstepping controller based acceleration feedback with equivalent disturbance observer, the unstable phenomenon of the low-speed system is suppressed, while tracking accuracy of flight simulator is improved, and dynamic friction torque and perturbed torque are compensated effectively.

5   Conclusions

Flight simulator is a kind of servo system with uncertainties and disturbances (such as nonlinear friction factors) which worsens the performance of the flight simulator especially when low frequency and small gain signal inputs the system. To obtain the high performance and good robustness for flight simulator, a acceleration compound control has been presented. Acceleration singal is obtained by establishing an effective acceleration observer. Acceleration feedback can overcome the effect of the system friction and disturbance.   Based on the Lyapunov stability theorem, the backstepping controller keeps the system globally asymptotically stable. Simulation results indicate that the compound controller is capable of giving excellent position tracking and velocity tracking for the flight simulator. The effect of friction to the system is overcome effectively.

References

1. Lischinsky, P., Canudas de Wit, C., Morel, G.: Friction compensation for an industrial hydraulic robot. IEEE Control Systems Magazine 19, 25–30 (1999)
2. Zhu, Y., Pagilla, P.R.: Static and dynamic friction compensation in trajectory tracking control of robots. In: Proceedings of the 2002 IEEE International Conference on Robotics & Automation, pp. 2644–2649. IEEE Press, Washington (2002)
3. Noorbakhash, S.M., Yazdizadeh, A.: A new approach for lyapunov based adaptive friction compensation. In: IEEE Control Applications (CCA) & Intelligent Control (ISIC), pp. 66–70. IEEE Press, Russia (2009)

4. Liu, G.: Decomposition-based friction compensation of mechanical systems. Mechatronics 12, 755–769 (2002)
5. Morel, G., Iagnemma, K., Dubowsky, S.: The precise control of manipulators with high joint-friction using base force/torque sensing. Automatica 36, 931–941 (2000)
6. Yuan, T., Zhang, R.: Design of guidance law for exoatmospheric interceptor during its terminal course. Journal of Astronautics 30, 474–480 (2009)
7. Shen, D., Liu, Z., Liu, S.: Friction compensation based acceleration feedback control for flight simulator. Advanced Materials Research 8, 1702–1707 (2010)
8. Nima Mahmoodi, S., Craft, M.J., Southward, S.C., Ahmadian, M.: Active vibration control using optimized modified acceleration feedback with Adaptive Line Enhancer for frequency tracking. Journal of Sound and Vibration 330, 1300–1311 (2011)
9. Jing, Y., Yong, F., Fei, Z.: Suppression of mechanical resonance based on higher-order sliding mode and acceleration feedback. Control Theory & Applications 26(10), 1133–1136 (2009)
10. He, Y.Q., Han, J.D.: Acceleration feedback enhanced robust control of an unmanned helicopter. Journal of Guidance Control and Dynamics 33, 1236–1250 (2010)
11. Bousserhane, I.K., Hazzab, A., Rahli, M., Mazari, B., Kamli, M.: Mover position control of linear induction motor drive using adaptive backstepping controller with integral action. Tamkang Journal of Science and Engineering 12, 17–28 (2009)
12. Alanis, A.Y., Sanchez, E.N., Loukianov, A.G.: Real-time discrete backstepping neural control for induction motors. IEEE Transactions on Control Systems Technology 19, 359–366 (2011)
13. Wang, Z.: Friction compensation for high precision mechanical bearing turntable. PhD thesis, Harbin Institute of Technology (2007)
14. de Wit Carlos, C., Olsson, H., Astrom, J., et al.: A new model for control of systems with friction. IEEE Transactions on Automatic Control 40, 419–425 (1995)

The Analysis of Reconnaissance Modeling and Simulation in Combat Simulation

Rui Fan[1], Hao Li[2], and Fang Liu[1]

[1] Department of Equipment Command & Administration Academy of Armored
[2] Weapon Equipment Demonstration Center Force Engineering
Beijing 100072, China
pillow2000@tom.com

Abstract. The modeling and simulation of reconnaissance is a important part of army combat simulation. The reconnaissance system is the complex combination of many reconnaissance equipments such as the ground vehicle and air vehicle, and includes different form like sound, light and electricity. Based on the basic conception, reconnaissance action and reconnaissance equipment, paper gives the modeling Analysis of this model. Then, paper gives the composing and structure of reconnaissance system model and uses it to simulation. The result indicates that the model has rational structure and can be used in the combat simulation.

Keywords: Reconnaissance, Combat Simulation, Modeling and Simulation.

1 Introduction

Under the condition of information, each kind of equipment has got development at very fast speed. It makes a great change of modality of current warfare. The leading effect of information is more distinctness. The Reconnaissance system with the core of information is the important tool to get information during fighting prepare and fighting process. This system is a complex system of every reconnaissance device. Because of complexity of equipment and using relation is more complex than before, and situation changes fast than before, it improves the request of time, veracity and continuity in reconnaissance intelligence. In order to improve the reconnaissance efficiency, it is a crucial matter in current time to explore using mode of reconnaissance system and influence of reconnaissance action to the combat. The modeling and simulation technology is a effect measure to study it.

Currently, there are different kind of reconnaissance equipment, but voluminous of these models do not consider the relation between reconnaissance system and other system under the joint operations, and are not suit to current reconnaissance research. It needs improve and this is also the main content in paper.

2 The Status of Reconnaissance System Simulation

Usually, the models of army combat simulation system include battlefield environment model, data prepare model, combat simulation model, display model and result statistics

T. Xiao, L. Zhang, and S. Ma (Eds.): ICSC 2012, Part II, CCIS 327, pp. 272–279, 2012.

model. Therefore, the combat simulation model includes command system sub model, support system sub model, weapon system sub model, electronic war system sub model, communication system sub model and reconnaissance system sub model. Obviously, reconnaissance system sub model is an important part. Based on the equipment, this model simulates reconnaissance action under the control of combat command, it gets enemy information to offer in-time and exact intelligence to command system such as position, type and so on. It gives help to form the next order or the hit action of weapon system, and drives the combat simulation process.

3   Analysis of Reconnaissance Action

3.1   The Basic Conception of Reconnaissance

According to our request, the basal means of reconnaissance includes armed reconnaissance, technology reconnaissance and military investigation. Among these means, the armed reconnaissance also has many kinds such as observation, listening, fight reconnaissance, fire reconnaissance, catching captive and searching. The technology reconnaissance includes wiretapping, wireless reconnaissance, radar reconnaissance, television reconnaissance, taking pictures, ground sensor reconnaissance, computer network reconnaissance, remote sensing, pilotless aircraft reconnaissance and night vision reconnaissance.

The content of reconnaissance mainly includes enemy's situation, friend' s situation, terrain, weather and climate situation.

According to different force, the organizing into groups of reconnaissance can be divided into reconnaissance detachment, absolute reconnaissance swarm, reconnaissance swarm, reconnaissance vehicle (squad), reconnaissance team and reconnaissance prearrangement.

According to different reconnaissance mode, the organizing into groups of reconnaissance can be divided into reconnaissance swarm at enemy's rear area, special reconnaissance swarm, television reconnaissance swarm, observation post, radar station, pilotless aircraft reconnaissance swarm and mobile reconnaissance swarm.

3.2   The Flow of Reconnaissance

The reconnaissance model is a high degree abstraction of the real reconnaissance action. The target of reconnaissance action is to support fight force completing prepare for combat pertinently and to help commander making right decision. So, In order to find the instance which is used to fulfill the combat prepare, reconnaissance commander should throw out reconnaissance force to scheduled fighting area in time according to the superior's indication.

The general flow of reconnaissance implementation is showed as following figure.

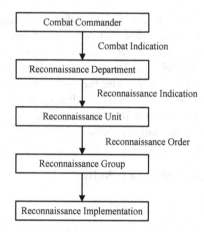

Fig. 1. Reconnaissance Implementation Flow in Combat

Based on the above flow, the simulation flow of reconnaissance action can be designed as following.

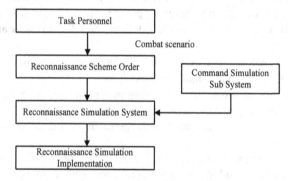

Fig. 2. Reconnaissance Implementation Flow in Combat Simulation

4   Modeling of Reconnaissance System

4.1   The Modeling Analysis of Reconnaissance System

Reconnaissance system is an organic whole of multiform reconnaissance equipment. The modeling of reconnaissance should carry out based on reconnaissance equipment. In the reconnaissance system model, we have two modes such as armed force reconnaissance and technology reconnaissance. At first, in order to depress complexity and make study expediently, we predigest the armed force reconnaissance to two type, there are fight reconnaissance and fire reconnaissance. The technology reconnaissance is predigested to radar reconnaissance, optics reconnaissance and pilotless aircraft reconnaissance.

After simulation task personnel inputting basic data such as army organization, equipment and so on, we can get the friend's data in combat simulation system which can be used by reconnaissance system model. The weather and climate situation can be set by task personnel at the system initialization phase. The particular degree is decided by the requirement of prophase.

The main result of reconnaissance system model is enemy's situation data and landform data. The enemy's situation data mainly includes enemy's position, type and formation status. The landform data mainly includes road, bridge and river, and so on.

The foundation of reconnaissance group data is combat scenario or combat plan. It can be confirmed by simulation personnel before combat simulation beginning.

During the combat simulation process, the simulation of reconnaissance system has two drive modes.

The one mode of getting drive is prepared by simulation task personnel, they use data prepare model to input reconnaissance order into reconnaissance simulation system. These orders are based on combat scenario or combat plan, they have a standard format in order to be understood by computer.

The other mode of getting drive is created by command simulation sub system. These orders is based on the enemy's situation which is offered by reconnaissance simulation system. Command simulation sub system uses these intelligence to create new order, then some of order is given to reconnaissance simulation system. When reconnaissance simulation system gets the order, it can behave with corresponding order.

4.2   The Composing of Reconnaissance System Model

From above analysis, the reconnaissance system model can be divided into five type, they are fighting reconnaissance model, fire reconnaissance model, radar reconnaissance model optics reconnaissance model and pilotless aircraft reconnaissance model. Because of simulation requirement, reconnaissance system model should include intelligence integration model.

So, we can get construction figure of reconnaissance system model as following.

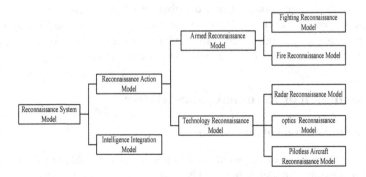

Fig. 3. Reconnaissance System Model Construction

The Function of intelligence integration model is disposing reconnaissance result, it mainly includes three type, such as collection and classification of intelligence, differentiation and judgement of intelligence and reporting and distribution of intelligence.

1) Collection and Classification of Intelligence

During the combat process, the source of intelligence data in reconnaissance system simulation is so many, it has some characters such as multi-platform of reconnaissance, multi-target and multi-information, and so on. Therefore, the data of reconnaissance system simulation has a lot of quantity and various kinds. Under this condition, we should establish appropriate classification of intelligence, so that we can get intelligence under this classification in the combat simulation by using reconnaissance simulation system.

In real combat, some reconnaissance platforms accomplish one task together. So, according to the character of data, intelligence integration model uses the method which is called line-classification method. This method also is called level-classification method. It divides the object into some levels by choosing attribute or regulation, and arranges them to form a system which has layered and deployed in rank framework. It can be realized easily in the simulation program.

2) Differentiation and Judgement of Intelligence

In real reconnaissance system, we get wrong and redundant data from it is unavoidable, as the mapping of reconnaissance system, the reconnaissance model also can offer some wrong and redundant result. For this reason, it needs differentiation and filter. Especially we get the inveracious result which has been sent by enemy purposely, the judgement is more important. So, the detection and control of data is a concernful content in reconnaissance modeling. The data needing differentiation and judgement includes target data, shooting data, damage data, ammunition consumption data, moving data and tactic exertion data.

3) Reporting and Distribution of intelligence

In the modern combat, each level has its own reconnaissance task, and also has its own reporting and distribution task. Based on definite combat principle, we make the content and purview of reporting and distribution of intelligence in reconnaissance simulation system. After the end of collection, classification, differentiation and judgement, it brings the intelligence to combat command model in each level, and also offers some intelligence to other sub model in combat system model.

5   Simulation of Reconnaissance System

5.1   The Initialization of Simulation

Before reconnaissance system simulation starts, it needs initialization for the data which reconnaissance model required. The initialization completes two function, one is inputting all data correlative with reconnaissance in the combat scenario, includes framework of reconnaissance, formation, reconnaissance equipment, deploy of reconnaissance force and reconnaissance plan order; the other is matching reconnaissance data in order to form equipment, simulation entity of reconnaissance force, it includes performance data of reconnaissance equipment and order data.

During the initialization process, the most difficult and important content is to get fixed format reconnaissance plan order to drive the reconnaissance simulation. These orders should be set down according to the reconnaissance task of combat reconnaissance and reconnaissance order of combat commander. These two sources should be transferred into fixed format according as the request of combat simulation system. After this step, we finally get usable order for simulation, it can be understood by computer and be used in reconnaissance simulation. This fixed format reconnaissance plan order can be called reconnaissance advance scheme.

The reconnaissance advance scheme is a modality of knowledge representation which has been abstracted. From angle of knowledge expression, it can be considered the producing rule, it is composed with three parts.

1) Basic Information
This part describes basic information of advance scheme, includes reconnaissance advance scheme number, reconnaissance command post, execution priority level and can be reused.

2) Condition part
This is an aggregation of precondition which can spring the execution. According to the military requirement, the condition part represents various intelligence information which can restrict and influence the reconnaissance action and reconnaissance command. This means conditions that some actions needed. It includes time, site, reconnaissance requirement, necessary enemy's situation, necessary own situation, reconnaissance force, reconnaissance range and range distance.

3) Conclusion part
This part is the action that be sprung by the advance scheme. The conclusion can be departed into two construction. The one is reconnaissance order, namely, this is reconnaissance task has been give to reconnaissance unit or element. The other is idiographic reconnaissance action, such action is carried out by diversified reconnaissance entities. Under current condition, the extractive rule of advance scheme should been abstracted from the reconnaissance theory of conventional mechanization troop and joint combat theory.

The following is an example.

The description in combat scenario is like this:

Reconnaissance swarm enforces order to reconnoiter enemy's brigade command post when the fight begins.

The description in reconnaissance advance scheme is like this:

Condition one: reconnaissance swarm carries out its task when the combat time equals to 1 second.

Conclusion one: television reconnaissance unit performs its task to spy enemy's brigade command post from X hour to X hour;

Conclusion two: electronic reconnaissance unit performs its task to spy enemy's brigade command post from X hour to X hour;

Conclusion three: pilotless aircraft reconnaissance unit performs its task to spy enemy's brigade command post from X hour to X hour.

By this step, we can get usable order in simulation system. The above example is described by using work. In simulation program, such reconnaissance advance scheme is described by using parameter and variable.

5.2   The Result of Simulation

When the simulation initialization has been finished, we can begin the combat simulation, the reconnaissance simulation joins it to run together.

During simulation process, the reconnaissance entity carries out its task based on the order, when it gets result, the entity transports data to command simulation sub system in time by passing the communication simulation sub system. Then, according to distribution regulation, reconnaissance simulation system gives the data to other sub models of combat simulation model.

The result data of above example is in the following table.

Table 1. Reconnaissance result data

Serial number	Transmission type	Transmission opportunity	Transmission content
1		When find undiscriminating target	Find command post, coordinate(X,X), Mph(X), distance(X)
2		After distinguish target	Brigade command post, coordinate(X,X), Mph(X), distance(X)
3	Target information	After distinguish target	Brigade command post, defense force(XX), work(XX), XX tank XX, coordinate(X,X)
4		After distinguish target	Brigade command post, XX command vehicle XX, coordinate(X,X), ···
5		After distinguish target	Brigade command post, frequency range(XX), strong signal
6		After distinguish target	Other target information in nearby area
7	Geography information	After distinguish target	Brigade command post, deploy area(XX), valley, no wood
8		After distinguish target	Brigade command post, road XX, bridge XX, ···

6   Conclusions

Reconnaissance simulation is important in combat simulation system. It offers enemy's situation and landform data to combat simulation. Because of complexity, paper just gives the simple description of pare content of reconnaissance system modeling and simulation. Paper brings forward frame and structure of reconnaissance model. This model is under actualization and consummation phase in current time. The next work is rebuilding reconnaissance model focused on reconnaissance simulation efficiency, model type and model amount in order to improve the usability and creditability.

References

1. Hu, X.-F.: The Simulation Analysis and Experiment of Combat Complex System. National Defence Publishing Company (2008)
2. Liu, Z.-X.: The Conspectus of Compositive Army Reconnaissance Intelligence work. National Defence Publishing Company (2001)
3. Ying, D.: The Construction of Armored Force Reconnaissance conception Model based on Request Function Mapping. Computer Simulation (December 2007)
4. Cheng, W.: Research on Advance Scheme Initialization of Digital Division Command Decision Model. Master Degree thesis of Academy of Armored Force Engineering (2007)
5. Hui, Z.: The Simulation Analysis of Reconnaissance Surveillance System based on UML. Command Control and Simulation (June 2007)

An Approach of Targets Selection in the Battle of Attacking Targets S-o-S Wrecked

Yi Liang[1,2], Yequan Cai[1], Xiaoming Luo[2], and Lei Hu[3]

[1] Science and Technology on Complex Systems Simulation Laboratory,
100101, Beijing, China
[2] Company of Postgraduate, The Academy of Equipment,
101416, Beijing, China
[3] Nanjing Military Deputy Bureau,
210024, Nanjing, China
{Yi Liang,Yequan Cai,Xiaoming Luo,Lei Hu}wwlylww@126.com

Abstract. Achieving objectives of the operation could be promoted quickly by choosing the targets system leading to worse affected overall situation. However it was difficult to quantify these effects. The targets system-of-system (S-o-S) potential energy was constructed by referring to Quantum states and related concepts in Quantum Theory. A function of potential energy was established by monadic cubic equation, by which the effects of targets systems wrecked were able to be quantified with the value of transition of potential energy. Through the simulation experiments, several points, in which potential energy of target systems descending substantially, are similar to four points in five grades of Battle Damage System : 0.10, 0.35, 0.60 and0.85. The velocity of transition of potential energy can be illustrated by the distance of simulation steps between the potential energy points, which shows that the network structure of targets S-o-S is no-scale as well as the transition of potential energy of system is according with Power Law.

Keywords: Attacking S-o-S wrecked, Quantum State, Targets Choice, Potential Energy of Targets S-o-S.

1 The Foundational Question of Targets Selection Based on Attacking S-o-S to Disintegrate Campaign

1.1 The Question of Measuring S-o-S Combat Effect

The meaning of Target is that an object shot or attacked in *Modern Chinese Dictionary*[1]. The definition of military targets is that objects with military character or with military value need to be stricken or defended in *People's Liberation Army*

---

[1] Academy of Social Sciences Institute of Linguistics Dictionary Editorial Office, Modern Chinese dictionary, Beijing: The Commercial Press, 1996, pp.903. (In Chinese)

T. Xiao, L. Zhang, and S. Ma (Eds.): ICSC 2012, Part II, CCIS 327, pp. 280–289, 2012.
© Springer-Verlag Berlin Heidelberg 2012

Military Terms[2]. The definition of military targets means that objects with serious effect for the whole battle or with material means for strategic aim need to be stricken or defended, such as political centers, economical centers and military centers, heavy corps, military bases and important facilities. Referring to the explanations, "target" was defined as some objects in this paper, which was stricken to destroy bodies or abilities and to achieve the effect of S-o-S combat for campaign aims. So there are meanings of four aspects for the effect of S-o-S combat:

Firstly, S-o-S combating was conflict between two or more battle system-of-systems. Xiaofeng Hu, who is the professor of Chinese Defense University, said that battle S-o-S is composed of countries or all kinds of S-o-S in nations participating in this battle, and each grade of battle S-o-S consists of different grade targets[3]. The professor Zuiliang Zhang of Academy of Military Sciences had given a conclusion in reference[4] that a battle S-o-S was made up of military system, polity system, economy system, society system, facility system and information system. He also pointed out that making a campaign decision should center on "Attacking S-o-S to disintegrate or combat effect".

Secondly, S-o-S combat implicitly means abilities. Professor Xiaofeng Hu said, "Ability is a power to make expectation come true. It is a kind of capability which can complete a series of missions and achieve these aims by all kinds of methods, tools and information in special standards and conditions."[3] The general Jixun Yu of the PLA Second Artillery Corps said that "Battle Power" was the most approximate to battle S-o-S in PLA military terms, and "it shows that violence exporting is foundational capability of objects" in reference[5]. So the essential of S-o-S combat was that confrontations performed to respective capabilities in battle, as shown in Fig. 1.

In figure 1, there was a construction about battle S-o-S with sub-grade six S-o-S. On the top of the figure 1, these six abilities of S-o-S aggregated into the monolithic battle ability. These six abilities were the whole S-o-S integrated ability rather than linear addition.

Thirdly, destroying ability of S-o-S was showed by "effect" after attacking. "Effect is an influence on the object after actions as well as a change of state produced by systematic influence, including condition, behavior, and privilege." So the effect of aim is the link between battle intent and actual action as well as an important part on decision of battle. For example, before U.S. Air Force raided Libya, they had attacked air defense radars, anti-aircraft missile's bases and so on to get air supremacy by cruise missiles. In this course, action was the operation of attacking targets S-o-S; effect was that air defense ability had been destroyed; the aim was U.S. Force had grabbed the air supremacy of Libya.

---

[2] Academy of Military Sciences, People's Liberation Army military terms , Beijing:Military Sciences Press, 1997, pp. 7,69. (In Chinese)

[3] Xiaofeng Hu,Jingyu Yang, Guangya Si, etc, War complex system simulation analysis & experimentation, Beijing: Defense University Press, 2004:281,288,349. (In Chinese)

[4] Zuiliang Zhang, etc. Military strategic operation research analysis methods, Beijing: Academy of Military Sciences Press, 2009, pp.208. (In Chinese)

[5] Jixun Yu, etc. Defeated war will—targets choosing in information warfare, Beijing: People's Liberate Army Press,2009, pp.43-44, pp.46-47. (In Chinese)

At last, attacking S-o-S to break-down is one of the most actual operation models in S-o-S combat. This action aims at the whole ability in battle, which applies itself to make enemy lose some abilities in changing the unitary ability in battle. Taking effects of campaign depends on optimized choosing targets and attacking them. Effects of S-o-S combat are formed to disintegrate networks, make S-o-S paralyze, and make enemy lose battle heart. The break-down network mainly includes information network.

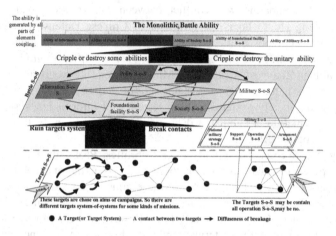

Fig. 1. The generating process of effect of S-o-S combat

So, effects will be taken by attacking some targets in S-o-S, which is composed of some targets or targets systems. Targets systems are some parts in battle S-o-S with some abilities, as figure 1 shown. In the figure, these black points stand for targets or targets systems, belonging to operation S-o-S or the others. It is an essential content of operation decision to attack targets and destroy some parts or the whole ability in battle S-o-S. "Targets S-o-S is the set of center, key nodes or joint nodes in battle S-o-S......It is an integer which carries off life from the mind of battle." said General Jixun Yu.

According to the reference, we define that the targets S-o-S is a complex huge system for enemy with a holistic ability, consisting of all targets on the attacking list. And these elements of targets are not always center, key nodes or joint nodes. For example, a normal solider is not a center in a battle to America, however, U.S. government would rather give up the battle as the number of normal soldiers' death is too large on the battlefield to bear, just as Korean War.

Two concepts of targets S-o-S destroyed effect and potential energy of targets S-o-S were defined in this study for making the hidden structure clearly and contacting the effect of S-o-S combat with operation missions. Targets S-o-S destroyed effect means that when one target (or target system) has been attacked at least, this structure of battle S-o-S will be broken down, and these elements, functions and behaviors will be changed. This crumbling S-o-S leads to performance degradation of the unitary ability of targets S-o-S, even lost. The influence of the results from assault is able to be measured referring to the concept. And the effect of bankruptcy can derive from subversion of paradigm relationship, disappearance of dependent relationships of substance, energy and information. The potential energy of targets S-o-S is a numerical description for a complex huge system with a unitary ability. So the destroyed effect of targets S-o-S is the computing value of the collapse process of potential energy of targets S-o-S.

1.2   A Semantic Explicit Formula of Quantum States Reveal a Measure Metaphor of Targets S-o-S Potential Energy

The study is referring to "a physical property may be 'quantized'"[6] from Quantum Theory. Usually, a quantum state is a set of mathematical variables that fully describes as a quantum system. Some physical effects convert quantum system from an initial state to a ground state, and this process is called "quantum state collapse". The process of releasing quantum system energy from high to low is called "transition".[7]

Potential energy of targets S-o-S, the same as quantum state, shows a unitary ability which can not be divided. When there is nothing in targets system (value of energy is 0), this situation is called ground state. As the scale and construction of targets S-o-S have completed, the initial state is fixed. After being attacked, a potential energy will transform from the initial state with a high energy to a middle state with a low energy, just do once. Potential energy can be affected by scale of targets and optimizational degree of S-o-Ss' structure. The value of potential energy and values of influence factors can be achieved, and the relations between them can be analyzed by statistic methods as the courses of transition are in "Black Box". The process of attacked can be viewed as either parts of quality (substance of targets) peeled off or energy (function of targets S-o-S) released from targets S-o-S, as shown in Fig. 2.

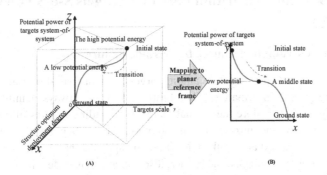

Fig. 2. Collapse of potential energy of targets S-o-S schematic diagram

---

[6] B. Hoffmann. The strange story of the quantum , Pelican ,1963.

[7] Shiyong Li, Panchi Li. Quantum computation and quantum optimization algorithms, Haerbin: Haerbin Institute of Technology Press, 2009, pp.7. (In Chinese)

In the figure 2, the z axis is potential energy which cannot less than zero, and x axis and y axis vary with external force. That is they are non-negative values as one-way of time. The figure 2 is just a situation in non-negative space.

It is extensively randomized for potential energy, comparing with uncertainty of quantum state. From the microcosmic aspect, randomness is generated by information supported, and function instability and structure adjustment in S-o-S. Set influence factors as independent variables and potential energy as dependent variable, the function of potential energy of targets S-o-S can be constructed. The function is multidimensional and non-linear, as shown in Fig. 2(A). All kinds of factors can be synthesized to one independent variable, so the multidimensional function converts to two-dimensional, as shown in Fig. 2(B). In this figure, potential energy transition of targets S-o-S indicates a relationship between independent variables and dependent variable, which can be assumed as multi-segment cubic equation. One of the segment cubic equations can be described as:

$$y = \alpha + \beta_2 x^2 + \beta_3 x^3 \tag{1}$$

Variables of x and y can be achieved based on the relationship between each element and the whole targets S-o-S, the targets and tables formulated for every kind of effects of military operations, the experimentations, the exercises, and operation statistical data. Put these data into equation (1), and each coefficient can be gotten. Set segments of potential energy as five grades (demolish, serious damage, moderate damage, minor damage and intactness) of targets damage in reference[8], there is a five segment cubic equation. Every coefficient is different in each segment.

2   The Selection Algorithm Based on Targets S-o-S Potential Energy

2.1   Structure Crumbling Caused by Cascade Failure

There are relevant network structure among targets systems based on transmission of substance, energy and information. The ability of S-o-S is always manifested in the networks. And cascade failure means that there are cascading failures of transmission of substance, energy and information in network. At the beginning, one or a few targets nodes are attacked and conked. Malfunction spreads one by one and causes the whole network collapse. As cascade failure, also called "snowslide", in line with these features concluding "a unitary model, behavior or dynamic structure, and a process of self-organization transition, irreducible and independent" [9] and so on; it is considered

---

[8] Jiangping Wen, etc. Military application technology of satellites , Beijing: National Defense Industry Press, 2007, pp.69, (In Chinese)

[9] Xinrong Huang, Complex science and philosophy. Beijing: Central Compilation Press, 2007,pp.12, (In Chinese)

as an emergent course. All kinds of targets are considered as nodes, the abilities of targets of which undertake are viewed as "load". These abilities are formed by functions of themselves and structure of network.

When damage of targets appears, cascade failure of targets network, which is a form of transformation from targets damage effects to targets S-o-S damage effect, is able to be described by "load" without any dimension. When targets have been attacked, failure results are prior to ruining these nodes with higher degree, whose degree is low while right is high in reality. Propagation of damage in network can be showed better by load of potential energy.

First step, define a network G=(V,E), setting points V={$v_1,v_2,...,v_n$,} and links E={$e_1,e_2,...,e_m$}. v_i is a target node, and maximum quantity is N. The number of initial nodes is m_0, and real-time number of nodes is n=|V| in network. e_j is used to describe relation among each target. Initial input is the data of the mission and space information supported. In the mission, there is information of targets and operational plans which have been collected and produced, from which the number of targets and connectivity to construct initial targets S-o-S network can be offered. Provided reconnaissance, surveillance and communication for the network as real-time condition variables, it is viable to construct the network in which a node state at any time can be modeled as:

$$x_i(t+1) = \left| (1-c_H^{\ W})f(x_i(t)) + c_H^{\ W} \sum_{j=1, j\neq i}^{N} \frac{a_{i,j}f(x_j(t))}{k_i} \right| + e^{\xi} E_{com} \qquad (2)$$

In this formula, i=1,2,...,N, $x_i(t)$ is the load state of ith node at t time, the information of N nodes is signified by matrix $A=(a_{ij})_{N\times N}$. If there was a link between node i and node j , then $a_{ij}=a_{ji}=1$; or else, $a_{ij}=a_{ji}=0$. k_i is degree of node i. f indicates dynamic behaviors of nodes which are Logistic mapping described as $f(x)=4x(1-x)$. In the formula, the absolute value sign ensures that states of all nodes are non-negative. $e^{\xi}E_{Com}$ is an external disturbance value as well as a factor on exerting function on weapons. When the value is 0, all nodes are in normal states. When targets are being attacked, cascade failure will appear in the network. ζ is the parameter on supporting precise striking and E_{Com} is the parameter on communication efficacy, both of which are variables on the condition of time. Usually, $e^{\xi}E_{Com} \geq 1$. $c_H^{\ W}$ is clustering coefficient, achieved by formula (3) as $c_H^{\ W} \in (0,1)$.

$$c_H^{\ W}(i) = \frac{\sum_{jk} w_{ij}w_{jk}w_{ki}}{\max_{ij} w_{ij}\sum_{jk} w_{ij}w_{ki}} \qquad (3)$$

The algorithm about cascade failure can be exhibited as four steps:

First step, there is potential energy load for each node i as integer$\left[x_i(t)\right]$; at the same time, nodes are assigned threshold z_i, and the minimal integer is set $[z_i]([z_i] \leq k_i)$ which is not less than z_i.

Second step, choose the node i with maximum degree as initial target to be attacked, and $e^{\zeta} E_{Com}$ is added in.

Third step, if $\left(x_i(t)\right) > z_i$, the state of node i is instable just as failure, and "Delete" action is done; $[z_i]$ nodes should be selected from k_i neighbor nodes. To j, which is one of selected nodes, do $\left[x_i(t)\right] \leftarrow \left[x_j(t)\right] + 1$ as well as $\left[x_i(t)\right] \leftarrow \left[x_i(t+1)\right] - [z_i]$.

Fourth step, if new instable nodes were still yielded, the "Delete" action would be done until there were none.

The second step to the fourth step should be repeated until the distribution scale of cascade failure is accomplished.

2.2   Mapping Potential Energy Collapse

The collapse process of targets S-o-S structure can be presented on time axis by cascade failure along with striking.

Potential energy $\varphi(t)$ is set at t time, and the model can be constructed as:

$$\varphi(t) = \sum_{1}^{n} x_i(0) \times e^{\frac{\overline{e}_{ij} Z_i}{E_{Net}}} - \int_{0}^{\infty} \left(\sum_{i}^{n} x_i(t) \times e^{\frac{\overline{e}_{ij} Z_i}{E_{Net}}} \right) dt \tag{4}$$

In the formula, $\sum_{1}^{n} x_i(0) \times e^{\frac{\overline{e}_{ij} Z_i}{E_{Net}}}$ is initial state of targets S-o-S potential energy at 0 time. Z_i is the community inner degree of i, which maps the character of group aggregation in real targets network, and can be calculated by formula (3). The meaning of E_{Net} is efficacy in network, gathered by statistic data mapping the connectivity of network. $\overline{e}_{ij}$ is the average value of rights of node i and $i \neq j$ of links. For showing the step times in simulation, the formula (4) can be discretizated as:

$$\varphi(t') = \sum_{1}^{n} x_i(0) \times e^{\frac{\overline{e}_{ij} Z_i}{E_{Net}}} - \sum_{1}^{m} \left(\sum_{1}^{n} x_i(t') \times e^{\frac{\overline{e}_{ij} Z_i}{E_{Net}}} \right) \tag{5}$$

t' is time length of one step, $-\sum_1^m \left(\sum_1^n x_i(t') \times e^{\frac{\bar{e}_{ij} Z_i}{E_{Net}}} \right)$ is the whole potential energy value of

transition. And the each value of transitions is $\sum_1^n x_i(t') \times e^{\frac{\bar{e}_{ij} Z_i}{E_{Net}}}$, which can be

simplified as $\beta_k x^k$ ($k \geq 1$). It can be seen that the initial state of potential energy is a constant $|\alpha|$ (the value of α is negative) as scale of targets nodes and S-o-S structure are fixed, according to the formula (5).Just set $y = \varphi(t')$, and the potential energy can be simplified as $y = \alpha + \beta_1 x + \beta_2 x^2 + \cdots + \beta_n x^n$, the model of which corresponds with the assumption of formula (1). The unitary ability of the targets network follows power rule and these targets networks are no-scale, which can be certificated by the inverse process of targets S-o-S damage effect.

The targets S-o-S damage effect can be quantitatively analyzed by the above process in an S-o-S combat campaign. And then, contributions of nodes to transitions at every simulation steps are able to be calculated on the contrary by the values of potential energy and targets nodes state. At last, targets are sequenced by contribution, and the list of targets is drafted.

3   The Example and the Analysis

Experiments were done with Component based Integrated Modeling and Simulation Environment (CISE). A target choosing module was made for a project of Science and Technology on Complex System Simulation Laboratory (STCSSL). So there were some models coming from this project. An inputting data interface is shown in Fig. 3. Let the initial state value is 1, the quantity of targets systems is 351, scale of a target system is [0,1], the threshold of failure is 90%, the parameter of space reconnaissance efficacy is 0.65, the parameter of communication efficacy is 0.65, simulation times are 100, and the results of potential energy value distribution are shown as Fig. 4.

Fig. 3. The module of targets choosing

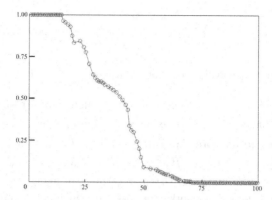

Fig. 4. A result of potential energy collapse of targets S-o-S

In figure 4, a transition appeared at the 18th step. It was considered that potential energy varied from intactness to minor damage. At the 25th step, there was a little crest, and the value was 0.85 approximately. So it was considered as appearance of minor damage. From the 31th to the 35th step, these values were about 0.58, and moderate damage could be confirmed. At the 46th step, it reached serious damage, and the value was about 0.35. At the 51th step it reached demolish degree, and the value was about 0.1. At the 70th step, the value was 0. The whole course of transition was similar to a waterfall. The curve of waterfall was more identical with the assumption at the first section in this paper. As the step times of simulation showed that a certain amount of attacking was permitted at the beginning in S-o-S. 18 steps attacking were allowed as S-o-S was redundant. The value decreased from 0.85 to 0.1 (from minor damage to demolish) just through 26 steps. Especially, there were only 5 steps from 0.35 to 0.1 (from serious damage to demolish). It meant that when the scale of damage important targets was enough, cascade failure led to snowslide in S-o-S. As shown in Fig. 3(B), these middle stats were approaching to 0.1, 0.3, 0.65 and 0.9, which were empirical data of network paralysis. At the end of experiment, the targets list was produced by reverse calculation of potential energy of targets S-o-S.

4   Conclusion

In this paper, the concept of potential energy of targets S-o-S was defined referring to quantum state. And based-on collapsing of potential energy of targets S-o-S an algorithm of targets choosing was established. The result of simulation showed that abilities of battle S-o-S could be quantificational described by potential energy of targets S-o-S. This destructing situation of targets S-o-S inner structure was displayed by transition of potential energy preferable after attacking, and it accords with experiential data. Because of dynamic character of targets S-o-S, potential energy values are distribution in some probability. In order to get the important values of the accurate values about targets, a mass of experimentations are necessary. This approach can support computing of targets chosen in campaigns of attacking S-o-S wrecked, and supply thinking for quantificational research S-o-S combat abilities based on information system.

References

1. Academy of Social Sciences Institute of Linguistics Dictionary Editorial Office, Modern Chinese dictionary, p. 903. The Commercial Press, Beijing (1996) (in Chinese)
2. Academy of Military Sciences, People's Liberation Army military terms, pp. 7,69. Military Sciences Press, Beijing (1997) (in Chinese)
3. Hu, X., Yang, J., Si, G., et al.: War complex system simulation analysis & experimentation, p. 281, 288, 349. Defense University Press, Beijing (2004) (in Chinese)
4. Zhang, Z., et al.: Military strategic operation research analysis methods, p. 208. Academy of Military Sciences Press, Beijing (2009) (in Chinese)
5. Yu, J., et al.: Defeated war will—targets choosing in information warfare, pp. 43–44, 46–47. People's Liberate Army Press, Beijing (2009) (in Chinese)
6. Hoffmann, B.: The strange story of the quantum. Pelican (1963)
7. Li, S., Li, P.: Quantum computation and quantum optimization algorithms, p. 7. Haerbin Institute of Technology Press, Haerbin (2009) (in Chinese)
8. Wen, J., et al.: Military application technology of satellites, p. 69. National Defense Industry Press, Beijing (2007) (in Chinese)
9. Huang, X.: Complex science and philosophy, p. 12. Central Compilation Press, Beijing (2007) (in Chinese)
10. Liang, Y., Xing, J.: An approach to battlefield data management of targets and environment. In: IEEE 2011 International Conference of Information Technology, Computer Engineering and Management Sciences, vol. 2, pp. 191–192. IEEE Press (December 2011) EI.2012.0614754271

Evaluation of Injure Effect Based on the Pixel Simulation

Dengan Chen, Guowei Wang, and Hongri Cong

Department of Command, Naval Aeronautical and Astronautical University,
264001, Yantai, China
ridiculousathena@126.com

Abstract. In view of evaluating the injure effect, a new method based on the real irregular-shaped target image is proposed in this article by analyzing on the distribution of the pixels before and after the shooting test. Through using different gray level to represent the different importance of the target, this article expatiate the basic steps of the pixel simulation method in Matlab, and take an example to validate the proposed method, and the simulation results verify the efficiency and feasibility of the proposed method.

Keywords: pixel simulation method, target gray image, injure effect, basic steps, application of Matlab.

1   Introduction

The injure effect of the weapon is often supposed to be the integral for the product of the hitting probability and the damage function[1]. But the analytical method for calculating the injure probability is very complex in fact. A new method to evaluate the injure effect based on the target grayscale is proposed in the paper, through which we can evaluate the injure effect simply by means of statistical analysis.

Pixel simulation method based on the target gray image to evaluate the injure effect, which is shooting on the gray image in the simulation environment directly. After shooting test, all the hitting points were set to the particular color on the computer screen. So we can obtain the shooting probability by counting and analyzing the distribution of the hitting points which were set to the particular color.

The importance of the different part of the target is different, so the injure effect by the shooting is different in different part. Then we can identify the parts of the target gray image by the different importance, and take the different gray scale to distinguish. Through analyzing the distribution of the hitting points on the different important parts, we can evaluate the injure effect accurately.

2   Obtain the Basic Data of the Target Image

2.1   Acquire the Target Image and Process Preliminary

Acquire the target image as clear as you can.
Distinguish the target in the background and set the background color to white.

T. Xiao, L. Zhang, and S. Ma (Eds.): ICSC 2012, Part II, CCIS 327, pp. 290–295, 2012.

Transform the target image to the gray image, and identify the different importance of the target by the different gray scale in the image.

2.2   Acquire the Target Image and Process Preliminary

In Matlab, numerical array is the basic data type, which is very fit to express the image. So the data of the image should be imported easily.

Fig. 1. Square Gray Image

We can obtain the data of the image in Matlab command window by using [2]
A=imread('d:\square.bmp')
Array A is acquired, represented the data of the bitmap which was named as square and saved in the D partition.

Now many data are displayed in Matlab command window. Every data represented the gray scale of the pixel point in the image 'square.bmp'. Analyze the array A, it consist 3 values, the value of part 1 is 0, the value of part 2 is 128, and the value of part 3 is 200.

In Matlab, the data of the gray image is a simple two dimensional array, and the value of the array element represents the gray scale of the pixel point in the image. For example the value 0 represents black and the value 255 represents white, and the value between 0 and 255 represent the different gray scale.

Analyze the array A in the command window by using
S = size(A)
We can get S=[95,95], which means that the length of the image is 95 pixels and the width is 95 pixels.

3   Shooting in the Simulation Environment Based on the Target Gray Image

Aiming at the center of the target gray image, and shooting in the simulation environment, and set the hitting points to the particular color. After the shooting test, we can obtain the distribution figure of the hitting points on the screen.

The distribution of the hitting points obey Gaussian distribution[1]. We can get the coordinates of the hitting points by Monte-Carlo Method, in which generate the random numbers by calling the random number generators of Matlab. Then we can plot the hitting points on the target gray image directly and set the color of the hitting points to white in Matlab.

4   Steps of the Injure Effect Evaluation

Now the background of the target gray image is white, and the color of the hitting points is white too.

Step 1: count the pixel points of the different important parts which are set to the different gray scale before the shooting test.

Step 2: aiming at the center of the target, and shooting in the simulation environment. Calculating the coordinates of the hitting points through Monte-Carlo Method, then plot the hitting points on the target gray image directly and set the color of the points to white in Matlab.

Step 3: after the shooting test, count the pixel points of the different important parts which was set to the different gray scale again.

Step 4: after the shooting test, we subtract the number which obtained by the second count from the number which obtained by the first count, then we obtain the value which is equal to the number of the hitting points in fact.

Then evaluate the injure effect by the established conditions.

5   Analysis of the Case

Detect the enemy frigate by the sea reconnaissance beyond 3000 meters, we acquire the target image and process preliminary as shown in Figure 2. Shoot at the frigate with the naval gun. Set the systematic error to 0, the coordinates of the hitting points follow Gaussian distributions because of the radon factors. On the premise that the shells hit on the frigate, if the key region of the frigate such as the command room or the engine room is hit by more than 3 shells, then the frigate lost the total combat ability. If the key region is hit by 2 shells and the important region such as the main weapons or the control room is hit by more than 2 shells, then the frigate is seriously hurt and lost most combat ability. Otherwise the frigate is slightly hurt. Then if fire 100 shells, evaluating the injure effect.

Step 1: possess the target image
Distinguish the frigate in the background and set the background color to white. Set the image to the gray image, and identify the different importance by the different gray scale in the image, as shown in Figure 2. The region A represents the command room, the region B represents the engine room, the region C represents the main weapons, the region D represents the control room and the region E represents others on the frigate gray image.

Set the gray scale of the region A and the region B to 0, set the gray scale of the region C and the region D to 80, set the gray scale of the region E to 132, then we can get the frigate gray image as shown in figure 2.

Fig. 2. Frigate Gray Image

Step 2: import the data of the frigate gray image in Matlab
We can obtain the data of the frigate gray image and analyze the data in Matlab command window by using

A=imread('d:\frigate.bmp')
size(A)

The data of the image which was saved in the D partition should be imported in Matlab, and the array A is acquired. Size(A)= [219,758], which means that the two dimensional array A represented the 219-by-758 matrix, and it also means that the height of the image is 219 pixels and the width is 758 pixels. The value of the element in the matrix A represents the gray scale of the pixel point, and the subscript of the element represents the coordinate of the pixel point on the gray image[2].

In Matlab, exercise axis-ij on the image, axis ij places the coordinate system origin in the upper left corner and the i-axis is vertical, with values increasing from top to bottom, the j-axis is horizontal with values increasing from left to right. The unit of the coordinate is pixel. So typed A （181,377） in the command window, we got 80, which means the gray scale of the pixel （181,377） on the gray image is 80.

Step 3: count the pixel points of the different important parts which is set to the different gray scale in Matlab
We can obtain the number of the pixel points of the different important parts which was set to the different gray scale in Matlab command window by using

x_1=size(A(find(A= =0)))[3]
y_1=size(A(find(A= =80)))[3]
z_1=size(A(find(A= =132)))[3]

In the command window, we can obtain x_1=8398. Then we determine the quantity of the pixels in region A and B by counting the quantity of the elements whose value was 0 in matrix A.

In the same way, y_1=9629, z_1=38803, which means the quantity of the pixels in region C and D is 9629 and the quantity of the pixels in region E is 38803.

Step 4: aim at the center of the frigate, shoot in the simulation environment and plot the hitting points on the target gray image directly
Display the frigate gray image and hold the image in Matlab by using
imshow(A);
hold on
Aiming at the center pixel (110,380) of the frigate image and shooting, the distributions of the hitting points obey Gaussian distribution[4]. The coordinates of the hitting points should be obtained through the random numbers which were generated by calling the random number generators in Matlab.

Set the systematic error to 0, and set the horizontal deviations to σ_x, and set the vertical deviations to σ_y, generate the random numbers η_1 and η_2 in Matlab[5]. Thus, the coordinates of the hitting points are

$$\begin{cases} x_i = \sigma_x \eta_1 + \mu_x \\ y_i = \sigma_y \eta_2 + \mu_y \end{cases}$$

In this equation, i stand for the shooting times, $i=1,2,3\ldots,n$, μ_x and μ_y stand for the aiming point and $\mu_x=110$, $\mu_y=380$, σ_x and σ_y stand for the deviations and $\sigma_x=200$, $\sigma_y=400$.

For this paper, set $n=100$, we obtained the coordinates of the hitting points, then plot the points on the frigate gray image directly. So we got the dropping points distribution as shown in figure 3.

Fig. 3. Dropping Point Distribution Image

In order to calculate easily, set the color of the points to white and the size of the points to 1by using

plot(X,Y,'.w', 'MarkerSize',1)

Then we can get the shooting effect image as shown in figure 4.

Fig. 4. Shooting Effect Image

Step 5: evaluate the shooting effect

After the shooting test, count the quantity of the pixel points in the different important parts which are set to the different gray scale again, then we have

$x_2=8396$, $y_2=9627$, $z_2=38798$

So we have got the quantity of the shots hit the different important parts.

Then we have

$Shoot_{AB}=x_1-x_2=2$

$Shoot_{CD}=y_1-y_2=2$

$Shoot_E=z_1-z_2=5$

It means that the value of the hitting points in the region A and B are 2, in the region C and D are 2, and in the region E are 5.

Step 6: evaluate the injure effect
In this shooting test, fired 100 shells, hit the key region of the frigate 2 shells, hit the important region 2 shells, and hit other region 5 shells. Based on the basis of the fixed principle, we can determine that the frigate is seriously hurt and lost most combat ability.

6   Conclusions

In this paper, a new method which evaluate the injure effect based on the target gray image was processed. It is advantageous that we can obtain the results directly and avoided the analytic derivation for the formula complexly. The basic steps of the method were introduced in this paper. Finally the simulation result verify that the proposed method can evaluate the injure effect conveniently and feasibly.

At the same time, we can also obtain the hitting probability easily through counting the quantity of the hitting points in the particular region by the method.

References

1. Zhang, Y.-P.: The Base of the Combat Simulation, pp. 284–324. Academic Press, BeiJing (2004) (in Chinese)
2. Gonzalez, R.C., Woods, R.E., Eddins, S.L.: Digital Image Processing Using MATLAB, pp. 202–222. Tsinghua University Press, BeiJing (2007) (in Chinese)
3. Zhang, Z.-Y.: Master MATLAB 6.5, pp. 38–76. Beihang University Press, Beijing (2003) (in Chinese)
4. Pei, L.-C., Wang-Zhongting: Monte-Carlo Method and Its Application, pp. 211–268. China Ocean Press, Beijing (1998)
5. Shi, F., Cheng, B.-S., Chen, B.: Handbook of the MATLAB Function, pp. 410–448. China Railway Press, Beijing (2011) (in Chinese)

Research on IETM Interaction Based-On Multi-agent

ZongChang Xu[1], Bo Li[1], ShuFeng Huang[1], and Yun Zhao[2]

[1] Academy of Armored Forces Engineering, 100072 Beijing, China
[2] National University of Defense Technology, Changsha 410073, China
everlibo@sina.com

Abstract. On the basis of analysis of the information crisis we have met in products supporting action, this paper described the characteristics of IETM Interaction, and explained the hierarchy of the achievement of IETM interaction in detail. After studying the characteristics of products supporting information systems, in order to improve the information-interaction ability of information systems, the paper introduced the Multi-Agent into the supporting actions, and researched the framework of interaction and the method of information-interaction.

Keywords: IETM, Interaction, Multi-Agent, Information System.

1 Introduction

With the continuous development of information technology, in our social actions, the effects of information become more and more important. In field of products support, the major impact of information technology is the appearance of many kinds of information-based supporting measures, and these measures have brought positive impact on the management, repairing, supplying and training. In information-based environment, the most remarkable characteristic of products supporting action is that we have a lot of information systems to support the products [1].

Interactive electronic technical manual (IETM) is a technical publication in which the contents such as general theory, operation and maintenance are stored with digital format. The contents can be interactively showed with characters, figures, tables, audios and videos [2]. Due to the integrity and variety of its data content, IETM overcomes the disadvantages of traditional papery technical manual, and contributes a lot in digital and electronic method of product technical data, and provides the timely and accurate data source for maintenance and training of products. But, because of the development of IETM and the independence of other information systems, the result is that the formats of data are different too, and there aren't the uniformed specification used for data interchange and compatible interfaces between these systems. The aftereffect is that the share of data between these systems is very difficult, and then, many information islands appear. Accordingly, how to use the data of these systems scientifically and reasonably is the problem we must solve, this is because that the share of data is where the shoe pinches to improve the whole supporting ability of the products.

T. Xiao, L. Zhang, and S. Ma (Eds.): ICSC 2012, Part II, CCIS 327, pp. 296–303, 2012.

IETM interaction is the ability that the IETM users obtain information and knowledge about products via operating the IETM systems. It is the inherent characteristic showing the major technical characteristic of IETM. At the same time, IETM interaction is the sticking point of improving the effectiveness and efficiency of product maintenance and operator training.

2   The Characteristics of IETM

At present, IETM has become one important research focus of product supporting; it has some notable characteristics as follows [3].

2.1   IETM Has a Whole System of Technical Standard

IETM was born in the United States; the standardization of IETM has caught the researcher's attention since its generation. Now, it has formed the whole system of technical standards about IETM. The United States is the country who issued the IETM technical standards firstly; the IETM work group modified them on the basis of the practical requirement and the development of technology. These standards constituted a system of IETM Specification. Some European countries are attaching importance to the standardization of IETM. Several European countries worked together and issued the IETM specification ASD/AIA/ATA S1000D, International Specification for technical publication utilizing a common source database, and updated this specification continuously. Now, S1000D has become the most popular IETM technical standard; its content covers the air products, sea products and land products. In addition, many other countries have developed the native IETM technical standards according to the practice of their countries.

2.2   The Data Included in IETM Is Accurate and Authoritative

The purpose of researching IETM is to build an integrated data environment. The integrated data environment can provide the data supporting for all kinds of actions of products and reduce the cost. The IETM data come from the activity relating to the product producing, using and supporting. The data sources include the using specification, maintaining manual, technical drawing and other contents. According to the requirements in IETM technical standard, the IETM authors process and store these data, and classify them into several types. Only the validated data can be processed. And then, these data are published into IETM and used for the daily products supporting actions. All of these can assure the accurateness and authoritativeness of the IETM data.

2.3   The Contents of IETM Involve Other Supporting Elements

The products supporting actions include maintenance planning, manpower and personnel, equipment supporting, supporting device, technical information, training and training supporting, computer resource supporting, supporting facility, etc. On the basis of the IETM technical standard, the contents of IETM include many information types, such as description, procedure, fault, planning, parts, wiring, crew and training. In order to run the supporting action successfully, the people who take on the responsibility of supporting elements must cooperate with each other.

After analyzing the characteristics of IETM, we can find that there is a close relationship between IETM and other supporting actions. Moreover, IETM has an advantage over other information systems. In this condition, we can study IETM as a breach; especially we should study the IETM interaction in-depth.

3   The Achievement Hierarchy of IETM Interaction

Interaction is the process of information interchange between users and information systems. Apparently, it is that the IETM users obtain the required information by operating IETM systems, but, because the obtained information is pre-established, the fact is that this kind of interaction happens among the data of IETM. All of the data is organized by the IETM authors and is solidified in the contents of IETM. In other words, the data of IETM is static; it differs from the dynamic information. Nowadays, IETM interaction is limited by the whole degree of data and the experience of IETM authors. All of these restrict the development of IETM interaction and cannot meet the requirement of intellectualized IETM. Based on the different organization method of information, we can compartmentalize the achievement hierarchy of IETM interaction as follows.

3.1   Information Interaction in the Data Module

The interaction on this level concerns the reference relationship of text, table, figure and multimedia in the data module. Both the main body and object of reference are in the same data module. The purpose of this kind of interaction is maintaining the local integrality in the data module, and making sure the data module which is the smallest information unit can present the information clearly.

3.2   Information Interaction between Data Modules

The interaction on this level concerns the reference relationship among different data modules. By this method, the IETM authors connect several associated data modules as an organism which includes limited information about the products. After building the reference relationship, the IETM authors can provide the fully information about one component by these relative data modules, or form a publication module containing them, or issue them as a self-governed publication. The purpose of this kind of interaction is solving conflict between the scope of data module and required information.

3.3   Information Interaction among Publications/ Publication Modules

The interaction on this level is concerning the reference relationship among different publications/publication modules. The publication module contains several data modules and the publication contains one or more publication modules. Referring to the traditional technical manual and on the basis of the content scope of IETM, the publication/publication modules may be a part of one technical manual, or the whole technical manual. The purpose of interaction among publication modules is connecting the publication modules which relate to the unique product, and forming the technical publication about the product. But, the purpose of interaction among publications is providing information of some other correlative products for the users of a certain product.

3.4   Information Interaction between IETM and Other Information Systems

The interaction on this level has exceeded the limit of IETM and is used for the cooperation of different supporting information systems. It has not been achieved and is in the exploring stage. Because the product supporting actions needs the information supporting coming from other fields, the requirement for the timely supporting actions and information interactions among systems becomes more necessitous. In addition, intellectualized supporting measure is an important problem we must research. This is because that when we research the information interaction between IETM and other information systems, we will improve the intellectualized level of IETM, at the same time, we can provide reference for the building of the intellectualized product supporting environment.

The four levels of above follow a logical sequence. The higher interaction level can be achieved only when the lower level has been achieved. At present, we have obtained a lot of fruits, but all of them do not break through the fourth level. Especially, we are lacking the research result about the intellectualized IETM interaction.

4   IETM Interaction Based on Multi-agent

Intellectualized interaction is the key fact that affects the process of IETM and other supporting information systems. Nowadays, because the development of computer science is so fast, in the field of artificial intelligence and computer science, researchers pay more attention to Agent. Agent can simulate the behavior of human and is used in many social fields. Along with the increasing requirement for the product supporting, highly intellectualized grade, reliability and fleetly adaptability consist the goal of product supporting information systems. Furthermore, this goal conforms to the characteristics of Agent. But, the single Agent is limited by the environment and task, and has the narrow knowledge. The product supporting actions relate to many supporting elements, and need the collaboration from IETM and other systems. For this reason, we can utilize the advantage of Multi-Agent to research how to improve the level of IETM intellectualized interaction.

4.1   Multi-agent Technology

Multi Agent system (MAS) is a loose coupling system which contains several Agents. MAS wants to compartmentalize the complicated system into several smaller and concerted sub-systems; these sub-systems communicate with each other and obey the united management [5]. Such measure can offset the shortages of individual Agents, and can make the systemic ability exceed the total ability of all sub-systems. These Agents are dispersive, but the behavior is autonomous. When achieving the function or goal of the system, each Agent obtains its own function or goal in the interaction process. This can meet the requirement for the product supporting. Each independent supporting information system implements its task, and communicates with each other by the means of information and function sharing. Via this manner, all of the product supporting information systems work together and improve the readiness and availability of the products.

4.2   The Interaction Architecture of IETM Based on Multi-agent Technology

In this section, we will regard IETM and other information systems as Agents which have the intellectualized characteristics. These Agents have individual belief, knowledge and intention. They could feel the changes of the environment and will make a quick response. When needed, they will collaborate with other Agents and accomplish the supporting task together. The interaction architecture of IETM based on Multi-Agent technology is shown in figure 1.

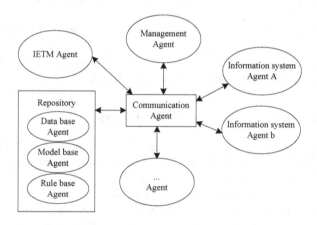

Fig. 1. The interaction architecture of IETM based on Multi-Agent technology

Except the IETM Agent and other information system Agents, this architecture also needs the management Agent, communication Agent and other Agents. Management Agent belongs to the control-type Agent; it is the decision-making section of the whole architecture; its goal is maximizing the efficiency of supporting actions; it receives the massages coming from other Agents. Management Agent processes the information and assorts with other Agents. Finally, it will give the final decision and distribute the decision to other Agents. Communication Agent provides other Agents with the communication method.

4.3   Example Analyzing

In order to explain the running principle of the interaction architecture of IETM based on Multi-Agent technology, this section will give an example and describe the process of information and function interaction between IETM and other information systems. The work flow will be shown in figure 2.

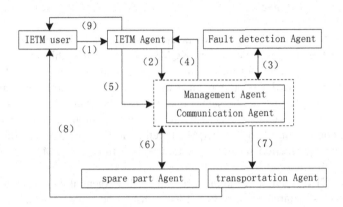

Fig. 2. Example for the interaction architecture

This example is about the process repairing action. When a product goes wrong, the IETM user seeks the fault via IETM, but the knowledge contained in IETM is not enough to confirm the fault exactly and cannot isolate the fault. At this time, the IETM user needs some help coming from exterior fault detection system. When the exterior fault detection system isolates the fault, the repairman needs the spare part to replace the damaged part. The brief description about the flow will be given below.

Step 1: the product goes wrong. IETM user interactes with IETM Agent and utilizes the knowledge contained in IETM to seek the fault.

Step 2: IETM cannot find the fault part and needs the help coming from the exterior fault detection system. IETM sends requirement to the management Agent via the communication Agent.

Step 3: management Agent assigns the task to the fault detection Agent. According to the fault phenomena, fault detection Agent begins the fault detecting work. When the fault is found and isolated, the fault detection Agent sends the result to the management Agent.

Step 4: the management Agent returns the detecting result to the IETM Agent.

Step 5: on the basis of the detecting result, IETM Agent sends the part requirement to the management Agent.

Step 6: the management Agent sends out the direction of supplying the part to the spare part Agent and gets an answer.

Step 7: the management Agent sends out the direction of transmitting the part to the transportation Agent.

Step 8: the transportation Agent carries the spare part to the repairman.

Step 9: when the spare part arrived, the IETM Agent guides the repairman to replace the damaged part.

4.4   Information Interaction of the IETM Agent Based on XML

Because of the different data formats, IETM and other information systems cannot transfer each other conveniently. So, in this section, we will give the method of information interaction.

Now, the popular language of Agent communication is Knowledge Query and Manipulation Language (KQML), but, KQML can be used within the same system only. It is difficult to use it for the communication among several Agents. EXtensible markup language (XML) is a popular language used to interchange information among different systems. At the same time, the popular standards of IETM require using XML as the language to record the product information. In this condition, this section will connect the XML and KQML together and use the XML as the language to interchange information in the interaction architecture of IETM based on Multi-Agent technology [4].

When the IETM Agent needs to interact with another Agent, it will generate a KQML massage about its requirement, and then, it will translate the KQML massage into a XML massage which can be understood by other Agents [6]. Then, the XML massage will be sent to the object Agent via the communication Agent. When the object Agent generates an answer in form of KQML massage, the answer massage will be processed in the same way and return to the IETM Agent. All of these have formed a loop of interaction between IETM and other information systems. Following is an example.

The KQML massage is:

```
( ask-one
: sender IETM Agent
: receiver Diagnosis Agent
: reply-with Result
: language XML
: content function(param 1, param 2)
...
 )
```

The translated XML massage is:

```
<performative>ask-one
<sender>IETM Agent</sender>
<receiver>< /receiver>
<reply-with> Result </reply-with>
<language> Result </ language>
<content>
<functionName parameter 1 = "param 1" parameter 2 =
"param 2">function</functionName>
</content>
```

5   Conclusions

With the development of the information-based supporting methods, the information and function interaction among different systems can improve the supporting efficiency and save the supporting cost. As an important tool of product supporting action, the interaction level of IETM affects the practical supporting task directly. In order to meet the requirement for the intellectualized supporting means, this paper tries to combine the IETM and Multi-Agent technology together and seek for the newly method to improve the interaction level between IETM and other information systems.

References

1. Xu, Z.: Supportability engineering. Arms Industry Press, Beijing (2002)
2. Zhao, A.: Research on Several Key Technologies of IETM for Equipment. Academy of Armored Forces Engineering (2009)
3. International specification for technical publications utilizing a common source database (Issue 3.0). ASD-AIA (July 2007)
4. Bin, Y.: An Agent Communication Framework Based on XML and CORBA Technique. Computer Technology and Development (December 2006)
5. Lin, L.: Research on Relative Theories and Technologies of Multi-Agent-based collaborative Manufacturing Resource Share. Wuhan University of Technology (2007)
6. Xiong, J., et al.: XML-based Muti-agent Communication System Architecture. Journal of Nanchang University(Natural Science) (July 2008)

The Wiener Model Identification
of Self-oscillation Actuator

Shuang Wei, Baiwei Guo, and Hong Xu

Key Laboratory of Dynamics and Control of Flight Vehicle, Ministry of Education ,
Beijing Institute of Technology, Beijing 100081, China
guobw@bit.edu.cn

Abstract. To study the saturation nonlinear phenomena of self-oscillation actuator caused by constructions, a two-step method was proposed to establish its mathematic model by linked Wiener structure. Firstly, the frequency of self-oscillation and effective output signal of system were obtained by analyzing its spectrum and designing filter. Then, through analyzing the characters of output signal, differential equations and polynomial basis functions were chosen for linear sub-system and non-linear sub-system of Wiener Model, and the parameters were determined by calculating. The validity of mathematic model was demonstrated by simulating.

Keywords: Wiener Model, self-oscillation linear actuator, system identification, saturation, non-linear.

1 Introduction

The actuator acts as the most important executive mechanism in guidance system, its dynamitic characteristics have direct impact on the overall performance of the aircraft. One of the main problems in the preliminary design of a missile guidance system is to establish the mathematic model of the program, the model not only requires the ability to accurately describe the intended program of static and dynamitic characteristics, but also can be analyzed and mathematically simulated during the designing process. Therefore, it is very necessary and valuable to establish mathematical model for an actuator in engineering applications. Self-excited oscillation linear actuator is a special kind of actuator used in missiles. This kind of actuator has a prominent characteristic in the working process, and the actuator rudder has high frequencies from 40 Hz to 50 Hz in self-excited oscillation. [1]Due to the existence of high-frequency oscillation characteristic, the actuator command response has great randomness, which caused considerable difficulties to the dynamitic performance of the actuator, such as the rudder reaction delay phenomenon caused by the uncertainly command response, and rudder feedback saturation phenomenon when the control command input is bigger. These nonlinear phenomenon make the linear steering model cannot accurately describe the dynamic characteristics. In this paper, an effective two-step method is introduced to accurately describe the dynamic characteristics in saturated case, through setting up the Wiener Model of self-oscillating actuator.

T. Xiao, L. Zhang, and S. Ma (Eds.): ICSC 2012, Part II, CCIS 327, pp. 304–310, 2012.

2   The Response Characteristics of Self-oscillating Actuator

The self-oscillating actuator is particularly suitable for use in small rotating tactical missile for its simple structure and low cost. As there is relay control in actuator system, it is a typical nonlinear system. In order to realize the linear control, low frequency control signal is overlaid on high frequency self-excited oscillation in the input terminal. When it is used in missiles, an essential low pass filter of the projectiles can filter out the high frequency signal to realize the equivalent linearization proportional control.

Spinning projectiles of single channel control are studied in this paper, and amplitude modulated sine wave are designed as control instructions. The responding curves of self-excited oscillation actuator are shown in Figure 1 and 2. It is shown that the sine wave is of amplitude 1V and the frequency 1Hz in figure 1, and the sine wave is of amplitude 2V and frequency 1Hz in figure 2.

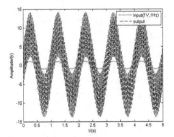   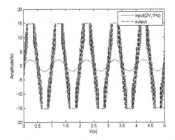

Fig. 1. Actuator sine instructions response   **Fig. 2.** Actuator sine instructions response
curve(a)   curve(b)

It can be shown in figure 1 that the actuator follows the sine instruction very well and start to make self-excited oscillation at the same time, when the instructions amplitude is 1V. However, it is shown in the figure 2 that the output signal begins to appear saturation phenomenon because of exceeding instruction amplitude 2V. Undoubtedly, the output saturation affects the dynamic characteristics of actuator. Moreover, the changing frequency of instruction will significantly increase the actuator delay compensation time. Therefore, it's of great value to set up a mathematical model to describe the actuator in saturation case and analysis the characteristics of actuator.

3   Model Identification Algorithm

3.1   Signal Processing

To establish a mathematical model of the system, the primary issue is to determine the input and output signal that can reflect the static and dynamic characteristics of system. For self-excited oscillation actuator, it needs to separate effective signal from the output, the effective signal is the first order harmonic with same frequency of control instruction. [2]As shown in figure 3 and figure 4, it's the spectrum analysis of output signal. The difference between the two pictures is that they have different input signal, the instruction in figure 3 is sine wave of 1V, 1Hz, and the instruction in figure 4 is sine wave of 1V, 5Hz. It can be seen from the figure that the output signal mainly consists of the 45Hz self-oscillation signal and the corresponding to the input signal such as 5Hz and 1Hz.

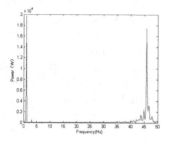

Fig. 3. Actuator output signal spectrum analysis(a)

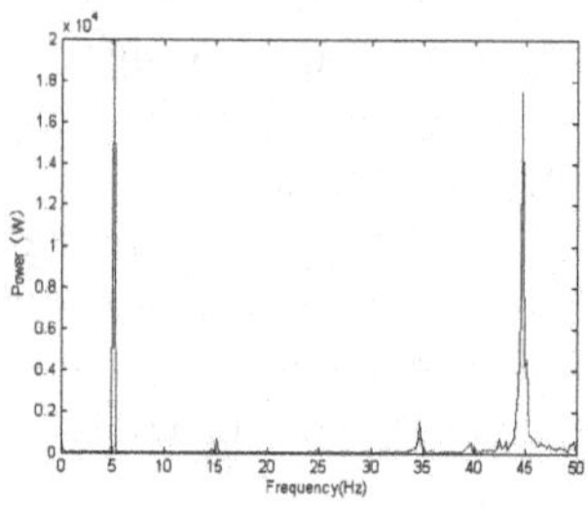

Fig. 4. Actuator output signal spectrum analysis(b)

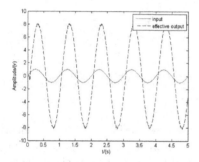 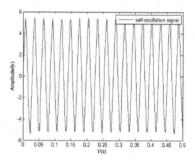

Fig. 5. The effective output signal of actuator

Fig. 6. The self-oscillation signal of actuator

A band-pass filter is designed to filter out the high frequency noise and self-oscillation signal from output signal, and the effective output can be obtained and shown in figure 5. It is determined that effective output has same frequency with the input instruction. The self-oscillation signal of the actuator is shown in the figure 6. The filter result is consistent with the spectrum analysis.

3.2   Wiener Model

The Wiener Model consists of a linear subsystem and a nonlinear subsystem. The dynamic characteristics of the object can be described by the linear subsystem, and the linear model can be rectified by nonlinear static subsystem. Therefore, the Wiener

Model is suitable for describing such actuator that contains both dynamic linear structure and static nonlinear structure.[3] According to the characteristics of self-excited oscillation actuator, the equivalent system is a series structure that the former is linear block and the follower is nonlinear block. The Wiener Model structure is shown in figure 7.[4]

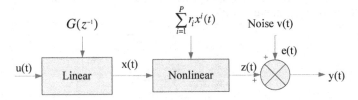

Fig. 7. The structure of Wiener Model

As is shown in figure 7, $u(t)$ is system input, the result of the linear subsystem, $x(t)$, is immeasurable middle variable. The output $z(t)$ of the nonlinear subsystem can be gotten. $e(t)$ is the noise signal of output terminal, and $y(t)$ is the output signal of system. The linear subsystem is expressed as an n-order difference equations and it is assumed that $b_0=1$.

$$B(z^{-1})x(k) = A(z^{-1})u(k) \quad,$$

$$A(z^{-1}) = a_0 + a_1 z^{-1} + a_2 z^{-2} + \ldots\ldots + a_n z^{-n}, \tag{1}$$

$$B(z^{-1}) = b_0 + b_1 z^{-1} + b_2 z^{-2} + \ldots\ldots + b_n z^{-n},$$

The nonlinear subsystem is expressed as a p order polynomial:

$$y(k)=r_1 x(k)+\ldots\ldots+r_p x^p(k)+v(k) \tag{2}$$

In the case of the stability of the system, the order n and p can be appropriately selected to make the gain of system fit the given nonlinear and linear block, and the parameters a_i, b_i, r_i, can be estimated by using the measurement data $\{u(k), y(k)\}$. Combine with formula (1) and formula(2), the equation of whole system can be achieved:

$$B(z^{-1})y(k) = r_1 A(z^{-1})u(k) + \sum_{i=2}^{p}\sum_{j=0}^{n} r_i b_j x^i(k-j) \tag{3}$$

In formula(3), the $x^i(k-j)$ is immeasurable middle variables, and it couldn't identify the required parameters using least square algorithm.

In reference[5], a multi-step algorithm was proposed to identify the Hammerstein model, and it is a combination of steady state identification and dynamic identification. The multi-step algorithm mentioned in the reference is as follows : first achieve the step response data, then conform the order of nonlinear subsystem and identify the parameter, according to the steady output data, after that, base on the characteristics of the Hammerstein model, identify the parameters of linear subsystem. Inspired by the reference, this paper proposes a two-step algorithm to identify the model of actuator in saturation case. But for the study object is self-excited oscillation actuator, the step input may be harmful to the actuator, so still use the sine wave as input. After that, add the self-oscillation signal to the linear output, combine the linear output with the output in saturation case, then identify the parameter of nonlinear subsystem depend on least square method, the process of algorithms and derivation are as follows:

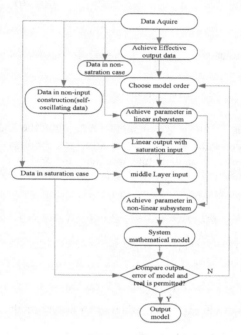

Fig. 8. The Process of Algorithms

Assume that $\{u_0, y_0\}$ is the input instruction and effective output data, which is unsaturated, and $\{u_1, y_1\}$ is the data in saturation case and $\{0, y_z\}$ is the self-oscillation signal in zero input instruction. If the system output is unsaturated, the nonlinear subsystem can be supposed as, $r_1=1$, $r_i=0$ ($i=2, 3, \ldots p$), as a result:

$$B(z^{-1})z_0 = A(z^{-1})u_0 \tag{4}$$

Just substitute $y(k)=z(k)+v(k)$ into formula(4), formula (5) will get immediately.

$$B(z^{-1})y_0(k) = A(z^{-1})u_0(k) + B(z^{-1})v(k) \tag{5}$$

Assume the equivalent noise is as follows: $\xi(k) = v(k) + \ldots + b_n v(k-n) = B(z^{-1})v(k)$, Assume that it includes not only input and output measument noise, but also system internal noise. The formula (5) can be transformed to formula (6) :

$$y(k) = -b_1 y_0(k-1) - \ldots - b_n y_0(k-n) + a_0 u(k) + \ldots + a_n u(k-n) + \xi(k) \qquad (6)$$

In formula (6), the parameter a_i, b_i can be identified depending on least square algorithm, substitute a_i, b_i to formula (1), if combine formula (1) and saturation input data, the linear output under saturation input instruction will achieve. Now add the self-oscillation signal to the linear output, it will get the middle variable, substitute it to formula (2), and it can be expressed as:

$$y_1(k) = r_1 x_1(k) + r_2 x_1^2(k) + \ldots + r_p x_1^p(k) + v(k) \qquad (7)$$

Assume that $v(k)$ is Gauss white noise, base on $n+N$ groups of data (x_1, y_1),identify the parameter r_i depend on least square algorithm twice. At last, substitute a_i, b_i, r_i into formula (1) and formula (2), the Wiener Model of whole system achieved.

4   Simulation Analysis

The following is experimental plan : on NI PXI platform, the request input instructions are generated and the rudder feedback signal are collected by LabView RT controller and NI 6230 high speed data acquire card, and the program language is Labwindows/CVI. Combine the saved data and the two-step algorithm mentioned above, the Wiener Model identification of the self-oscillation actuator realized. Use homogenization error RMS (Root Mean Square Normalized error) to judge the accuracy of the identification. $\{u_0, y_0\}$ is the data group under input construction 1V, 2Hz, $\{u_1, y_1\}$ is the data groups under input construction 2V, 1Hz, $\{0, y_z\}$ is the self-oscillation data groups under zero input construction. They are all in the same air pressure. Describe the linear subsystem as forth order $n=4$ and nonlinear subsystem order $p=3$. The RMS minimums are shown in table 1. The sample time is 0.001s, run time is 50s, and the parameters are obtained:

$$a_0 = -28.82, a_1 = 43.35, a_2 = -0.3298, a_3 = -14.19$$

$$b_1 = -2.278, b_2 = 1.0875, b_3 = 0.7287, b_4 = -0.5335$$

$$r_1 = 1.3578, r_2 = 7.67e^{-4}, r_3 = 3.73e^{-4}$$

Select the forth order ARX (Auto Regressive eXogenous) model, contrast with the Wiener Model in same condition. Due to the model output contains self-oscillation signal, the output graph is less comparative, and the model output and actual output error is given in table 2, which is shown in table 2. The Wiener Model is more accurate description than ARX model.

Table 1. RMS in different nonlinear order

p	2	3	4	5
RMS	4.4273	3.7652	4.4060	4.3818

Table 2. The RMS of model output error

Model	Wiener	ARX
RMS	3.7652	21.3426

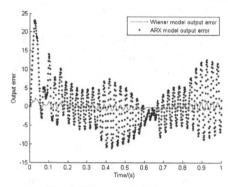

Fig. 9. Wiener and ARX output

5   Conclusions

A two-step method was proposed to establish its mathematic model by linked Wiener structure to study the saturation nonlinear phenomena of self-oscillation actuator caused by constructions. The frequency of self-oscillation and effective output signal of system were obtained by analyzing its spectrum and designing filter, and differential equations and polynomial basis functions were chosen for linear sub-system and non-linear sub-system of Wiener Model, and the parameters were determined by calculating. Through simulation and analysis, it is found that the characteristics of actuator can be described and identified. This research is useful in saturation case, time delay, dead zone, asymmetric relay characteristics etc.

References

1. Yu, J., Lin, F., Fang, Z.: Research on the Method to Deal with Delay Compensation Time of Self-oscillation linear Actuator. Acta Armamentar 30(5), 1–3 (2009)
2. Wang, L., Zhang, J.: Design of Phase-shift Detection Filter of Self-oscillation Linear Actutor. Tactical Missile Technology, February 2–4 (2010)
3. Wu, D.: Identification method for nonlinear dynamic system using Wiener neural network. Control Theory & Applications 26(11), 1–2 (2009)
4. Gui, W., Song, H., Yang, C.: Hammerstein-Wiener model identified by least-squares-support –vector machine and its application. Control Theory & Applications 25(3), 1–2 (2008)
5. Shen, T.: Research on System Identification of Auxiliary Power Unit of Electric Vehicle, pp. 44–89. Beijing Institute of Technology (2007)

Research on Virtual Design
and Man-in-Loop Simulation

Zhiming Song[1,2] and Shengxiao Zhang[1]

[1] Systems Engineering Research Institute, CSSC, Beijing 100036, China
[2] Beijing China Shipbuilding IT Co .ltd. CSSC,Beijing100861, China
szm72@163.com

Abstract. This paper focuses on the difficulties on the research of the modern industrial complex product. Based on the large-scale command and control system, some key technologies are achieved in this paper: the digital design and the human-in-loop simulation; the engineering method at the stages of the project establishment, the product design and the physical prototype test; the solution of some engineering applications.

Keywords: Virtual Design, Human-in-the-Loop, simulation, test.

1 Introduction

In modern industrial production, various products are getting more and more complex; this is implied by the large-scale, multi-application and high technology, etc. Roughly speaking, based on the physical prototype, the process of the traditional industrial design is: (1)according to task requirements,to carry out program design and technical design; (2)to produce in-kind previous prototype; (3)to test the previous prototype; (4)to improve the design, based on the test results;(5)and so forth until the completion of the design requirements.

However, for the physical prototype, the test runs in the real environment at the final phase of the project development, so to make the modification of the products difficult (even small modification causes the great lost of the time and expenditure), if there are the design drawbacks or serious errors.

In the area of the airport scheduling management, large-scale ship project, the C2 system requires lots of persons on duty, who is one part of the global system. Thus at the design stage, the setting of the persons' position, the functional design of the display and control station and the persons' cooperation should be synchronized and considered. In traditional design mode, the manipulative test of the persons can be achieved after the realization of the physical prototype, this makes some problems; besides, the C2 system is tested at the laboratory, which is totally different from the real environment (e.g. ships), because this test is only useful to the interface, the static function, the ideal workflow; next, the test in the real environment is necessary, in order to resolve the problems caused by the real environment.

T. Xiao, L. Zhang, and S. Ma (Eds.): ICSC 2012, Part II, CCIS 327, pp. 311–317, 2012.
© Springer-Verlag Berlin Heidelberg 2012

Thus, there are several problems in the physical-prototype-based industrial design mode: long development cycle; high development and testing cost etc. Especially for the novel complex system, more complex design causes more serious problem as mentioned above [1].

According to the characteristics of the C2 products, based on the digital modeling and simulation technology, this paper realizes the works as follows: (1)Building the virtual prototype, virtual working environment, and the virtual scene (served for the human operators) in the design process; (2)Realizing the simulation test of the human-in-loop, so to detect the design drawbacks efficiently and quickly; (3)Completing the design task by providing a reference for the design optimization; (4)Utilizing the virtual environment to simulate the real environment, especially after the realization of the physical prototype.(5)Improving the simulation for the environment, e.g. the navigation of the ship, the ocean weather conditions, etc.

By all the works as mentioned above, we can achieve the test in the laboratory, which should also be applied to the real environment, so as to significantly shorten the test cycle and improve the product quality.

2   Virtual Design and Test

2.1   Virtual Design Approach at the Stage of the Project Study

The development cycle of one product depends on the project study on the product feasibility, which is to describe the background, the significance, the necessity and the feasibility of the product. At the stage of the project study, there are two development modes: the traditional development mode and the virtual design mode. In the traditional development mode, which is based on the document and PPT, the work contents are hard to understand and may be missed, especially for the complex products. However in the virtual design mode, based on the preliminary assumptions and virtual reality technology, the target image can be described in the form of 3D flash at graphical PC; the novel target image can be generated quickly with the modification of the project. Comparing both the traditional development mode and the virtual design mode, we can see that the virtual design mode can improve the performance of the project study, accelerate the study progress, and define the global system and his composition.

2.2   Virtual Design at the Stage of the Project Design

After the product study, we go into the stage of the project design. For the distributed C2 system, the key technologies at this stage are, based on the predefined technical solution and HLA (a Distributed Interactive Simulation Technology), to build the analog prototype of the system (the digital prototype), develop the supportive environment for the prototype simulation, design virtual test and optimization algorithm.

2.2.1   The Necessity for Designing the Virtual Prototype of the C2 System Based on HLA

The C2 system is the distributed information system of "PC+software"; many designers thought that there is no need to work based on the distributed "PC+software". However, HLA can also apply to the development of the information system for the following reasons: (1)HLA is the best engineering standard to solve the "reusability" and the "interoperability" so far. In general, the complex information system is developed by a number of research units, which requires lots of modifications in the process, while the "reusability" and "interoperability" of HLA support the parallel design and the integration of the subsystems, so HLA can help us build a simulation prototype quickly, carry out dynamic real-time simulation and improve the design. Otherwise, the direct development of the software costs a large amount of work and long time, makes the product design hard to improve. (2)HLA-based simulation prototype only includes the main functions of the real system and the important interfaces, but does not involve the system details (e.g. the exception handling, the illegal input processing, the over demanding of the hardware, the system stability conditions, etc). Thus, this avoids unnecessary details at the preliminary design stage and greatly accelerates the development cycle. (3)In HLA simulation, software development environment is popular, e.g. the windows operating system, C++, C#, Java and other high-level language, a large number of popular software. More importantly, we need not to design the TCP/IP communication protocol thanks to the criterion and methods of HLA, which make us develop and improve a simulation prototype more quickly. Besides, in the industrial application, due to the stability, the security, the "real-time", the industrial norms, or design constraints, etc, the simulation is developed based on UNIX or VXWORKS operating system and C/C++ or even low-level language, this makes the development of the simulation less effective. (4)In the mode of HLA-based simulation prototype, we can achieve the program design as soon as possible for the specific model by the virtual prototype, and apply final program model to the products. Especially when the simulation and products use the same language, e.g. C, the simulation code can even be directly ported into the products.

2.2.2   Virtual Design and Test

Generally, the design process for complex product contains the project design and technical design. The virtual prototypes and virtual test environment can be built after the previous completion of the report of the program design mainly including the following parts: (1)By distributed HLA simulation, each console device establishes the corresponding the simulator (the independent federal node). (2)According to the working environment, on which the product runs, and the design test, we establish the models of environmental factors and build the supportive environment of the digital prototype simulation, e.g. the ship navigation simulator, the object-based C2 simulator. (3)By visual simulation technology, 3D visual scene is developed for the persons who have the visual operating demands.

In this way, at the project design stage we can obtain the prototype of future products; build the complete virtual product and its test environment. The operators of the C2 system operate the console simulator just as operating the real device; they can also carry out the human-in-loop simulation, evaluate the design and modify the bugs. And then according to the modification of the design, we modify the HLA-corresponding virtual prototype and supportive simulation environment, and so forth until the completion of the program design and the technical design.

The digital method at the design stage in presented in Figure 1.

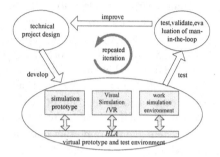

Fig. 1. Digital application at the virtual design stage

3   Virtual Test after the Development of the Product

As mentioned above, the virtual prototype is nearly to be ready at the end of the technical design. Thus, we will develop the physical prototype based on the final technical design, thanks to the modification by the virtual test at the design stage, the physical prototype need not to be improved greatly.

Compare to the virtual prototyping, the physical prototype is a real device, which will be tested in the digital virtual testing environment so to resolve the "adaptability" problems of the interface. The interface adapter (for the physical prototype of the console) can be achieved by: accessing the distributed virtual prototype testing environment based on the HLA criterion; accessing the real interface characteristics of the display and control console, e.g. UDP, CORBA, CAN, serial connection, etc. This is detailed in Figure 2.

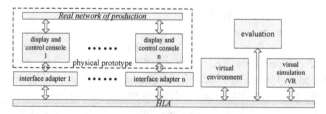

Fig. 2. Virtual test of physical prototype

The simulation test by accessing the physical prototype into the virtual testing environment can simulate the real environment; test the adaptability of the product for the real and poor working conditions. Besides, the physical prototype focuses on the reliability design, the fault tolerance and safety design of the product. We can invite the users to participate in the simulation test, so as to evaluate the reliability, the availability and the ergonomic in the virtual operating environment, give the comments. By this way, we can greatly reduce the works in the follow-up field tests, shorten the test cycle (especially in the traditional mode, this causes lots of problems), speed up the delivery schedule, reduce development costs, improve safety quality and reliability.

4   Key Technologies

4.1   The Integration for the Modeling and Simulation of the Distributed Virtual Prototype

The virtual design and simulation of the C2 system need the corresponding simulation system. There are two difficulties in the industrial application: (1)The HLA-based simulation of the C2 system, with the instrumentation tools, GIS tools, *etc*, forms the simulation console; this requires the matching design functions, and the accuracy of each simulation console. (2)The simulation of the external supportive environment is related to the running of the C2 system, which depends on the synthesized natural environment. Generally, the difference of the external environments will cause a great difference of the process and the results of the C2 system. Thus, in order to obtain correct and effective test results, the external environment must be modeled and simulated. Note that, the external environment is composed of various professional equipments, *e.g.* the mechanical, the electronic, the electromagnetic, and the natural environment, *etc*. there should be a professional research team to model and simulate the external environment based on the C2 system. Moreover, many factors affect the running of the C2 product, which is difficult to model: the synthesized natural environment, in which the sea state, the wind conditions, the visibility, the temperature, the humidity, the cloud amount and other factors are required, they are interrelated, and have some statistical characteristics in some particular regions and specific time, so how to model and simulate them precisely is still an open problem. From the point of the simulation form, they contain the all-digital simulation, the semi-physical simulation, and other forms, by the reflective memory technology, the serial communication and Ethernet; we can resolve the problems of the accessibility and the "real-time" in the semi-physical system.

4.2   Visual Simulation Technology

In the testing environment of virtual prototype, the visual simulation has the following applications: (1)For the visual C2 task, it makes use of the visual simulation to generate real-time visual scene; (2)The visual simulation can generate the real-time visual scene for the equipments of the video surveillance, the periscope observation, and the infrared detection; (3)In the testing system of the virtual prototype, it is necessary to set up an expert evaluation environment, which is connected to the simulation circuit, so to receive the simulation data, generate the virtual scene in real time for the experts who evaluate the system performance.

Due to the difference of applications, the forms of the visual simulation are totally different, e.g. the visual scene with a single key command position, which requires high-quality scene performance, utilizes a single spherical ring screen and the stereoscopic projection; for the visual simulation who depicts the scene outside the cabin, we usually adopt the method of the porthole physical compartment with TV splicing; the simulation of the multi-person evaluation utilizes the cylindrical ring screen with the multi-channels. Generally, different requirements demand different visual simulations.

For any visual simulation, the test of the C2 system requires the "real-time" and high-quality scenes. Generally speaking, we use the high-level 3D graphical software, e.g. Vega Prime. However, the practical applications usually require some special scene effects which can not be supported by the high-level graphical software, so the development based on OpenGL, Direct and graphics -card-based vector programming is necessary.

4.3   Virtual Reality (VR)

VR is an important branch of the modern simulation technology, compared to the visual simulation; VR not only improves the issue of the "see", but also gives human more feelings e.g. the "hear", the "touch", the "smell", this greatly improve the immersion sense in the simulation and further the third dimension [2].

In the C2 system, the person sometimes use the gesture to operate, this is a problem of the physical movements' command, which we should resolve in the simulation. By VR, we can introduce the persons' movements into the simulation; develop the special VR program for the operator with the gesture commands (including the hardware and the simulation software); give the equipments as the helmet, the data clothing, and data gloves to the operators, so to allow them to watch the virtual scene and the movements of other operators; the data clothing collects the movement signals and sends them to the simulation, and then generate the corresponding virtual movements.

To develop VR is not easy: (1)The VR system is complex, which contains the helmets, the data gloves, the data clothing, the position/tracking sensor, the control computer and the graphical computer. The development of VR involves how to manage these equipments. (2)Poor reliability; because of the poor performance of the VR position equipments on operators and VR position/tracking sensors, the VR programs have the problems on the "see" and the "watch", which reduce the VR performance. (3)The "real time", the synchronization and the interconnection of the VR programs are still open problems. (4)The development of the data clothing depends on the application, we need to transfer the real time information (the position/velocity of the operator) to the visual scene, and reproduce the position/velocity of the virtual operator. The difficulty of this process is how to arrange the sensors on the operator and build the relation between the output of the sensors and the human movements. (5)Other problems in the development of VR: the three-dimensional display; the synchronization of the data and computing; the motion estimation and smoothness [3].

4.4   Evaluation Technology

The virtual prototype and the virtual testing simulation system of the C2 system involve two types of evaluation: the evolution of the simulation system; the evaluation of the business in the simulation. It is impossible to design the virtual prototype and the virtual system totally same as the real system, with this problem, in the industrial application, we should determine the corresponding analog scope and credibility indicators firstly, evaluate the simulation models and systems by VVA, so as to ensure the validity of the virtual systems and the virtual test.

Besides, the objective of the virtual test for the virtual prototype is to test the technical design and the application of the product (e.g. the station deployment, the station function, the work processes, the capacity indicators, the ergonomics). In order to quantify the test results, we need to establish the evaluation of the models and system, record the data of the test process, and make an objective evaluation. Especially for more complex systems, to design an evaluation model with the comprehensive system and wide performance indicators is very important; the experts of the environment evaluation and the persons in the test can also evaluate the test intuitively and subjectively.

5   Conclusions

The method proposed in this paper, which has been applied to the research cycle of some project shortened the development cycle, reduced the development cost, and improved the product quality. By the application, the feasibility of the method in this paper has been proved. Besides, the foreign digital technology has reached the complex industrial products without drawings, completely virtual development [4]. Thus, combined these technologies as mentioned above, this paper has improved the application of the digital technology, established the administrative and management system, developed the digital research norm, and finally achieved the "virtual test" of the product.

References

1. Song, Z.: Research on digital development technology of complex systems. The Ship Demonstration Reference-the Yongfeng Construction Special Issue (August 2009)
2. Burdea, G.C.: Philippe Coiffet. Virtual reality technology. Publishing House of Electronics Industry, Beijing (2005)
3. Song, Z.: Research and applications in the VR technology in ship command and control system. Journal of System Simulation 23(8), 1729–1733 (2011)
4. Sun, H.: Review of digital modeling and simulation technology in the development of foreign weapons and equipment. Digital Military 2, 47–51 (2011)

Research on CSP Model
for Complex TT&C Task Scheduling

Zhen Zhu[1], Yongming Gao[2], and Bin Wang[2]

[1] Graduate School, The Academy of Equipment, Beijing 101416, China
[2] Department of Information&Equipment, The Academy of Equipment, Beijing 101416, China
Zhuzhen_wx_js@hotmail.com

Abstract. This paper focus on the high frequency of conflict and complex constraints in ground TT&C(Tracking Telemetering and Command) resources scheduling problems. A detailed analyze of resources and requests has been made. Tasks are divided into collections of requests classified by their phases with a sequent based on constraint to describe their logic. Six constraints including equipment matching constraint, time windows constraint, antenna confliction constraint, satellite competition, sequential logic constraint and consumable resource constraint are particularly expressed. To meet the vary preferences from usage of resources to accomplishment of requests by different users, three heuristic principals have been added to the CSP(Constraints Satisfaction Problem) model. In the end of this paper, the model is validated by a simulation.

Keywords: TT&C task scheduling, CSP, resource confliction, satellite consumable resources, request preferences, flexible principals.

1 Introduction

The ground resources for scheduling are becoming more and more precious while the TT&C tasks are exploding now. The TT&C scheduling aims at distributing limited resources and time windows to tasks, so that user requests can be fulfilled maximally. Current missions become complex that even a single task can be divided into logical phases and users' consideration differ from usage of resource to accomplishment of request. The problem changed and a traditional model may be insufficient.

The main methods for modeling TT&C scheduling are Mathematical Scheduling Model[1], Figure Model[2], Heuristic Model[3], Petri Model[4] and CSP Model. Paper [7] solved the problem of observation satellite scheduling. The memory limitation of satellite is taken into consideration, but the equipment cannot be replenished. Paper [8] builds a CSP model for observation satellite considering task, resources, event and constraints, but tasks are isolated with no connection. Paper [9] discusses SPOT-5, as well as a direct Multi-knapsack model is made considering satellite memory and energy is made. However, the model cannot describe the sequent and logic connections of tasks limited. Paper [10] views scheduling as a problem of distributing related and

T. Xiao, L. Zhang, and S. Ma (Eds.): ICSC 2012, Part II, CCIS 327, pp. 318–327, 2012.

exclusive resources. It gives 3 types of constraints, but the matching of satellite and antenna is not considered.

Besides, many researchers conversed TT&C scheduling problems into mature models in other fields, such as Parallel Machine Model[11], Vehicle Routing Model[12], Sequential Decision Model[13], etc. Most of their purposes are on the maximal the quantity of task or the summary of task weight. The author considers 6 constraints and 3 principals for a CSP model and validated it by a simulation.

2　The Description of Ground TT&C Resources

2.1　Ground Station Resources

Ground stations can do tasks of Tracking, Telemetering, Commanding and Transferring[14], Define grand station set as $GRS=\{GRS_1, GRS_2, ..., GRS_M\}$, M counts to total. Usually a station has 1-3 antennas, $GRS_i=\{ant_{i,\ 1}, ant_{i,\ 2}, ...ant_{i,\ G(i)}\}$, $i=\{1,2, ..., M\}$, G(i) is the quantity of GRS_i, so $\sum_{i=1}^{M}G(i)=G$. Antennas may have many types, while the author define them as A、B、C、D.

Antenna has attributes ant=(CLASS, PT, HEALTH), CLASS can be A,B,C and D, PT stands for prepare time, HEALTH express as the available time of antenna.

2.2　Satellite Resource

Define the set of satellite $SAT=\{sat_1, sat_2, ..., sat_S\}$, its attribute sat=(FUCTION, PT, STORAGE). A FUNCTION matches a CLASS of ant, PT stands for prepare time, STORAGE is the satellite's memory which can be replenished when the satellite downloads to a station and deplete when the satellite is observing or uploading.

2.3　Target Resource

Target can be described as a point or an area by scale, and dynamic or statistic by status. In this paper, the author simplified all targets as statistic points and view them as special antennas $TARGET \subset GANA$.

2.4　Visible Time Windows

Define visible time windows as $VW_{s,g}=\{vw_{s,g,1}, vw_{s,g,2}, ..., vw_{s,g,V(s,g)}\}$ for sat_s and $g.ana_g$. V is the total number of VW totally. $V=\sum_{s=1}^{S}\sum_{g=1}^{G}V(s, g)$, so the visible time windows can also be described as $VW=\{vw_1, vw_2, ..., vw_V\}$. The attribute $vw_i=(sat_s, gana_g, Begin, End)$, includes its satellites, antennas, begin time and end time.

3   Description of Request

Requests are transferred from tasks. Define TASK={TASK$_1$, TASK$_2$, ..., TASK$_T$}. A task can be divided into requests REQ={req$_1$, req$_2$, ..., req$_R$}. The attribute req = (TASK , sat , GRS , Begin , End , duration , cost , LA) .The attribute presents tasks the request belongs to, satellite, ground station, what time request begins, what time request ends, the duration, the cost of satellite memory, and the logic relationships of requests. When cost<0, it may be a deplete request. When cost>0, it may be a replenish request. LA={LA$_1$, LA$_2$, ..., LA$_{L(i)}$}. L(i) shows the number of related requests. Attribute LA$_i$= (req , Begin , End). It means this request must begin after req, but start in the Interval of [Begin , End].

Request is inseparable from the smallest task unit. Users proposes task type, orbit phases, task duration and other concrete demands in TASK which will finally be divided and transferred into REQ. For example, TASK$_1$"Satellite S observe target T for 10 minutes during its ascending node, and download the data to ground station G in 24 hours ". Task$_1$ is divided into two requests, req$_1$ and req$_2$. req$_1$ means "S observe T in [t1,t2]", and req$_2$ represents "S communicate with G in the interval [t3,t4]". The logic relationship can be constrainted by req$_2$.LA=(req$_1$, 0, 24).

4   CSP Model of Ground TT&C Resource Scheduling

4.1   Constraints

The TT&C scheduling problem can be considered as a configure set SCH={K$_1$, K$_2$, ..., K$_R$} where K$_i$∈{0, 1, 2, ..., V} to fulfill all constraints. Each request corresponds to a K in SCH. K$_i$=t means req$_i$ is scheduled in vw$_t$. A req$_i$ will not be scheduled when K$_i$=0. As soon as each request selects a proper time window, the scheduled set is made as {K$_1$, K$_2$, ..., K$_R$}.

As a result, the variable of ground TT&C resource CSP model can be described as $X=\{SCH\}$, and its domain is $\forall x \in X$, $D_x=\{\{K_1, K_2, ..., K_R\}\}$, where K$_i$∈{0, 1, 2, ..., V}. The author defines 6 constraints as follows:

$$C_1: \quad \forall vw_{s,g} \Rightarrow \begin{cases} MATCH_{s,g}=1 \\ VW_{s,g} \cap HEALTH_g = VW_{s,g} \end{cases} \tag{1}$$

$$C_2: \quad \begin{aligned} &\forall K_r=k , \ k \neq 0 \Rightarrow \\ &[req_r.Begin , req_r.End] \cap [vw_k.Begin , vw_k.End] \geq req_r.duration+PT \\ &\quad {}_{\substack{r=\{1,2, ..., R\} \\ k \in \{1\ 2, ..., V\}}} \end{aligned} \tag{2}$$

$$C_3: \quad \forall \text{gana}_g \in \{vw_{k_i}.\text{gana} \cup vw_{k_j}.\text{gana-TARGET}\} \Rightarrow$$
$$[\text{req}_i. \text{Begin}, \text{req}_i.\text{End}+\text{gana}_g.\text{PT}] \cap [\text{req}_j. \text{Begin}, \text{req}_j.\text{End}] = \phi \qquad (3)$$
$$\begin{array}{c} i \neq j \\ i, j = \{1,2, \dots, R\} \\ k_i, k_j \in \{1,2, \dots, V\} \end{array}$$

$$C_4: \quad \forall \text{sat}_s \in \{vw_{k_i} \cup vw_{k_j}\} \Rightarrow$$
$$[\text{req}_i. \text{Begin}, \text{req}_i.\text{End}+\text{sat}_s.\text{PT}] \cap [\text{req}_j. \text{Begin}, \text{req}_j.\text{End}] = \phi \qquad (4)$$
$$\begin{array}{c} i \neq j \\ i, j = \{1,2, \dots, R\} \\ k_i, k_j \in \{1,2, \dots, V\} \end{array}$$

$$C_5: \quad \forall \text{req}_i.\text{LA.req}=\text{req}_j \Rightarrow$$
$$[\text{req}_i. \text{Begin}, \text{req}_i.\text{End}] \subset [\text{req}_j.\text{End}+\text{req}_i.\text{LA.Begin}, \text{req}_j.\text{End}+\text{req}_i.\text{LA.End}] \qquad (5)$$
$$i, j = \{1,2, \dots, R\}$$

$$C_6: \quad \forall \text{sat}_s \Rightarrow \text{LEFT}_{s, si} = \text{Min}\{\text{LEFT}_{s, si-1}+\text{req}_{si}.\text{cost}, \text{sat}_s.\text{STORAGE}\} \geq 0 \qquad (6)$$
$$i = \{1,2, \dots, f(i)\}$$

4.1.1   Equipment Matching Constraint

The premise that an antenna can communicate with satellite successfully is their matching in function and performance. Define function $\text{MATCH}_{s, g}=1$ for sat_s and ant_g meet $\text{sat}_s.\text{FUCTION} \in \text{gana}_g.\text{CLASS}$, else $\text{MATCH}_{s, g}=0$.

Constraint (1) indicates that only married satellite and antenna can communicate and the equipment must be in normal operation.

4.1.2   Time Windows Constraint

Constraint (2) indicates that if req_r is scheduled in tw_k, the available time windows of req_r and tw_k intersection must be greater than the addition of request's duration and the equipment's prepare time.

4.1.3   Antenna Confliction Constraint

Constraint (3) indicates that under a configure of $x=\{k_1, k_2, \dots k_R\}$, if req_i and req_j applied for the same antenna, their execute time cannot be overlapped. C_3 makes sure that an antenna will never serve multi-satellite at the same time. Meanwhile, two requests by the same satellite cannot be scheduled in conflict time.

4.1.4   Satellite Competition Constraint

Constraint (4) is quite same as constraint (3) which ensured a satellite cannot respond multi-antenna at the same time.

4.1.5   Sequential Logic Constraint

Constraint（5）indicates the sequential and logical relationships of requests. A request req_i must begin in logic time window [LA.Begin, LA.End] after its C_5 request req_i ends. LA.Begin must be earlier than LA.End, and a negative value indicates that req_i begin earlier than req_j. MAX stands for a infinitely great. The relationship of requestA and requestB are described in Figure 1, and the 9 logical expressions are also listed in Table 1. As far as an "OR" relationship of two request means they need not appear in a schedule, the author views "OR" as mutual exclusion in this problem.

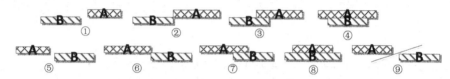

Fig. 1. Requests logic relationships

Table 1. Requests logic relationships expression

Logical relationships	LA.Begin	LA.End
①B ends before A starts	(-MAX, -A.duration-B.duration)	(-MAX, -A.duration)
②B ends at A starts	-A.duration- B.duration	-A.duration
③B end after A starts	(-A.duration- B.duration, A.duration)	(-A.duration, B.duration - A.duration)
④B in A	(-A.duration, - B.duration)	(B.duration- A.duration, 0)
⑤B starts after A ends	(0, MAX)	(B.duration, MAX)
⑥B starts at A ends	0	B.duration
⑦B starts before A ends	(-B.duration, 0)	(0, B.duration)
⑧B cntains A	(-B.duration, - A.duration)	(0, B.duration-A.duration)
⑨B OR A	MAX	MAX

4.1.6   Consumable Resource Constraint

Constraint（6）indicates memory of satellite positive. Sort $REQ_s = \bigcup_{\substack{sat_s \in req_i \\ K_i \neq 0}} \{req_i\}$ by req.Begin to get a set $REQ_s^* = \{req_{s1}, req_{s2}, \dots, req_{sf(s)}\}$, f(s) is the total number of requests in sats scheduled. Define $LEFT_{s,r}$ as the left memory after req_r of sat_s. The upper bound of LEFT is the STORAGE. $LEFT_{s,si}$. It will be modified after each req_r. Obviously, $LEFT_{s,0}$=sats.STORAGE at the beginning. Any requests attempt to minus LEFT below zero will not be scheduled.

4.2   Flexible Scheduling Principals

To solve the problem of low efficiency, task dispersion, imbalance loading etc. the author designed P_1, P_2 and P_3 3 types of principals and contribute（10） for the composition through configure their weight which realized a flexible scheduling control. The principals expressed as follows:

$$P_1 : \quad \frac{\sum_{t=1}^{T} P_t \cdot D(TASK_t)}{\sum_{t=1}^{T} P_t} \tag{7}$$

$$P_2 : \quad \frac{\alpha}{\displaystyle\sum_{i=\{1,2,\ \dots\ ,\ G\}} (\mathrm{Var}\{\ (\ req_r.\mathrm{Begin}+req_r.\mathrm{duration}/\,2\ )\}*req_r.\mathrm{duration}/\beta)}_{req_r.\mathrm{GRS=GRS}_i} \tag{8}$$

$$P_3 : \quad \sum_{g=1}^{G} \sqrt{\sum_{\substack{vw_{k_r}.\mathrm{ant=ant}_g \\ k_r \neq 0}} req_r.\mathrm{duration}} \tag{9}$$

$$P = \mathrm{Max}(\omega_1 P_1 + \omega_2 P_2 + \omega_3 P_3) \tag{10}$$

4.2.1   Priority Principal

Expression （7） has a function $D(TASK_t)=\begin{cases}1 & \forall req_r.\ TASK=TASK_t \Rightarrow k_r \neq 0 \\ 0 & else\end{cases}$ which shows the achievement of task. P_t is the priority of $TASK_t$ and it will be taken into calculation only when all requests in task successfully scheduled.

4.2.2   Task Gather Principal

Expression （8） guides tasks to schedule together for a same station in a collected period relatively. α,β are constant and Var stands for variance. $req_r.\mathrm{Begin}+req_r.\mathrm{duration}/\,2$ is the center of reqr's execute time. The duration here reflects the weight of request. Each time window will multiply $req_r.\mathrm{duration}/\beta$ before variance.

4.2.3   Equipment Load Balance Principal

The expression in radical sign expresses the total execute accumulative time of all requests. Knowing the bulge property of radical sign, the function will get its maximum in its domain where the concept of balance can be well described. Expression （9） guides tasks to schedule avoid cases of overloading or idle for equipment.

5   Simulation

The simulation consists of two satellite, two ground stations, one target, and 7 tasks. The author assumes that all stations have only one C type antenna and satellites match antennas. Tasks are divided into 18 requests as Table 2 below:

Table 2. Simulation parameters

Requests	Available time windows(m)	Resources	Duration	Logic constraints
GV 1.1	50~170	RE 1- BJ	110	GV1.2
	250~370	ER 1- BJ		0,max
	550~730	ER 1- BJ		
	900~1130	ER 1- BJ		
GV 1.2	320~500	ER 1- BJ	70	GV1.1
	1220~1310	ER 1- BJ		
GV 2.1	100~350	ER 1- BJ	100	
	620~820	ER 1- BJ		
GV 2.2	620~820	ER 1- BJ	150	GV2.3
	910~1255	ER 1- BJ		100,250
GV 2.3	250~600	ER 1- BJ	100	
	1200~1400	ER 1- BJ		
GV 3.1	710~1000	ER 1- BJ	155	
GV 3.2	100~250	ER 1- BJ	60	GV2.3
	150~250	ER 1- BJ		0,max
	330~650	ER 1- SY		
	1180~1000	ER 1- SY		
GV 4.1	525~630	ER 2- BJ	80	
GV 4.2	600~750	ER 2- BJ	55	
GV 4.3	435~495	ER 2- BJ	50	
GV 4.4	400~900	ER 2- BJ	40	
	400~900	ER 2- SY		
GV 5.1	220~400	ER 2- BJ	150	GV4.4
	550~790	ER 2- BJ		-540,-290
GV 5.2	920~1260	ER 2- SY	200	
GV 5.3	130~300	ER 1- SY	200	
	420~700	ER 1- SY		
	1100~1405	ER 1- SY		
GV 6.1	60~210	ER 2- TW	100	
	260~430	ER 2- TW		
	820~950	ER 2- TW		
GV 6.2	100~350	ER 1- TW	100	
	620~820	ER 1- TW		
GV 7.1	520~720	ER 1- TW	150	
	1010~1255	ER 1- TW		
GV 7.2	200~400	ER 2- TW	150	
	1200~1400	ER 2- TW		

The author uses Genetic Theory [15-16] to solve the problem, the request serial is made as gene, and the population scale is 20. The original population is generated randomly. After an inheritance of 100 times, a result is show as Figure 2:

Lines parallels x axis in Figure 2 stand for time windows and the deeper color ones are the execute time of requests. In this case, GV3.2 failed because it cannot meet the logic constraint of GV2.3, which results the failure of TASK3 and the release of GV3.1 resources. GV5.1 in TASK5 failed for lacking of satellite memories. The resources occupied by GV5.2 are also released and the unscheduled request GV5.3 is canceled. This result validated the feasibility of the CSP model.

(10) takes (7)~(9) into consideration and the author calculated a weighting summation for heuristic by 3 types of preferences that is A(0.8,0.1,0.1), B(0.6,0.2,0.2), C(0.5,0.4,0.1). The percentage of request complement (average of 10 simulations) is shown in Table 3, the curve of fitness is shown in Figure 3 and the usage of resources is shown as Figure 4.

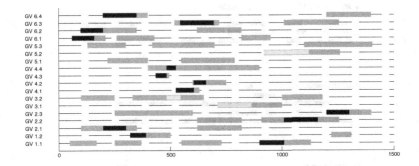

Fig. 2. Schedule result

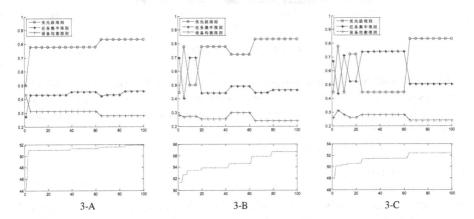

3-A   3-B   3-C

Fig. 3. Change of fitness

Table 3. Percentage of request complement

Preference	ω_1	ω_2	ω_3	Complete percentage
A	0.8	0.1	0.1	80.51%
B	0.6	0.2	0.2	77.33%
C	0.5	0.4	0.1	50.14%

Table 3 shows that (7) has an important influence on task complement. This result owing to the computing mode of (7) that only achieved request's weight can be calculated. This method can take account of both amount and priority of tasks. It's better than the pure maximum amount method.

Figure 3 shows that solution approaching to the best when fitness of population improved through the evaluation of genetic method. Comparing the curve in A, B and C of Figure 3, three results can be found: Firstly, a more weight principal can bring a greater profit for the main fitness; Secondly, the genetic method prefers guiding the more weight principal to others; Thirdly, different principals have conflicts and even contradiction to each other. It is shown previously in Figure 3-C.

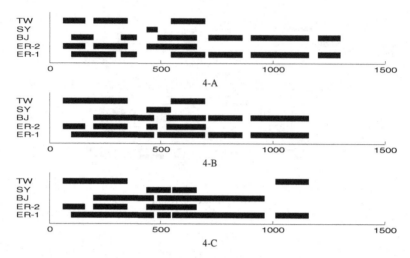

Fig. 4. Usage of resources

Figure 4 shows the usage of resources in three preferences. When the weight of P_2 increases, occupy time of resources changes from dispersion to continuation by which the effectiveness of P_2 is proved. However task complement percentage comes down for the weight of P_1 decreases.

6   Conclusion

Future space missions must be hard and complex. The author focuses on the model of current ground TT&C resource scheduling problem. To describe the problem simplified by researchers, the author designed a CSP model. The efficiency and validity are partly proved by the simulation. Three principals are designed to fulfill different users' preferences. Results in the simulation also show the contradiction of principals and prove the necessary of this flexible scheduling strange.

References

1. Gooley, T.D.: Automating the Satellite Range Scheduling Process. Air Force Institute of Technology Master Thesis, Ohio (1993)
2. Gabrel, V., Vanderpooten, D.: Enumeration and interactive selection of efficient paths in a multiple criteria Figure for scheduling an earth observing satellite. European Journal of Operational Research 139(3), 533–542 (2002)
3. Marinelli, F., Nocella, S., Rossi, F., et al.: A Languageian Heuristic for Satellite Range Scheduling with Resource Constraints[R/OL]. JPL Technical Report (2005), http://www.optimizationline.org
4. Wang, Y., Zhao, J., Nie, C.: Research of multi satellite and ground station system. Journal of Air Force Engineering University (Natural science edition) (4), 7–11 (2003)

5. Bensana, E., Verfaillie, G., Agnese, C.G., et al.: Exact and approximate methods for the daily management of an earth observation satellite. In: Proc of the 4th International Symposium on Space Mission Operations and Ground Data System, pp. 3–12 (1996)
6. Guang, J.: CSP model for satellite and ground station TT&C resource scheduling problems. Systems Engineering and Electronics 29(7), 1117–1120 (2007)
7. Wolfe, W., Sorensen, S.: Three scheduling algorithms applied to the earth observing systems domain. Management Science 46(1), 148–168 (2000)
8. Pemberton, J.C., Greenwald, L.G.: On the Need for Dynamic Scheduling of Imaging Satellites. In: Pecora 15/Land Satellite Information IV/ISRRS Commission I/FIEOS 2002 Confernce Proceedings, Denver (2002)
9. Vasquezm, H.D.: Solving the selecting and scheduling photoFigures problem with a consist neighborhood heuristic. In: Proc of the 16th IEEE International Conference on Tools with Artificial Intelligence. IEEE Computer Society, Washington DC (2004)
10. Liu, Y., Chen, Y., Tan, Y.: Modeling and Solving A Multi-resources Dynamic Scheduling Problem with Time Windows. Operations Research and Management Science 14(2), 47–53 (2005)
11. He, R.: Research on imaging reconnaissance satellite scheduling problem. National University of Defense Technology, Chang Sha (2004)
12. Li, J., Tan, Y.: Modeling and Solving Observation Satellite Scheduling as a Pickup and Delivery Problem. Systems Engineering-Theory & Practice 24(12), 65–71 (2004)
13. Damiani, S., Verfaillie, G., Charmeau, C.M.: An Anytime Planning Approach for the Management of an Earth Watching Satellite. In: Proc of the 4th International Workshop on Planning and Scheduling for Space (2004)
14. Xie, H., Zhang, M.: Space TT&C Systems, pp. 54–106. The Publisher of National University of Defense Technology, Chang Sha (2000)
15. Barbulescu, L., Howe, A.E., Whitley, L.D., et al.: Understanding algorithm performance on an oversubscribed scheduling application. Journal of Artificial Intelligence Research 27(12), 577–617 (2006)
16. Sun, J., Xhafa, F.: A Genetic Algorithm for Ground Station Scheduling. In: 2011 International Conference on Complex, Intelligent, and Software Intensive Systems, pp. 138–145 (2011)

Research of the Random Noise Compensation of MEMS Gyro

Xiaowen Wu and Qing Li

Institute of Intelligence Control of BISTU, Beijing, 100101

Abstract. Feature of Unscented Kalman Filter(UKF) is systematic analysed, and UKF is used in the compensation of MEMS Gyro random noise.Discussion the compensation of MEMS Gyro static random noise and dynamic random noise,The specific use of neural networks and Support Vector Machines in the compensation of MEMS Gyro random noise is proposed.Described in detail how MEMS Gyro random noise is compensated in the project.There is some defective when the time series used to build dynamic mathematical model of MEMS Gyro random noise,advantages and disadvantages of the compensation methodology of the MEMS Gyro random noise used by foreigner are pointed out.

Keywords: MEMS Gyroscope, Unscented Kalman Filter(UKF), Time Series, Neural Network, Support Vector Machines(SVM).

1 Introduction

MEMS concept is first proposed by the famous American physicist Feyman,He pointed out that a problem of the MEMS technology development is how to use low-precision tool manufacturing high-precision products.Error compensation of MEMS inertial devices is an important means to improve the accuracy,Therefore, focus of the study is was transferred to error modeling and error compensation method of the MEMS gyroscope structure by many research institutes leading in MEMS technology in order to improve the performance and robustness of the gyroscope.

2 The Unscented Kalman Filter

Unscented Kalman filter is proposed by JULIER and UHLMAN.A central and vital operation perfor- med in the Kalman Filter is the propagation of a Gaussian random variable (GRV) through the system dynamics.The UKF use a deterministic sampling approach.The state distribution is again approximated by a GRV, but is now represen-ed using a minimal set of carefully chosen sample points.These sample points compl-etely capture the true mean and covariance of the GRV,and when propagated through the true nonlinear system captures the posterior mean and covariance accurately to the 3rd order (Taylor series expansion) for any nonlinearity[1].

T. Xiao, L. Zhang, and S. Ma (Eds.): ICSC 2012, Part II, CCIS 327, pp. 328–335, 2012.
© Springer-Verlag Berlin Heidelberg 2012

The unscented transformation(UT)is a method for calculating the statistics of a random variable which undergoes a nonlinear transformation.consider propagating a random variable x (dimension L)through a nonlinear function, $y = g(x)$. Assume x has mean $\bar{x}$ and covariance P_x .To calculate the statistcs of y,we form a matrix χ of 2L+1sigma vectors χ_i (with corresponding weights W_i),according to the following:

$$\chi_0 = \bar{x}$$

$$\chi_i = \bar{x} + \left(\sqrt{(L+\lambda)P_x} \right)_i \quad i=1,...,L$$

$$\chi_i = \bar{x} - \left(\sqrt{(L+\lambda)P_x} \right)_{i-L} \quad i=L+1,...,2L$$

$$W_0^{(m)} = \lambda/(L+\lambda)$$

$$W_0^{(c)} = \lambda/(L+\lambda)+(1-\alpha^2+\beta)$$

$$W_i^{(m)} = W_i^{(c)} = 1/\{2(L+\lambda)\} \quad i=1,...,2L$$

(2.1)

Where $\lambda = \alpha^2(L+\kappa) - L$ is a scaling parameter, α determines the spread of the sigma points around $\bar{x}$ and is usually set to a small positive value. κ is a secondary scaling parameter which is usually set to 0,and β is used to incorporate prior knowledge of the distribution of x (for Gaussian distributions, β=2 is optimal). $(\sqrt{(L+\lambda)P_x})_i$ is the is the ith row of the matrix square root.These sigma vectors are propagated through the nonlinear function,

$$y_i = g(\chi_i) \quad i = 0,...,2L \tag{2.2}$$

and the mean and covariance for y are approximated using a weighted sample mean and covariance of the posterior sigma points,

$$\bar{y} \approx \sum_{i=0}^{2L} W_i^{(m)} y_i \tag{2.3}$$

$$P_y \approx \sum_{i=0}^{2L} W_i^{(c)} \{y_i - \bar{y}\}\{y_i - \bar{y}\}^T \tag{2.4}$$

The deceptively simple approach taken with the UT results in approximations that are accurate to the third order for Gaussian inputs for all nonlinearities.For non-Gaussian inputs,approximations are accurate to at least the second-order,with the accuracy of third and higher order moments determined by the choice of α and β .

The most important characteristics of the UKF is Unscented conversion,the conve- rsion of the mean and variance information are provided a direct and obvious mechan- ism by Unscented conversion which are expected to solve the deficiencies of lineariz- ation.Kalman linear filtering framework is used by UKF,the specific form of sampling is deterministic sampling.the number of particle points (sigma points) sampled by   UKF is very few,according to the chosen sampling strategy,The specific number of samples are determined.symmetric sampling of the 2n +1 sigma points is most comm- only used.the calculation amount of UKF and EKF are almost equal,but its performa- nce is better than EKF's.

3   Error Modeling and Error Compensation Method for MEMS Inertial Devices

When random noise of MEMS inertial devices is compensated,error model need to be established and model parameters need to be identified,then the compensation is implemented.

Random drift is an important feature of the Gyroscope,a lot of work in the testing and modeling of Gyro drift has been done at home and abroad.mathematical and physical model of the MEMS Gyro are established from mass,spring system of Gyro, etc(resonant structural level),then the error are compensated,you can achieve better results. However,in most cases,due to lack of information about manufacturing structure of MEMS gyroscope,Most of us use the time series, statistical modeling methods, etc,including the Allan Variance Analysis,the ARMA model, neural networks,wavelet analysis,etc.Those methods have been used to model the random error of the Gyro. The Support Vector Machine is considered to be the best "off-line" supervised learning algorithm,it also can be applied to model random error of MEMS Gyro:

Allan variance method is the standard method for analysis of Gyro noise,Through the use of Allan variance method,various error sources and its contribution to statistical properties of the entire noise can very easily detailed expressed and identified.

Auto-regressive moving average(ARMA) method is that the random error of the Gyro output was fitted through use of the linear combination of AR and MA model which is driven by white noise,a variety of random noise of the gyroscope are overall considered through that method.through the use of models of different order,statistical properties of the gyroscope random errors can be modeled with different precision in the time domain.

In the process of modeling of Gyro random drift and prediction research,Gyro random drift has two characteristics:Slow time-varying, weakly nonlinear,the analysis methods of time series are considered from linear,This is bound to affect accuracy of the established model.In theory,Neural networks and Support Vector Machines have the ability to approximate nonlinear functions with arbitrary precision, and have nonl- inear transformation of features and a high degree of parallel computing power, they provides a very effective way for nonlinear modeling of gyro random drift. There are two programs to establish the model of gyroscope random drift using Neural Networks:

One:Filtering method are based on Neural Network,Gyro error are corrected through software filtering.

Two:The technology of Multi-sensor data fusion,a group of environmental sensors are used to detect operating temperature and ambient humidity of sensor studio,power supply fluctuations and other factors. output of these environment sensors and the compensated sensor are considered as the input of neural network,The output of sensor is corrected through the neural network's capability of nonlinear mapping, the output of sensor network is correction value of the compensated sensor.

Support Vector Machine is that statistical learning theory considered as basis is developed as machine learning algorithms by the Vapnik Professor of the Bell Labs. The basic principle is to build optimal hyperplane of the sample space or the feature space,in order to make the maximum distance between the hyperplane and the different types of samples.the statistical properties of random error of the Gyro can be modeled through regression support vector machine.the performance of Support Vector Machines is better than Neural Networks,especially in the accuracy and the mapping ability of the nonlinear characteristics,therefore,the above two programs are also suitable for Support Vector Machine.

Wavelet Transform is particularly suitable for processing non-stationary signals for its excellent multi-resolution features, it's widely used in the signal denoising of Gyro.

In summary,First,random drift of the inertial devices is studied through analysis of ARMA model, has been some progress,propose Neural Networks,Support Vector Machine, Wavelet Analysis Method to study.

4   The Noise Compensation of MEMS GYRO

4.1   The Compensation of Static Noise of MEMS GYRO

Compensation process of static noise of MEMS Gyro as shown below:

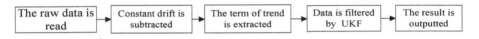

Fig. 1. The static noise compensation of MEMS Gyro

Static data of a MEME gyro are selected to test,The sampling frequency is 20HZ, collecting 100,000 data,output data of Y-axis is removed the constant term, trend and cycle.Time series model is established using the AIC criterion as an ARMA(2,1):

$$x_k = 1.4916x_{k-1} - 0.6134x_{k-2} + e_k + 0.3460e_{k-1} \qquad (4.1)$$

To convert it into a state space model as follows:

$$\begin{bmatrix} x_k \\ x_{k-1} \end{bmatrix} = \begin{bmatrix} 1.4916 & 1 \\ -0.6134 & 0 \end{bmatrix} \begin{bmatrix} x_{k-1} \\ x_{k-2} \end{bmatrix} + \begin{bmatrix} 1 \\ 0.3460 \end{bmatrix} w_k \qquad (4.2)$$

$$Z_k = \begin{bmatrix} 1 & 0 \end{bmatrix} \begin{bmatrix} x_k \\ x_{k-1} \end{bmatrix} + v_k \qquad (4.3)$$

Each of w_k and v_k is an quantity scalar, which are respectively considered as process noise and measurement noise.the trend term of the data is removed and then the processed data is filtered.the measurement noise, α, β are adjusted to make noise of the filtered data become small,as shown below:

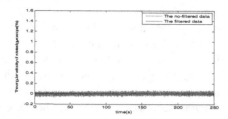

Fig. 2. The Static Noise Compensation of MEMS Gyro

In Figure 2,Red is the not being filtered data,blue is the being filtered data.Obviously the standard deviation of the filtered data is much less than the not-filtered data's, obtained that noise compensation effect of static data can be very good using UKF, The reason is that static data of Gyro has a strong Gaussian statistical properties,Compensation of the static noise is that standard deviation of the pure noise is reduced to minimum,and other factors do not be considered.

4.2   The Compensation of Dynamic Noise of MEMS GYRO

The compensation of dynamic noise is much more complex than static noise's. The reduction of dynamic noise is very important.the compensation method of dynamic noise as follows:

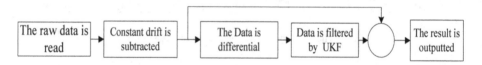

Fig. 3. The dynamic noise compensation of MEMS Gyro

Figure 3 shows the method of dynamic noise compensation of MEMS Gyro,the data needs to be differential in this method,the no-differential data minus the filtered data in order to reduce noise,The principle is:in the process of system data generated,the data of k time and the data of k-1 time should be equal,if the two are not equal,that is the error(The error is considered to be noise), after the error is filtered (The role of doing so is to amend),the no-differential data minus the filtered data in order to redu- ce noise.

Gyroscope is rotated by angular velocity of 5°/s,The input data is multiplied by a scale factor, Figure 3 shows the method of compensation of dynamic noise of MEMS Gyro,Parameters is being debugged, the results are as follows:

we can obtained from figure 3 that after the noise of dynamic data is compensated, the noise is reduced much,indicating that the noise compensation effect of MEMS gyroscope of uniform rotation is well.

An extreme situation is to be considered,Gyro is turned by rate of ±10°,±20°,±30°, ±50°,±75°,±90°, ±100°/s in one experiment.the output data is processed by the metho- d shown in figure 3. Figure 6 is the result of the noise is compensated,figure 5 is enla- rged to figure 6.

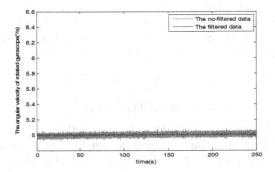

Fig. 4. The noise compensation of constant angular velocity of MEMS Gyro

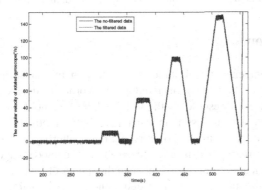

Fig. 5. The dynamic noise compensation of MEMS Gyro

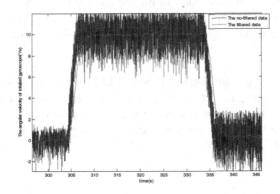

Fig. 6. The dynamic noise compensation of MEMS Gyro

From figure 5,we can obtain that after the data is processed by the method shown in figure 3,the noise of data is reduce with a greater degree,However, from figure 6, we can know that there is a time lag in the filtered data.What causes the time lag, mathematical model of the previous needs to be considered here:

$$x_k = 1.4916x_{k-1} - 0.6134x_{k-2} + e_k + 0.3460e_{k-1}$$

The model here is a time series model,Time series model is essentially a linear model,where x_k is almost linear superposition of x_{k-1} and x_{k-2},that led to the model is similar to a circuit of second-order lag,signal through the approximation second-order lag of circuit,which will inevitably produce a time lag in the filtered data ralative to the original data.of course ,the way of increase the frequency can reduce the time lag, but also make the bandwidth increase,making an increase in noise,especially high frequency noise,So now,we could only compromise to deal with the time lag of data.

5   Conclusion

The method of compensation of static noise and dynamic noise are different.in the project,the method of Segmentation is adopted in order to decide which method of compensation is used, threshold method is used,the threshold is set,If the absolute value of the output data is less than the threshold,the method of static filtering is adopted,on the contrary,the method of dynamic noise filtering is used.

The method of time series is used to establish the model of dynamic noise of ME-MS Gyro will lead to time lag of the data.the model of time series is essentially a line- ar model,but the model of actual system is nonlinear in majority.the nonlinear of dyn- amic noise data of MEMS gyroscope is strongly,so time series is not suitable for the modeling of dynamic noise of MEMS Gyro.the random noise of the MEMS Gyro is compensated by Butterworth filter in Europe and the United States,the principle is that bandwidth of the random noise and useful data are different,noise is filtered out by high-pass filter or low-pass filter,this method does not produce time lag,but the accuracy is not high.

Acknowledgments. First and foremost,I would like to show my deepest gratitude to my supervisor,Dr.Qing Li,a respectable,responsible and resourceful scholar,who has provided me with valuable guidance in every stage of the writing of this thesis.Without his enlightening instruction, impresive kindness and patience, I could not have completed my thesis.

References

1. Wan, E.A., van der Menve, R.: The Unscented Kalman Filter for Nonlinear Estimation. J. AS-SPCC, 153–158 (2000)
2. Julier, S.J., Uhlmann, J.K.: Unscented Filtering and Nonlinear Estimation. J. Proceedings of the IEEE 92(3), 401–422 (2004)

3. Kang, C., Su, Z.: Design of Data Acquisition and Processing System for IMU. J. IITA 2008 12, 585–588 (2008)
4. Grewal, M.S., Andrews, A.P.: Applications of Kalman Filtering in Aerospace 1960 to the Present. J. Control Systems 30(3), 69–78 (2010)
5. Gordon, N.J., Salmond, D.J., Smith, A.F.M.: Novel approach to nonlinear/non-Gaussian Bayesian state estimation. J. Radar and Signal Processing 140(2), 107–113 (1993)
6. Julier, S.J., Uhlrnann, J.K., Durrant-Whyte, H.F.: A New Approach for Filtering Nonlinear Systems. In: Proceedings of the American Control Conference, vol. 3, pp. 1628–1632 (1995)

Human Behavior Representation Theory Progress in Constructive Simulation

Shaoyong Shi, Zaijiang Tang, Quanfeng Ma, and Jingye Wang

Department of Equipment Command and Administration, AAFE,
100072 Beijing, China
bjdssy@126.com, tangzaijiang@sina.com,
{yyshadowing,wang_jingye}@yahoo.com.cn

Abstract. There are higher requirements for human behavior representation (HBR) in constructive simulation. After analyzing the military domain requirements and theory requirements of individual and organization behavior modeling, the basic theory progress of HBR were discussed including motivation theory, behavior decision-making theory, four main cognition schools and four typical cognition structures-SOAR, ACT-R, EPIC and 4CAPS. Their advantages and limitations were indicated. Then, the state of the art of HBR was summarized including the contribution and deficiency of former research. Some recommendations to HBR researchers are listed in the end.

Keywords: human behavior representation, behavioral decision-making, cognition psychology, validation.

1 Introduction

In current military operational models, the human aspect is still often represented in a mechanistic way, bearing little resemblance to observations, as if all humans always act the same way in a situation much as a machine would. This situation exists in various military simulations more or less, including live simulation, virtual simulation and constructive simulation. In reality, human behavior is not deterministic. Without proper representation of behavior, and the reasons behind the behavior, the validity of the model may be seriously flawed, making its performance and predictions questionable, which has brought negative influence to the creditability of modeling and simulation [1]. Therefore, building better simulation systems and decision support tools, which include human behavior representation (HBR), is of primary importance.

Along with the development of application requirement to simulation, especially as information system technology and behavior modeling technology advance themselves, people has managed to a universal viewpoint that more attention should be paid to human behavior representation in military modeling and simulation. After analyzing the requirements of HBRs in military, the purpose of this paper is to review general framework, theories, technologies and advanced applications of HBRs that could be integrated in military simulations. The intent is to provide the modeling and

T. Xiao, L. Zhang, and S. Ma (Eds.): ICSC 2012, Part II, CCIS 327, pp. 336–344, 2012.

simulation (M&S) community recommendations of specific HBR models. Those emerging theories and technologies will have a great impact on the implementation and on the military use of simulation systems in the future.

2   Requirements

HBR models were demanded on various military simulations extensively and deeply. U.S. Department of Defense has set as an objective to "develop authoritative representations of individual human behavior" and to "develop authoritative representations of the behavior of groups and organizations". Several special panels and workshops [2,3] sponsored by DMSO and NATO address themselves to HBR theories, technologies and applications researches [4,5,6,7]. The panel interprets this finding as indicating the need for representation of larger units and organizations, as well as for and teams and that of real forces; for less predictability of modeled forces, to prevent trainees from gaming the training simulations; for more variability due not just to randomness, but also to reasoned behavior in a complex environment, and for realistic individual differences among human agents; for more intelligence to reflect the behavior of capable, trained forces; and for more adaptively to reflect the dynamic nature of the simulated environment and intelligent forces. Authoritative behavioral representations are needed at different levels of aggregation for different purposes. Concretely, at various times, representations are needed for the following at least [8]:

1) Individual combat vehicles;
2) Individual combatants, including dismounted infantry;
3) Squad, platoon, and/or company;
4) Groups of combat vehicles and other combat support and combat service support;
5) Aircraft and Aircraft formations;
6) The output of command and control elements;
7) Large units, such as Army battalions, brigades, or divisions; Air Force squadrons and wings; and Navy battle groups;

3   Basic Theories Progress of HBR

The intent of HBR is to build a computational model of a human being to achieve embodied goals and predict performance, expressing observed variability in behavior attributable to differences in the person's characteristics, to differences in the situation or to the interplay of both, mapping characteristics of empirical phenomena into values of parameters and models in an artificial world.

HBR is a syncretic domain across many subjects,   whose basic theory includes behavior science theory, cognition science theory, computer science theory. Furthermore, specialty basic theories also are needed to support their behavior modeling such as sociology theory, military science theory, and economics theory and so on.

3.1   Behavior Science Theory

Motivation Theory. According to psychology, human behaviors are under the control of motivation, while motivation comes from need. When some human need cannot be satisfied, a mentally tension state occurs, then it becomes one of internal drives which is called motivation in psychology. After owning the motivation, human should select or search for goals which lead to actions. The need was satisfied and the mentally tension state was relieved after effectual actions. And then a new need drives another behavior, which goes round and round until the life is stop. The figure below illustrates seven movement phases of need [9].

Fig. 1. Seven movement phases of need

Motivation is the desire and ideality of human which drives behaviors and actions. It drives and induces human behaviors and also hints the direction of behaviors. There were two origins of motivation, one is internal need, and another is external stimulation. The internal one is called need which describes a mentally state when human lack something. And the external one is stimulation comes from the environment. The diversity of need determines the diversity of motivation. In practical life, the intension of motivation undulates along with internal and external factors at any moment. The one owning uppermost intension determines human behavior among all motivations, which is called advanced motivation. Once the goal is achieved, the intension of this motivation weakens and another motivation intensifies. It drives other behaviors of human. Some motivations maybe be suffocated frequently and their intension are likely to become more and more lower until be abandoned.

There were three functions of motivation:

1) Drive Function. Motivation drives human behavior.
2) Select Function. Motivation induces the action into some certain direction and prospective goal.
3) Intensify Function. The result of behavior has an influence on motivation. Well result could make motivation more enhanced, while bad result would make it weaker until disappear.

Behavior Decision-Making Theory. Unlike normative decision-making paradigm, behavior decision-making is a descriptive paradigm which is more similar to human decision-making. The normative paradigm build on the assumption that decision maker is a perfect human who seeks to attain optimization target. In fact, it is impossible to obtain the best answer frequently in ordinary decision-making. The table below analyzes the differences between normative decision-making paradigm and descriptive one [10].

Table 1. Contrast of normative paradigm and descriptive paradigm

Contrast Content	Normative paradigm	Descriptive paradigm
Principle	Rational	Cognition based
Objective	Building optimization decision-making model	Comprehend reality decision-making process
Methods	Mathematics model and computing	Knowledge representation
Application	Optimization	Training and Improving
Science base	Economics /Statistics	Psychology/Sociology

The characters of descriptive decision-making paradigm are:

1) Limited rationality
2) Dynamic game
3) Time pressure

3.2   Cognition Psychology Theory

Different Cognition Schools. According to psychology, human behaviors are under the control of motivation, while motivation comes from need. When some human need cannot be satisfied, a mentally tension state occurs, then it becomes one of internal drives which is called motivation in psychology. After owning the motivation, human should select or search for goals which lead to actions. The need was satisfied and the mentally tension state was relieved after effectual actions. And then a new need drives another behavior, which goes round and round until the life is stop. The figure below illustrates seven movement phases of need [9].

Physics Symbolism
Physics symbolism [11] is the cognition science theory foundation of artificial intelligence. It regards cognition as a process of physics symbol comes from external inputs. It believes the external intelligent behaviors could be explained by internal cognition process. Works of mind was seen as an analogy for works of computer. It explains cognition as a symbol operation system including information process and information assimilation courses.

Physics symbolism integrates merits of cybernetics, information theory and system theory, which makes mind research strict in experimentation and coincident in theory. At the same time, its mechanical limitation is also obvious. Human can deal with various meaning under different linguistic conditions, while machine demand meaning is independent of linguistic condition.

Connected theory
Connected theory comes of artificial nerve network research at 4th decade 20th century. The cognition active mechanism is based upon the continuous change of connection intensity between nerve cells. This process is continuous changeful

parallel distributed simulative computing, which is different from physics symbol computing.

Module Theory
It was suggested by computer programming and hardware module, Fodor put forward cognition functional module model at 1983. Module theory believes that the structure and function of human brain makes up of highly specialized and single modules. The complex but artful combination of these modules is the foundation of complex and fine cognition function. Module theory obtains sustainment of many other subjects in memory research.

Ecology Actualism
The core viewpoint of ecology actualism is environment functional theory. It emphasizes cognition is determined by environment. More than occurs in the brain of individual, the cognition occurs in the interactional environment.

Typical Cognition Structures. There are many cognition structures have been described. The ordinary fours are discussed as follow [12]:

SOAR Structure
SOAR is theory architecture of state, operator and result. Through searching the problem space, an operator or a process was used for one state to get a result. SOAR has different meaning to different people. When used for artificial intelligence it could form integrative intelligent agent, and it can accomplish cognition simulation when used for cognition science.

SOAR structure includes :

1) State and operator. State refers to the entire information of current scene. Operator refers to the adopted method in problem space.
2) Working memory. Working memory refers to perception arrangement of state and its correlative operator, which is convenient for searching in long memory and actions.
3) Long memory. Long memory is the resource library of problem correlative content.
4) Perception-action interface.
5) Decision-making cycle.
6) Deadlock. Deadlock refers to lack of knowledge.
7) Learning mechanism. There are four learning mechanism:

   a) Once deadlock gives birth to new result, add a new rule into long memory accordingly;
   b) A new rule is added to map working memory into long memory in order to avoid the similar scene deadlock recur;
   c) Strengthen learning to change operator deflection;
   d) Scene learning saves some gone experience.

ACT-R Structure

Like other influential cognitive architectures, the ACT-R （Adaptive Control of Thought-Rational） theory has a computational implementation as an interpreter of a special coding language. The interpreter itself is written in Lisp, and might be loaded into any of the most common distributions of the Lisp language.

There are two types of modules:

1) Perceptual-motor modules, which take care of the interface with the real world. The most well-developed perceptual-motor modules in ACT-R are the visual and the manual modules.

2) Memory modules. There are two kinds of memory modules in ACT-R: declarative memory and procedural memory.

All the modules can only be accessed through their buffers. The contents of the buffers at a given moment in time represent the state of ACT-R at that moment. The only exception to this rule is the procedural module, which stores and applies procedural knowledge. It does not have an accessible buffer and is actually used to access other module's contents.

EPIC Structure

EPICis an integrated information process course. EPIC can form single operational model and multi-operational model, namely, interaction of executive-process. EPIC makes up of some interactive memory storage and process cells.

1) Memory. EPIC has three different types of memory, namely, long memory, procedure memory and working memory.

2) Process cells. EPIC has much visual, aural and tactual process cells. Each perception process cell output what it into working memory, and cognition process completes various tasks.

4CAPS Structure

4CAPS is an evolution structure of 3CAPS, which is a capacity-constrained collaborative activation-based production system. 4CAPS introduces the concept center, a 4CAPS model makes up of many collaborative centers. Each center is a mixed symbol and association system, which builds upon capacity-constrained resource supply.

3.3   Behavior Validate Theory

Unlike physics-based models, HBR models are not strictly mathematically-based making them difficult. The methodology for validating human behaviors draws upon three distinct yet related fields: models and simulations; behavioral science; and cognitive psychology. Each discipline has a unique perspective on creating viable HBR models, while has little in common with the other two. The reason validation standards of physics-based models are not well suited for validating HBR models is due to several factors [13]:

1) The nonlinear nature of human cognitive processes;
2) The large set of interdependent variables making it impossible to account for all possible interactions;
3) Inadequate metrics for validating HBR models;
4) The lack of a robust set of environmental data to run behavior models for model validation;

Like models of complex physical processes, HBR models can be validated at many different levels of abstraction. The table [13] below illustrates six levels of model correspondence for HBRs. In effect, these levels define six levels of referents. An accurate HBR will correspond to human behavior at six levels of representation: domain, sociological, psychological, physiological, computational and physical. An HBR with correspondence at all six levels is often better than an HBR with correspondence in fewer. Results show that no HBR currently exists with complete correspondence at all six levels.

Levels of HBR Correspondence and Referents
• Domain Correspondence
• Sociological Correspondence
• Psychological Correspondence
• Physiological Correspondence
• Computational Correspondence
• Physical Correspondence

Fig. 2. Levels of HBR Correspondence and Referents

4   Summarization and Recommendations

4.1   Contributions and Deficiencies of Former Research

Contributions

1) Define the research requirement of HBR. There were many organizations, workshops and seminars sponsored by government and national defense department participating in HBR research. Their research scope includes basic theory, approaches, modeling architectures and validation technology.
2) Behavior characters analyzed. The individual behavior character and organization behavior character of different domain were researched combining with behavior science.
3) Key behavior factors modeling. The computable model of some key behavior factors were researched based on cognition science including perception, cognition, emotion, fatigue, error.
4) Applications. The research benefit has been applied in military, society, biology, economy forecast and other domains tentatively.

Deficiencies

The state of the art indicates that people attach much more importance to individual behavior research. And more attention should be paid to organization behavior research. The main deficiencies as follows:

1) The current individual behavior models are hardly adaptable to various decision-making environments in advanced simulation, for instance:

   a) The adaptability of current behavior moderator is weak, and the reasoning result is divinable;
   b) Limited learning ability;
   c) Lack effective situation evaluation and decision-making process model;
   d) Lack integrative architectures of cognition process.

2) Lack of description methods for organization behaviors, for instance:

   a) Organization computable model;
   b) Organization character description methods;
   c) Organization communications mechanism;
   d) Lack of effective HBRs validation methods.

4.2   Recommendations

Some recommendations to HBR researchers in constructive modeling and simulation are:

1) Basic research of cross science should be enhanced to prove result translation including social science, cognition science and computer science. Specialists from different domains including military, analysts and human sciences should discuss together to ensure that appropriate models are being used to represent the human element of military simulations, or if this is not practicable, then to recognize the limitations of the models being used.

2) Establish a mechanism to collect and disseminate operational or training data that are suitable for developing and validating models of individual and orgnazation behaviors and performances, particularly data that supports modeling.

3) Promote the development of an open architecture or interface specification that supports interaction of operator models from a variety of sources within synthetic environments, particularly those environments that deal with the broader issues of HBR.

4) Promote the development and publication of formal models that support the analysis of HBR based problems, including the influences of culture, motivation and public opinion on individual and orgnazation behavior.

5) Promote the use of HBR modeling approaches in M&S for which the actions of individuals and teams play a critical role in the observed behaviors and outcomes.

References

1. Barry, P., Bjorkman, E.: The Human Behavior Challenge Problem. Proceedings of the 10th CGF&BR Conference (2001)
2. SISO Conferences & Workshops, http://www.sisostds.org
3. WSC Conferences & Workshops, http://www.wintersim.org
4. Dubois, R.D., Might, R.J.: Conceptual Modeling of Human Behavior. In: Proceedings of the 9th CGF&BR Conference (2000)
5. Tan, K.-M.T., Hiles, J.E.: Modeling the Human Decision Making Process in Maritime Interdiction Using Conceptual Blending Theory. 08-BRIMS-008 (2008)
6. Burgess, R.: A New Architecture for Improved Human Behavior in Military Simulations. U.S. Army War College Thesis (2008)
7. Eileen, A., Blemberg, P.: Review of the Denfense Modeling and Simulation Office Human Behavior Program. 01S-SIW-080 (2001)
8. Richard, W.P., Anne, S.M.: Modeling Human and Organizational Behavior: Application to Military Simulations, pp. 216–236. National Academy Press, Washington (1998)
9. Su, D.: Modern Western Behavior Science. Shandong Press, Jinan (1986)
10. Russo, J.E., An, B., Xu, L.: Behavioral Decision Making. Beijing Normal University Press, Beijing (1998)
11. Shi, Z.: Cognitive Science. University of Science and Technology of China Press, Hefei (September 2008)
12. Wang, Y., Liu, Y.: High-level cognition research-cognition structure, langage understanding and similarity. Science Press, Beijing (2009)
13. Goerger, S.R., McGinnis, M.L., Darken, R.P.: A Validation Methodology for Human Behavior Representation Models. United States Military Academy West Point, New York (2005)

Research on Simulation Method of Material Demand Forecast

Quanfeng Ma[1], Shaoyong Shi[1], and Ying Liang[2]

[1] Simulation Laboratory, The Academy of Armored Forces Engineering, Beijing, China
[2] College of Computer and Information Engineering,
Tianjin Normal University, Tianjin, China
{Quanfeng Ma,Shaoyong Shi,yyshadowing}@yahoo.com.cn

Abstract. A method of material demand forecast by adopting simulation approach is discussed in this paper. Difficulties in material demand forecast are also analyzed from four aspects of information, method, analysis and judgment. Simulation, as a means of material demand forecast, has its own advantages. Based on the analysis of requirements for material demand forecast, a kind of combat simulation model architecture for material demand forecast is constructed, and the important models are analyzed. Then several design principles and methods for material demand forecast are listed out. Finally, some typical issues about the experiment results are set forth.

Keywords: material demands, demand forecast, simulation.

1 Introduction

Material support plays a very important role in battles, and which has a direct influence on the process and ending of battles. Modern battles are non-linear ones under high techniques, the pace and process of battles is speeded up, so types of materials supported should be diverse and the supported amount should be sufficient. The battle is continuing growth, coupled with the severe destruction of the enemy blockade, resulting in the increase in material consumption rate.

Viewing from the recent local wars, national armies have done comprehensive and scientific analyses of material consume forecast, and which play a strong decision support role in battlefield needs [1]. Determine a reasonable consume limit by the battlefield condition, and establish a corresponding storage standard are both realistic needs in saving funds and meeting wartime needs [2]. Over the years, methods adopted in material support forecast varied a lot, they are empirical method, multiple linear regressions method, time series method and artificial neural network method [3].

Material demand forecast is an important part in support forecast. In material demand forecast, ammunition and equipment consumption are both the important ones, and their reasonable forecast are very difficult [3].

T. Xiao, L. Zhang, and S. Ma (Eds.): ICSC 2012, Part II, CCIS 327, pp. 345–352, 2012.

2   Difficulties in Material Demand Forecast

Future information warfare will be cooperative operations with multi-armed services, and their composition will be rather complicated. In which, there are many war units, and their nature and combat missions vary a lot, and so are their geographical location environments. Suddenness of a mission and uncertainty of its scale, results in a great random of support tasks.

In accordance with the four prediction elements (information, method, analysis, judgment), the wartime demand forecast are facing several main difficulties, and they are,

Difficulties in information or data. Due to the different levels of troop strength and different combat mission, combat fund supports in armies are different. Combat fund is closely related to combat mission, troop and weapon arrangement, combat duration, and combat geographical environment, so a huge number of various types of information are needed.

Difficulties in forecasting method. Due to the non-repeatability of battles, fund forecast experiences is hard to accumulate and hard to forecast intuitively. By using statistical methods, the mathematical models of combat fund forecast are different because of the different missions (attack, defend, land battle, air battle, sea battle) of armies, that is to say, different armies, even one army taking different missions, are both requiring different mathematical models. Each army need to establish a separate mathematical model based on the following parameters, such as their combat mission, combatants strength, war strength, combat duration, strategic material storage, combat geographical environment. Many types and a large number of mathematical models are to be established.

Difficulties in analysis. It is hard to analyze and evaluate the forecast result, due to the non-repeatability of battles.

Difficulties in judgement. First, to choose the required information needs to be judged, but it just can be judged by predictor's experience and theoretical accumulation. Second, to choose a forecasting method needs to be judged. The level of prediction accuracy is closely related with the selection of prediction methods. Third, whether to use the prediction result or not needs to be judged, and so does the modification of prediction result by the newest combat funds expenditure.

3   Adaptability Analysis of Material Support Demand Forecast in Simulation Method

3.1   Content Analysis of Material Demand Forecast

Contents of material demand forecast generally includes forecasts of the types and amount of materials. Further forecast should include the consideration of time and location of material demand [4]. The usability of forecast results will be greatly decreased if just given the type and amount of material, without its spatial and temporal distribution.

The key of material demand forecast is the prediction of material consumption. That is because that the amount of material demand is based on the material consumption, with further consideration of the loss and mobility amount of material.

3.2   Main Task of Forecast

Material consumption is affected by many factors, such as the mission, type, style of combat, war forces, the types and quantities of each war troop, and the target protection [5]. Material consumption includes the ammunition consumption during attacking a target, and that of being attacked by the enemy, and loss during support.

By analyzing the above factors, main task of material forecast can be confirmed to predict the quantities and types of combat troops' material consumption, including the quantities of consumed materials, the damaged materials and the loss at a certain time in a certain combat troop, among which the consumption prediction is an important part.

3.3   Prediction of Material Support Demand Based on Simulation

Consider to combat the various stages, the direction of possible operations against the degree of use of computers and other modern means and related formulas, by simulating combat situation, the battlefield environment, means of combat maneuvering range and engagement process, projected out to combat the various stages of equipment damage [6].

One kind of prediction method includes the following necessary steps. First, conform to the basic theoretical data of the military theories, weapon and equipment quantity, and tactical technique performance in the two sides of a combat. Second, take the possible combat manoeuver and rival degree from each stage and each direction into consideration. Third, utilize computers or other modern means and correlative calculation formula. Fourth, simulate the situation, environment, means, maneuvering range and engagement of the battle, and then calculate the weapon and equipment damage in various war stages.

Result of the above prediction method is more accuracy, but this method is greatly affected by technical conditions and levels, corresponding hardware, software and database should be established in advance so as to be used rapidly and conveniently in wartime.

Under a certain operation plan, in which the military forces are deployed, the enemy actions, the combat missions and stages are specified, combat simulation means to simulate the whole combat process, which includes command, communication, scout, electronic countermeasure, maneuver, fire attacking, and support, in virtual complicated battlefield and calculate equipment damage in each side of the battle.

Generally, before combat simulation, it is necessary to analyze the combat scenario from superior, understand the operational intentions, develop cooperative plans, and to supplement the lack in the operational plan, such as refining operational scheme, designing enemy action schema and so on. After analyzing the simulation result, a conclusion of combat effect can be obtained, so the equipment damage of the both sides in the battle can be calculated.

4   Construction of Combat Simulation Model of Support Demand Forecast Oriented

4.1   Requirements of Combat Model

A.   Requirements of Support Demand Forecast
Requirements to meet support demand forecast mainly include several factors relative to support demand, such as factors about type, quantity, time and geographical distribution.

B.   Requirements of Simulation Time
A large number of simulation experiments should be done to do support demand forecast. One simulation experiment lasts relatively short, and it should be limited at 0.5-5 hours.

C.   Requirements of Simulation Step
It should be able to meet the requirement of a variable step size for one second, so when carrying out rapid simulation, step requirements of 10 seconds, 30 seconds, 60 seconds and 600 seconds, can be satisfied.

4.2   Principles of Model Architecture

A.   Reusability Principle
Reusability of model's structure and usage, such as data model, if it is reusable, then new data format does not to be set separately, that is to say, if it can be obtained from existed alternating information, then it doesn't need to be subscribed and issued.

The leading idea of model reusability is to avoid establishing models repetitively, in order to decrease the costs of simulation development. Model reusability is the basis of constructing large and complicated model. According to the process of simulation activities, it can be divided into conceptual model reusability, mathematical model reusability and computer model reusability. To realize model reusability, each model in model architecture should be represented by uniform model structure and in normalized and standardized form.

B.   Completeness Principle
In mathematics and its relative fields, once an object is of completeness, that is, it is self-contained or complete without adding any other elements. Completeness of model architecture means that the established simulation model completely covers the described objects, and it can complete the service-oriented battlefield environment simulation.

C.   Coherence Principle
Models can be divided according their different types and uses, models of different type may be different in model frame architecture. Design of model architecture is the

key to determine whether the model is reusable, restructuring, expansible and maintainable. To assure the currency, reusability and re restructuring of a model in military range, the hierarchy and classification need to be uniform, that is to say that model architecture is of coherence.

D.   Parallelism Principle

Model is a reflection of real combat system. Real combat system is parallel, so models should satisfied the requirements of parallelism. The description of hierarchy and classification of model in model architecture must reflect parallelism. At the same time, in order to realize parallel simulation in a distributed computation environment, the hierarchy and classification of model must be convenient in realizing restructure and call of various models by parallel simulation environment, so as to realize dynamic combination of various parallel mission allocation conditions, and improve the speed of parallel simulation.

Material consumption is affected by many factors, such as the mission, type, style of combat, war forces, the types and quantities of each war troop, and the target protection [5]. Material consumption includes the ammunition consumption during attacking a target, and that of being attacked by the enemy, and loss during support.

By analyzing the above factors, main task of material forecast can be confirmed to predict the quantities and types of combat troops' material consumption, including the quantities of consumed materials, the damaged materials and the loss at a certain time in a certain combat troop, among which the consumption prediction is an important part.

4.3   Model Architecture

Material demand forecast model architecture based on simulation mainly include three parts, demand forecast models, forecast simulation models and simulation foundation models. Fig. 1 gives the detail of model architecture.

A.   Demand forecast models

These models are based on simulation results of forecast simulation models, and describe the principles between simulation result and forecast result. Credible and correct forecast results are made through second simulation result data processing.

B.   Forecast simulation models

Forecast simulation models can give original simulation result, through entities and operations in battle description, under certain input conditions.

Models can be divided into different parts, under different views and standards. Considering self-contained, oneness and parallel, the models architecture can be divided into two levels.

First, these models can be divided into three types, equipment models, command models and integrated environment models. Second, these models can be divided into particular types.

Equipment modes include six parts, command, maneuver, reconnaissance, communications, defenses and operation model. According to different arms of services characteristics, the operation models can be divided into armored infantry, tank, artillery, antiaircraft force, helicopter, command, communication, engineering, logistics, etc.

Command models include three parts, commander models, under-commander models and command means models. In command system, most commanders are both commanders and under-commanders.

Integrated environment models include service models, weather environment models, space environment models and electromagnetism environment models.

C. Simulation foundation models

Simulation foundation models include damage process simulation model and maintain process simulation model. However these models cannot participate in simulation experiment inline, complex simulation models should be constructed and the fundamental data forecast simulation model needed came from the complex simulation models.

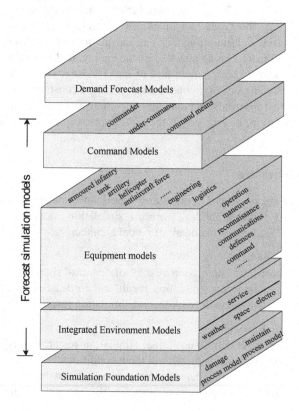

Fig. 1. Model Architecture

4.4   Damage Process Simulation Model

The damage process simulation model describes the process of target attacked such as equipment and blindage attacked by ammunition. The input elements include ammunition type, target attacked type, incident angle and incident speed. The outputs include damage components, damage level and attricist.

The simulation processes as follows, a) design parts of equipment attacked by ammunition, b) get the basic damage result of different ammunition through finite element analyses, c) analyze the relationship between the fragments and equipment inner components, and list the damage equipment components, e) give the attricist, f) give the battle effectiveness left.

4.5   Maintain Process Simulation Model

The maintain time and maintain material can be got from the maintain process simulation model. First, divide the equipment into irrelative components. Second, through simulation experiment, get the maintain time and maintain material of different sets of damage parts, position and damage style. Third, construct data inquire model which inputs are damage components count, position and damage style, and outputs are maintain time and maintain materials.

5   Simulation Experimentation Design and Result Analyses

It has much computation to forecast material demand using simulation. Simulation experiments must be designed considered the forecast object facts to using limited compute resources effectively. The simulation experiment was design as follows, a) analyze the factor of material demands, b) analyze the importance of the factors and eliminate the less important factors, c) analyze the factor range and select representative values, d) analyze the rationality of factors sets and eliminate obviously irrationality factors sets, e) experiment with these factors sets, f) import more values of focused factors, and rep e).

To forecast the material demands, the simulation experiment results must be analyzed. The general analyses should include, maximal material types and counts, min material types and counts, the fit samples rate, sensitivity analyses of factors, give the possible demand types and counts with believe scope.

6   Conclusions

This paper analyses the problem of material demand forecast, and discusses a series of relative problems about material demand forecast oriented on simulation method. Using the method in this paper, one can forecast the type, amount of material demand, and also can tell the temporal and special distribution of material demand. However, due to the complexity of combat system, and the simplicity of the simulation model, the accuracy and trustworthiness of the forecast result obtained from the simulation experiment will still need further analysis and study.

References

1. Wang, S.X., Yu, J., Xia, X.M.: Dynamic Model Research on Ammunition Demand in Combination of Firepower Blow. J. Fire Control and Command Control. 10, 101–101 (2009)
2. General Accounting Office: Operation Desert Storm Distribution of Ammunition and Supply Chain. AD-A293454 (1993)
3. Bergeron, S.M.: Revolution Military Logistics. AD-A396328 (2000)
4. Hou, S.X., Deng, Z.J.: Estimation of Maintenance Requirement for Naval Joint Maneuver Formation Based on Combat Simulation. J. Demonstration and Research. 1, 43–45 (2009)
5. Unlu, N.T.: Improving the Turkish navy requirements determination process: an assessment of demand forecasting methods for weapon system items. D. Naval Postgraduate School (2001)
6. Zhao, F.G., Sun, J.S., Zhang, L.W.: Research on Weapon Spare Parts Demand Forecasting Based on System. J. Computer Simulation. 3, 36–39 (2011)

Weapon Target Assignment Decision Based on Markov Decision Process in Air Defense

Yaofei Ma[*] and Chaohong Chou

School of Automation Science and Electronic Engineering, Beihang University,
100191 Beijing, China
mayaofei@gmail.com, chouchaohong@163.com

Abstract. This paper proposed a MDP based approach to resolve the weapon target assignment (WTA) problem in air defense domain. Considering the dynamic and stochastic nature of this problem, WTA is firstly decomposed into several sub-problems, the optimal strategy of which is easily to compute since the state space is very small. The strategies of sub-problems are combined to form global assignment strategy, in that a Minimum Marginal algorithm is employed for conflicts resolution. By this way, an approximate optimal WTA policy is obtained with reduction of computation complex.

Keywords: WTA, MDP.

1 Introduction

The WTA problem is a fundamental defense application of military operations. Generally, the problem consists of optimally assigning a given number of weapons to a set of targets, so that the total expected rewards of the sequential engagement is maximized.

At present, the WTA problem is generally divided into two categories: the static WTA, and the dynamic WTA. The static WTA [1] assigns weapons to targets only based on the current situation at allocating time without considering the whole process of the defense. There are literatures to study static WTA using linear integer programming [2,3], Maximum Marginal methods [4], simulated annealing(SA) algorithm [4], et. al. The dynamic WTA [5] assign weapons to targets in a sequential process, expecting to maximize the total reward within finite or infinite time horizon. In [6], a "shoot-look-shoot" policy is studied and weapon-target assignment at every step relies on the engagement results of previous assignment.

In this paper, we will study the dynamic WTA problem. We employ a MDP based approach to resolve this problem. WTA is firstly decomposed into a series of sub-problems, which only describe "single fire unit to single target" situation. Each sub-problems is viewed as a MDP with small state space, and we can easily calculate state

---

[*] Yaofei Ma, born in Henan Province in 1981, lecturer.

T. Xiao, L. Zhang, and S. Ma (Eds.): ICSC 2012, Part II, CCIS 327, pp. 353–360, 2012.

value and hence the optimal strategy. In the following process, a minimum marginal algorithm is employed to form the global assignment strategy.

2   The Formulation of WTA

2.1   The Definition of WTA Problem

An air defense system has N fire units, and each unit can launch m_i weapons without reload, $1 \le i \le N$. There is C attacking targets, which can be identified into H types. The number of targets belong to type h is l_h, i.e., $C = \sum_{h=1}^{H} l_h$. For convenience, we use "type" function to determine the target type: $type(j) = h$, where j is the index of targets.

To simplify the problem, we assume the defense weapons are all the same type, and are located in a compact area, such that the geometry and distance of intercept are the same for all weapons and targets. Based on this assumption, the kill probability of weapons is constant and only depends on target's type. KP_h is the kill probability to target type h.

When attacking targets approaching to the defense area, the intercept engagement begins at time t_{start} when targets enter the fire unit's shooting range, and ends at time t_{end} when targets leave the range. The interval $[t_{start}, t_{end}]$ is the time window for interception. Each target's time window can be estimated by its velocity and flight path, so we assume it is known once the interception begins. The time window will reduce with the defense process.

Within the interception window, our goal is to get maxim reward applying sequential weapon-target assignments. Reward consists of several components. Firstly, there is a value v_h associated with target type h. if the target is destroyed, v_h will be add to the total reward. Secondly, each consumed weapon owns a value of c. At last, if the target escapes from interception, a negative reward would be given to indicate the possible damage made by that target. During the engagement, we also consider some constraints as followings:

i.   In one step, a fire unit can launch weapons no more than $m_i^l (m_i^l \le m_i)$ simultaneously. This limitation reflect the defense capability of a single unit, and imposes a local constrain at each step when assign weapons to targets.

ii.   The weapon number assigned to one target j in one step should not exceed a limited number w_j. This constrain prevents abusing defense resource to single target, thus reduce the overall effectiveness of the defense system.

2.2   The Decomposition of Sub-problems

Before resolving the whole WTA problem, the "one fire unit to one target" situation is firstly considered. A fire unit i has m_i weapons currently, is going to intercept a target identified as type h. The fire unit launches weapons continually to the target, until the following state is reached: i) target is destroyed; ii) target's time window is closed; iii) all weapons are consumed. An optimal assignment sequence needs to be found to get the maxim reward, considering the cost of weapon consumption and possible interception failure.

This engagement process is viewed as a Markov Decision Process, since each shoot is independent and whether it will destroy the target is random. A general MDP problem-solving process is a trial and error loop. The agent (decision maker) decides best action according to current environment. Once the action is executed, the agent will obtain an instant reward and the environment experience a transition from a previous state to the new state. The agent continues this loop, aiming to find an optimal action sequence (strategy) to get the maxim total rewards in a long term.

The MDP can be represented as a tuple $<S, A, T, R>$, where S is a finite set of states; A is the finite set of actions; T is the transition distribution $T: S \times A \rightarrow S$, in that $T(s, a, s')$ is the transition probability from state s to s' if action a is took in state s. $R: S \times A \times S \rightarrow \mathcal{R}$ is the reward function, which calculate the instant reward given state s, action a and next state s'.

Given a MDP, the objective is to find a policy $\pi: s \rightarrow a$, which maximizes the expected accumulated reward in finite or infinite time horizon. In this paper, the subproblems can be formulated into simple MDP with finite time horizon. Its optimal policy depends on time, i.e., the optimal launching weapon number to a target will change with the passing of time.

The "one fire unit to one target" can be described as $< S_i, A_i, m_i, t_i, T_i, R_i >$, where i is the index of fire unit, and:

- $S_i = \{d, nd\}$. d means the target is destroyed, nd means the target is still survive.
- $A_i = \{a = m | m \leq m_i\}$: fire unit i can launch m ($0 \leq \mathrm{m} \leq m_i$) weapons to the single target at each time step. The more weapons launched at one time, the higher possibility to kill the target. However, the side effect is that there are fewer weapons left for future interceptions.
- m_i, t_i: m_i is available weapon number in fire unit i currently. t_i is the time step since t_{start}. The interception to a target will stop if $t_i \geq t_{start} - t_{end}$.
- T_i: the transition model in state space. After every launch, the engagement result has two outcomes: the target is destroyed (d), or not destroyed (ud). We just need to consider the transition start from state ud, as described as following:

$$T_i = \begin{cases} q_h{}^m, ud \rightarrow ud \text{ with m weapons} \\ 1 - q_h{}^m, ud \rightarrow d \text{ with m weapons} \end{cases} \tag{1}$$

Where: $q_h = (1 - KP_h)$ is target's survive probability after one weapon launched. KP_h is the kill probability to target type h.

- R_i: the instant reward after each launch:

$$R_i = \begin{cases} v_h, t_i \in [0, t_{start} - t_{end}], \text{target is destroyed} \\ 0, t_i \in [0, t_{start} - t_{end}], \text{target is survive} \\ -K, t_i > t_{start} - t_{end}. \end{cases} \quad (2)$$

Where: $-K$ is the punishment for target's escape.

With above formulation, the sub-problem can be solved by traditional dynamic programming. The value function can be iterated as following:

$$V_i(s, m_i, t_i) = \max \sum_{a \leq m_i, s, s' \in S} T_i(s, a, t_i, s') \times [R_i(s, a, t_i, s') +$$

$$V_i(s, m_i - a, t_i + 1)] - c * a \quad (3)$$

Given $V_i(s, m_i, t_i)$, the optimal policy of this sub-problem can be obtained:

$$\pi_i^*(s, m_i, t_i) = \arg \max_{a \leq m_i} V_i(s, m_i, t_i) \quad (4)$$

For each type h, we can compute the value function V_i^h and optimal strategy π_i^{h*} respectively. This knowledge will be used to construct the global assignment strategy.

3   Resolving Global Assignment Strategy

3.1   Possible Conflicts in Combination of Sub-strategies

In section 2.2, we consider the "one fire unit to one target" sub-problem, in that the value function $V_i^h(s, m_i, t_i)$ is computed and the optimal interception strategy is derived. V_i^h can be used as the heuristic knowledge to get the global assignment strategy, i.e., N fire units vs. C attacking targets.

The computation of global strategy can be divided into 2 steps.

Firstly, value function $V = \{V_i^h, i = 1, ..., N, h = 1, ..., H\}$ is used to form an initial global assignment, in that each fire unit assigns weapons to each target in a duplicated way. For example, fire unit i assign $m(i, j)$ weapons to target j ($h = type(j)$), according to its sub-problem optimal strategy π_i^{h*}. Every such assignment is denoted as: $x_{ij} = \{m(i, j) | h = type(j), \pi_i^{h*}\}$, thus the initial global assignment is $X = \{x_{ij} | i = 1, ..., N, j = 1, ..., C\}$.

Currently, the global assignment is just a collection of sub-problem strategies, where the engagement constraints (section 2.1) are not considered, hence the conflicts occur:

i.   For fire unit i, the amount of weapons assigned to all targets may exceed m_i^l:

$$\sum_j m(i, j) > m_i^l \quad (5)$$

which means the assignment is beyond the capability of fire unit i;

ii.   For target j, the total amount of weapons assigned to it by all fire units may exceed w_j:

$$\sum_i m(i,j) > w_j \qquad (6)$$

which means too much weapons are used for a single target.

3.2   Minimum Marginal Algorithm

Conflict resolution is the second step to compute the global assignment strategy. Some assignments should be canceled, under the criterion that these cancellations will minimize the total reward loss. We use Minimum Marginal algorithm to achieve this task, which is just the opposite of Maximum Marginal (MaxM) algorithm [4].

Conflict (5) is considered firstly. Assuming fire unit i have m_i weapons now. With the initial assignment, there are $m(i,j) = \pi_i^*(s, m_i, t_i)$ weapons are assigned to target j. The state value after this assignment is:

$$V_{ij} = V_i(s, m_i - m(i,j), t_i), \text{ with assignment to target } j \qquad (7)$$

If 1 weapon is reduced from $m(i,j)$, the state value becomes to:

$$V'_{ij} = V_i(s, m_i - m(i,j) + 1, t_i) \qquad (8)$$

Thus the change of state value is :

$$\Delta V_{ij} = V_{ij} - V'_{ij} \qquad (9)$$

It's easy to get ΔV_{ij}^{-1} since state value has been calculated in section 2.2). The same process is performed to each target. Target j^* satisfying (10) will be selected as the one whose assignment will be canceled:

$$j^* = \arg\min_j \Delta V_{ij}^{-1} \qquad (10)$$

Thus the amount of weapons assigned to target j^* will be:

$$m(i,j^*) = m(i,j^*) - 1 \qquad (11)$$

Recycling (8)-(11), until the initial assignment of fire unit i is adjusted to satisfy its local constrain:

$$\sum_j m(i,j) \le m_i^l \qquad (12)$$

The pseudo code for local constrain resolution is listed in Fig.1.

```
ResoluteWeapon(Set FireUnits, Set Targets,
                        Set& InitialAssign){
Input Variables:
  FireUnits: {fire unit i|i=1,…,N};
  Targets: {target j|j=1,…,C};
  InitialAssign: {m(i,j)| i=1,…,N, j=1,…,C};
Local Variables:
  mil: m^l_i, the local constrain of fire unit i;
  Vi: V_i(s,m_i,t_i), the pre-calculated state value;
  TotalAssign: temporary local variable;
  DetVij,mi,ti: temporary local variables;
  INFINITE: ∞;
  UNKNOWN: an enum constant;
Code:
For each fire unit i in FireUnits
  While(1), Do:
    TotalAssign :=0;
    For each target j in N
      m(i,j):= Assignment(i,j);
      TotalAssign := TotalAssig + m(i,j);
    End;
    IF (TotalAssign <= mil)
      Break;
    End
    Var MinLoss = INFINITE;
    Var CanceledIndex = UNKNOWN;
    For each target j in Targets
      DetVij = Vi(s,mi,ti) - Vi(s,mi+1,ti)
      If(DetVij<MinLoss)
        MinLoss = DetVij;
        CanceledIndex = j;
      End
    End
    m(i,CanceledIndex) = m(i,CanceledIndex) - 1;
  End
End
}
```

Fig. 1. The local constrain resolution algorithm

After conflict resolution for each fire unit, it's ensured that each fire unit will not launch too many weapons that beyond its capability in one time step. Next, we consider to resolute the constrain (**6**). According to similar approach, we limit the total amount of weapons assigned to every target. The pseudo code is list as Fig.2.

```
Set ResoluteTarget(Set FireUnits, Set Targets,
                   Set& Assign){
  Input Variables:
  FireUnits: {fire unit i|i=1,…,N};
  Targets: {target j|j=1,…,C};
  Assign: {m(i,j)| i=1,…,N, j=1,…,C}, which has been
          adjusted by ResoluteWeapon();
  Local Variables:
  wj: wⱼ, the constrain for weapon j;
  Vi: Vᵢ(s,mᵢ,tᵢ), the pre-calculated state value;
  TotalAssigned: temporary local variable;
  DetVij,mi,ti: temporary local variables;
  INFINITE: ∞;
  UNKNOWN: an enum constant;
  Code:
  For each target j in Targets
    While(1), Do:
    TotalAssigned =0;
    For each fire unit i in FireUnits
      m(i,j):= Assign(i,j);
      TotalAssigned := TotalAssigned +m(i,j)
    End;
    If(TotalAssigned <=wj)
      Break;
    End;

    MinLoss = INFINITE;
    CanceledIndex = UNKNOWN;
    For each fire unit i in FireUnits
      DetVij = Vij(s,mi,ti) - Vij(s,mi+1,ti)
      If(DetVij<MinLoss)
        MinLoss = DetVij;
        CanceledIndex = i;
      End;
    End;
    M(CanceledIndex,j) = M(CanceledIndex,j) - 1;
    End;
End;
```

Fig. 2. The targets' constrains resolution algorithm

4   Conclusion

With the decomposition of WTA problem into simple, easily computed sub-problems, the computation complexity is greatly reduced. The following work will be focused on two sides: i) To conduct experiments to verify proposed method; ii) to further improve the quality of global assignment, giving the quality guarantees at least.

References

1. Hosein, P., Athans, M.: An asymptotic result for the multi-stage weapon target allocation problem. LI DSP-945. MIT (1990)
2. Chen, D., Lei, Y.: The threat assessment and sorting model of air strikes target. Systems Engineering and Electronics 27(9), 1597–1599 (2005)
3. Wang, J., Lou, S.: Research on threat assessment and sorting model of the air raids target flow. Modern Defence Technology 29(6), 29–33 (2001)
4. Madni, A.M.: Efficient Heuristic Approaches to the Weapon–Target Assignment Problem. Journal of Aerospace Computing, Information, And Communication (6), 405–414 (2009)
5. Hosein, P., Athans, M.: Preferential defense strategies, part2: The dynamic case. LIDS-P-2003. MIT (1990)
6. Glazebrook, K., Washburn, A.: Shoot-Look-Shoot: A Review and Extension. Operations Research 52(3), 454–463 (2004)

Study of CGF Task Simulation System Based on HLA

Fei Jie, Fengxia Li, Zhaohan Lu, and Binghui Geng

Beijing Key Laboratory of Digital Performance and Simulation Technology,
Beijing Institute of Technology, Beijing, China
jiefei2008@hotmail.com

Abstract. This paper analyzes the importance of the task information in military simulation, discusses the different multi-resolution modeling (MRM) methods, designs and realizes a MRM simulation system based on HLA. Combat entities were modeled with aggregation-disaggregation method and the task information of the entities was built MRE models. The task MRE could maintain consistency of tasks in different levels of resolution strictly by maintaining all task details among all levels of resolution. And the combat entities would not consume too much simulation resources in the aggregation-disaggregation model. In the simulation federation, a task manage federate was constructed to maintain the task information in the whole simulation process which could interact with other federates by distributing task information and receiving feedbacks. Moreover, the task information in the task manage federate was used to visualize the task of combat entities in the 3D scene which could intuitionally show the intentions of entities.

Keywords: task model, multi-resolution modeling (MRM), computer generated forces (CGF), High Level Architecture (HLA).

1 Introduction

Modern military simulation system, based on modeling & simulation technologies and virtual reality technology, built the military simulation model with abstracting the process, phenomena and environment. With a simulated battlefield environment, the experiments of strategy and plans were used to verify the effect and inspire new ideas. Computer generated forces (CGF) means some simulation entities which are created and controlled by the computer in the battlefield simulation environment [1]. In a CGF simulation system, the CGF entities could respond to the battlefields situation and events when they occur by modeling the combat entities and their behaviors. The task of a CGF entity, which usually describes the entity's intention or the orders it received, largely determines this entity's subsequent behavior. Moreover, the description of a task often includes some information about entity attributes, such as position, formation, etc. Thus, task is a special and important attribute of an entity [2].

However, with the development of the computer techniques and the constant expansion of the simulation scale, the simulation model with fixed level of resolution can no longer meet the demand of simulation fidelity and complexity in the modern

T. Xiao, L. Zhang, and S. Ma (Eds.): ICSC 2012, Part II, CCIS 327, pp. 361–369, 2012.

military simulation. Multi-Resolution Modeling (MRM) is applicable when simulation entities at different levels of resolution are required to interoperate. Of many MRM methods, aggregation-disaggregation was most widely used, and was considered to be the most capable of manifesting the essence of MRM. But, it also incurs problems such as temporal inconsistency, chain disaggregation, etc. As discussed above, task is an important entity attribute which is related to other entity attributes. So the loss of task information and inconsistency of the representation about one task in different levels of resolution will impact on the simulation system hugely. In the process of MRM, maintaining the consistency among the task representation in different levels of resolutions is one crux of MRM.

This paper researches on the problem of MRM, models the combat entities with aggregation-disaggregation method, and builds Multi-Resolution Entity (MRE) model for the task of entities according to specific request in military simulation. Then, a distributed simulation system was built based on High Level Architecture (HLA). This simulations system could maintain consistency of the tasks of entities in different levels of resolution, provide interoperability between different simulation entities, increase the development efficiency, make the simulation more efficient, and have excellent expansibility.

2   HLA

HLA was proposed by Defense Modeling and Simulation Office (DMSO) in the Department of Defense (DoD) Modeling and Simulation Master Plan (MSMP) in October 1995 [3]. HLA is the primary content in the first goal of MSMP which is to develop a universal technology frame for realizing the interoperability and reuse of distributed simulation. HLA is the current leading system architecture of distributed interactive simulation. It sets up simulation system according to the object-oriented thinking. HLA focus on the work of system integration based on simulation members and designing interactions between those simulation members to fulfill the simulation.

In a simulation system based on HLA, federation, which consists of several interactional simulation members, is a distributed simulation system that is used to realize a given simulation purpose. The application program and component engaged in federation are called federates. In a federation, there are different kinds of federates. For example, a data recording federate is used to collect simulation data; an entity agent federate is used to interact with some entity; a manager federate is used to manage the simulation service. The most typical federate is a simulation application federate which generates a simulated entity's dynamic behavior based on a given simulation model. The design of HLA simulation model is primarily to design Object Model Template (OMT) which is used to define the Federation Object Model (FOM) and the Simulation Object Model (SOM). FOM describes the data exchange of federates in a universal and standard way. SOM describes the inherent ability what a single simulation application could provide to the federation.

Run Time Infrastructure (RTI) is a core component of HLA, it separates the simulation server layer from the bottom layer network function and realizes data exchanging among different federates with objects and interactions.

3   The Studies on MRM Methods

At present, there are three main methods of MRM, which are selective viewing, aggregation-disaggregation and MRE. In these methods, the aggregation-disaggregation was most widely used, and was considered to be the most capable of manifesting the essence of MRM. But, this method was easily lead to inconsistency between the low-resolution model which was to show macroscopic information and the high-resolution model which was to show model details. MRE method always maintains attributes of an entity in all levels of resolution, and could maintain consistency at the expense of more resources.

In military simulation, an entity's task could decide its sequent behavior to some extent, and the process and status of a task could also affect the process of decision making. So we model the combat entities in federates with aggregation-disaggregation method which designs some mapping functions to change the model in different levels of resolution, and build MRE model for the task information of the entities which could maintain all task details among different levels of resolution. This design will not consume too much resource, but also maintain consistency of tasks in different levels of resolution.

3.1   Aggregation-Disaggregation Model for Combat Entities

In aggregation-disaggregation method, a simulation entity was built multi-resolution model which could dynamically change its level of resolution in simulation process [4]. In general situation, the simulation entities were executing in low-resolution level. When simulation needed more model details, the model changed itself to high-resolution level. After that, the model could also change back to low-resolution level when those details were not needed any more.

Consistency means the running results of simulation models in different levels of resolution which are built for the same entity in the same condition. Consistency could be categorized into strong consistency and weak consistency, for which more detailed discussion and improved model can be found in document [5]. In traditional aggregation-disaggregation method, the mapping functions were constructed to transfer information for the models in different levels of resolution in the aggregation process and disaggregation process. However, lots of detail information in high-resolution model was lost during the aggregation process of high-resolution models. To improve the mapping functions, we design an additional information structure which is shown in figure 1 to dynamically add some necessary information for maintaining consistency.

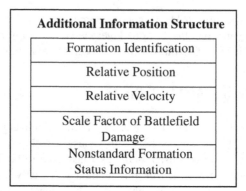

Additional Information Structure
Formation Identification
Relative Position
Relative Velocity
Scale Factor of Battlefield Damage
Nonstandard Formation Status Information

Fig. 1. The additional information structure in the disaggregation process

The additional information structure, which mainly included some common attributes of a combat simulation entity, was constructed when an entity formation triggered an aggregation process. The formation identification in the structure shows the formation type which may be a standard formation in the standard formation database or a temporary nonstandard formation.

Taking the simulation entity's position as an example, we give the improved mapping functions as follows. The aggregation process of position uses core entity location method. Firstly, the formation information of the entities was checked. If the current formation was not standard formation in the database, the mathematic description of current formation would be saved in the additional information structure and the formation identification would be set as temporary formation. After that, the mapping function was executing. Suppose that the core entities among entities $E_1, E_2, ..., E_n$ in the formation were $E_{c+1}, E_{c+2}, ..., E_{c+n}$ $(c \geq 0, m \geq 1, c, m \in N, c+m \leq n)$, the mapping function is:

$$E.p = f_A (E_1.p, E_2.p, ..., E_n.p) = \sum_{i=1}^{m} E_{c+i}.p / m$$

In the disaggregation process of positions, formation was firstly checked. If current formation was temporary formation, it would be disaggregated with the relative position information in the additional information structure, or the disaggregation process would reference the standard formation information in the database to generate positions for the new high-resolution entities. Suppose the position of high-resolution entity E_i' would be generated as $E_i'.p$. The mapping function is:

$$f_D(E.p; L) = \begin{cases} (E.p + sp_1, E.p + sp_2, ..., E.p + sp_n), & L = temporary \\ (E_1'.p, E_2'.p, ..., E_n'.p), & L = standard \end{cases}$$

3.2   MRE Model for Tasks

The task multi-resolution model and its maintaining consistency depend on task MRE. Task multi-resolution process depends heavily on applications. Some low-resolution tasks could be assigned to high-resolution entities directly, and some others must be disaggregated before assignation. This process needs the support of military experts. Once some attributes of a task was lost during the aggregation-disaggregation process, it was very difficult to generate them again because of the complexity of tasks. However, the tasks attributes in different levels of resolution could be updated with consistency functions if these attributes were recorded.

The MRE method, which always maintains attributes of a task in all levels of resolution, makes a task exist in multiple levels of resolution [5]. The figure 2 is the structure of a task MRE, which was constructed by aggregated model, disaggregated model, Consistency Enforcer (CE) and Interaction Resolver (IR).

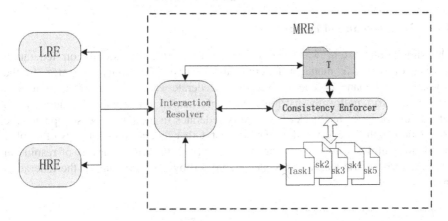

Fig. 2. The structure of an task MRE for combat entities. This shows 4 components in an MRE: aggregated model, disaggregated model, CE and IR.

A Consistency Enforcer is a component of a task MRE which ensures that the representations of a task in different levels of resolution are consistent. The consistency required that the multiple representations in a task MRE keep consistent when interactions changed some attributes. The kind of adjustment process to maintain consistency was done with consistency mapping functions. Mapping functions could translate the attributes in a representation to this attributes in another. This translating includes translating value or type. For example, a tank platoon was ordered to capture one area, so every single tank's task target should be one position coordinates or one enemy entity. The disaggregation mapping function could translate the tank platoon's task information into the tanks' task information, and the aggregation mapping function could also translate all the tanks' task information into the tank platoon's task information. Besides, every translation by mapping functions would complete before the time-step ends.

One other problem of task MRE is to resolve concurrent interactions in different levels of resolution. In the actual simulation, these concurrent interactions often were dependent. The component 'Interaction Resolver' is to solve this problem. In each time-step of simulation, all interactions received would be categorized into 4 types which were response interactions with certain outcomes, response interactions with uncertain outcomes, request interactions with certain outcomes and request interactions with uncertain outcomes. In the 4 types of interactions, response interactions were independent with request interactions because they described the information what had happened. In the response interactions, those which had certain outcomes were handled first, and some interactions information would be discarded which affected previous interactions. The request interactions were handled after response interactions, and the handling strategy was similar to the response interactions.

4   Task Simulation System Based on HLA

4.1   The Structure of Federation

The simulation system was built based on HLA [6]. The simulation federation consists of one task manager federate and several CGF entity federates. In the federation, task manager federate is a special federate who gets task information from combat scenario, uniformly distributes task information to every entity federate in an interaction, receives feedbacks from entity federates in the task process, updates the completion status of every task in the task list. Other federates are all sorts of combat simulation entities who simulate aggregated entities in different levels of resolution according to specific simulation scale. Figure 3 shows the structure of the federation in this system.

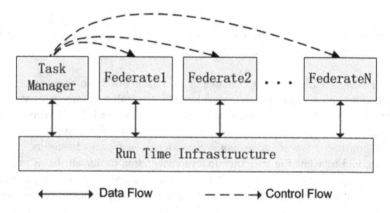

Fig. 3. The structure of the federation. The simulation federation consists of several classical federates and an additional task manage federate.

The simulation process could be described as follows. When simulation begins, the task manager federate packages original task information in the combat scenario into interactions, and sends to other federates through RTI. The entity federate will resolve the interaction after receiving it, disaggregates the task to the level of resolution in which the tasks could be completed by every entity, and transferred these tasks to every entity to execute. Every generated task in entity federates will send a 'new task' interaction to the task manager federate to establish a record in the task list. Analogously, the newly generated task information in all levels of resolution which may be generated by the decision-making mechanism of an entity in some level of resolution or may be preset in the combat scenario or some task update information will also be sent to the task manager federate. In addition, an 'end task' interaction will be sent to the task manager federate when the entity's task has completed or could not complete for various reasons. Finally, when the simulation ends, the task manager federate will evaluate the simulation results according to the task status information in the task list.

4.2   The Task Manage Federate

In the simulation process, task manager federate maintains a task list which records all task and their status information in the federation, including some completed tasks and some tasks in process. For each task in the task list, we establish such a record which is shown in table 1. In every record, the attribute 'Task_ID' is task identification which is integer and primary key in the list. The attribute 'Entity_Num' means how many entities are ordered to complete this task, and every entity's identification is recorded in the container 'Entity_ID'. The attribute 'Begin_Time' record the time when this task begins, and 'Last_Time' means how long this task will last. The 'Task_Type' is a set of predefined type identification of tasks, its integer value means the task type such as mobile task, attack task, surrounded task, patrol task, defense task, etc. There is a position coordinates in the 'Target_Area' which means differently in different task type, such as target location in a mobile task or the defensive area in a defense task. The attribute 'Task_Parameter' includes some additional information about a task which are used to control the task executing process. For example, an attack task need some information about the target entities and predefined attacking strategy, and patrol task also need some information about the patrol method. The attribute 'Agg_Task_ID' records the task identification from which this task was disaggregated (if this task is not in the lowest level of resolution). Correspondingly, the attribute 'Disagg_Task_Num' and the container 'Disagg_Task_ID' jointly describe that which tasks were disaggregated from this task (if this task has). At the end of this table, 'Task_Process'

Table 1. The attributes of a record in the task list

Attribute	Type	Comment
Task_ID	int	Task identification
Entity_Num	int	Number of the entities to perform this task
Entity_ID[ ]	Int[Entity_Num]	Identifications of the entities to perform this task
Begin_Time	Double	The time this task begins
Last_Time	Double	The duration of this task
Task_Type	Int	Type identification of this task
Target_Area	Double[x, y]	Target area of this task
Task_Parameter[ ]	Int[N]	Some additional information of a task
Agg_Task_ID	int	Identification of the aggregation task of this task
Disagg_Task_Num	int	Number of the disaggregation tasks of this task
Disagg_Task_ID[ ]	Int[Disagg_Task_Num]	Identification of the disaggregation tasks
Task_Process	float	Completion capability of this task
Task_Status	float	Percentage complete of this task

and 'Task_Status' are two percentages. The former estimates the ability that the task performers could complete this task in the current simulation time, and the latter is the percentage complete of this task.

4.3   Visualization of Task Information

According to the description of task information in the table 1, we realized the visualization of tasks in the simulation system with traditional military plotting. Visualization of the task information could intuitionally show the behavior information and the intentions of entities. And the visualization process would use different information which depended on the different task type.

Taking an attack task as an example, the visualization process based on the information of entities to perform this task, target location, and task control information which corresponded to the Entity_ID, Target_Area and Task_Parameter in the table 1. The figure 4 shows the visualization result of an attack task in the simulation system. The red rectangles marked the entities which were performing the current task. And the red arrow started from the aggregative position of the entities which was decided by the core entity as we mentioned in section 3.1. The end of the red arrow pointed at the target area of current attack task, and the radian of the arrow depended on the control information of current task which were waypoint in our system. Otherwise, the arrow should be drawn in the vertical plane of the line of sight, and the contours would be changed during the task process.

Fig. 4. The visualization of an attack task. This task was being performed by the left three tanks which were marked by red rectangles.

5   Conclusions

This paper analyzes the importance of the task information in military simulation, discusses the different MRM methods, designs and realizes a MRM simulation system based on HLA. The problem behind the simulation system is that how to find a fairly reasonable MRM method for the modeling of the entities and their tasks in different levels of resolution in the military simulation. Compared with the entities, the multi-resolution models of the entities' tasks needed to maintain consistency more strictly. Consequently, the difficulty of the MRM process is the conflict of maintaining consistency and economizing the simulation resources. Our approach to resolve this conflict was to model the combat entities with aggregation-disaggregation method and to build MRE model for the task information of the entities. On one hand, the task MRE could maintain consistency of tasks in different levels of resolution well through maintaining all task details among all levels of resolution. On the other hand, the combat entities would not consume too much simulation resources in the aggregation-disaggregation model.

In the simulation federation, we construct a task manage federate to maintain the task information in the whole simulation process. This federate could interact with other federates through distributing task information and receiving feedbacks. Moreover, according to the task list in the task manage federate, we tried to visualize the task information of combat entities in the 3D scene which could intuitively show the intentions of entities. The simulation process of the system could validate the validity of our modeling method.

References

1. Petty, D.M.: Computer Generated Forces in Distributed Interactive Simulation. Critical Reviews of Optical Science and Technology CR58, 251–280 (1995)
2. Yang, L., Guo, Q., Zhang, W.: Mission Decomposition and Mission Disaggregation for Aggregated Force Simulation. Journal of System Simulation. 18, 186–188 (2006)
3. IEEE Std 1516 -2010 IEEE Standard for Modeling and Simulation (M&S) High Level Architecture (HLA) - Framework and Rules (2000)
4. Li, M., Bi, C., Liu, X., Niu, D.: Research on Rules of Aggregation and Disaggregation for Aircraft Entity Models in Air Force Combat Simulation. In: Asia Simulation Conference-7th International Conference, pp. 1286–1290 (2008)
5. Reynolds, F.P., Natrajan, J.: A, Srinivasan, S.: Consistency Maintenance in Multiresolution Simulations. ACM Transactions on Modeling and Computer Simulation 7(3), 368–392 (1997)
6. Tan, G., Ng Ngee, W., Moradi, F.: Aggregation/Disaggregation in HLA Multi-Resolution Distributed Simulation. In: Fifth IEEE International Workshop on DS-RT, pp. 76–83 (2001)

Research of Aiming Error and Its Application in CGF Tank Firing Model

Changwei Zheng, Qing Xue, Xiaoming Ren, and Guanghui Li

College of Armored Force Engineering, Beijing, China
zhw_byh@163.com

Abstract. Based on the effecting factors of aiming error on firing precision in the gunner shooting procedure, it builds the aiming error model and shooting reaction delay model which compose the CGF tank aiming model with high precision. It makes the aiming action more realistic in CGF tank model which improves the fidelity and validity of system and it is conducive to enhance the efficiency of gunner's shooting and tactical training system.

Keywords: arget center judging error, aiming error, target motion error, shooting reaction delay, CGF aiming shoot model.

1 Introduction

CGF (Computer Generated Forces) It is one of crucial technologies in distribution interactive simulation, its major purposes lie in: It offers battle competitor or friend army for person in loop of the weapon simulation entity, raises actuality and the complexity of virtual battlefield environment, strengthens the trainees' immersing [1]. CGF tank entity model as enemy or friend enter in many operational simulation systems has been applied extensively, but the aim shooting model is simple and judges the firing outcome by random according to weapon performance without considering the factor of operational personnel. It can only embody the mutual weapon performance, and can not reflect the confrontation between armies, for tank gunner's shooting trains and company tactical training it is inconsistent with reality and not proper for training.

Modern tank's weapon system is straight aiming and has advanced fire control computer. After gunner discovers target, gunner selects the shell and load it then aims, trails and range finding, fire control system automatically collects vehicle states, distance, goal state and environmental parameters, calculates the gun's angle in vertical and horizontal direction and position the cannon, sets the firing parameters. After the gunner shoots, the shell will fly in the determined projection until hitting the target. From this procedure it is determined by fire control system, sensor error and shell distribution to whether hitting the target. It is major influencing factors such as the gunner aiming precision and shooting reaction time. Therefore reflecting the actual shooting realistically, it should consider the factor of gunner fully and build related model to perfect the shooting modular of CGF tank.

T. Xiao, L. Zhang, and S. Ma (Eds.): ICSC 2012, Part II, CCIS 327, pp. 370–374, 2012.

2   Operator Description Model

When the gunner uses aiming device to target the goal Owning to the effects of physiology, psychology, operating ability and equipment performance it can not aim goal's center accurately, the test proofs that it affects the hitting rate more than the error of shell distribution [2]. Therefore it should establish the aim operating error model, this model based on gunner's aim operating error generates simulation aiming point which offers reference for the calculation of shell distribution.

The time between the gunners find the target in aiming device and cannon fires is shooting reaction time [3]. Shooting reaction time is an important parameter in real cannon firing which is closely related with the gunner's operating ability. During the shooting reaction time if the target is disappeared or the more threaten target shows, it probably needs to cancel the shooting and re-aiming. Therefore finding target does not mean firing. It should build the shooting reaction time model to simulate the gunner's aiming operation time.

3   Analyses of Aiming Operation Error and Modeling

Aiming operation error is human caused and random which is composed by target center judging error, aiming error and target motion error [2].

3.1   Target Center Judging Error

Target center judging error makes the gunner hard to find the target center which means the aiming center is not the target center. Related data show that the target center judging error obeys the normal distribution [2].

$$f(x) = \frac{1}{\sigma\sqrt{2\pi}} e^{-\frac{(x-\alpha)^2}{2\sigma^2}} \tag{1}$$

In 1 α is the average value, normally is 0.

σ is Mean Square Error, it is related with α as follow:

$$E = 0.6745\sigma \tag{2}$$

Middle error E is the half length of variable in the interval by 0.5 possibilities [4]. When E is used to denote the aiming distribution, it is called calculation deviation. Table 1 is the calculation deviation of some type tank in different shooting form [2].

Table 1. Aiming calculation deviation

| | Shooting form | | | |
	s-s	s-m	m-s	m-m
horizontal	0.06 mil	0.5 mil	0.15 mil	0.52 mil
vertical	0.06 mil	0.3 mil	0.15 mil	0.34 mil

Target center judging error simulation can adopt the method of Monte Carlo, with target central point as the base combining the random accord with normal distribution of target center judging error which can generate the aiming point with introducing target center judging error to.

The random follows the normal distribution can get by Box—Muller method [5].

Setting the ξ', ξ'' are variables in $[0, \ 1)$, then

$$\eta' = \left(-2\ln\xi'\right)^{\frac{1}{2}}\cos 2\pi\xi'' \tag{3}$$

$$\eta'' = \left(-2\ln\xi'\right)^{\frac{1}{2}}\sin 2\pi\xi'' \tag{4}$$

Ordinary normal variable X and standard normal variable η is related as:

$$X = \sigma \cdot \eta + \mu$$

So it can from random in even distribution generate the random number that accords with general normal distribution.

Generating two numbers: R1, R2 between 0 and 1, then

$$\eta_x = \cos(2\pi R_2)\sqrt{-2\cdot\ln R_1} \tag{5}$$

$$\eta_y = \sin(2\pi R_2)\sqrt{-2\cdot\ln R_1} \tag{6}$$

The above numbers are following the standard normal distribution and transforming as follow:

$$X = 1.4826\cdot E_x\cdot\eta_x + \alpha_x \tag{7}$$

$$Y = 1.4826\cdot E_y\cdot\eta_y + \alpha_y \tag{8}$$

In 7 and 8, E_x is the middle error in vertical;

E_y is the middle error in horizon;

α_x is the average value in vertical;

α_y is the average value in horizon;

After getting the above-mentioned aiming angles which deviate the center of target, according to the distance between cannon and gunner it can figure out the aiming points coordinate finally.

3.2   Aiming Error

Aiming error is the random error caused by gunner's eye and operating difference which is the length of aiming device. Owning to the minimum of aiming device is less than 0.1mil, the aiming error is 0.1mil [2].

When the target center is settled, adding 0.1mil in the coordinate of target center.

$$X = X_0 \pm L_{PM} \cdot \sin(0.1 \cdot \frac{360}{6000}) \qquad (9)$$

$$Y = Y_0 \pm L_{PM} \cdot \sin(0.1 \cdot \frac{360}{6000}) \qquad (10)$$

L_{PM} is the distance between cannon and gunner.

In 10 the plus or minus is settled by generating the random between 0 and 1. When the random is less than 1/2 the minus will be chose, else the plus will be chose.

3.3   Target Motion Error

Target motion error is from the trailing target instability when measuring target angular velocity, therefore also called tracking error. It is the embodiment of gunner's tracking the moving target. Actual experience shows the tracking error is related with trail angular velocity. Usually when the trailing goal's speed is low, tracking error is larger than 5%; when the speed of trailing goal is above middle, tracking error is smaller than 5% [2].

From the distance between cannon and gunner, observing direction, target speed and direction it can get the trail angular velocity, trail angular velocity multiply with the correction coefficient of tracking error to get the trail angular velocity standard. Revising again with gunner training level, psychological quality coefficient to get different CGF entity's trail angular velocity, and then calculate ballistic direction in advance.

4   Shooting Reaction Delay Model

Shooting reaction delay is composed by [2]:

(1) The time between finding target and aiming target $(2\sim3s)$;
(2) The time of tracing target, judging distance, fire control computer calculation $(2\sim3s)$;
(3) Accurately aiming and firing $(0\sim2s)$ 。

The shooting reaction delay of trained gunner with simple and stabilizer fire control system is shown in table 2 [2].

Table 2. Shooting reaction delay

Fire control system	Shooting form		
	s-s	s-m	m-m
simple	5s	10s	no
stabilizer	5s	7s	10s

With the shooting reaction time in Table 2, revising with gunner training coefficient and gunner psychological quality coefficient, it can simulate different CGF tank entity's firing time from finding target to firing.

5   Applications

The method in this paper has been successfully applied in the tank fire control system dynamic simulator which provides the enemy for trainee, after the usage of elementary students, second level shooters and first level shooter it proves that it can embody the train level of shooter correctly and get good effects. Below is the enemy CGF tank fire observed in gunner mirror of simulator.

Fig. 1. Enemy CGF Tank firing

References

1.   Guo, Q., Yang, L.: Introduction of CGF. National Industry Press (2006)
2.   Zhu, J., Zhao, B.: Modern Tank Firing Control System. National Industry Press (2003)
3.   PLA. Tank Firing. PLA Press (1985)
4.   Zhang, Y.: War Simulation. National Industry Press (2004)

Command and Decision-Making Model for Armored Weapon Platform Based on Multi-agent

Changyi Chen, Xinjun Zhao, Yongxian Zou, Baili Qi, and Lingjie Kong

Beijing Special Vehicle Research Institute, Beijing, China, 100072

Abstract. After study on the character of the weapon platform, a new command and decision-making model based on multi-agents is presented in this paper. Through discussing the producing process of commanding activity, this paper put forward the cooperation model of multiple weapon platform based on KQML language in order to realize cooperation between multiple agents. At last, decision-making agents are given autonomous decision and self-inference abilities in the new command and decision-making model by using Artifical Neuro-Network Fuzzy Inference System.

Keywords: armored weapon platform, command and decision-making model, multi-agent, cooperation model, KQML language.

1 Introduction

Agent technology which rose in 1970s has been an important approach for studying complicated systems. Agent is generally recognized as a computational entity which can perceive its surroundings and act on the surroundings in line with its own goals. Multi-Agent system is a system that consists of several independent Agents which can accomplish some tasks or achieve some goals through collaboration. The intelligence of single Agent is limited, however, Agents can be organized via appropriate architecture so as to cover the shortage of every single Agent and reflect the intellectualized system behavior through competition, collaboration and negotiation, and thus being able to proceed large-scale problem solving activities and enable the capability of the whole system to exceed the capability of any single Agent. These Agents are theoretically or logically distributed, their behaviors are autonomous, but they all obey some protocols and are connected to accomplish certain task or achieve some goal together. Through interaction and cooperation, they can work out problems beyond the capability or knowledge of single Agent. Since Multi-Agent system is suitable for simulating human social system and characteristics of social activities, it has been used extensively in many War Simulation Systems of USA and many other western countries, such as IFOR, WARSIM2000, CFOR, OneSAF and so on. Besides, the movability and self-learning characteristics of Agent are also helpful for simulating the behavior of the fighting entity in battlefield more vividly.

T. Xiao, L. Zhang, and S. Ma (Eds.): ICSC 2012, Part II, CCIS 327, pp. 375–382, 2012.

2   Collaboration Model among Weapon Command Platforms Based on Agent

During the course of combat, as all weapon platforms have their own organizations, a command relation exists between the upper-lever weapon platform and the lower-level weapon platform. Every organized troop has its own command and control mechanism, such as the platoon-level combating unit is commanded by the platoon leader, and the regiment-level combating unit has its own command post. There are information like orders, reports and notices needed to be interacted among different combating units, therefore, the element of organization (also can be called affiliation relationship among weapon platforms) is quite important. This paper put forward the collaboration model among weapon platforms based on interchange language KQML of Agent. The grammar of KQML language is based on balanced parentheses table similar to LISP language, with the first element is operation name, and the other parts are parameters, each parameter is a match of parameter name/parameter. The following is a simple example of a single tank reports to the platoon leader about finding an enemy tank:

```
(report: find-enemy(category? tank)
    :receiver row-leader
        :sender 2-tank
        :language normal)
```

Among which, report is the operation name, the value of parameter name find-enemy is the content of this communication, meaning that tank is what found; the value of parameter receiver indicates the Agent name receiving this report, and the value of parameter sender indicates the Agent name of who sending this message.

The communication among weapon platform models adopts KQML language, and it roughly can be divided into 4 situations: report, request, order and notice. The former two situations are normally sending information by lower-level weapon platform to upper-level weapon platform, while the latter two situations are normally sending information by upper-level weapon platform to lower-level weapon platform. As during the course of combat, the normal situation is to command level by level, but there are also overstepping command sometimes, so the command model under normal situation is shown as Figure 1. The collaboration model among weapon platforms is established by the organizations, converging upon higher lever combat unit gradually from every single weapon platform. The command and decision-making system of lower-level combat unit will send reports and requests to the upper-level information blackboard, and receive orders and notices sent by upper-level command and decision-making system. Under normal situation, the information is passed level by level, but the upper-level command and decision-making system can bypass the immediate leadership to send information to subordinate combat units. And the KQML language can support this situation well.

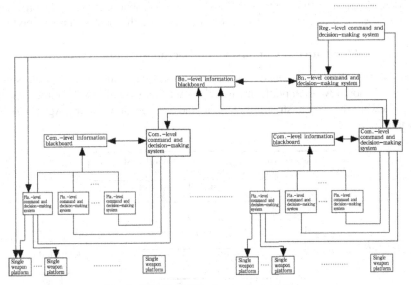

Fig. 1. Collaboration of command relations

3   Command and Decision-Making Model Based on Multi-agent

3.1   Behavior Description of Command and Decision-Making Agent

1) The combat unit receives the order, which will be explained and classified, and confirmed as the order-type information from the upper-level; then it will be stored in the incident list and be handled as high priority.

2) Through the scene-wish matching rule stored inside the knowledge base, it will trigger the matching rule and generate detailed ammunition support wish aggregate; without outside threat and incompatibility with current (or initial) intention, the wish aggregate will have the only wish to execute the order immediately, and store the wish sub-aggregate (that is the target aggregate) into the wish base. The above mentioned thought process is the lines of reasoning.

3) Screening in line with the cost or difficulties of achieving the goal and the capabilities of its own, it will take the optimized wish which can accomplish the task as the instant intention, that is to execute the combat order immediately, and store it into the intention base. The above mentioned thought process is called as the decision-making behavior. Intention base is a storage place in which the intentions to be executed will be stored according to generation sequence or execution priority.

4) Disassemble the intention to be executed (the most optimized plan), that is to execute the combat order immediately, into detailed action plan, and confirm the parameters of action plan. Plan is a structural body, which includes target, task, triggering terms, success terms and invalidation terms. As there successful examples (cases) of the orders of this type within the knowledge base, it can be selected directly from the base. The action parameters of this offence task are as follows: X combat unit, load at time of X:X, depart at time of X:X, pass through

route X, arrive at the location of X and execute combat task of X. Then the action plan will be assigned to relative combat units through task distribution module.

3.2   Logical Structure of Command and Decision-Making Agent Model

Based on the above-mentioned description of the capabilities and processing of modeling armored weapon platform, as well as the analyses of commanding behavior, we put forward the logical structure of command and decision-making Agent model as shown in Figure 2.

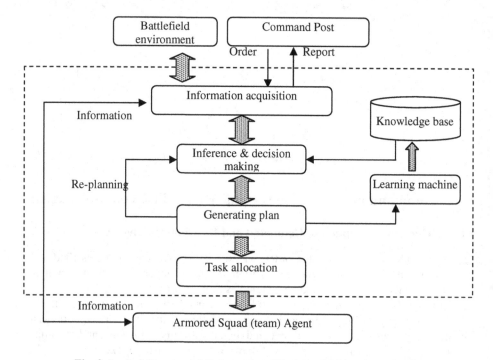

Fig. 2. Logical Structure of Command and Decision-Making Agent Model

4   Reasoning Process of Command and Decision-Making Model

This model utilizes layered reasoning approach. Considering the fuzzyness of human's thought process during the course of decision-making, as well as the fuzzyness of data which have similar rules, we adopt fuzzy logic to proceed inference. The planning layer utilizes artifical neuro-network fuzzy inference system (ANNFIS), decides which action to be used, with each sort of actions matching one ANNFIS. Execution layer uses optimized control law as per the controlled quantity to be calculated, so as to achieve the expected status and accomplish selected action.

The planning layer uses ANNFIS as shown in Figure 3 to accomplish fuzzy rule inference. In line with five procedures of fuzzy reasoning course, the ANNFIS is a five-layered forward network: input layer, fuzzification layer, fuzzifying rule layer, conclusion layer and output layer.

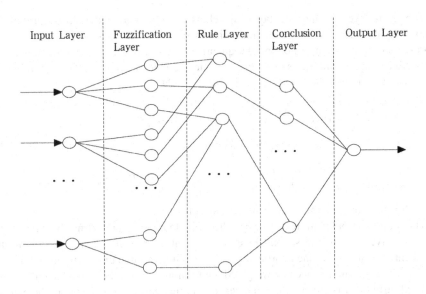

Fig. 3. ANNFIS Structure

The first layer is the input layer. Each neuron represents an input variable, its quantity equals to the number n of variables which exist in the preconditions of fuzzifying rule, that is, N1 = n. It will transfer the input value to the next layer, and the transfer function is 1. As per the preconditions of each sort of rules, the input variable is a subaggregate of rule preconditions aggregate.

$$f_i^{(1)} = x_i^{(0)} = x_i \tag{1}$$

$$x_i^{(1)} = g_i^{(1)} = f_i^{(1)} \qquad i = 1,2,...,n \tag{2}$$

Among which, xi(1) is the initial input variable; gi(i) is the network transfer function; and fi(i) is rule relevance grade function.

The second layer is fuzzification layer. Each neuron represents a language variate-value, to calculate the membership grade function μji of each input subvalue in the fuzzy set of language variate-value, we adopts bell shaped function:

$$f_{ij}^{(2)} = -\frac{(x_i^{(1)} - c_{ij})^2}{\sigma_{ij}^2} \tag{3}$$

$$x_{ij}^{(2)} = \mu_i^{\ j} = g_{ij}^{(2)} = e^{f_{ij}^{(2)}} = e^{-\frac{(x_i - c_{ij})^2}{\sigma_{ij}^2}} \tag{4}$$

$$i = 1,2,..n \qquad j = 1,2,..m_i \qquad N_2 = \sum_{i=1}^{n} m_i$$

In the formula, n represents the number of dimension of the input variable, mi is the fuzzy partition number for the ith input variable, N2 is the number of neurons in the second layer. Cij and σij represent the center and width of membership function respectively.

The third layer is the rule layer, which is used to match the preconditions of fuzzifying rule and to calculate the relevance grade of each rule. Each neuron represents one fuzzifying rule, and the quantity of neurons equal to that of fuzzifying rules. Since the preconditions of fuzzifying rule is connected by and, the neuron in this layer will accomplish the fuzzifying calculation AND.

$$f_k^{(3)} = \min\{x_{1i_1}^{(2)}, x_{2i_2}^{(2)}, ..., x_{ni_n}^{(2)}\} = \min\{\mu_1^{i_1}, \mu_2^{i_2}, ..., \mu_n^{i_n}\} \tag{5}$$

$$x_k^{(3)} = g_k^{(3)} = f_k^{(3)} \tag{6}$$

$$i_1 \in (1,2,...m_1) \qquad i_2 \in (1,2,...m_2)$$
$$i_n \in (1,2,...m_n) \qquad k = 1,2,...m$$

In the formula, m is the number of fuzzifying rules.

The total node N3 = m in this layer. The weighted value connecting the neurons in the third layer and in the second layer is constant 1 or 0. If the rule preconditions represented by a certain one neuron has the fuzzifying variable matching one neuron in the second layer, the connection weighted value should be 1, otherwise it should be 0.

The fourth layer is the conclusion layer. Each rule neuron is connected to the neuron representing relevant conclusion in this layer. The number of neurons in this layer N4 is the number of actions for each sort of rules. Each rule even having the same conclusion will effect the reasoning result, thus the transfer function of conclusion neurons is designed as S function:

$$f_l^{(4)} = \sum_k \omega_{kl} x_k^{(3)} \tag{7}$$

$$x_l^{(4)} = g_l^{(4)} = \frac{1}{1+e^{-f_l^{(4)}}} = \frac{1}{1+e^{-\sum_k \omega_{kl} x_k^3}} \tag{8}$$

$$l = 1,2,... \quad N_4, \qquad i = 1,2,...r_j \quad k = 1,2,..r_l$$

r_l represents the number of the nodes in the third layer matched by the lth node in the fourth layer. Among which, ω_{kl} means the weighted value between the kth neuron in the rule layer and the lth neuron in the conclusion layer.

The fifth layer is the output layer. The number of output neuron equals to that of output variable, and the output of this reasoning network is the sequence number of actions adopted, thus N5 = 1. the neurons in this layer will complete clarified calculation and output precise value. The process of clarification adopts weighted average method.

$$f^{(5)} = \frac{\sum_{l=1}^{N_4} (x_l^{(4)} \times l)}{\sum_{l=1}^{N_4} x_l^{(4)}} \tag{9}$$

$$x^{(5)} = y = g^{(5)} = f^{(5)} \tag{10}$$

Then conduct rounding calculation to y and will get the sequence number of the solution.

5   Example of Decision-Making on Tank Platoon Formation Selection

There are many factors affecting tank formation, such as terrain, enemy's situation, etc., the tank platoon should take all factors into consideration when selecting formation, and it should be considered carefully when formulating rules. This paper has stored the decision-making rules of selecting tank platoon formation so as to perform matching during reasoning. For example,

When the mission of tank platoon is marching, which generates the marching fact, and the rule is as follow:

```
IF (marching) THEN formation is column
```

When encountering enemy during marching, the mission is changed to reencounter, which generates rencounter fact, and the rule is as follow:

```
IF (rencounter) THEN formation is del
```

When the tank platform find an enemy target which make our side need to change formation accordingly, it should send report to the information blackboard, the KQML grammar should be:

```
( report: find-enemy (category? Enemy-tank3)

        :receiver row-blackboard

    :sender 1-tank

  :language normal)
```

As for the selection of formation, it should be decided in line with formation changing rule inside the inference machine and select the optimized formation, then send orders to every single platform, the KQML grammar should be:

```
( command: change formation(category: triangle)

        :receiver 1-tank

    :sender row-leader

  :language normal)
```

6   Concluding Remarks

Through the above-mentioned discussion, we can see that the interactive language KQML model based on Agent is comparatively suitable for simulating behaviors of command and control of CGF entity. Because it clearly portrayed the mental status (belief, wishes, intentions etc.) of single Agent, which decides the behavior of CGF entity, and the mental status of CGF entity provides a visualized explanation for its behavior, and it is comparatively easy to describe the generating mechanism of CGF behavior. This paper set Agent as a method to analyze problems and as a base unit of modeling to establish command entity. Here we still adopt the modeling frame based on interactive language KQML of Agent to establish the behavior model of command and decision-making Agent, using fuzzy logic to perform inference and generate command and decision-making behaviors like command and mission monitoring.

References

1. Duan, G., Qian, L., Wang, J., et al.: Multi-Intelligent-Agents System——A New Production Run Mode. Chinese Mechanical Engineering 9(2), 23–27 (1998)
2. Yang, L., Guo, Q.: Progress on the Study of Computer-Generated Forces. Computer Simulation 17(3), 4–7 (2000)
3. Kim, B.-I., Heragu, S.S., Graves, R.J., et al.: A Hybrid Scheduling and Control System Architecture for Warehouse Management. IEEE Transactions on Robotics and Automation 19(6), 991–1001 (2003)
4. Pew, R.W., Mavor, A.S.: Modelling human and organization behavior: Application to Military Simulations, pp. 335–341. National Academic Press, Washington, D.C (1998)
5. Barry, G.S.: Unifying Expert System AND The Decision Science. Operational Research (1), 12–17 (1996)

Research on the Distributed Environment Module of SPMM

Shengjie Wang[1,2,*], Fengju Kang[1,2], Huizhen Yang[1,2], and Hong Han[1,2]

[1] Marine College of Northwestern Polytechnical University, Xi'an, China
[2] National Key Laboratory of Underwater Information Process and Control, Xi'an, China
xxm1960@126.com

Abstract. To solve the big traffic problem caused by centralized environment model in the Simulation Platform of Military-intelligent-UUV based on MAS (SPMM), proposed a distributed environment model, extracted the environmental elements for concept modeling by taking the environment as an intelligent and dynamic object, designed the operation system structure of the distributed environment model, and advanced a method that combined the distributed environment with interest management. The simulation verified that the method can effectively reduce the traffic between UUV and the environment, and help keeping the space consistency. The research provided technical support for SPMM.

Keywords: Military-intelligent-UUV, distributed environment, environment concept model.

1 Introduction

In the SPMM, the perception of UUV comes from the environment and its action has effect on the environment, so the modeling of the environment is one of the most important technologies problems during the process of building the SPMM, and it plays a key role in the formation of the system complexity. In the traditional distributed simulation [1], the models of military-intelligent-UUV are deployed in computers respectively, while the environment model is deployed in one computer, which is called centralized environment model. In the distributed simulation, every UUV node needs to interact with the environment model, which will bring huge network traffic and cause communication delays and congestion more easily. At this time, the centralized environment model will limits the system size and performance. Therefore, the distributed environment model is considered [2] for reducing the communication traffic between the UUV node and the environment node. In this paper, after the concept modeling of environmental elements, a distributed environment operation system structure is designed, and a method that combining the distributed environment and the interest management is putted forward to help keeping the space consistency.

---

* Shengjie Wang (1985-),female, doctoral graduate student, research in computer simulation.

T. Xiao, L. Zhang, and S. Ma (Eds.): ICSC 2012, Part II, CCIS 327, pp. 383–389, 2012.

2   The Underwater Environment Conceptual Model of Military-Intelligent-UUV

Everything out of the military-intelligent-UUV is considered as its environment, which mainly contains the natural environment and the battle environment. The natural environment includes topographical environment and water environment, and the battle environment includes enemy environment and our environment. During the UUV's mission, all kinds of environment have certain degree of threat on it: it will be damaged if the distance from reefs of topographical environment is shorter than its turn radius; the temperature and salinity of water environment will influence its sonar system, control system, and the acoustic communication [3]; it will be attacked after entering the detection zone of enemy's weapon platform of enemy environment; in our environment, it may damaged by collision in formation.

The environment considered here is not a passive, unchanged object [4], it is an intelligent and dynamic object that carries the following functions:

(1).Space position and sequence function: provides the relationship of the spatial position and sequence of individuals in the environment; ensures the related behavior can be carried out as normal, such as transform and keep formation.

(2). Information guidance function: provides local environment information for individual behavior decision and guides the UUV to complete its mission. For example, the topographical environment informs UUV there is a reef nearby and gives guidance for obstacle avoidance.

(3).Effect function: the environment will have effects on the UUV under certain condition, for example, if the obstacle avoidance does not happen in time, the reef will damage the UUV. And the attack of enemy also will damages or even destroys the UUV.

Meanwhile, UUV can effect the environment too. Taking the effect as the result of UUV's action, that is to say, UUV changes the environmental states by executing actions. In order to describe action, we introduced the current environment table, delete table and add table. In this description, each action includes four major elements: (1) Name: the ID of the action; (2) Current environmental state table: describes the parameters of the current environmental state, which is the precondition of the execution of action; (3) Delete table: describes the environmental states that turn into false after the execution of action; (4) Add table: describes the environmental states that turn into true after the execution of action.

So the action can be described by a quaternion. Assuming that UUV can execute a fixed set of action, $Action = \{\alpha_1, ..., \alpha_n\}$, any action $\alpha \in Action$ can be described as follow:

$$< ID, Sta_\alpha, Del_\alpha, Add_\alpha > \tag{1}$$

In which, ID represents the name of action, Sta_α represents the current environmental state table, Del_α represents the delete table, Add_α represents the add table.

3   The Key Technology of the Distributed Environment Construction

3.1   The Construction of the Environmental Elements Model

In the distributed environment, the environment model needs to be rebuilt in every computer node by using the transferred environment information. According to the above analysis, not only the geographical attributes, but also the physical attributes, the functional attributes and other information need to be transferred. So, In order to facilitate the interaction of the environment model between nodes, a unified format should provide for describing the characteristics of environment. Comprehensive consideration of the dynamic environment function and the effect UUV make to the environment, and other factors, abstract the environmental elements model as follows:

$$E =< ID, Pos, Type, Attr, Eff, Sta > \qquad (2)$$

Among them,

ID is the only mark for the element, used to differentiate the different elements of the environment;

Pos is the position information of the element, recorded by the boundary data of the elements of three-dimensional environment;

$Type$ is the type information of the element, used to distinguish different kinds of elements of the system;

$Attr$ contains all kinds of attribute information of elements, different elements can define different attribute information, but all the definition must follow the same data format. Here is the format for defining attribute: $Attr =< Name, Type, Value >$, in which, $Name$ represents the name of the attribute, $Type$ represents the data types of the attribute's value, $Value$ represents the attribute's value;

Eff is the effect of the element. It represents the effect that the environmental element did to UUV or other elements, mainly used to represent UUV's physical attributes changes caused by environment. Define $Eff =< Name, Con, Res, Cons >$, in which, $Name$ is the name of the effect, Con is the condition needed to accomplish the effect, Res is the result caused by the effect, $Cons$ is the additional constraints;

Sta is the mark of the state of the environment.

By using this environment modeling method, we extract the general character of the environmental elements, making environment data modeled in a unified format, causing the hierarchical relationships between the parameters more clearly, and meanwhile, embodying the functional and dynamic of the environment.

3.2   Interest Management

The particularity of military-intelligent-UUV's environment decides that if it is detected by enemy's weapon platform, it might be attacked, at this time, there will be a lot of interactions between two sides, and all the interactions will have effect on the environment. Under this condition, if we still use distributed environment only, the huge amount of communication will still affect the real-time of network. Besides, the traditional method of testing whether other entity is within the detecting scope needs to scan all entity information before judging whether any entity is in the detection radius. This will seriously affect the real-time of simulation. Therefore, a method that combines the distributed environment and interest management is putting forward.

There are two main purpose of interest management [5]: firstly, in order to reduce the taking up of the network bandwidth, reducing the unrelated data; secondly, reduce the processing costs of the simulation nodes caused by accepting redundant data. In order to achieve the above two purposes, interest management decides which objects can communicate and what information need to be transformed between the objects that exist communication relationship.

Define the interest space as the environment space contained within a circle, which taking object position as centre and the detection range as radius. If object A's interest space intersects object B's, we say that object A is interested in object B.

When the simulation operated into the situation that enemy weapons platform can detects UUV, that is to say, the enemy weapons platform is interested in UUV, dividing a new environment model, whose represented area covers both sides, and distributing it for both sides' node for updating, and because the range of the environment loaded by this module is mainly where the conflicts concentrated, it will help reducing the number of update. Then, establishing a communication link between the interest objects to transport the related data directly, which can reducing network communication traffic.

3.3 The Operation System Structure Design of the Distributed Environment Model

The simulation systems developed nowadays often use parallel and distributed technology to solve the problem of calculation of simulation entities, they distributed the simulation entities to different computers in order to improve the performance, however, the environment model is often operated in one computer node. The advantage of this structure is the process of the environment is simple, and the disadvantage is obviously too: all the other entities need to interact with it, as the number of entities increase, the communication load of the system will increasing. So, here the environment module becomes the bottlenecks of system performance, and limits the size of the simulation.

In order to reduce the communication between the entities model and the environment model during the operation, dividing the environment model and distribute them on different nodes, the local environment model is responsible for providing environment information, interacting and real-time adjusting of the local UUV. The main functions of local environment model are:

(1) Simulating the environment of the divided area according to the data distributed by environment node;

(2) According to the subscribing of UUV, retrieving the environmental parameters of the subscribe node object's position, calculating the environmental constraints of the object and sending them to the subscribe node. If the parameters subscribed are beyond the scope, it requires the environment manager for data updating, and gets the environmental parameters of the new divided area;

(3) Uploading the changes of the area's environmental state caused by UUV to the environment node to complete the data exchange and the updating of the environment information during the simulation process.

The designed distributed environment operation system structure is showed in Fig.1.

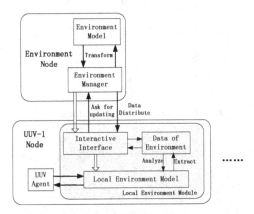

Fig. 1. Structure of distributed environment operation system

The figure only shows the relationship between environment node and the UUV-1 node, and all the other UUV node's relationship with the environment node is same. After the simulation begins, a square area, which takes UUV' position as centre and six times detection range as sides, is divided as local environment by the environment node. Then, the environment information of this area is distributed through the interface to local environment module on the UUV node for building the local environment model and communicating with UUV. If UUV has effect on the environment, the changed environmental states will be extracted and uploaded to the environment node through the interactive interface to real-time update the entire environment. When UUV is about to run out of the area, local environment model will send the update requirement to the environment manager through the interactive interface. During the simulation, if the movement of other UUV nodes will affect the local environment of the UUV, but it's not the time for updating the data and the changed environmental states can not be informed in time, so the space no-consistency problem will occur. For example, if the enemy's weapon platform which UUV take as target is destroyed by other UUV, but the local environment module's data has not been updated, therefore, it will attacks the entity that is not exist. In order to avoid happening this no-consistency problem, design a communicate route between environment manager and the interactive interface, and distribute the changed environmental states information to the local environment module through interactive interface directly (showed by the 45°arrow in the Fig.1).

4   Simulation Result

Building the distributed SPMM based on HLA, and the system structure is showed in Fig.2. The platform adopted the designed distribute operation system structure of environment model, every simulation entity node has its local environment module, and both the environment node and the local environment module are built by the extracted elements.

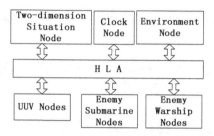

Fig. 2. Simulation System Framework

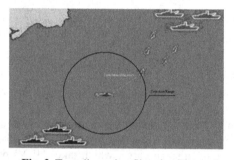

Fig. 3. Two-dimension Situation Picture

When the enemy's weapon platform detects UUV, as it showed in Fig.3, the two-dimension situation picture, introduces the interest management and builds the communication route between the enemy submarine and the detected UUV for transforming related data directly, by which reducing the network communication amount.

5   Conclusion

Through the simulation test, using the proposed structure as the environmental operation part of the distribute SPMM can effectively reduce the network communication burden brought by the interaction between intelligent UUV and environment model, lessen the network load, and relieve the consistency problem caused by distributed environment model. And this structure provides technical support for the simulation platform building.

Acknowledgments. This paper is supported by the foundation of "National key laboratory of underwater information process and control Foundation (9140c2305041001)", "Foundational Research of Northwestern Polytechnical University (NWPU2011JC0242)", and "Supporting Technology of Shipping Pre-research (11J4.1.1)".

References

1. Uhrmacher, A., Gugler, K.: Distributed, Parallel simulation of multiple, deliberative agents. In: Proceedings of Parallel and Distributed Simulation Conference (PADS), pp. 101–110 (2000)
2. Ye, C.-Q.: Research on Key Techniques of Multi-agent Platform for Distributed Simulation of Complex System. National University of Defense Technology, 36–40 (2006)
3. Kang, X.-D., Li, Y.-P.: A Kind of Virtual Implementation Method of Ocean Temperature and Salinity. J. Computer Simulation 27(5), 239–242 (2010)
4. Yang, Z.-M., Si, G.-Y., Li, Z.-Q., Zhang, F.: ARE: New Conceptual Model for Social Crowd Behavior Modeling. Journal of System Simulation 24(2), 435–440 (2012)
5. Morse, K.L.: An Adaptive, Distributed Algorithm for Interest Management. University of California, USA (2000)

Modeling and Simulation of Pilot Behavior Interfaced with Avionics System

Huaxing Wu[1,*], Fengju Kang[1], Wei Huang[2], and Yi Lu[2]

[1] Marine College, North Western Polytechnical University, Xi'an, Shanxi, 710072, China
[2] Aeronautics & Astronautics Engineering College, Air Force Engineering University, Xian, Shanxi, 710038, China
Wuhuaxing1978@163.com

Abstract. To represent the complex behavior of a human pilot operating a fighter aircraft, an agent-based modeling and simulation method is proposed in this paper. First a live virtual constructive simulation platform including an agent-based avionics system model is introduced as a test-bed. Through refining the interface information flow between a pilot and avionics system, employing fuzzy reasoning to mimic the information processing of human, and applying Bayesian network to situation assessment, then using fuzzy Petri-net to make decisions and plan actions, the hybrid agent-based pilot model will sense, think, learn and act as a human pilot do. The ongoing effort indicates its feasibility and validity.

Keywords: Pilot Behavior Representation, Avionics System, Agent-based Modeling, Situation Assessment, Decision Making.

1 Introduction

As more and more air combat simulation systems are developed for training and warfare analysis, the cost spending on human and asset is increasing, especially in the areas of military exercises that usually have many pilot-in-the-loop simulators joined[1]. To reduce the cost and make the simulating progress easy to organize and manage, a cost effective way is to replace the manned simulator with computer generated force (CGF) [2-3]. To simulate a manned fighter aircraft, the most important thing is to develop an aircraft system model and a pilot model driving it.

In an ongoing effort, we are creating an agent-based avionics system model which is able to realistically stand in for the whole aircraft platform including flight control system and weapon system [4]. And at the same time we begin to develop a general pilot model for testing it in a live virtual constructive simulation (LVCS) environment. Our system design approaches have been proved feasible and informal results so far are promising. Many pilot models mainly emphasizes on its situation assessment, decision making, or maneuver control, omitting the detailed interaction between pilot and

---

* Huaxing Wu (1978-), male, PhD Candidate, research on system simulation technology, theory and application of fire control system.

T. Xiao, L. Zhang, and S. Ma (Eds.): ICSC 2012, Part II, CCIS 327, pp. 390–398, 2012.
© Springer-Verlag Berlin Heidelberg 2012

system. It often leads to lack of fidelity. To increase the human-system fidelity, this paper presents an agent-based modeling (ABM) and simulation method to model a pilot behavior, and describes the detailed interaction interfaced with this avionics system model.

2   Test-Bed for the Avionics System Model and Pilot Model

Originally, we developed a type of simulation software for training to manipulate manually most aircraft equipments. Since onboard avionics system is the most important system a pilot interacts with, so we construct a multi-agent based avionics system model to represent the whole aircraft platform.

Figure 1 shows the structure of agent-based avionics system model (ABASM) and its interface relation to other agent in the LVCS environment. By decomposing avionics system model into more concrete and subtle sub-models with respect to its hierarchy structure, and creating a distributed communication agent model complying with actual 1553B data bus, the system model can achieve a high fidelity from the bottom up.

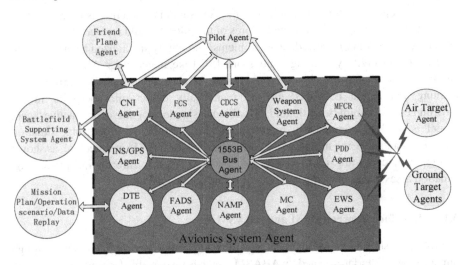

Fig. 1. Multi-agent Structure of Avionics System Model

Centralized on the ABASM, a distributed LVCS test-bed software architecture is constructed for test, as Figure 2 shows. Previous work was emphasized on modeling subsystem with enhanced fidelity, and partly verified the validity and utility of the whole avionics system model. In addition, to replace former pilot agent controlled by human in the test-bed, now computer generated agent model is designed for pilot behavior representation with the little modified interfaces to other components. In the following section, this pilot agent model (PAM) is described.

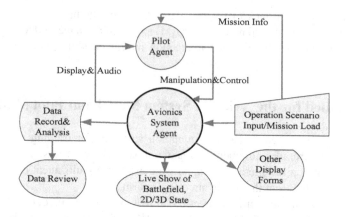

Fig. 2. Structure of LVCS Test-bed

3   Agent-Based Pilot Model Structure

As explicit representations of pilot behavior, PAM should offer a means for replicating many of the abilities, attributes, and features of the pilot it would replace [1]. ABM has been used to model numerous diverse problems, and highly specialized agents perform realistically in military training simulations [5]. Like many other ABM systems, a credible PAM should also incorporate various AI algorithms such as reinforcement learning and neural networks, etc., to realistically depict pilot behavior in the environment of complex battlefield. Traditional simple, cognitive or reactive agent model is hard to competently represent human information processing, situation assessment and decision making. So PAM employs hybrid ABM architecture, as shown in Figure 3, consisting of four layers of behavior model: Information processing, situation assessment, decision and planning, and action execution.

3.1   Interface between PAM and ABASM

As figure 3 shows, PAM interacts with the simulated environment only through human-system interface owned by ABASM which is responsible for sensing and acting on the environment. It means necessary to refine the interface information flow between a pilot and avionics system.

In a real cockpit, a pilot mainly sense information via sight of instrument, head-up display (HUD) and multi-function displays (MFD), along with audios from earphones or other sound devices. All this video and audio information is originated from subsystem owned by ABASM, such as cockpit display and control subsystem (CDCS). So we have to trace back to original subsystem data, to represent these videos and audios.

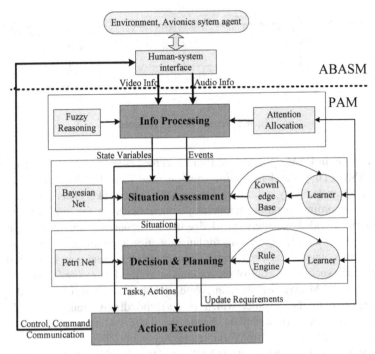

Fig. 3. Hybrid ABM architecture of Pilot Agent Model

For example, Table 1 lists a part of information from PAM to ABASM model, it also exposes a few parameters representing important information a pilot may see in HUD video, and these parameters are possibly originated from various sub-system but can be acquired directly from CDCS model.

Table 1. Example of Data Flow between PAM and ABASM

Data name	From	To
Throttle Position	PAM	ABASM
Stick X Position	PAM	ABASM
Stick Y Position	PAM	ABASM
Main Mode Switch	PAM	ABASM
Heading angle	ABASM	PAM
Pitch angle	ABASM	PAM
Roll angle	ABASM	PAM
Air Speed	ABASM	PAM
Altitude	ABASM	PAM

3.2   Information Processing Based on Fuzzy Reasoning

On the basis of interface information, PAM uses fuzzy logic to mimic the human information process, that are more compatible with the way a pilot tend to reason qualitatively. Fuzzy reasoning turns real-valued sensor data into fuzzy linguistic values, and then uses them to reason and make decision, as shown in Figure 4.

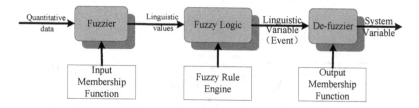

Fig. 4. Process of Fuzzy Reasoning

For example, in PAM, quantitative flight parameters such as air speed and altitude from ABASM (They stand in for information seen form HUD or instruments in a cockpit) are translated by a fuzzier to linguistic values, like faster, slower, higher, lower, etc., according to input membership functions. Such functions and linguistic values can be provided by expert knowledge in air-combat domain. Fuzzy logic is used to produces state variables and events for later situation assessment. Especially in some emergent cases where real-time continuous maneuver execution is needed, PAM should produce successive control on stick and throttle. For example, when escaping from a missile, PAM may directly manipulate stick to turn left or right according to the position relative to the missile, which is correspondingly translated to linguistic variables such as left, right, up or down, etc. Then the manipulation on stick is translated into continuous control variable ranging from -1.0 to 1.0.

As regards audio information, it can be directly translated into notification event and some quantitative values which can also be processed on fuzzy logic. In addition, to mimic human realistically, attention allocation decided by mental state is added to limit pilot awareness at a certain time.

3.3   Situation Assessment Based on Bayesian Network

At the layer of Situation assessment, PAM uses all system state variables and stochastic events to infer and assess current situation, which refers to recognition-primed decision making. Since traditional production-rule based situation assessment is hard to present human cognition process facing uncertain environmental condition, hence, Bayesian belief network based modeling method is employed to represent the information fusing ability and reasoning ability for a human pilot to judge target threat and estimate own attacking opportunity along with incomplete and ambiguous perception. Considering that as time goes a pilot can make exact and stable assessment when cues cumulate, it is necessary to employ dynamic Bayesian network than traditional static network. So here we uses discrete fuzzy dynamic Bayesian network (DFDBN) to deal with this probability reasoning process with respect to input fuzzy state variables and former discrete slices of time.

The basic ideal of DFDBN includes that [6]: it first constructs the network structure incorporating observed nodes and hide nodes that represent key state variables and their relation; it creates discrete fuzzy sets for input fuzzy state variables (fuzzy linguistic values) based on special knowledge bases, then uses them as observed values and determine their membership to diverse state with probability. For the DFDBN with n hide nodes and m observed nodes, the joint distribution probability function can be described by Equation (1) [7]:

$$P(x_{11}, x_{12}, \cdots, x_{1n}, \cdots, x_{T1}, x_{T2}, \cdots x_{Tn} \mid y_{11o}, y_{12o}, \cdots, y_{1mo}, \cdots, y_{T1o}, y_{T2o}, \cdots y_{Tmo})$$

$$= \sum_{y_{11}, y_{12}, \cdots, y_{Tm}} \frac{\prod_{i,j} P(y_{ij} \mid P_a(Y_{ij})) \prod_{i,k} P(x_{ik} \mid P_a(X_{ik}))}{\sum_{x_{11}, x_{12}, \cdots, x_{Tk}} \prod_{i,j} P(y_{ij} \mid P_a(Y_{ij})) \prod_{i,k} P(x_{ik} \mid P_a(X_{ik}))} \times \prod_{i,j} P(Y_{ij} = y_{ijo}) \,, \; i \in [1, T], j \in [1, T], k \in [1, n] \tag{1}$$

Where, X_{ij} means a hide node, Y_{ij} means a observed node, in which j is the node number and i is the time slice number. x_{ij} is a value state of a hide node x_{ij}, y_{ij} is a observed value of node Y_{ij}. $P(Y_{ij} = y_{ijo})$ is the probability when the observed value of node Y_{ij} is y_{ijo}.

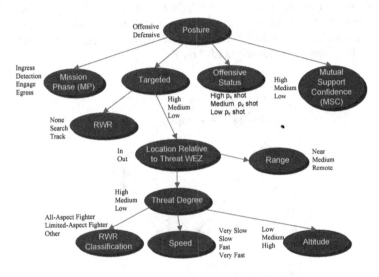

Fig. 5. Bayesian Network Used in PAM

In PAM, we uses Bayesian network mainly to assess whether the mental posture of pilot is offensive or defensive, as shown in Figure 5. In addition, we can also use layered Bayesian network to deduce whether he is targeted by the enemy aircraft, as well as his location relative to threat WEZ (weapon engagement zone) and the threat degree. However, too many nodes and time slices will reduce the computing efficiency and tractability that are both important for real-time application of PAM. So in PAM the number of time slice is limited to three, and the amount of nodes used is decreased by simplification. The structure and initial membership of Bayesian network are determined by domain experts, and they are stored in a knowledge base. Additionally, they can be leveraged by a learner according to experimental results and real-time update requirements in special condition where PAM will cater to some new added functions which may be available in the future avionics system.

3.4   Decision and Plan Based on Fuzzy Petri-Net

At the layer of decision and planning in PAM, the assessed situations are regarded as fuzzy input variables to select appropriate responses and actions as a human pilot do. Since traditional rule-based technology is hard to process uncertain and incomplete situations, we employs fuzzy Petri-net (FPN) to model pilot's behavior of decision making and mission planning. FPN provides visual graphical models for fuzzy production rules, which are usually associated with membership, credibility, certainty and probability [8]. Here the FPN is expressed as [9]

$$FPN=(P, T, C, I, O, Mp, Th, W) \tag{2}$$

Where, the place P represents the set of input situations and output conclusion. The transition T represents the rules including "AND" and "OR". The predicate C is a set of proposition used to represent real situations and decisions. The predicate I and O represent the link between P and T. The predicate Mp is the membership value of P, Th is the value of T, and W is the weight of P on T.

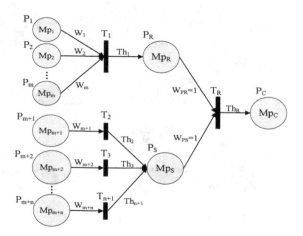

Fig. 6. Two-layered Structure of FPN in PAM

In practical applications of PAM, decisions and plans are made based on certain rules associated with a conjunction of many conditions and situations. The assessed situations may be uncertain and partial, and PAM should use a human-like method to process them combining with supporting conditions and restrictive ones. So we construct a hybrid FPN for each rule and associated situations, which employs a layered structure as shown in Figure 6.

In this FPN, "Mp_R", "Mp_S" and "Th_R" are three fixed hidden nodes to fire the rule. "Mp_R" represents the restrictive conditions, "Mp_S" represents the supporting conditions, and the weight for them is constant 1. "Th_R", a value between 0 and 1, is used to represent the certainty of the rule, which can be determined by domain experts and altered by learner. "Mp_C", the value of output place "Pc", represents the membership or probability of selecting a task or action under the input situation and this rule, and it can be computed as

$$Mp_c = Mp_R \times Mp_S \times Th_R \tag{3}$$

Thus, the final value of "Mp_C" can be computed as

$$Mp_c = Th_R \times \left(Th_1 \prod_{i=1}^{m}(W_i Mp_i) \right) \times \left(\sum_{j=1}^{n}(Th_{j+1}W_{m+j}Mp_{m+j}) \right) \tag{4}$$

Here, both the weight W and the value Th are determined by domain expert knowledge, and they can also be leveraged by a learner in PAM to create a more suitable rule engine [10].

4   Application of PAM

The development of both PAM and ABASM is an ongoing effort that is far from completion because of inherent complexity. For the nonce, in the LVCS test-bed as shown by Figure 2, we create an application of PAM to acquire data from another application of ABASM, process information, assess situations, make decisions, plan actions, and then drive the model of aircraft. Figure 7 shows an example of PAM, in which PAM drives ABASM to intercept the enemy aircraft.

Fig. 7. Example for PAM Used to Drive ABASM

In this application, we demonstrate the feasibility of the software architecture of PAM and its layered modules and the PAM application can realistically interact with ABASM. It also proves the validity of the key arithmetic approaches, such as fuzzy logic, Bayesian Network, and Petri-net. But we also find the real-time performance and intelligence of model are not satisfying in current test environment, where the learners for APM are not completed yet.

5   Conclusions

In this paper, we have presented an agent-based method for modeling and simulating the complex behavior of a human pilot interfaced with avionics system. We also outline the LVCS test-bed with the avionics system model and pilot mode. Especially, the pilot agent model is detailed from the architecture to the adoptive methodologies. Pilot study and its application prove that this agent-base pilot model is valid and it can be used to realistically drive aircraft models. Besides continued development of details in this model, future effort will be emphasized on the improvement of the real-time performance and intelligence of this model. The promising results have great application value for large-scale simulation events that often need participation of many human pilots.

References

1. Brett, B.E.: Developing Human Performance Model-Driven Synthetic Teammates for Command and Control Simulation: CART Virtual Warriors. In: Proceedings of the 15th Conference on Behavior Representation in Modeling and Simulation (2006)
2. Wallenstein, C., Reilly, S.N., Harper, K.A.: Building a Human Behavior Model for a Collaborative Air-Combat Domain. In: Proceedings of the 15th Conference on Behavior Representation in Modeling and Simulation, Orlando, Florida (2006)
3. Craig, K., Doyal, J., Brett, B.: Development of a Hybrid Model of Tactical Fighter Pilot Behavior Using IMPRINT Task Network Modeling and the Adaptive Control of Thought – Rational (ACT-R). In: Proceedings of the 11th Conference on Computer Generated Force and Behavior Representation, Orlando, Florida (2002)
4. Wu, H., Wei, H., Kang, F., Lu, Y.: Research on Operational Simulation for Avionics System Based on Multi-Agent. In: Proceedings of Thirteenth Chinese Conference, SSTA 2011, Huangshan, China, pp. 427–431 (2011)
5. Sonnenshein, J., Ratonel, M., Keller, C., Wong, L.: Integrating Agent-Based Models into Warfare Assessment Simulations to Enhance Human Decision Making Modeling. In: 2009 Summer Simulation Interoperability Workshop Papers (2009)
6. Wu, T., Zhang, A., Li, L.: Study on the Threat Assessment in Air Combat based on Discrete Fuzzy Dynamic Bayesian Network. Fire Control & Command Control, 56–69 (2009)
7. Shi, J., Gao, X., Li, X.: Modeling Air Combat Situation Assessment by Using Fuzzy Dynamic Bayesian Network. Journal of System Simulation 18, 1093–1096 (2006)
8. Yuan, J.: Petri-net based Modeling for Reliability of Complex System and Its Intelligent Analytical Method. National Defense Industry Press, Beijing (2011)
9. Shi, Z., Zhang, A., Liu, H.: Study on Air Combat Tactics Decision-making Based on Fuzzy Petri Nets. Journal of System Simulation 19, 63–66 (2007)
10. Sui, Q., Yeo, Y.-C., How, K.-Y.: An Advanced Rule Engine for Computer Generated Forces. In: Proceedings of the 17th Conference on Behavior Representation in Modeling and Simulation (2008)

Research and Application of Tank Gunners' Skills Model in Operation Simulation

Guanghui Li, Junqing Huang, Jian Han, and Yanping Fan

Department of Equipment Command and Administration,
Academy of Armored Force Engineering, 100072 Beijing, China

Abstract. Troops' forces not only have a relationship with weaponry equipment, but it is also related to operation skills of equipment-users tightly. Battle models using in operation simulation reveal weaponry capability, furthermore, skill element of warriors must be taken for account. By using the man-in-loop simulation experiment modeling method which the gunner takes participate in, this article analyses distribution principles of aiming-point, building the gunner's aiming precision model. Moreover, through exploring differences of gunner's individual skills on the basis of the mentioned work, gunners' operation skills distribution model including aiming-point judgement capability difference model and manipulation capability difference model is built. Moreover, by applying this model in operation simulation, the fidelity of operation simulation can be enhanced.

Keywords: tank gunner, operation skill, experiment modeling, operation simulation.

1 Foreword

Operation simulation is one of important application domains in simulation science and technology. Nowadays, firepower model based on equipment performances is utilized prevalently in operation simulation. No considering the element of operation staff, the simulation result can only reveal the merits and defects of both sides weaponry performances, the differences of troops battle forces can not be reflected, so as to influence the fidelity of operation simulation results[1][2].

Literature [3] brings forth a tank gunner model which need a huge amount of data to be calculated and a long simulation periods based on transferring function. Furthermore, how to make sure the differences among gunners in tank units is too hard, result in the requirement of operation simulation can not be satisfied.

Carrying through the research on differences of tank gunners aiming accuracy and manipulating skills, tank gunners manipulating skills models being the same with tactical large scale operation simulation application are built. Therefore, the result of operation simulation can reflect the difference of operation staff, revealing the contradiction of tank units battle forces.

T. Xiao, L. Zhang, and S. Ma (Eds.): ICSC 2012, Part II, CCIS 327, pp. 399–406, 2012.

2   Experimental Research on Tank Gunners Aiming Deviation Distribution Principles

There are lots of problems in experiment style adopted actual forces and equipments: the first, experiment system construction is very hard, and experiment organization is complicated. The second, the influence that comes from exterior environment elements is huge, it is hard to make sure the consistent of experimental parameters imported. The third, equipment can not be provided with the real time record experimental data capability, extra data recording apparatus is needed.

Advanced computer simulation technology is utilized fully. Aiming accuracy experiment on Gunners shooting is implemented in actual forces manipulation simulator. The main data of gunners aiming manipulation procession is recorded by program. Then, the experimental data is analyzed. The method is very effective in the research on gunners shooting aiming accuracy distribution regulation and individual skills differences.

(1) Design of experimental scheme

① Participator: Selecting A and B two different technological levels of tank gunners about 50 persons whose age is from 20 to 25, good health condition, excellent eyesight (above 1.0) in the same unit, the individual selected should undertakes equipment application for a long time, bearing certain ball cartridge shooting experiences.

② Experimental facilities: A suit of tank static shooting simulator which can not simulate dynamic shooting effects of vehicles, fire power control console is composed of accessories, manipulator, observing apparatus and chairs whose relative position is consistent with real vehicles. Computer real time graphic technology comes into being view. The summer forest, natural sunray, no shading, good atmosphere visibility are simulated. Experimental temperature is ranging from 20 to 25 degree, and the environment noise less than 50db.The fact that every performance which is identical to actual vehicles of simulator is qualified by testing is accepted by participators.

③ Visual shooting field: Referring to the collocation of tank shooting range terrain which is flatness, in this field, tanks are always in the state of horizontal level. Both tanks and targets that is a white square about 16 square meters are still. Target center and gunner trunnion are at the same height. Target distances are 1500 meters and 2000 meters separately.

④ Experimental times: Referring to paramilitary battle shooting experiment condition of first shoot straight experiment, each gunner should aiming the target 100 times in the distance of 1500 meters and 2000 meters separately. Each trigger action indicates the finishing of this aiming behavior.

⑤ Records of experimental data: Simulators can record data real time and save into disk in type of text file. The record contents includes aiming-point horizontal coordinate (x), aiming-point upright coordinate (y). Both x and y are floating point numbers (unit: meter), zero point is the center of target, x positive coordinate is rightwards and y positive coordinate is upwards.

⑥ Proceeding of experimental data: On the basis of deleting unqualified experimental data by data pretreatment, the experimental data is analyzed by Matlab software and Excel tool, achieving the distribution character value which involving mean value and belief degree range, mean variance and its belief degree range, hypothesis checkout results of distribution type in horizontal level and upright level. Distribution parameter estimate: adopting maximum similarity estimate method, the default value $\alpha = 0.05$, the value equaling to 95% of belief degree range is gotten. Hypothesis checkout of normal school: J-B(jbtest) and lillietest checkout method are selected, prominence level $\alpha = 0.05$.

(2) Experimental data statistics analysis
① Same individual aiming distribution regulation analysis
The data of x coordinate 192 group and y coordinate 193 group pass J-B(jbtest) or lillietest method. See Table 1 as follows.

Table 1. Experimental Data Distribution Regulation Statistics

Grade	Effective Number	X Coordinate		Y Coordinate	
		Normal Distribution Number	Percent	Normal Distribution Number	Percent
A	98	96	98.0%	96	98.0%
B	99	96	97.0%	97	98.0%

Conclusion: the shoot-aiming accuracy distribution single-direction of tank gunner obeys normal school.
② Different individuals otherness analysis
Treating statistical measure of A and B grade gunners aiming experiment in the distance of 1500 meters and 2000 meters separately. Through analyzing the principles of mean value and mean variance among different individuals, the individual differences among different gunners are gotten.

1) Mean value (μ) distribution analysis
Taking every aiming experimental mean value (μ) as sample, distribution regulation is researched, the result of which can be seen in Table 2 and Table 3.

Table 2. "X Coordinate Mean Value" Distribution Analysis

Grade	Distance	Scope	Mean Value	Mean Variance	Distribution and Checkout
A	1500	[-0.24, 0.17]	-0.045	0.107	normal pass
	2000	[-0.29, 0.18]	-0.070	0.116	normal pass
B	1500	[-0.31, 0.16]	-0.072	0.112	normal pass
	2000	[-0.38, 0.32]	-0.058	0.118	normal pass

Table 3. "Y Coordinate Mean Value" Distribution Analysis

Grade	Distance	Scope	Mean Value	Mean Variance	Distribution and Checkout
A	1500	[-0.25, 0.42]	0.060	0.181	normal pass
	2000	[-0.44, 0.41]	0.050	0.202	normal pass
B	1500	[-0.68, 0.89]	0.071	0.310	normal pass
	2000	[-1.02, 1.14]	0.093	0.453	normal pass

Conclusions:

- In the same distance, the mean value of the same technology rank individual aiming deviation distribution obeys normal distribution in horizontal and upright directions.
- Mean value represents the judgement deviation of target centre for gunners, which is mean value of all aiming-point deviation. As the increase of samples, the mean value inclines to zero.

2) Mean variance (σ) distribution analysis

Taking the mean variance (σ) of each aiming experiment as samples, the distribution regulation is analyzed, the result of which is showed as Table 4 and Table 5.

Table 4. "X Coordinate Mean Variance" Distribution Analysis

Grade	Distance	Scope	Mean Value	Mean Variance	Distribution and Checkout
A	1500	[0.11, 0.77]	0.364	0.188	normal pass
	2000	[0.09, 0.95]	0.417	0.219	normal pass
B	1500	[0.13, 0.99]	0.460	0.198	normal pass
	2000	[0.14, 0.88]	0.496	0.221	normal pass

Table 5. "Y Coordinate Mean Variance" Distribution Analysis

Grade	Distance	Scope	Mean Value	Mean Variance	Distribution and Checkout
A	1500	[0.13, 0.77]	0.415	0.152	normal pass
	2000	[0.05, 0.87]	0.402	0.192	normal pass
B	1500	[0.18, 1.01]	0.499	0.227	normal pass
	2000	[0.05, 0.93]	0.509	0.232	normal pass

Conclusions:
- In the same distance, the mean value of the same technology rank individual aiming deviation distribution obeys normal distribution in horizontal and upright directions.
- The mean value influence of "mean variance" is not huge for distance. Technology grades have a certain effect on mean value of "mean variance", the mean variance of "mean variance" is smaller for better-skill gunners.
- The mean variance of "mean variance" increases as distance augments. In the same distance, the mean variance of "mean variance" is smaller for better-skill gunners.

3   Tank Gunners Skill Model Construction

The diversity among tank gunners can be described by aiming-point judge capability diversity and manipulation capability diversity. On the basis of experiment analysis, the tank gunner skill models can be constructed as follows.

(1) Aiming-point judgement capability diversity model
Aiming-point judgement capability diversity models describe the distribution principles of aiming-point judgement accuracy in different shooting distances among different gunners, which are aiming-point judgement capability description of different gunners. Aiming-point judgement model obeys normal school whose mean value equals zero.

$$f(\mu) = \frac{1}{\sigma_\mu \sqrt{2\pi}} e^{-\frac{x^2}{2\sigma_\mu^2}} \tag{1}$$

(2) Manipulation capability diversity model
Manipulation capability diversity model describes the principle of transfer aiming graduation to aiming accuracy in different distance among the different skill gunners. Gunners manipulation capability model can be ensured in normal school probability density.

$$f(\sigma) = \frac{1}{\sigma_\sigma \sqrt{2\pi}} e^{-\frac{(x-\mu_\sigma)^2}{2\sigma_\sigma^2}} \tag{2}$$

(3) Tank gunners skill model
Considering lots of elements, except formula (1) and (2), tank gunners skill models include another two formulas as follows.

$$\mu_c = f_1() \cdot f_3() \cdot \mu \tag{3}$$

$$\sigma_c = f_2() \cdot f_4() \cdot \sigma \tag{4}$$

f1(): amending measure of gunners view deviation influence element, which is related to target brightness, contrast, size, distance, atmosphere environment visibility, movement status, color diversity with background, shady effect etc. elements, it is integration of view sensitive degree and sight angle[4-5].

f2(): amending measure of gunners aiming manipulation control deviation influence elements, which reflects the effect of target movement element on aiming error, it is a linear or non-linear function of target movement status. In the practical application, the deviation augmentation coefficient is introduced. The numerical value of general amending measure is about 1.05. The value is larger than 1.05 in the state of low speed. The value is less than 1.05 in the state of medium or even higher speed[6].

f3(): the influence of gunners view judgement error because of interior environment, attitude and emotion change

f4(): the influence of gunners manipulation error because of interior environment, attitude and emotion change

Comparing results of formula (1), (2), (3), (4), combining the experimental analysis conclusion, tank gunners skill model can be represented.

$$f(x) = \frac{1}{\sigma_c \sqrt{2\pi}} e^{-\frac{(x-\mu_c)^2}{2\sigma_c^2}} \tag{5}$$

4   Application of Unit Level Operation Simulation

(1) Tank shooting distribution model

Not only does accuracy of tank gun shooting have something to do with weaponry system performance, but also has a tight relationship with tank gunners' skill. Hereby, tank shooting distribution model includes tank gunners skill model and gun shell distribution model.

Tank gunners skill models can be seen in formula (5)

Gun shell distribution regulation obeys normal school whose mean value equals zero, therefore, gun shell distribution model can be represented by formula (6) and (7).

$$f_p(x) = \frac{1}{\sigma_p \sqrt{2\pi}} e^{-\frac{x^2}{2\sigma_p^2}} \tag{6}$$

$$\sigma_p = E / 0.6745 \tag{7}$$

In this formula, σ_p is mean variance of gun distribution, E represents calculation deviation or median deviation which can be inquired from shooting list.

(2) Simulation flow

① From formula (1),(2) distribution characteristic parameter μ,and σ (only initialized in operation simulation, all of gunners individual skill characteristic parameter can be produced in one time) are coming into being separately, as the different grade gunners.

② In accordance with the specific condition, four amending parameters f1(), f2(), f3(), f4() are calculated or estimated. From formula (3), (4), distribution characteristic parameters μ_c, σ_c can come into being (if no considering the influence of environment element, those parameters can be calculated once in initialization period of simulation).

③ According to the requirement of simulation procession, each aiming shooting should be simulated for every gunner, so as to producing each shooting deviation of every gunner. Shooting simulation one time includes:

1) Producing four independent uniform distribution random (r1, r2), (r3, r4) in [0,1] range.

2) From (r1, r2), (r3, r4), four independent random (xm, ym), (xp, yp) from two groups which obey the formula (5) and (6) are produced by coordinate changing method. These random represents horizontal deviation and upright deviation aiming-point, and also represents gun shells distribution horizontal deviation and upright deviation.

3) According to formula x= xm +xp, y= ym + yp, the value of horizontal coordinate and upright coordinate of shells landing point are calculated separately.

4) Judgement about whether hit the target. If |x| less than half of target frontispiece width and |y| less than half of target frontispiece height, the target is hit, or else, it is not being hit.

(3) Application exemplification

① Simulation initial condition

In the application of actual operation simulation, the influence elements of gunners and equipment are designated in simulation initialization. The influence elements of environment are designated by battlefield environment simulation system in simulation procession. In this instance, all of conditions are appointed in simulation initialization.

1) Supposing the environment condition as standard condition, that is, all of amending parameters of f1(), f2(), f3(), f4() is 1.

2) Equipment is some type of tank. Supposing gun deviation as Ex and Ey, Ex=0.29, Ey=0.31, the distribution mean variance is $\sigma x=0.43, \sigma y=0.46$;

3) The square of target which is still frontispiece is 2.3m×2.3m. The target distance is about 1500 meters.

4) Selecting three gunners whose performance can be distinguished as "good", "fairly" and "badly" separately in experiment, the values of aiming distribution characteristic parameter as follows:

"good": $\mu x=0.013, \mu y=0.041, \sigma x=0.1744, \sigma y=0.2403$.

"fairly": $\mu x=-0.0719, \mu y=0.1706, \sigma x=0.4597, \sigma y=0.4995$.

"badly": $\mu x=-0.1484, \mu y=0.2523, \sigma x=0.5893, \sigma y=0.979$.

② Simulation result statistics analysis

According to the flow of simulation, as it is known every gunner aiming distribution characteristics parameter, so the distribution characteristic parameters cannot be calculated by formula (1) and (2).

Implementing 10 times simulation among different grades gunners, in each simulation time, the amount of shell is 1000, mean shell hit the target rate is recorded. Those are statistical results as follows:

• No considering error of gunners aiming distribution, mean hit the target rate is 95.14%;

- Mean hit the target rate of good skill gunners is 92.24%;
- Mean hit the target rate of fairly skill gunners is 92.24%;
- Mean hit the target rate of badly skill gunners is 92.24%;

From results of simulation, gunners elements are introduced. The probability of hit the target rate is cut off. The reduction extent of hit the target rate has something to do with skill level of gunners. The reduction extent is nearly 36%, which reflects the influence of staff skills on operation.

If considering influence of mentality quality and environment element on gunners shooting aiming accuracy in simulation, the rate of hit the target can be reduced in some extent.

5   Conclusions

Tank gunners individual skills diversity is researched, in the way of experimental modeling method and man-in-loop semi-practicality simulation experiment technology. The individual diversity of tank gunners is explored, and tank gunners skill models are built, which can apply for the requirement of operation simulation.

- The single direction shooting aiming accuracy distribution of tank gunners obeys normal school. Aiming-point judgement of tank gunners obeys normal school whose mean value equals zero. Manipulation capability of tank gunners obeys normal school whose mean value doesn't equal zero.
- In the operation, weaponry equipment utilization performance and manipulators training level, environment elements etc. are indispensable. Therefore, modeling and simulation for operation staff capability should be emphasized in operation simulation.

For tanks etc. which kinds of direct aiming weaponry equipment are at a low level of automatization, staff manipulation error and equipment performance error are in the same quantity level. If you want to enhance the shooting accuracy of weaponry equipment dramatically, the automatization degree of weaponry equipment needs boosting, so as to reduce the intervention of manipulators.

References

1. Sun, B.-l., Jin, D.-A.: Modeling & Simulation Summarize of World Army. Computer Simulation (1), 4–8 (2002)
2. Diao, L.-W., Yang, J.-Y., Wang, Z.-Y.: Gunner Model for Tactical Simulation of Armored Force. Computer Simulation (6), 29–31 (2004)
3. Zhou, Q.-H., Chang, T.-Q., Qiu, X.: Fire Control System and Command Control System of Combat Vehicle. National Defence Industry Press (2003)
4. Ding, Y.-L.: Man-Machine Engineering. BeiJing Institute of Technology Press (2005)
5. Zhu, Y.-G., Shao, D.-C., Zhang, D.-M.: Analysis of the Tank Firing Accidents Based on Man-machine-environment Factor. Fire Control & Command Control (2), 103–106 (2005)
6. Zhu, J.-F., Zhao, B.-J., Wang, Q.-Z.: Modern Tank Fire Control System. National Defence Industry Press (2003)

Research of Army Battle Parallel Simulation Method Based on Function Modules

Yalong Ma, Qingjun Huang, and Ming Sun

Armored Forces Engineering, Beijing, China, 100072
Monlon1973@tom.com

Abstract. There is huge computing in the modern battle simulation, for the models with so many amounts and so small granularity, complex hiberarchy of simulation system. Adopting parallel simulation is the current method. The paper gives the parallel scheme based on function modules from present function and structure of simulation system. The method needs division and coalition of function modules based on the time of computing and communicating. The example suggests that the method has a certain efficiency and good value from the existing system.

Keywords: parallel simulation, function module, division.

1 Introduction

It makes battle simulation slenderize to nodes of information that ability of information exerts double effect in modern battle. This can fully embody effect of information. Complex of structure, huge types and numbers of equipment, person and organ brings on simulation count capacity increase as geometric series. There is an example of scale of 5000 noumenons, the scope covering command communicate, information, reconnaissance, fire, electron rivalry, combat ensure, logistics ensure, equipment ensure, the simulation object including armor, infantry, artillery, aerial defense, engineer sapper, chemical defense. This simulation has the specialty of excess real time and great count quantity. For resolving the matter of compute capacity and communication capacity, there are two methods. One is enlarging the scale of simulation system, or increasing the number of simulation nodes. The other is using the computer with high capability. The former problem brings is that distributed simulation system cannot be infinitely enlarged. [1]To a certain extent, simulation efficiency will fall instead of increasing. At the same time, this problem brings great difficulty to simulation management; the system reliability is not high. The trend of large scale battle simulation development is that the high speed parallel simulation is realized by applying high performance computers. Parallel simulation based on cluster is mainly discussed in this thesis. The cluster is composed of computer nodes connected by high-speed communication network. The node might be workstation or PC. The transmission delay is shorter, which belongs to tight coupling connection manners, low cost and good enlarge ability, this kind of simulation can meet the requirement of large scale simulation.

T. Xiao, L. Zhang, and S. Ma (Eds.): ICSC 2012, Part II, CCIS 327, pp. 407–413, 2012.

2   Parallel Simulation

[2]Parallel simulation is compared to serial simulation. Serial simulation is that every part of simulation system executes simulation in time order. When one step finished, then next step goes on. But outstanding characteristics of parallel simulation are simultaneity and intercurrence. Simultaneity is two or more affairs occurring at the same time. Intercurrence means that two or more affairs can appear at a same time interval.

Parallel simulation is in two forms mainly under the cluster pattern.

(1)Multi-sample parallel simulation
Multi-sample parallel simulation means that, under the condition of non-divided simulation system, samples (simulation system) are distributed to each processor node equally, and the parallel simulation is realized by running lots of samples among several processors in the same way, as figure 1 follows. This kind of form can be realized easily. System is not necessary to be decomposed. The problem is that the node which has finished mission in advance cannot be redeployed to share the work of other nodes, leading to the phenomenon that calculation resources cannot be utilized fully.

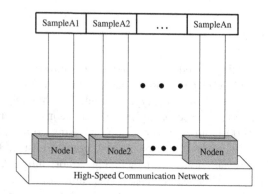

Fig. 1. Multi-sample parallel simulation

(2) Single-sample parallel simulation
Single-sample parallel simulation means this kind of simulation running that, samples are divided according to mission, then decomposers are submitted to parallel processor cluster. [3] The essence of this form simulation is that mission is dealt with in parallel in order to reduce the sample running time. Users can treat cluster computers as one super high speed computer, no considering number of nodes, as figure.2 follows. Because the dissection of sample is at a level of mission, the workload of dissection is light, in result the speed of samples processing is high. However, the program design is complex and interaction between missions is existed, which may lead to some amount of rollback.

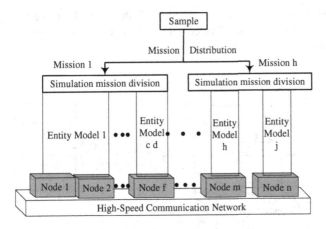

Fig. 2. Single-sample parallel simulation

In this paper, the method which realizes the operation parallel simulation based on current operation simulation system is researched. There are two aims, the first one is using the current conclusions to cut off the explore periods, the second one is exploring the most direct and feasible manner which is practical way to realize parallel simulation at present based on this current system.

3   Army Battle Parallel Simulation Method Based on Functional Modules

[4] Functional modules refer to operation simulation mission classified by simulation staffs according to function and structure of battle system.

Red-blue's operation command, network communication, reconnaissance intelligence, electronic confrontation, firepower confrontation, operation support, logistics, equipment support etc. actions are simulated in army battle simulation system, in view of function requirement. Simultaneously, various operation entities will execute these operation behaviors which are parallel between each other. So parallel attributive of these function modules can be utilized and applied to parallel simulation.

3.1   The Ideology of Simulation Based on Functional Modules

The basic ideology of functional modules parallel is that the disposal time and communication time are merged into even functional modules, on the basis of whole battle simulation system function modules division, in accordance with computing time characteristics and communication characteristics of each functional module. Then, these functional modules will be distributed to different processor and running at the same time. The total simulation procedure running time will be reduced and the simulation speed will be quickened. As figure.3 shows, if there are four processors, red functional modules can be divided into four processors, and parallel simulation will be realized.

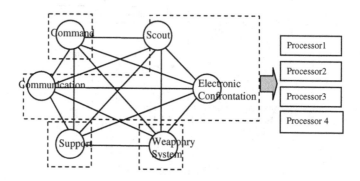

Fig. 3. Basic guideline of functional modules parallel simulation

3.2   Functional Modules Division Method

When the big functional module cannot meet the parallel requirement, this module needs to be divided. As figure.4 shows, the computing time of eighth functional module is longer, the eighth one need to be divided further. By analyzing function structure, the eighth module is divided into three sub-function modules. The communication between the three modules with former seven modules should be rearranged.

One system can be divided limitlessly. The division of simulation system function modules serves for function combination. Therefore, the number of processors is limited. As long as the combination requirement can be met, the goal of division will be reached.

In fact, the division of function modules is to enhance the parallel degree of simulation system. At the same time, the communication cost of simulation system will be increased. It is conflict between each other. The division can be put forward as the condition mentioned as follows:

(1)   Dividable condition
Calculating the function module balance degree:

$$\alpha = \frac{Max(c_i)}{\sum_i c_i \Big/ n}, (i = 1,2,\cdots,m) \tag{1}$$

the ratio of maximum and mean value of each functional module computing time c_i, when α larger then 1, some certain functional module computing time has surplus the mean value, that means this functional module can be divided further.

Computing ratio of calculation and communication, that is value of calculation time divides communication time. When γ of a certain functional module is very small, redundancy disposal can be taken into account. Namely, the mission will be replicated. When a functional module is copied, the corresponding relationship between this module and other modules can be dealt with well. If the ratio value of calculation and communication is large, we can take copy and divide into account first, then copy this module and divide it.

(2) Undividable condition
While designing the functional module, some functional modules certainly are not fit for being divided. If these modules are divided forcedly, this condition will lead to the communication increase. So there are lots of modules to be divided, this phenomenon is embodied in the whole balance performance, after combination, the requirement of functional modules parallel simulation cannot be met. In another words, the parallel attributive of simulation cannot be reached, the functional modules which are related to long computing time or communication time should be divided.

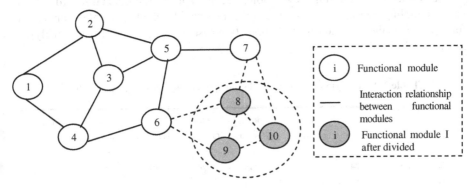

Fig. 4. Functional module mission division manners

4   Group Army Battle Parallel Simulation on Realizations

Among eight blades in blade server, the battle simulation between one red army and blue brigade is carried out. Parallel simulation method adopting functional modules is utilized to further divide the simulation missions. Corresponding to the processor number, through merging functional modules, eight simulation missions are classified; there are command simulation module, intelligence simulation module, weaponry system simulation module, battle environment simulation module, operation support and equipment support modules in both red and blue. In both red and blue simulation models internal, reconnaissance, communication, electronic confrontation modules are merged into one simulation mission, which is called information module, as figure 5 follows.

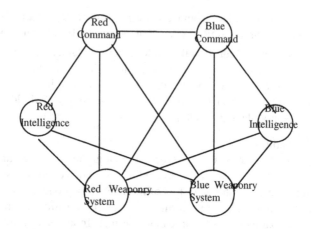

Fig. 5. Red-blue functional module interaction picture

Because the operation time is very long, the amount of experimental record data is large, sampling process will be made, the margin of sampling is 500 simulation frames. This is the specific result of simulation system parallel performance analysis, as Chart.1 follows.

Table 1. Equipment operation simulation sub-system performance statistics

	Red Command	Red Intelligence	Red Weaponry System	Blue Command	Blue Intelligence	Blue Weaponry System	Sum Total
Calculate Time	30164	13751	72086	8883	5059	46679	176622
Communication Time	1473	5063	1154	306	782	226	9004
Total Disposal Time	31637	18814	73240	9189	5841	46905	185626
Leisure Time	51833	86857	37939	77432	106065	63613	423739
Processor Efficiency	37.90	17.80	65.88	10.61	5.22	42.44	
Acceleration Rate							1.8

From chart.1, the parallel efficiency of visible simulation system is only 1.8 times, which need to enhance. In considering that the computing time of each blade are not same, red's time is much longer than blue's. Especially, the red communication intelligence is much more than blue's. Using rate of every processor is not higher than expected. Because the serial and parallel affairs simulation are not considered in this existed system, affairs appearing in every step are strictly occurring at same time, which will lead to the influence of simulation step on serial or parallel affairs inevitably including some key serial affairs can not be tracked accurately. So the parallel efficiency is affected. When parallel simulation system is newly designed, serial and parallel affairs simulation method should be thought over plenty. The demand about serial and parallel affairs simulation should be obeyed strictly. These logical errors can be reduced radically.

The simulation running speed is quickened. Every computing and communication ratio of simulation mission in this simulation system is very large, the mission division is successful. Whereas, the fact that distribution of mission computing amount is not equal leads to parallel simulation efficiency is low. Analyzing in the last, red-blue weaponry system functional module can be divided further. Simulation mission can be divided newly. This can improve the parallel performance of simulation system and enhance the simulation computing speed further.

5   Conclusions

Army battle parallel simulation is based on functional modules which are divided and assembled. Comparing others with considering parallel in system design, the amount of improving work is less. Translatability and refer ability are better, especially the fact that improving the existing system can be proved having certain effects. Parallel simulation is a large scale simulation which is the most potential research direction, and it provides development of simulation industry with energy.

References

1. Qiao, H.: Parallel simulation engine and correlate technology research. National Defense Science and Technology University, Changsha (2006)
2. Hu, X.F., Yang, J.-Y.: Simulation Analysis and Experiment of War Complex System. National Defense University Press (2008)
3. He, Y.: Parallel Computer Environment Based on Transferring Message. Journal of Xiangtan University (Social Science Edition) 27(5) (2003)
4. Zhang, M.: Research of System Rivalry Interactive Models faced with Informationization War Simulation. Journal of Navy Engineer University (5) (2006)

Multi-aircraft Cooperative Target Allocation in BVR Air Combat Using Cultural-Genetic Algorithm

Ni Li, Wenqing Yi, and Guanghong Gong

School of Automation Science and Electrical Engineering
Beihang University
Beijing, China
yiwq1987@126.com

Abstract. According to the characteristics of BVR (Beyond Visual Range) air combat, a mathematical model of multi-aircraft cooperative target allocation problem was built. Also a Cultural-Genetic Algorithm is proposed to solve this problem, which integrates cultural algorithm and genetic algorithm effectively. Based on the framework of Cultural Algorithm, Genetic Algorithm is selected as the evolutionary algorithm of population space. The knowledge of reasonable allocation plans is extracted from population space and stored in a belief space, which will influence the selection and mutation operation of Genetic Algorithm to make the optimization fast and accurate. Simulation results on typical application instances show that this algorithm is more efficient in performance than traditional Genetic Algorithm.

Keywords: Cultural Algorithm, Genetic Algorithm, BVR Air Combat, Target Allocation.

1 Introduction

With the increase of detection range of airborne sensor equipment and effective range of air to air missiles, BVR air combat is becoming a main operation of modern air combat. Multi-aircraft cooperative target allocation is one of the problems in air combat decision-making process, which aims at allocating targets more reasonably according to battlefield situation. It tries to avoid the duplication of attack, and give full play to combat effectiveness of aircrafts. Many scholars have made research into the model of this problem and related solving methods [1, 2]. Gao Yong, Zheng Xiaohong and Hou Zhiqiang discussed the optimal strategy of target allocation and established an air combat model based on differential game theory [3]. And they adopted integer programming to solve the problem. Xiao Bingsong, Fang Yangwang and Xu Yunshan built a new model from the perspective of weapon types, so as to minimize answer dimensions [4]. And the model was calculated by particle swarm optimization algorithm.

In human societies, culture can be viewed as a vehicle for the storage of information that is potentially accessible to all members of the society, and that can be useful in guiding their problem solving activities. Based on this theory, Reynolds put

T. Xiao, L. Zhang, and S. Ma (Eds.): ICSC 2012, Part II, CCIS 327, pp. 414–422, 2012.
© Springer-Verlag Berlin Heidelberg 2012

forward CA (Cultural Algorithm) in 1994, the main idea of which is to build a dual inheritance system with evolution taking place at the population space and the belief space. The belief space is a repository for knowledge concerning the self-adaptation process. The knowledge stored in the belief space can be used to direct the evolution of the population space. A large amount of studies on CA have been carried out by scholars. Reynolds and Chung adopted the architecture of the integration of evolutionary programming and GENOCOP (Genetic algorithm for Numerical Optimization for Constrained Problems) and successfully applied CA in global optimization problem [5]. Ricardo Landa Becerra and Carlos A. Cello firstly used CA to solve multi-objective optimization problem and achieved good results [6].

GA (Genetic Algorithm) is a stochastic search algorithm that simulates the evolution process and mechanism in nature to solve optimization problems [7]. GA is simple, universal and strong in robustness, which is a powerful tool to solve global optimization problems. However, in the process of evolution, there are also problems, such as, the global convergence is not good enough and sometimes easy to trap into local minimum. A lot of researches have been focused on improving this situation. Here we hope to make use of the knowledge generated during evolutionary process to guide the direction of evolution.

This paper comes up with a CGA (Cultural-Generic Algorithm) to solve multi-aircraft cooperative target allocation problem in BVR air combat and the related key work is described in the following sections. GA is selected as the evolutionary algorithm of population space. And a belief space is designed to store good individuals in the population space. The knowledge in belief space influences not only the selection operation, but also the mutation operation in GA. At last, a simulation is conducted to test the feasibility and effectiveness of CGA.

2   Description of Multi-aircraft Cooperative Target Allocation

With the development of battlefield detection technology and C4ISR technology, as well as the advances in weapons and equipment, modern air combat is tending to meet the demand that multiple aircrafts within formation cooperatively and precisely attack targets under the condition of BVR. The major problem is to select an optimal and reasonable weapon-target allocation plan to achieve the best combat effect [8]. Thus the threat between the two combat sides should be evaluated first, including air combat capability threat and situational threat. Air combat capability reflects the comprehensive performance of the aircraft. However, situational threat is to calculate angle threat, distance threat and velocity threat according to the position and attitude of both sides. The final evaluation result is the weight sum of the two kinds of threats. What this paper concerns is mainly about the final threat evaluation result, but not related evaluation method and process. Therefore, it is assumed that the threat of friendly aircraft i to enemy aircraft j is T_{ij} and $\overline{T_{ji}}$ is the threat of enemy aircraft to friendly aircraft. Then the advantage index v_{ij} of friendly aircraft i to enemy aircraft j is depicted in formula (1)

$$v_{ij} = T_{ij} - \overline{T_{ji}} \tag{1}$$

Suppose that the number of friendly aircrafts is m and the number of enemy aircrafts is n. Then the matrix of advantage indexes is described in formula (2)

$$V = \begin{bmatrix} v_{11} & v_{12} & \cdots & v_{1n} \\ v_{21} & v_{22} & \cdots & v_{2n} \\ \vdots & \vdots & \ddots & \vdots \\ v_{m1} & v_{m2} & \cdots & v_{mn} \end{bmatrix}. \tag{2}$$

The decision-making process is to achieve the greatest advantage of friendly aircrafts over enemy aircrafts. According to the matrix of advantage indexes, the mathematical model of target allocation is described in formula (3).

$$Z = \max(\sum_{i=1}^{m} \sum_{j=1}^{n} v_{ij} X_{ij} U_{ij}) \cdot \tag{3}$$

In the model, X_{ij} is 1 when friendly aircraft i attacks enemy aircraft j, and 0 or else. U_{ij} is a punishment factor. This model satisfies the following constraints.

$$\begin{cases} \sum_{j=1}^{n} X_{ij} \le Q_i, i = 1, 2, ..., m \\ \sum_{i=1}^{m} X_{ij} \le P_i, j = 1, 2, ..., n \\ X_{ij} = 0, i \ne r, if \ v_{rj} \ge v_f \\ X_{ij} = \begin{cases} 1, \lambda v_{i,\max} + (1-\lambda)v_{i,\min} \ge v_i \\ 0, else \end{cases} \\ U_{ij} = \begin{cases} 1, v_{ij} > 0 \\ -2, v_{ij} < 0 \end{cases} \end{cases} \tag{4}$$

The first constraint means friendly aircraft i can attack no more than Q_i enemy aircrafts. The second constraint means enemy aircraft j can be attacked by no more than P_i friendly aircrafts. The third constraint indicates if the advantage of friendly aircraft i over enemy aircraft j has reached the satisfaction v_f, then other aircrafts need not to be assigned to this enemy. $0 \le \lambda \le 1$ in the fourth constraint reflects the pilot's balance on attack or evasion, 1 for completely attack and 0 for completely evade. The last one is to punish the allocation plans that assign the weak to attack the strong. If friendly aircraft is in a dominant position, then $U_{ij} = 1$, or else $U_{ij} = -2$.

3   Cultural Algorithm

The framework of CA is illustrated in Fig.1. It is consisted of three components: population space, belief space and the protocols between them. Population space is constructed by individuals, each of which represents a solution to the problem. Any computational model can be used in population space as the evolutionary mechanism for social population. Belief space represents the bias that has been acquired by the population during its problem solving process. Special knowledge and experience are also stored in belief space, which can guide the evolutionary direction of population space. The two components communicate with each other through protocols between them. In this way, the population component and the belief space interact with and support each other. As such, CA is a dual inheritance system where both the population and belief evolve over time in parallel.

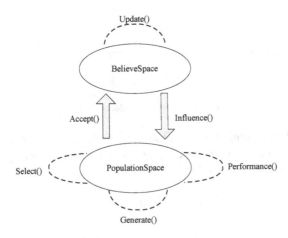

Fig. 1. The framework of CA

When applying CA to solve practical problems, the key point is how to design belief space and the influence function. In other words, it is important to determine what kind of knowledge belief space is composed of and how the knowledge influences the evolution in population space. In continuous optimization problems, the solution set is in continuous Euclidean space and belief space commonly stores knowledge about range value. However, multi-aircraft cooperative target allocation is a discrete optimization problem. The solutions are discrete points in searching space. Thus CGA, proposed here, selects individuals with good fitness to build belief space as templates to construct best individuals. Compare individuals in population space and the templates in belief space and adopt k-nearest neighbor method to affect selection and mutation operation. The following section will discuss this method in detail.

4   Cultural-Genetic Algorithm

4.1   Code Design

Code design is the primary problem to be solved when GA is applied, and it is also a key step when GA is designed. As target allocation is a discrete problem, integer code is selected here. It is supposed that the number of friendly aircrafts is m and the i_{th} aircraft can attack no more than Q_i targets, which is also the amount of missiles the aircraft carries. Therefore, the length of each individual, also called chromosome, is L, represented as

$$L = \sum_{i=1}^{m} Q_i \ .$$ (5)

Assume the number of enemy aircrafts is n, and then the range of each gene in the chromosome is from 0 to n. A typical chromosome is illustrated in Fig.2.

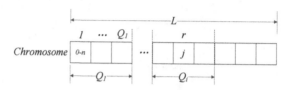

Fig. 2. A typical chromosome

$Chromosome[r]=j$ means the r_{th} missile attacks the j_{th} target, but if $j=0$, then no target is assigned to this missile. The r_{th} missile is defined to correspond with the i_{th} friendly aircraft, and the relationship is restricted to

$$\sum_{f=1}^{i-1} Q_f < r \le \sum_{f=1}^{i} Q_f \ .$$ (6)

4.2   Belief Space

The individuals with good fitness in population space are selected to establish belief space which is represented as $<G, L(t)>$. G stores the best individual ever since the evolutionary process starts. It influences the mutation operation of GA by means of k-nearest neighbor. $L(t)$ is constituted of a certain amount of good individuals from the current population space, which affects the selection process and updates every several generations.

Accept function is responsible for selecting individuals which are used to update belief space. The number of individuals to be selected can be permanent or vary with the evolution progress. Here the accept number is defined according to current iteration as follows

$$n_{accept} = p * \beta + \lfloor p * \beta / t \rfloor \ .$$ (7)

In formula (7), p is the size of population space, t is the current iteration, and $\beta = 0.2$. The individuals with good fitness increase with the evolution progress, and as a result, the corresponding number to accept decreases to accelerate the convergence of the algorithm.

4.3 Selection

Selection is the survival of the fitness, and commonly the process is random. Thus, it is necessary to guide the selection operation with knowledge stored in belief space to accelerate the convergence speed. Firstly, generate child populations by roulette method before selection. CGA adopts k-nearest neighbor theory [9] and compares individuals in child populations with the good ones in $L(t)$ to calculate the similarity index according to formula (8)

$$S(chm1, chm2) = \sum_{r=1}^{L} chm1(r) \otimes chm2(r) .$$ (8)

$chm1$ and $chm2$ are two chromosomes. r is the location of the genes. The operator $\otimes$ means to compare the two genes and return 1 when they are the same, or else 0. The similarity index S measures the degree of similarity of two chromosomes. The greater the similarity index, the higher the similarity. And then, individuals with greater similarity index are chosen to replace the poor individuals in the child population.

4.4 Crossover

In GA, crossover is used to exchange part of the genes in one chromosome with another to generate next generation. Two-point crossover is adopted here. Firstly, chromosomes are stochastically paired. And then randomly select two points in a chromosome and swap the genes between the two points with the other paired chromosome.

4.5 Mutation

Mutation is effective in preventing genetic algorithm from falling into local optimum, improving the ability of global search and maintaining the diversity of species. The mutation of traditional GA is conducted randomly. This paper improves the mutation operation with neighbor search mutation, guided by the knowledge G stored in belief space. Neighbor search mutation is to list all the possible permutation and combination of the genes located in the mutation points, the number of which is generally no more than 3. And then calculate the fitness of each individual that is newly generated, among which the best one is chosen as the final result of the mutation. According to the mutation probability P_m, a chromosome is selected from the child population and compared with the best one in belief space. And the positions of the different genes are recorded, as well as the number. The detailed mutation operation is described as follows:

(1) If $q<3$, randomly choose several points to conduct neighbor search mutation.
(2) If $q>3$, firstly, a random sequence from 1 to q is generated. Suppose u is the number of genes to conduct neighbor search mutation, v is the current cycle number and w be the maximum cycle number, calculated by $w = \lfloor q/u \rfloor$. In the first place, u is assumed to be 3 and v is 1. Take three elements orderly from P to determine the mutation points. And then conduct neighbor search mutation and let $v=v+1$. Repeat the above process until $v=w$.

In selection and mutation operation, there may be infeasible individuals occurred which are unacceptable. To punish these individuals, the fitness of them is set to be a low value and then they will gradually be eliminated in the evolution process.

4.6   CGA Design

The basic process of CGA is illustrated in Fig.3 and described in detail as follows.

Step 1: Initialize population space and evaluate the fitness of individuals.

Step 2: Initialize belief space.

Step 3: Selection operation. Firstly, generate initial child population with roulette method. Secondly, select certain individuals and calculate similarity index with belief space $L(t)$. And then replace poor individuals with good individuals.

Step 4: Two-point crossover operation.

Step 5: Mutation operation. Compare the individual to be mutated with G in belief space and conduct neighbor search mutation according to the number of different genes.

Step 6: Evaluate child population and judge if it reaches the update frequency or not. If it meets, update belief space and return to Step 3, otherwise, continue to Step 7.

Step 7: Terminate operation judgment. If the termination condition is satisfied, go back to step 3, otherwise, stops.

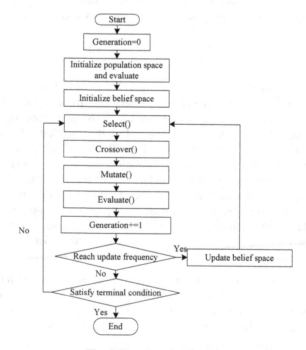

Fig. 3. The process of CGA

5   Simulations and Analysis

In this simulation, the number of friendly aircrafts is supposed to be 2, each of which can attack no more than 2 targets. And the number of enemy aircrafts is 4, each of which can be attacked by 2 aircrafts to avoid abusing advantages. Other parameters are set as follows: $\lambda = 0$, $v_t = -0.1$, $v_f = 0.1$. The advantage indexes of our aircrafts over enemies are shown in Table 1.

Table 1. List of advantage indexes

Friend	Enemy			
	1	2	3	4
a	0.112	0.060	0.021	-0.015
b	0.046	0.054	0.024	-0.036

To illustrate the effectiveness of the algorithm, we apply CGA and traditional GA to solve this problem and compare the performance of the two algorithms under the same parameters. It is set that the size of the population is 30, the maximum evolutionary generation is 200, the crossover probability $Pc=0.7$, the mutation probability $Pm=0.3$. The belief space in CGA updates every 10 generations, thus the update frequency is 10. The objective function is shown in formula (3). The two algorithms respectively run 100 times. The simulation results are compared in Table 2, in respect to the final result, accuracy and evolution generation.

Table 2. Simulation results

	Final result	Accuracy	Generation		
			Max	Average	Min
CGA	(1,4,2,3)	99%	62	25	4
GA	(4,1,2,3)	95%	110	56	15

The chromosome of the final allocation plan is (1,4,2,3) or (4,1,2,3). It means that when plane a attacks the 1st and 4th target and plane b attacks the 2nd and 3rd target, the combat advantage is the largest. Both the two algorithms get the correct result, but the accuracy of CGA is higher than that of GA. Furthermore, CGA needs less iteration than GA to reach the optimal value. It will reduce the running time and meet the real-time requirements in air combat.

6   Conclusion

BVR air combat will be a main operation of modern air combat. This paper analyzes multi-aircraft cooperative target allocation problem according to the characteristics of BVR air combat. A mathematical model of this problem is built from the point of view of air combat threat between two sides. Referring to the framework of CA, a new algorithm named Cultural-Genetic Algorithm is proposed, which effectively combines CA and GA. The knowledge is abstracted from population space and stored in belief space, which can be used to guide the evolutionary direction of GA. The simulation results show that CGA performs better than GA in convergence speed and accuracy rate in solving the problem. However, the battlefield environment is changing all the time. More constraints should be concerned to modify the model and the algorithm in future works.

Acknowledgments. This study was supported by National Nature Science Foundation of China, and the supporting project is "Study on parallel intelligent optimization simulation with combination of qualitative and quantitative method" (61004089). It was also financially supported by the Graduate Student Innovation Practice Foundation of Beihang University in China, which is "Research of an efficient and intelligent optimization method and application in aircraft configuration design".

References

1. Paddon Harry, G.: Maneuvering Target Simulation for Testing the Terminal Guidance of Air-to-Air Missile. AD-A039757/OSL (1977)
2. Ring, T.: US Airborne Command and Control System. World Air Power 36, 40–57 (1999)
3. Gao, Y., Zhen, X., Hou, Z.: Optical Target-Assignment Strategy in BVR Air Combat based on Integer Programming. Journal of System Simulation 23(1), 72–75 (2011) (in Chinese)
4. Xiao, B., Fang, Y., Xu, Y., Zhang, P., Wang, P.: Research on coordinated formation target assignment model for beyond visual range air combat. Systems Engineering and Electronics 32(7), 1476–1479 (2010) (in Chinese)
5. Reynolds, G., Michalewicz, Z., Cavaretta, M.: Using Cultural Algorithms for Constraint Handling in GENOCOP. In: Proceedings of the Fourth Annual Conference on Evolutionary Programming, pp. 298–305 (1995)
6. Becerra, R.L., Coello, C.A.: Evolutionary Multi-objective Using a Cultural Algorithms. In: 2003 IEEE Swarm Intelligence Symposium, pp. 6–13 (2003)
7. Holland, J.: Adaptation in natural and artificial systems, pp. 35–67. University of Michigan Press, Ann Arbor (1975)
8. Delin, L., Zhong, Y., Haibin, D., et al.: Heuristic particle swarm optimization algorithm for air combat decision-making on CMTA. Trans. of Nanjing University of Aeronautics and Astronautics 23(1), 20–26 (2006)
9. Berger, J., Barkaoui, M.: A parallel hybrid genetic algorithm for the vehicle routing problem with time windows. Computers & Operations Research, 2037–2053 (2004)

Secure and Semantic Repository for Weapon Models in the Cloud

Hyunhwi Kim, Chanjong Park, and Kangsun Lee

Department of Computer Engineering, MyongJi University, MyongJiRo 116, YongIn,
Kyunggi-Do, South Korea
ksl@mju.ac.kr

Abstract. Simulation-based weapons analysis requires significant efforts to
represent the complex structure and dynamics of weapon systems on the
computer. A model repository can help model developers to save their
development costs and time by utilizing predefined and already validated
weapon models. In this paper, we introduce OpenREM (Open REpository for
weapon Models) which has been developed to store weapon models in the
cloud data storages. OpenREM provides a semantic search service to reuse
semantically similar models, despite of their structural and textual differences.
OpenREM also prevents and detects possibly security probes, and employs an
intrusion tolerant mechanism to be able to survive through security threats.

Keywords: Reuse Repository, Semantic Search, Security, Weapons
Effectiveness.

1 Introduction

Analyzing modern weapon systems becomes a hard task as their dynamics and
structures become complex. Simulation-based weapons analysis requires significant
cost and time, since we need to go through intensive modeling tasks to represent
weapon systems on the computer [1-2]. A model repository can help model
developers to save their development costs and time by utilizing predefined and
already validated weapon models [3- 4].

Many research works have provided model repositories for various M&S
applications [5-7]. Although they have been successful in managing reusable models,
such as registering and retrieving models, their utilization has been limited partly due
to the following reasons:

- Lack of semantic matching: Most of the existing repositories employ key-word
  based search techniques to find reusable models. They lack flexible matching
  services regardless of structural discrepancies between weapon models. Also, they
  are not powerful in taking into account the contextual similarity between similar
  weapon models [8-9].
- Low utilization: Utilizing the reuse repositories may be limited, if users are unable
  to access the stored models from anywhere on various execution environments

T. Xiao, L. Zhang, and S. Ma (Eds.): ICSC 2012, Part II, CCIS 327, pp. 423–433, 2012.
© Springer-Verlag Berlin Heidelberg 2012

[10]. Since weapon models are usually developed by many experts from various disciplines possibly dispersed over the network, a distributed repository can greatly facilitate collaborative modeling among the weapon engineers [11].

- Vulnerability to security threats: Weapon models have attributes and operations that only authorized people can access and reuse. In the presence of security probes and attacks, the repository should be resilient in providing secure repository services. Unless the security concerns are resolved, the functionality of the reuse repositories can be useless [12-13].

In this paper, we introduce a cloud model repository to reuse weapon models for simulation-based effectiveness analysis. In order to maximize reusability, our reuse repository recommends a model that has maximum similarity in structure and behavior. We construct ontology to organize similar weapon models and assess structural similarity between models. Thesaurus dictionaries are also managed to resolve textual discrepancies appeared in the names of attributes and operations for weapon models. Our reuse repository has been implemented in the cloud computing environment to store large amount of data for representing weapon models. Utilization of the reuse repository can be improved, since users can access the weapon models from anywhere and on various execution and operating systems with the help of cloud data storage and services. Also, our repository provides high levels of security by allowing authorized users to exchange encrypted data and delivering intrusion-resilient services in the presence of security attacks.

OpenREM(Open REpository for weapon Models) is our implementation which has been developed as a reuse repository of our integrated M&S environment, OpenSIM (Open Simulation Engine for Interoperable Models) [14]. With the help of openREM and tools/services of OpenSIM, model developers can efficiently conduct their weapons effectiveness analysis by improving reusability of predefined weapon models.

This paper is organized as follows. Section 2 presents the architecture of our model repository, OpenREM, with detailed explanation on the components. Section 3 presents a semantic search process to locate reusable weapon models in OpenREM. Weapon ontology, thesaurus dictionaries and the semantic search algorithm are explained in Section 3. Section 4 presents tools and services to manage the repository with implementation details. We conclude in Section 5 with summary and future research works to achieve.

2   The Architecture of OpenREM

Figure 1 sketches the overall architecture of OpenREM. Clients can access the reuse repository from anywhere with the help of *Storage Manager*. Storage services help clients to register their models and search reusable models according to their simulation objectives. With the help of *Resource Registrant*, each model is registered to the model repository with syntax (e.g. interface information) and semantic (e.g. weapon category) information. All these information are zipped with an index bitmap to save space. In order to support semantic search for weapon models, queries are analyzed in *Query Analyzer*. Morphological analysis is performed on the weapon models to resolve textual discrepancies in the names of attributes and operations. The *Searcher* ranks candidates with the help of *Ranking Module*, and recommends reusable models to the client. OpenREM also employs security modules including *Security Detector* and *Recovery Manager*. Details on these modules will be discussed in Section 4.

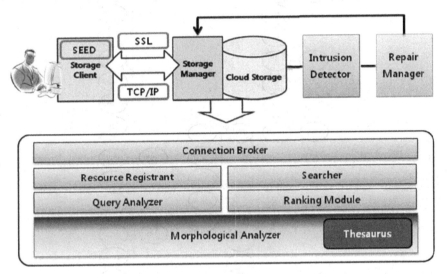

Fig. 1. Architecture of OpenREM in OpenSIM

3   Semantic Search Process of OpenREM

Although weapon models exhibit different forms in development programming languages and platforms, they are *similar* in their structures and behaviors. Since weapon systems are usually developed in order to improve parts of the old ones, there are very high chances to reuse the existing weapon models for analyzing the effectiveness of new weapons. In order to maximize reusability of weapon models, OpenREM recommends a model that has maximum similarity in structure and behavior. Structure similarity is assessed based on our weapon ontology, while behavioral similarity is assessed by looking up the thesaurus dictionary for weapon systems and resolving textual discrepancies appeared in the names of attributes and methods. Section 3.1 – 3.3 present the details.

3.1   Structure Matching Process

Ontology formally represents knowledge as a set of concepts within a domain, and the relationships between those concepts [9]. We construct weapon ontology to organize weapon models. Figure 2 shows a part of weapon ontology to organize guided missiles. Guided missile models are represented and related to others according to

426   H. Kim, C. Park, and K. Lee

military organizations (i.e. Air force, Army, Navy), engagement types (i.e. air-to-air, air-to-ground, ground-to-air, etc.), range (i.e. short, middle, long), guidance method (i.e. radar, laser, optic, GPS, etc.), development details (i.e. platform, programming language), and resolution (i.e. high, medium, low).

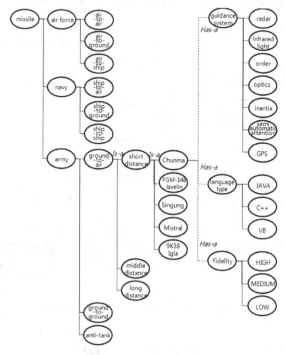

Fig. 2. Weapon Ontology for Guided Missiles

An index bitmap is associated with a weapon model, in order to represent the ontology information space-efficiently. All the structural information, including military organization, warfare type, range, fidelity, programming language, and guidance systems, are represented with 25 bits as shown in Figure 3. These bitmap indexes provide significant performance advantages over traditional value-list indexes for complex queries, such as searching for reusable models [15]. Structural similarity can be assessed by logical operations (e.g. and (&)) between the index bitmaps.

Given a user model X, structural similarity with other model, Y, is calculated by the following equation:

```
S_Similarity(X,Y) =
    Σ (Index (Xi) & Index (Yi))*wi
   ∀i=1..25
```

where, Index(Xi) is the ith bit in the index bitmap of model X, and w_i is a weight factor for comparing the ith bit, and & is logical and operation.

25 bits

Military (3bit)	Warfare (3bit)	Range (3bit)	Fidelity (3bit)	PL (3bit)	Guidance (10bit)

Field Name	Example
Military	Army(001), Navy(010), AirForce(100)
Warfare	Air-to-Air(001), Ground-to-Air(010)
Range	Short(001), Medium(010), Long(100)
Fidelity	High(001), Medium(010), Low(100)
Programming Language	C++(001), Java(010)
Guidance Type	Radar(0000000001), Infrared light(0000000100)

Fig. 3. Structure Index Map (in part)

3.2   Behavior Matching Process

Models may have attributes and operations with different names, even though they have similar meanings. We construct a weapon thesaurus dictionary in order to group models that have similar meanings in attributes and operations. Figure 4 shows a part of our thesaurus dictionary for guided missiles. For example, *hit rate*, *hit_rate, hit ratio, hit* and *accuracy* may have the same meaning, even though their textual appearances are different. By looking up the names of attributes and operations in the thesaurus dictionary, we can assess how a model is similar to other models regardless of their textual appearances.

X	Wingspan	Altitude	Accuracy	Length
x	wingspan	altitude	accuracy	Length
currentx	wingspread	flightaltitude	accuracyrate	Scope
current_x	wingwidth	flight_altitude	accuracy_rate	Spread
coordinate	wing_width	flightlevel	hit	lineardimension
coordinate_x	wingbreadth	flight_level	hitrate	lenear_dimension
Speed	Diameter	Length	Altitude	Ceiling
speed	caliber	spread	flightlevel	Serviceceiling
pace		lineardimension	flight_altitude	practicalceiling
velocity				

Fig. 4. Weapon Thesaurus Dictionary for Guided Missiles (in part)

Two models can be considered as similar if they have many attributes in common. In order to resolve morphological discrepancies between attributes, we first look up the thesaurus dictionary to replace an attribute name with the representative name in the thesaurus dictionary. Then, attributes similarity, A_Similarity(X,Y), between model X and model Y can be calculated by cross-checking all attributes of model X and model Y, and counting the number of attributes that belong to both of the models. O_similarity(X,Y), the measure for assessing similarity on operations between model X and model Y, can be determined with the same process as in A_Similarity.

Finally, the search algorithm determines the overall similarity, Similarity, by calculating the weighted sum of S_Similarity, A_Similarity, and O_Similarity. Models with high Similarity values are recommended to users as reusable candidates.

4   Intrusion Tolerant Mechanism in OpenREM

OpenREM employs multi-layer approach to deliver security against illegal intrusions and attacks. The following are the three layers, each of which addresses security concerns in the aspect of prevention, detection and tolerance.

- Prevention: OpenREM establishes SSL (Secure Socket Layer) [16] connection to prevent unauthorized data exchanges between users and the repository. OpenREM assigns a unique session key to a client when he logs in the repository and employs the public-key encryption techniques to generate shared data exchanges by using OpenSSL and SEED [20].
- Detection: OpenREM detects security attacks by analyzing usage patterns. OpenREM performs protocol analysis, content searching and content matching by employing Snort, an open source network-based intrusion detection system, to detect probes or attacks, such as, operating system fingerprinting, common gateway interface, buffer overflows, etc [17].
- Tolerance: OpenREM extends traditional secure systems to be able to survive or operate through attacks. A name node maintains a set of metadata to locate a weapon model which may be distributed into three data nodes. In order to survive unpredictable and undetectable security attacks, OpenREM manages secondary name node. OpenREM employs mechanisms to manage snapshots and recover from data replications. Figure 5 depicts a set of sequences to recover from security attacks.

5   Implementation

A cloud M&S resource storage has been constructed in OpenSIM based on Apache Hadoop and HDFS (Hadoop Distributed File System) [18]. Apache Hadoop is a software framework that supports the distributed processing of large data sets across clusters of computers.

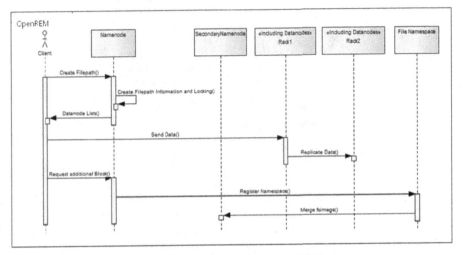

Fig. 5. Recovery Process of OpenREM

HDFS is a distributed, scalable, and portable file system written in Java for the Hadoop framework. HDFS provides services to replicate data across multiple hosts for high reliability, to rebalance data by moving copies around, and to keep the replication of data high [19]. Weapon models and their associated data resources are stored across three machines with the help of HDFS. Clients can transparently access weapon models stored in the OpenSIM repository through secure TCP/IP communication by using OpenSSL and Snort [16,17,20]. Also, repository services can be remained secure by managing snapshots and data replications. Section 4.1 – 4.3 illustrate how we can reuse weapon models in OpenSIM repository through an example of Mistral missile.

5.1 Registration

Users register their weapon models to the repository in OpenSIM. Figure 6 shows a registration tool in OpenSIM. Attributes, Operations, and general information (e.g. model name, creator, publisher, implementation details (e.g. programming language, operating system), component type (e.g. C++, DLL, etc.), ownership) can be selectively published for users discretion. For example, attributes such as (x, y, z) position of a missile, and operation names, such as fireTarget, are published by users.   All published data are then automatically represented in XML and RDF data files as shown in Figure 7. Also, an index bitmap is also associated with the registered model based on the weapon ontology discussed in section 3.1.

Suppose the Mistral model has been developed by army to analyze the effectiveness of short-range, infrared ray missile in the anti-air warfare. Also, suppose this model has been developed by C++ with detailed dynamics and attributes (high resolution). By matching this information with the weapon ontology in Figure 2, the index bitmap of this model is defined as 001001001001001000000000100. This index bitmap is specified in the last row of the RDF data file in Figure 7.

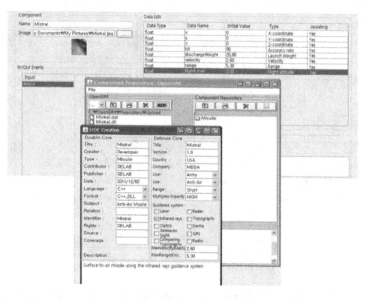

Fig. 6. Registration Process in OpenSIM

```
<?xml version="1.0" encoding="EUC-KR"?>
<MissileData>
  <attribute>
    <attributeCount>8</attributeCount>
    <coordinateXName>x</coordinateXName>
    <coordinateXValue>0</coordinateXValue>
    <coordinateYName>y</coordinateYName>
    <coordinateYValue>0</coordinateYValue>
    <coordinateZName>z</coordinateZName>
    <coordinateZValue>0</coordinateZValue>
    <accuracyRateName>hit</accuracyRateName>
    <accuracyRateValue>90</accuracyRateValue>
    <launchWeightName>dischargeWeight</launchWeightName>
    <launchWeightValue>25.80</launchWeightValue>
    <lengthName>-</lengthName>
    <lengthValue>-</lengthValue>
    <caliberValue>-</caliberValue>
    <speedName>velocity</speedName>
    <speedValue>2.60</speedValue>
        :
        :
  </attribute>
  <operation>
    <operationCount>1</operationCount>
    <operationName>fireTarget</operationName>
    <operationDescriptione>Calculates (x,y,z) to encounter a targer
                </operationDescriptione>
        :
  </operation>
</MissileData>
```

(a) XML data file

```
<?xml version="1.0" encoding="EUC-KR"?>
<RDF
xmlns="http://www.w3.org/TR/WD-rdf-syntax#"
xmlns:dc="http://selab.mju.ac.kr#"
xmlns:inducement="http://selab.mju.ac.kr/inducement/"
>

<Description about="Mistral.dll">
      <dc:Title>Mistral</dc:Title>
      <dc:Creator>Taesup</dc:Creator>
      <dc:Type>Missile</dc:Type>
      <dc:Contributor>SELAB</dc:Contributor>
      <dc:Publisher>SELAB</dc:Publisher>
      <dc:Date>2011/11/21</dc:Date>
      <dc:Format>C++_DLL</dc:Format>
      <dc:Subject>anti-air weapon</dc:Subject>
            :
      <dc:Name>Mistral</dc:Name>
      <dc:Version>1.0</dc:Version>
      <dc: Fidelity>HIGH</dc:MultiFidelity>
      <dc:Country>USA</dc:Country>
      <dc:Company>MBDA</dc:Company>
      <dc:Military> Army</dc:Army>
      <dc:Use>Anti-Air</dc:Use>
      <dc:Distance>Short</dc:Distance>
      <dc:Guidancet>
<Description>
<inducement:Laser>Used</inducement:Laser>
      <inducement:Radar>Unused</inducement:Radar>
      <inducement:Infrared>Unused</inducement:Infrared>
      <inducement:Order>Unused</inducement:Order>
      <inducement:Optics>Unused</inducement:Optics>
      <inducement:Inertia>Unused</inducement:Inertia>

</Description>
      </dc:Guidancet>
      <dc:maxSpeed>2.60</dc:maxSpeed>
      <dc:maxRange>5.30</dc:maxRange>
            :
      <dc:BitMap>001001001000000100001001</dc:BitMap>
</Description>
</RDF>
```

(b) RDF data file

Fig. 7. Data files for registering weapon models – in part

During the registration process, all data exchanges between clients and the OpenREM are encrypted based on the cipher suite in SEED [20] through secure network communications [16,20].

5.2   Semantic Search

Semantic search in OpenSIM is performed by matching structure and behavior. Suppose a modeler wants to reuse available missile models that have been developed by army for analyzing weapons effectiveness in anti-air warfare.

Suppose the modeler also wants to reuse short-distance and infrared ray guided missiles. Upon selecting the search criteria, such as military organization, and warfare type, SQL query is automatically generated with the corresponding index bitmap. Structure matching is performed by the steps specified in section 3.1. Table 1 summarizes structure matching results in descending order. The three models with highest structure matching score are selected for further attributes and operations matching. Based on the missile thesaurus dictionary, attributes with similar meanings are grouped. In this example, KP-SAM, Mistral, and 9K38 are selected from the structure matching, and their attributes are cross-checked after resolving their textual differences with the help of the missile thesaurus dictionary.

Table 1. Structure Matching Results – in part (Top 10)

Missile	Index bitmap	Matching Score
Sin-Goong (KP-SAM)	001 001 001 001 010 0000000100	13
Mistral	001 001 001 001 001 0000000100	13
9K38 Eaglar	001 001 001 010 001 0000000100	13
FGM-148	001 001 001 001 100 0001000000	12
BGM-71 TOW	001 000 001 010 100 0000010000	12
Chun-Ma (KSAM-1)	001 001 001 010 010 0000000010	12
KM-SAM	001 001 000 100 100 0000101010	9
9K115-2	001 000 001 100 010 0000010000	8
HyunMu-2	001 010 100 001 100 0000100000	5
HyunMu-1	001 010 100 001 001 0000100000	5

Figure 8 shows the OpenSIM tools to show the results from the structure and behavior matching. Based on the modeling and simulation objectives, users can choose reusable models that have desired attributes. Operation names are also checked based on the thesaurus dictionary, and operations with the similar meaning are grouped for users to select reusable models. Detailed descriptions on the operations are also available to help users choose reusable models.

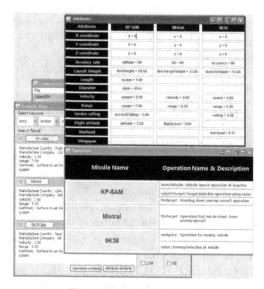

Fig. 8. Behaviour Matching

6   Conclusion

In this paper, we introduced OpenREM, a cloud repository for improving reusability of weapon models. OpenREM recommends semantically similar models by matching structure information based on the weapon ontology. Behaviour matching is performed to resolve textual differences in the names of attributes and methods by looking up the weapon thesaurus dictionaries. All the services in OpenREM are intrusion-tolerant by detecting security probes from unauthorized users and recovering from security threats based on the snapshots and data replications.

We would like to further apply the semantic matching process to reuse the small-grained units, for example, subcomponents of a weapon model, and operations. Various relationships, such as assembled-by, related-to, implemented-by, can be added for accurate semantic discovery. We also would like to research various metrics to properly quantify similarity between weapon models.

Acknowledgements. This work was supported by Defense Acquisition Program Administration and Agency for Defense Development under the contract UD080042AD, Republic of Korea.

References

1. Cho, B., Kim, D., Kim, S., Youn, C.: Real-Time Distributed Simulation Environment for Air Defense System Using A Software Framework. The Journal of Defense Modeling and Simulation: Applications, Methodology, Technology 4, 64–79 (2007)

2. Hong, J., Seo, K., Seok, M., Kim, T.: Interoperation between Engagement and Engineering-level Models for Effectiveness Analysis. JDMS (The Journal of Defense Modeling and Simulation: Applications, Methodology, Technology) 8, 143–156 (2011)

3. Benali, H., Saoud, N.: Towards a Component-Based Framework for Interoperability and Composability in Modeling and Simulation. Simulation 87, 133–148 (2010)

4. Sommerville: Software Engineering, 9th Edn. Pearson

5. Guo, J., Luqu: A Survey of Software Reuse Repositories. In: IEEE ECBS (Engineering of Computer Based Systems) Proceedings, pp. 92–100 (2000)

6. Lloyd, C.M., Lawson, J.R., Hunter, P.J., Nielsen, P.F.: The CellML Model Repository. Bioinformatics 24(18), 2122–2123 (2008)

7. Koegel, M., Helming, J.: EMFStore - a Model Repository for EMF models. In: ICSE 2010 (2010)

8. Yilmaz, L., Paspuleti, S.: Toward a Meta-Level Framework for Agent-Supported Interoperation of Defense Simulations. The Journal of Defense Modeling and Simulation: Applications, Methodology, Technology 2, 161–175 (2005)

9. Silver, G., Miller, J.: DeMO: An Ontology for Discrete-event Modeling and Simulation. Simulation 87, 747–773 (2010)

10. Franklin, M., Halevy, A.: From databases to dataspaces: a new abstraction for information management. Sigmod Record 34, 27–33 (2005)

11. Fiho, W.A., Hirata, C.M., Yano, A.T.: GroupSim: A Collaborative Environment for Discrete Event Simulation Software Development for the World Wide Web 80(6), 257–272 (2004)

12. Pingle, Y., Kohli, V., Kamat, S., Poladia, N.: Big Data Processing using Apache Hadoop in Cloud System. In: National Conference on Emerging Trends in Engineering & Technology (2012)

13. Palankar, M.R., Iamnitchi, A., Ripeanu, M., Garfinkel, S.: Amazon S3 for Science Grids: a Viable Solution? In: DADC 2008 Proceedings of the 2008 International Workshop on Data-Aware Distributed Computing, pp. 55–64 (2008)

14. Lee, K., Park, J., Park, C.: OpenSIM (Open Simulation Engine for Interoperable Models) for Weapons Effectiveness Analysis. In: The 2011 International Conference on Modeling, Simulation and Visualization Methods, MSV 2011, pp. 116–120 (2011)

15. O'Neil, P., Quass, D.: Improved Query Performance with Variant Indexes. In: SIGMMOD 1997 (1997)

16. Bhiogade, M.S.: Secure Socket Layer, InSITE - "Where Parallels Intersect" (2002)

17. Roesch, M.: SNORT – Light weight Intrusion Detection for Networks. In: Proceedings of LISA 1999: 13th Systems Administration Conference (1999)

18. Apache, Hadoop, The Apache Software Foundation (2011), retrieved http://hadoop.apache.org/

19. Chuck, L.: Hadoop in Action, 1st edn. Manning Publications (2010)

20. OpenSSL, crytography and SSL/TLS Toolkit, http://www.openssl.org/

Finite Element Analysis of Mice Tibia under Impact Loading

Nan Chen, Qing Luo, and Qiguo Rong[*]

College of Engineering, Peking University
100871 Beijing, P.R. China
pku.chennan@gmail.com, qrong@pku.edu.cn

Abstract. Fracture is one of most common injuries in the clinical diagnosis, mainly existed by the kind of stress fracture. With the fast development in sports area, not only the olds but also more and more young athletes may suffer the disease, usually happening under an impact. Currently there are only limited tests to predict the fracture such as BMD (bone mineral density) testing or biopsies of microdamage, but none of them was specific enough. Under such circumstance, this study will try the FEM (finite element method) to find out the process of impact fracture. A free-fall device was set up and a geometry model of mice tibia was created based on a real one. The results show that under the condition of no fracturethe maximum stresses occurred at two crooks, 1/3 below the knee joint of the tibia and 1/3 above the ankle joint, which were the same with clinical diagnosis statistic. In addition, an experiment was conducted with the same device, and the results were matched with the FEM simulation. Therefore this model of simulation was well suitable for the study on impact fracture, and would help in future fracture prediction.

Keywords: bone damage, tibia, impact, FEM.

1 Introduction

Fragility fracture is one of the major concerns in health care of current society, with an increasing trend of 1.26 million annually world-wide, predicting to achieve 4.5 million by end of 2050. [1] Also there is a high probability of bone fracture in the elder, costing expensive treatment and resulting in significant morbidity and mortality[2,3]. Besides, the fracture of basketball players or high jump athletes or soldiers was occurred at the 1/3 below knee joint, while that of the running or long jump athletes was occurred at the 1/3 above ankle joint. Also fracture has become a common epidemic disease in army.some FEM simulation showed that the stress was not well-distributed in tibia of running soldiers, and the max stress 115MPa occurred also at the 1/3 below the knee joint [4].The fragility fracture ratio was about 2-4%in global athletes, and the recurrence ratio after 4 years was about 2-13%[5].It is indicated that in the context of bone fracture, not only the old are easily to suffer it,

---

[*] Corresponding author.

T. Xiao, L. Zhang, and S. Ma (Eds.): ICSC 2012, Part II, CCIS 327, pp. 434–441, 2012.
© Springer-Verlag Berlin Heidelberg 2012

the young athletes or soldiers may also suffer fracture from strong impact force while training. That's why fracture has gradually become the heat of bone tissue medical, and gained more and more attention from researchers.

There are two reasons for fracture. One is the effect of the quality deterioration of bone from the change of cells and molecular causing by things like aging and disease, which is reflected on the components and sub-microstructure of bone. The other one is the instant impact from powerful energy which exceeds the bone's bear range and leads to fracture. The former one is usually caused by osteoporosis for its decreased toughness and the latter one is often caused by car crash or landfall for the transient huge force.

Presently, BMD (bone mineral density) loss is the mainly clinic guideline to diagnose osteoporosis and predict the fracture[6,7]. The higher level of BMD, the lower level of danger was in fracture. But more and more studies showed that this standard is no longer dependable[6,8].In addition, the decreasing of fracture ratio had no relationship with the change of BMD from the observations of osteoporosis people who had taken the medicine to prevent BMD decrease [8].

Bone quality is determined by multiple factors, such as architecture, mineralization, and microdamage accumulation[9].The mainstream consensus is that when the reconstruction speed cannot catch up with that of microdamage accumulation, the bone tissue will accumulate more and more microdamage, decreasing the bone's mechanical properties and breaking the structure. Two main types of microdamages have been observed in human's bone, linear microcrack and diffuse damage. Microdamage is closely related to bone tissues internal structure, material properties and forced state. Hence, research on the structural characteristics and microdamage mechanisms under impact can help explain the causes for fracture and predict the fracture risks for different bone's microstructure under different impact. However, the detection of microdamage in living human individuals is technically challenging and relies currently on invasive sampling by biopsies[10,11].

In despite of the limit of predicting the degree of microdamage of bone, we could use the FEM to simulate. With the development of cross-disciplinary research in recent years, FEM has been widely applied in the biomechanics. The main advantage of FEM is that it can show the stress, strain and displacement in any part of the model.

Although there are plenty of researches on microdamage focusing on bone fatigue[12-15], few were focused on the influence of impact[16,17]. For high-intensity training athletes, the impact exposed them to higher risks of fracture than the common people. This study will set up a free-fall impact FEM simulation (Ansys Workbench 12.1) for bone, and the result will be compared with the experiment, to discuss the feasibility of the FEM model.

2   Material and Method

Early studies have shown that female B6 mice are fully mature at the age of 4 months, since when their cross-sectional area, thickness and weight of cortical bone no longer changed greatly [18]. So they were suitable for researching on the properties of bone tissue. Fig.1 showed one of mice tibia taken from the mice at 4 months' age and cleaned of soft tissue. According to the shape of real tibia bone, a geometry model was made with the same curve for finite element simulation. The model of cortical bone, with 15mm distance at longitudinal direction, was a shape of a thick-wall cylinder cavity with a cross-section composed with ellipse (outer) and circle (inter). The two left solid parts werecancellous bone with totally 5mm distance at longitudinal direction.

A free-fall impact device was set as Fig.2. An aluminum cylinder was used as the impact source for the free-fall, and vertically hit the loading tap, which was made of PMMA, with similar elastic modulus with tibia. The proximal of tibia (near knee joint) was fixed with a big steel plate, and the distal (near ankle joint) was contact with loading tap (a 4mm^2 area). There were three contact areas in this system: the aluminum to the loading tap (rough), the loading tap to distal of tibia (rough) and proximal of tibia to steel plate (bonded). All components are meshed, and the statistic of node and element of the whole system are showed in Table.1.

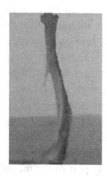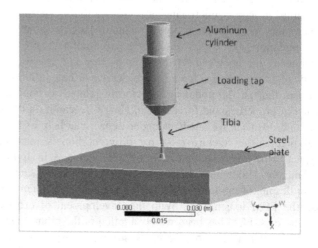

Fig. 1. mice tibia   **Fig.2.** Geometry diagram of free-fall impact system

Table 1. Number node and element of free-fall impact system

	Cancellous bone (distal)	Cortical bone	Cancellous bone (proximal)	Loading tap (PMMA)	Aluminum cylinder	Steel plate
Number of node	3736	59244	3522	9948	8595	56631
Number of element	741	11562	710	2210	1860	12348

Table.2 showed all material parameter and component parameter of the system. Asa free-fall system ,$v$was 2.8m/s when h was 40cm. So the initial impact speed from aluminum cylinder to loading tap is 2.8m/s and the steel plate is fixed.The whole impact process last 450μs, and each time step was about 4.5μs.

Table 2. All parameters for free-fall impact simulation of FE system

	Cancellous bone (distal)	Cortical bone	Cancellous bone (proximal)	Loading tap (PMMA)	Aluminum cylinder	Steel plate
Volume (mm³)	3.28	8.86	6.64	3.43×10^3	1.02×10^3	8.32×10^4
Density (kg•m^-3)	270	1700	270	1160	2770	7850
Young's modulus (GPa)	2.0	15.0	2.0	3.85	71.0	200.0
Possion's ratio	0.3	0.3	0.3	0.3	0.33	0.3
Mass (g)	8.87×10^{-4}	1.51×10^{-2}	1.79×10^{-3}	3.98	2.83	653.44

3   Results

Fig.3 showed the stress-time curve in free-fall impact simulation, and the maximum stress 544MPa occurred at 245μs of the whole process. At the moment, the maximum stress was showed up at the two crooks of the model in the vonMises stress distribution (Fig.4 (a)). So the two cross-sections at the two crooks (Fig.4 (b) and Fig.4(c)) were cut to observe the situation of the impact. At one crooks, the max stress appeared in the compressive region but within a small area, and the stress at both ends of y-axis were larger than at the both ends of x-axis. Also the stress of most areas of the cross-section was below 120MPa. The other crook showed the same result.

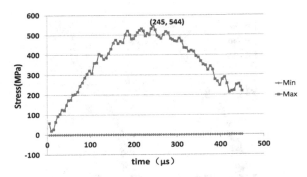

Fig. 3. von Misesstress-time curve in free-fall impact simulation

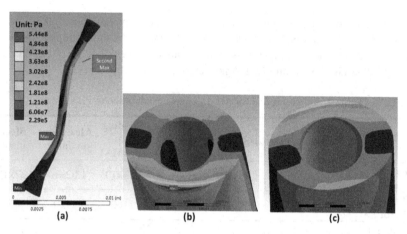

Fig. 4. Von Misesstress distributionat 245μs: (a) the whole tibia, (b) cross-section1, (c)cross-section2

Fig.5 showed the strain-time curve in free-fall impact simulation, in which there were two maximum strain 52.8% (at 200μs) and 52.2% (at 232μs). Checking the vonMisesstrain graphs at the two time points (Fig.6), the maximum strain occurred at the edge of the connection areas between loading tap and cancellous bone (distal), and the strain of the whole cortical bone was less than 2.3%.

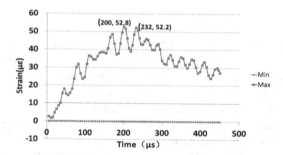

Fig. 5. Strain-time curve in free-fall impact simulation

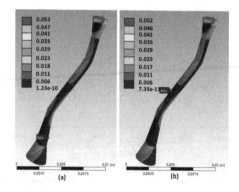

Fig. 6. Strain of the whole tibia at(a) 200μs, (b) 232μs

According to the deformation-curve, the longer the time lasts, the larger deformation was shown. So at the end of the whole impact processthe after-impact position of all the components were performed. The total deformation of system was showed in Fig.7, and the maximum deformation happened at the contact area between cancellous bone (distal) and loading tap, indicating that the bone was bending in the impact process. And the deformation of the place is about 0.5mm, and the strain was 2.5%, in-line with the max strain in the same place showed in Fig.6. Fig.8 showed the three directional deformations (x, y and z axis) of the bone model. The displacement of x-axis was too small for further analysis, while the max displacement of y-axis was on the crook near the proximal of bone, and the max displacement of z-axis was on the distal of bone.

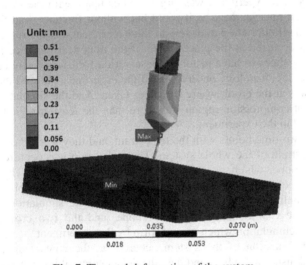

Fig. 7. The total deformation of the system

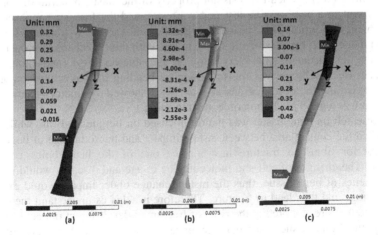

Fig. 8. Three directional deformations of bone model (a)z-axis, (b)x-axis, (c)y-axis

4   Discussion

A model of mice tibia has been established to study the mechanical behavior of bone tissue under bending impact via FEM. In general, bone would have a fracture when its stress was about 140-160MPa. Fig.4 showed that the stress of at least half of the bone was about 60 to 120MPa, which meant the bone would not have a fracture. Meanwhile the stress range of the two cross sections of the bone was 60 to 544MPa, but most of the area was under 120MPa, which meant the fracture would not likely happen. Besides Fig.3 showed that at time point 126μs, 187μs and 218μs, the high stress was around 520MPa at somewhere of the bone. Butthe stress of the whole cross section was not above 140MPa, so the bone tissue under the initial condition would not be fractured. An experiment was targeted to compare with the simulation, which required as much microdamage as it could but without fracture. And this simulation could provide the important parameters to the experiment. As the result showed, the max stress was occurred at the place of 1/3 of the tibia near the knee joint. And the place was cut to slices to have histology observation forit was easily caused clinical fracture. In addition, histology observation of the experiment showed that most of the microdamagewas at the crook where the slices taken. And the simulation showed the microdamage of compression region was more than the tension region, which could also be observed in the experiment.

There were two time points with the max strain, and they were chosen as the basis to observe the strain of the whole system. The max strain was occurred at region of the cancellous bone, which was sharply the same with the fact. The strain of the crooks of the bone was below 1.8%, but was higher than any other place of the bone. Consider the nonlinear effect of the transient impact, the simulation cloud express clearly the process of bending impact of bone, and the two crocks have much microdamage accumulation which was confirm by the experiment.

The total deformation of the system occurred at the contact area between the loading tap and distal of the boneand then the deformation of bone at z-axis decreased slowly, which was matched the resistant property of the elastic material of bone. The tibia was sent to a compressive test under a tester, and the fracture happened at the displacement of 0.6mm. This meant the displacement caused by transient force was less than that caused by quasi-static force, in line with their mechanical properties. At x-axis, the displacement was very tiny, at the micron level, and quite evenly distributed. Because bone was transmutation by bending of y-axis and compression by the z-axis, and the deformations at x-axis was showed symmetry. Therefore this simulation was a good prediction on bone impacting.

The research on bone tissue was mainly focused on fatigue analysis, while only a few studied the contact area between instant impact and microdamage of bone tissue, especially for tibia.The fracture has become one of the heat topics in clinical medicine. The changes of cell and molecule due to age and diseases would influence the proprieties of bone tissue, thus the instant change under impact would exceed its tolerant range and thus lead to fracture. Therefore it helps us understand the cause of bone tissue fracture and predict the risks of fracture under different impact sources by studying the bone tissue microdamage under impact. Also, there are still some improving opportunities for future study, such as constructing a 3-D structure of tibia via micro-CT, and simulating under different material proprieties. Or a fatigue simulation would be started and then an impact test would be followed to study the impact strength of bone tissue under a more realistic situation.

Acknowledgments. This work was supported by The National Natural Science Foundation of China (10872007).

References

1. Gullberg, B., Johnell, O., Kanis, J.A.: World-wide projections for hip fracture. Osteoporosis International 7, 407–413 (1997)
2. Johnell, O., Kanis, J.A., Oden, A., et al.: Mortality after osteoporotic fractures. Osteoporosis International 15, 38–42 (2004)
3. Melton 3rd, L.J.: Adverse outcomes of osteoporotic fractures in the general population. Journal of Bone and Mineral Research 18, 1139–1141 (2003)
4. Liao, D.H., Han, H.C., Kuang, Z.B.: Finite element analysis of human tibia. Journal of Biomedical Engineering 15(1), 53–57 (1998)
5. Johnson, A.W., Weiss, C.B., Wheeler, D.L.: Stress fractures of the femoral shaft in athletes-more common than expected. Am. J. Sports Med. 22, 248–256 (1994)
6. Fazzalari, N.L., Forwood, M.R., Smith, K., et al.: Assessment of cancellous bone quality in severe osteoarthrosis: Bone mineral density, mechanics, and microdamage. Bone 22, 381–388 (1998)
7. Cefalu, C.A.: Is bone mineral density predictive of fracture risk reduction? Current Medical Research and Opinion 20, 341–349 (2004)
8. Wynnyckyj, C., Omelon, S., Savage, K., et al.: A new tool to assess the mechanical properties of bone due to collagen degradation. Bone 44, 840–848 (2009)
9. NIH: Osteoporosis prevention, diagnosis, and therapy, in NIH Consensus Statement, March 27-29, pp. 1–45. National Institutes of Health (2000)
10. Chapurlat, R.D., Arlot, M., Burt-Pichat, B., et al.: Microcrack frequency and bone remodeling in postmenopausal osteoporotic women on long-term bisphosphonates: a bone biopsy study. J. Bone Miner Res. 22, 1502–1509 (2007)
11. Chapurlat, R.D., Delmas, P.D.: Bone microdamage: a clinical perspective. Osteoporos Int. 20, 1299–1308 (2009)
12. Frost, H.M.: Presence of microscopic cracks in vivo in bone. Henry Ford Med. Bulletin 8, 27–35.(1960)
13. Wang, X., Nyman, J.S.: A novel approach to assess post-yield energy dissipation of bone in tension. Journal of Biomechanics 40, 674–677 (2007)
14. Dong, X.N., Leng, H.J., Ran, Q.T., et al.: Finding of microdamage morphology differences in mouse femoral bones with distinct mineralization levels. Journal of Mechanics in Medicine and Biology 11, 423–432 (2011)
15. Burr, D.B., Turner, C.H., Naick, P., et al.: Does microdamage accumulation affect the mechanical properties of bone? Journal of Biomechanics 31, 337–345 (1998)
16. Reilly, G.C., Currey, J.D.: The effects of damage and microcracking on the impact strength of bone. Journal of Biomechanics 33, 337–343 (2000)
17. Verteramo, A., Seedhom, B.B.: Effect of a single impact loading on the structure and mechanical properties of articular cartilage. Journal of Biomechanics 16, 3580–3589 (2007)
18. Price, C., Herman, B.C., Lufkin, T., et al.: Genetic variation in bone growth patterns defines adult mouse bone fragility. Journal of Bone and Mineral Research 20, 1983–1991 (2005)

Author Index